·PRAISE·

"Wit, wisdom, and verve—these are only three of Irena Chalmer's most wonderful traits. So many of us in the food world have benefited from her intelligence and enthusiasm, whether through a collaboration or simply a stimulating conversation. Now she is sharing her talents with a new generation of young people. Long live Irena Chalmers!

—DARRA GOLDSTEIN,
EDITOR IN CHIEF, *GASTRONOMICA*

"I know of no one who knows as much about food and the industry as [Chalmers] does. Certainly no one writes with as much candor and humor."

—RICHARD GRAUSMAN, FOUNDER & PRESIDENT,
THE CAREERS THROUGH CULINARY ARTS PROGRAM (C-CAP)

"Irena Chalmers should be right up there with Julia and Jim in spreading the word about good food in America. As the First Lady of Food books for three decades, Chalmers presence on the page or in a lecture hall charges the atmosphere with vitality, wit and wisdom."

—BETTY FUSSELL, FOOD HISTORIAN AND AUTHOR OF
THE STORY OF CORN, MY KITCHEN WARS AND RAISING STEAKS

"Irena Chalmers knows her stuff. Over the years she has reinvented herself as an award-winning cookbook author, restaurant consultant, cooking school teacher, speechwriter and CIA instructor. Who could be a better and guide to finding a job in the food business?"

—DIANE JACOB, AUTHOR OF WILL WRITE FOR FOOD: *THE COMPLETE GUIDE TO WRITING*
COOKBOOKS, RESTAURANT REVIEWS, ARTICLES, MEMOIR, FICTION, AND MORE

"Irena Chalmers is a prolific publisher, author, teacher and food consultant—a very versatile and witty enlightener"

—BEVERLY STEPHEN
EXECUTIVE EDITOR *FOOD ARTS*

"Irena Chalmers brings insights and information to the enormous world of food enthusiasts like no other voice in the arena. Her writing is as interesting and refined as a carefully crafted meal."

—AUTHOR OF *START UP MARKETING, JUST SAY YES,*
BRAINDING COMMENTATOR FOR NATIONAL NEWS AND
COLUMNIST FOR NEWSPAPERS AND MAGAZINES THROUGHOUT THE WORLD

"Irena and I had the good common fortune to work with the greatest restaurateur of the 20th century, Joe Baum. We both spent years trying to anticipate his response to our proposals. Irena was one of the few personalities able to cool his fevered brow and make him happy. This is a gift she brings to most encounters. After all, she was once a nurse. Her sunny disposition and good will, both in her writing and her presence, make you want to spend time with her. You'll feel better afterwards."

—MILTON GLASER, DESIGNER (OF I LOVE NY LOGO)

"Irena's column is a perennial favorite of *Chef Magazine* readers. There's a reason why it's the very last page in the magazine—to ensure they read the rest."

—ABBIE JARMAN, EDITOR, *CHEF MAGAZINE*

"Irena is one of my favorite people in life. She is warm, witty and . . . a brilliant cook. She thinks with a first-rate mind and writes with an angel on her pen."

—CHEF DAVID JAMES ROBINSON
EXECUTIVE CHEF/OWNER
BEZALEL GABLES FINE CATERING & EVENTS

"For the past 25 years, with both wit and wisdom, Irena Chalmers has been instructing us on the culinary world's virtues, which she is always quick to trumpet, and its vices, which she skewers with delicious accuracy. Her keynote addresses to major food-related conferences have pinpointed trends that have significantly shaped an entire industry, noting both its promise and potential and its possible pitfalls. Her many books have enlightened and entertained thousands of devoted culinary practitioners."

—PHILLIP S. COOKE AND DANIEL D. MAYE
MANAGING PARTNERS (RETIRED), FSA GROUP & PALS

"Irena Chalmers is a masterful cook, a dazzling intellect, a beloved teacher, a sparkling writer and more, much more. She brings everything she has to the table of life and dispenses it all bountifully and generously. Her food, her knowledge, her know-how, her insights. They're there for all of us to have and enjoy. So, pull up a chair and have a seat at Irena's table. You'll have wonderful time. You will be nourished. You will be filled. It's a promise."

—ELAINE YANNUZZI
FORMER PRESIDENT, EXPRESSION UNLTD.

"The distinguished and absolutely delectable Irena Chalmers always has her finger on what is important in our lives. She knows, for instance, what the world needs now are jobs, including those in the culinary world. *Food Jobs* makes a valuable contribution at the right time."

—PETER D. FRANKLIN, FOOD COLUMNIST,
UNIVERSAL PRESS SYNDICATE.

"I think every incoming student should be exposed to at least one class with Ms. Chalmers, It will be a truly enlightening experience that no one should be deprived of."

—RANDY WALTERS
CULINARY STUDENT, CULINARY OF AMERICA

• **PRAISE FOR** •
The Food Professional's Guide
Compiled by Irena Chalmers, Foreword by Julia Child

"Here in one place are all the names that we used to have to find by hunting through a dozen different directories. You no longer have to spend hours on your own tracing down a fact, a service or a person, the editors of this directory have done the work for you. I can't imagine how we have all lived without it."

—JULIA CHILD

"The thought of even attempting to compile such a volume is mind-boggling."
—Los Angeles Daily News

"Those with a fervid interest in food will take real delight in this book, and serious cooks will find it invaluable."
—John Mariani

"This kind of giant, comprehensive national directory of people, products and services in the food and wine industries which many have long wished for has finally been published."
—Restaurant Digest.

• PRAISE FOR •
The Great American Food Almanac

"*The Great Food Almanac* is a feast to read—helpful, healthy data in an easy format."
—Robert Mondavi, Chairman of the Board, Robert Mondavi Winery

"With this book, Irena Chalmers provides ravening food-fact foragers with something richly meaty or delectably odd to chew on every day of the year."
—Michael & Ariane Batterberry
Founding Editors, *Food Arts Magazine*

"Irena Chalmers has the quickest mind in the food world. Facts and fantasies crowd the ever-lively pages, carefully annotated. What really sets The Great Food Almanac apart is its diversity and humor. The PC Thought Police run for cover when Irena hits town. And those who feel the fun has been removed from our food along with the fat and frosting have a welcome opportunity to binge on smiles and chuckles."
—William Rice
Food and wine Columnist, *Chicago Tribune*

"I haven't had so much fun with a book since the long-lost days of *The Whole Earth Catalog.* Thanks from all of us out here who are hopelessly compulsive browsers, relentless fact and figure collectors, amateur muckrakers, gossip hounds and of course, food lovers. You've left a treasure chest on our doorsteps."
—Nach Waxman
Founder and owner, Kitchen Arts and Letters, New York City

"Nobody does it better than Irena Chalmers in this new almanac of fascinating and juicy tidbits seasoned with her famous irrepressible humor."
—Maggie Waldron
Executive Creative Director, Ketchum Food Center

"For me, receiving a new book from Irena Chalmers is always thrill. *The Great Food Almanac* bursts with wit, charm and Irena's delightful information. What a way to learn!"
—Sheila Lukins
Co-author of *The Silver Palate* cookbooks

food JOBS

Irena Chalmers

150 GREAT JOBS

FOR CULINARY STUDENTS,

CAREER CHANGERS AND FOOD LOVERS

BEAUFORT BOOKS

NEW YORK

Library of Congress Cataloging-in-Publication Data
Chalmers, Irena.
    Food jobs : 150 great jobs for culinary students,
career changers and food lovers/ Irena Chalmers.
        p. cm.
    Includes bibliographical references and index.
    ISBN 978-0-8253-0592-4 (alk. paper)
    1. Food service--Vocational guidance. I. Title.

    TX911.3.V62C42 2008
    647.95023—dc22

                                        2008026124

Published in the United States by Beaufort Books, New York
www.beaufortbooks.com

Distributed by Midpoint Trade Books
www.midpointtradebooks.com

Interior design by Pauline Neuwirth, Neuwirth & Associates, Inc.

10 9 8 7 6 5 4 3 2 1

Printed in the United States of America

For butchers and bakers   *For winers*
And tillers of acres   *And diners*
And food-trivia players   *And buyers making deals by the bunch.*
And carrot purveyors   *For eaters of noodles*
And wielders of woks.   *And bakers of strudels.*
For food fashion leaders   *For post-midnight snackers*
And recipe readers   *And packers*
And fitness-freak jocks.   *And craters*
And salesmen   *And vanishing head waiters*
Who breakfast on lox,   *And food innovators who act on a hunch.*
For taste counterfeiters   *For sommeliers with tastevin flying*
And writers of letters   *So clearly implying*
And restaurateurs   *They'd like a gratuity*
And entrepreneurs   *Akin to an annuity*
And connoisseurs.   *And then a drop more.*
For greeters   *For cake decorators*
And seaters   *And cookbook creators*
Of meeters for brunch   *And people who munch.*
And ladies who lunch.   *In short, this is neat*

For all who eat . . .

Most of all, this book is dedicated to my darling, hard-working daughter, Hilary; incomparable son, Philip; and charming daughter-in-law, Emiko. To Freddie, who encouraged me to buy all those copper pans and joyfully shared the first cooking efforts.
And for Elaine, who was at my side every step of the way.

Some dream of things that are and ask, Why?

Others dream of things that never were and ask, Why not?

—Robert F. Kennedy

contents

150 food jobs

Executive Chef	Restaurant Consultant	Military Chef
Banquets Chef	Caterer	Arctic Chef
Chef de Cuisine	Event Planner	Public-School Kitchen Chef
Sous Chef	Celebrity Chef	College-Dining-Hall Chef
Line Cook	Humanitarian	Association Manager
Prep Cook	Egg Peeler	Product Promoter
Butcher	Omelet Maker	Product Spokesperson
Sausage Maker	Pizza Chef	Product Demonstrator
Beef Manti Maker	Pizza Deliverer	Food Retailer
Dishwasher	Hot-Dog Vender	Entrepreneur
Pastry Chef	Firehouse Chef	Retail Shop Owner
Cake Designer	Boutique Chef	Cheese Maker
Cupcake Creator	Airline Chef	Cheese Connoisseur
Master Chef	Private Plane Chef	Artisanal Bread Baker
General Manager	Personal Chef	Deli Owner
Maître d'	Butler	Sandwich-Shop Owner
Waitstaff	Corporate-Dining-Room Chef	Cooking School Owner
Dining Coach	Country-Club or Lodge Chef	Ice-Cream Namer
Busboy	Bed-and-Breakfast Owner	Coffee Shop Owner
Bartender	Cruise-Ship Lecturer	Tea Shop Owner
Sommelier	Cruise-Ship Chef	Wholesaler
Restaurant Owner	Spa Chef	Gift Basket Maker
Diner Owner	Hospital Chef	Designer/Art Director
Restaurant Consultant	Retirement-Home Chef	Graphic Designer
Chief Financial Officer	Prison Chef	Exhibition Curator

Food Photographer	Archivist	Olive oil Taster
Food Stylist	Publisher	Ice Cream Taster
Prop Stylist	Cooking Contest Judge	Tea Taster
Menu Designer	Food Cartoonist	Coffee Taster
Kitchen Designer	Food and Restaurant Critic	Dietitian
Food Writer	Blogger	Nutritionist
Fortune-Cookie Message Writer	Food Radio Host	Seed Scientist
Columnist	Media Trainer	Citron Farmer
Biographer	Culinary Television Producer	Boutique Crop Farmer
Editor	Journalist	Hydroponic Farmer
Literary Agent	Publicist	Herb and Specialty Crop Farmer
Cookbook Author	Marketer	Biotechnology Researcher
Cookbook Collaborator	Press Agent	Fish Farmer
Copyeditor	Researcher	Caviar Producer
Proofreader	Newsletter Producer	Wild Game Farmer
Fact Checker	Futurist	Cowboy
Indexer	Ethicist	Bee Keeper
Recipe Developer	Psychologist	Honey Producer
Recipe Tester	Garbage Anthropologist	Mushroom Grower
Cookbook Doctor	Anthropologist	Chef Instructor
Historian	Obesity Researcher	Culinary School Teacher
Culinary Bookseller	Product Developer	Culinary Tour Guide
Cookbook Reviewer	Research Chef	Culinary Librarian
Recipe Writer	Flavor Maker	
Rare Book Collector	Vinegar Taster	

acknowledgments

HEY SAY IT is lonely being a writer. What rubbish! When I look at my network of cherished friends, I realize I am part of a lovely, celebratory, constantly hungry crowd of food lovers. This makes me rich beyond my wildest dreams.

There is no possible way to thank the entire merry band of experts and colleagues who so willingly agreed to help compile this book. Almost every author thanks their literary agent and editor, and I want to join that chorus, too. Jane Dystel is the New York agent I share with many other fortunate writers. Jane encouraged and supported *Food Jobs* with constant kindness and generosity of spirit. Ultimately it was Eric Kampmann, Margot Atwell and Erin Smith who immediately understood the spirit of the book and became the best publishers I have ever known. Pauline Neuwirth, Beth Metrick and the others at Neuwirth and Associates were also instrumental in putting this book together.

It is my editor, Mary Goodbody, to whom I am most indebted. Mary shaped my unwieldy (not-so-magnum) opus so it could fit comfortably between the covers and flow coherently. Her careful, painstaking work has again been invaluable. My admiration for her grows exponentially. Only a fellow author could begin to guess how d——d difficult it can be to get a simple idea into publication! Together we agonized over every word and mourned those that were so reluctantly trimmed for reasons of space. Peter Jacoby refined the final copy. I owe a great debt of gratitude to Lisa Ekus-Saffer who is the book publicist extraordinaire.

Elaine Yannuzzi provided me with the original idea for the book and patiently read every draft of the manuscript. Elaine owned Expression unLTD, a huge gourmet store in New Jersey. She is my dear friend and adviser about everything important in life. I owe her a greater debt than I can ever repay. I also owe special thanks to Jerry Fischetti, an associate professor at the Culinary Institute of America (CIA) and a treasured friend, and Doyle and Ricky Ford, who created a darling home for me.

Many generous colleagues contributed their words of wisdom and breathed life into the narrative. I am grateful for all the inspiring quotes from Pat Adrian, the former editorial director of the Good Cook Book Club; Bruce Aidells, the sage of sausages; Gary Allen, author of *The Resource Guide for Food Writers* and *The Herbalist in the Kitchen*; super soup maker David Ansel; and Michael Batterberry, editor in chief/publisher of *Food Arts* magazine. Thank you to restaurateur extraordinaire Joe Baum, for whom I worked for many grand and glorious years. Applause is due to Barbara Beery; Rose Levy Beranbaum; Lois Bloom and Pat Boyer; Freida and Karen Caplan; folk hero Julia Child; distinguished scientist Shirley Corriher; master food stylist Delores Custer; good food purveyor Ariane Daguin, founder/owner of d'Artagnan; and brilliant-beyond-compare television producer Geoffrey Drummond. And to John Edge—the southern sage—and culinary students Alison Fong and Sasha Foppiano. And to Brent Frei, director of public relations, marketing, and editorial development for food-service companies. And to Miriam Goderich of Dystel and Goderich Literary Management. And thank you, Stephan Hengst, director of public relations at the CIA, for your thoughtful essay.

A large thank you is owed to my former culinary student Molly Kendall, who inspired me to call on my pals to share the infinite wisdom that forms the backbone of the book. Deserving of literary sainthood are Cynthia Glover, *Bon Appétit*'s Kristine Kidd, and Abigail Kirsch—caterer to the fortunate—and the esteemed Harold McGee. I am so happy to include agricultural biotechnologist Michael Lawton, rare book collector Jan Longone, anthropologist Sidney Mintz, and another outstanding former student, Erica Murphy.

I am particularly proud to share the words of Daniel Maye, the visionary association manager who was single-handedly responsible for the vast expansion of the International Association of Culinary Professionals (IACP); beloved restaurateur Danny Meyer; Dr. Kathy Merget, dean of liberal arts and management studies at the CIA; Dr. Denise Bauer, associate dean for curriculum and instruction for liberal arts at the CIA; and Anne McBride, who received her PhD in food studies at NYU and wrote about her experiences for this book. Anne also helped me enormously by conducting several interviews with food celebrities.

I am delighted indeed to have the opportunity of including words from restaurateur Michel Nischan, writer Carol Penn-Romine, and culinary pioneer Jacques Pépin.

William Reynolds, provost of the City Colleges of Chicago, is one of the great wise men of our profession and the best interviewer I have ever met. Thank you, Bill, for your insights.

Thank you to Bill Rice of the *Chicago Tribune* and the brilliant restaurant critic Alan Richman, who teaches food writing at the French Culinary Institute in Manhattan. Thanks to Phyllis Richman, former *Washington Post* restaurant critic and author of the mystery *The Butter Did It: A Gastronomic Tale of Love and Murder*.

I am grateful to Carrie Robbins, theatrical costume designer and waitstaff uniform designer for the Rainbow Room and Windows on the World. Thank you, John Roberts: you have guided the growth of the Specialty Foods Association with a steady hand for many years. And sincere thanks to Ron Tanner, the other special—indeed, specialty—food guru. Thank you, Rick Rogers.

I am fortunate to count among my dear friends cookbook editor Elizabeth Crossman, Betty Fussell, Darra Goldstein, Anne Willan, Irene Sax, and Elizabeth Schneider—the revered grand dame of vegetables and author of *Uncommon Fruits and Vegetables: A Commonsense Guide* and *Vegetables from Amaranth to Zucchini: The Essential Reference*. They are among our finest food writers.

Thank you to Mimi Sheraton, who knows more or less everything about everything; Richard Sherlock, the ethical ethicist; the venerable Jeffrey Steingarten; writer Sandy Szwarc, who is the conscience of the food universe; and Marguerite Thomas, who has made a specialty of compiling a Who's Who of the culinary world. Thanks too to Calvin Trillin, Alice Waters, and Tim and Nina Zagat.

I am grateful for all the talented and good-natured friends who have contributed lovely essays to this work: Todd Coleman, now food editor at *Saveur* magazine; and Phillip S. Cooke, Dale De Groff, Lisa Ekus-Saffer, Andrew Freeman, Milton Glaser, Cynthia Glover, Barbara Haber, Jim Howard, Dianne Jacob, David Joachim, Chris Kimball, Shirley Kirkpatrick, David Leite, Patti Londre,

Dana Minuta, Pam Parseghian, the divine David Robinson—and Tom, Jim Scherzi, Francine Segan, Andrew Smith, Joyce Marcley Vergilli, Denise Vivaldo, Candy Wallace, Nach Waxman, Sylvia Weinstock, Faith Willinger, Lisa Forare Windbladh, and Sue Zelickson. Thank you. As Tiny Tim said, "Bless you every one" for sharing your infinite knowledge with me and our readers.

I have made every effort to gratefully acknowledge each person who provided information and guidance. I am particularly fortunate to know so many students and members of the faculty at the Culinary Institute of America. You bring to my life gifts beyond compare.

The original book contract called for this work to be completed in one year, but in the end, it took considerably longer—and actually encompasses a lifetime of toil in many, many food jobs.

IRENA CHALMERS
irena@foodjobsbook.com
www.foodjobsbook.com

foreword

WHEN I LOST my job several years ago, I received an important piece of advice from my friend Paula Wolfert. I told her I was thinking about reopening my cooking school. She was appalled. "Are you nuts?" she asked incredulously. "When you started your cooking school there was no competition. Now there are plenty of other people who can teach as well—probably much better than you. Don't be an ant in an anthill. Do something different."

Following her good advice, I used a telescope instead of a microscope to see what other opportunities beckoned beyond the horizon. I became a cookbook publisher. Milton Glaser, the renowned graphic designer, was the art director for the books that I named the Great American Cooking Schools series.

Among the titles I published were the first books written by several cooking-school teachers who later achieved dazzling success. I assigned both the subject and the title for each book, and to my astonishment all the authors agreed to get to work right away. Rose Levy Beranbaum wrote a little book called *Romantic and Classic Cakes*, which evolved into the groundbreaking *The Cake Bible*, and she has continued to write numerous other award-winning and classic cookbooks. Nathalie Dupree wrote *Cooking of the South* and became the belle of southern cooking long before the arrival of

Paula Dean. Barbara Kafka, the widely acknowledged all-around genius, compiled *American Food and California Wine*. Among her many other publications are the award-winning *Microwave Gourmet and Roasting: A Simple Art*, *Party Food*, *Soup: A Way of Life*, and, most recently, with Christopher Styler, *Vegetable Love: A Book for Cooks*.

I asked Richard Sax to write *Old-Fashioned Desserts*, and he eventually created *Classic Home Desserts*, the definitive work on this subject. Gary Goldberg, who wrote *Successful Parties,* is now the director of the Manhattan-based New School Culinary Arts Program. The late Peter Kump wrote *Quiche and Pâté* for my publishing company. At the time he owned a small cooking school that, under the wise guidance of its current owner, Rick Smilow, has grown into the hugely successful Institute of Culinary Education in New York City.

These cookbooks won many awards for both text and art direction, and in the process I lost almost every penny I had. In exchange I got a life; I think that's a pretty good trade off.

Before my exhilarating but ultimately ill-fated publishing adventure, I worked with David Grimes, the visionary risk taker and founder of Potpourri Press. We were both living in Greensboro, North Carolina, where he owned a large gourmet store in a shopping mall and I had a more modest cookware and specialty food and wine shop from which I conducted cooking classes. We got together to publish dozens of small cookbooks that, in the beginning, were all related to cooking utensils.

We like to think we were pioneers of single-subject cookbooks that were distributed (in multiples of a dozen, all nonreturnable) to the gift and gourmet market. The first in a collection of many was *Fondue*, a little booklet that, embarrassingly in hindsight, cost one dollar retail—fifty cents wholesale. It sold a million copies . . .

I actually began my circuitous culinary journey at Lexington Market in Baltimore. It was the home of the DelMarVa (Delaware, Maryland, and Virginia) Chicken Festival. The festival's promoters hired a woman, sight unseen, to demonstrate the prize-winning fried chicken recipe. When she arrived there was no mistaking the fact she was absolutely gorgeous. The organizers were shocked. "Oh dear, this won't do at all," they declared. "What we need is somebody ordinary." That's how I got the job.

Before Baltimore, I had been a nurse in England and Scotland. I arrived in New York City without knowing a single person. I was appointed to teach neuroanatomy and neurophysiology to nurses at Columbia-Presbyterian Neurological Institute.

Until recently, I lived in midtown Manhattan. I planned to stay there forever. I love big cities, but my life changed suddenly when I again lost my job, this time at the World Trade Center's famous restaurant, Windows on the World, where I had worked as a so-called consultant for the restaurant chairman, Joe Baum. (Craig Claiborne described Joe as "the restaurateur of our century." Almost everyone agreed with that opinion.) I functioned as the general scribbler in residence, writing Joe's speeches, helping to compose menus and press releases, working on the Web site, and producing brochures. I was a small part of the "brains trust team" that compiled proposals for the restaurant's many new ventures.

At the same time I was employed by the International Food Information Council, a Washington, D.C.–based nonprofit foundation whose mission is to communicate science-based information on food safety, nutrition, and biotechnology to health and nutrition educators, government officials, and the media. My assignment there was to talk and write about agricultural biotechnology.

I was also teaching a class in professional food writing one afternoon a week at the Culinary Institute of America. After September 11, 2001, I decided to move closer to the school. I bought a small cottage in Kingston, New York, and took some driving lessons, as I hadn't driven a car for more than twenty years. Now I'm teaching, writing, and speaking at food conferences more than ever before. I've even planted a rose garden.

I have briefly recounted my own experiences to show how my seemingly unrelated paths have turned out to be surprisingly interrelated and have converged to form this book. I have actually tackled many of the food jobs described in these pages. I've found ways to turn my greatest passion into a career (many careers, in fact). My fondest hope is that you, too, will find ways of using the things you *love* to do to guide you to the work that Joseph Campbell so eloquently called your *bliss*.

introduction

I **GET AN** enormous amount of satisfaction and pleasure from teaching at the Culinary Institute of America. At the first meeting of my professional-food-writing class, I ask the students to tell me something about themselves that will surprise me. I know they are all attending the school because they love to cook and are passionate about food. I also know not all of them will choose to become professional chefs upon graduation. So what else do they *love* to do?

Recently, a rather grumpy-looking girl folded her arms and glared at me. In response to what she clearly thought was a dumb question, she answered, "I *love* to go shopping." Everyone laughed, but I thought this was a really useful piece of information.

I told her about a former colleague at Windows on the World who is a tabletop consultant. She scours manufacturers' showrooms for the latest designs of china, glassware, and distinctive serving plates for several upscale restaurants. My student now does the same thing. She works part-time as a tabletop counselor and is also a prop stylist for a food photographer. She too goes shopping everyday. When a chef wants a tagine, mandoline, or any other specialized piece of equipment, she knows exactly what it is and can lay her hands on it immediately. She found her *bliss*—her perfect food job.

Another student arrived early to class carrying the *Wall Street Journal*. After graduation, he joined an investment banking firm that paid his way to become a financial analyst specializing in food companies. He combined his culinary knowledge with his interest in finance and embarked on a career for which he was uniquely qualified.

A student in the culinary program responded to my question by saying, "I want to be a rock star." I couldn't help him become a great musician, but instead I suggested he find a job as a personal chef for his favorite rock group. He did. When he cooks something good for them to eat, they sometimes let him play with them. He found himself a really cool job; he had the courage to offer his food knowledge and the leader of the band was happy to give him a seat on the bus.

A Korean culinary student whose English-speaking ability did not quite match his exemplary cooking skills found work as a private chef at the Korean Embassy in Washington, D.C. The diplomats were delighted to have "home-cooked" food prepared by someone who spoke their language.

These are examples of using your knowledge, experience, and passion to find your perfect food job. None of these students, or many others I have met, knew these jobs existed. And if they had, they wouldn't know where to begin to apply for such positions. Even experienced food professionals are largely unaware of the dazzling range of career paths that will enable them to find work that is interesting, challenging, and fulfilling.

You may not know that there's an ice-cream company that employs a full-time taster. You may not know how to become a tea or coffee taster or an account executive promoting beef, pork, peaches, pears, or other commodities. You may be unaware that the United States Postal Service employed a chef to provide meals for the cycling team that it sponsored. *American Idol* engages a personal chef to feed the secluded finalists. An experienced cook may earn eighty thousand dollars a year—tax-free—working on a luxury yacht cruising the Greek islands. Chefs work at NASA developing food for astronauts. A food lover with no formal training may find success as a restaurant critic if he possesses a vibrant palate and can write well.

There is always plenty of work to be found in restaurants, but food lovers could explore other opportunities and think about becoming a private chef for a movie star, a sports hero, or a television anchor. Have you thought about a career as a literary agent, cheese-shop owner, food-travel writer, bartender, artisanal bread baker, wedding-cake designer, food photographer, recipe tester, food-trends researcher, radio interviewer, publicist, bed-and-breakfast owner, cooking-school teacher, media trainer, or any one of literally hundreds of other ways to earn a living in the food world?

Whether you are interested in science or supermarkets, in engineering, accounting, human relations, or flower arranging for fancy parties, in cookbook reviewing or judging cooking contests, there is a job in the food field for you. Or you can dream up something that has never before been done and make it happen.

YOUR CAREER IN FOOD

Sir Francis Crick, who with Dr. James Watson unraveled the DNA code, once declared that if you are not prepared to take a risk you should never get married, you shouldn't have children, and you most certainly should never risk changing jobs.

You, dear reader, are taking a huge risk. You are thinking about starting a new career. Simply reading these words is a measure of your bravery, your sense of adventure, and your willingness to take charge of your life.

Whether we know it or not, we are all taking risks all the time. Even if we are classified as full-time employees, we are really free-lancers. The axe hangs over our head by a slender thread. The only security we have is our ability to transform our knowledge and experience into stepping stones to the next opportunity.

Rather than thinking about permanence and security, we should all be thinking about—and hoping for—change. Change is the only constant in the continuum of our lives.

If you stop pedaling, you'll fall off your bike. If you keep going, no matter how slowly, you will eventually arrive at the place you want to be. If you stand still, there is an illusion you are coasting, but in fact you are falling back. Keep reading and keep networking. You never know when the next opportunity will come your way, and you must always be ready to welcome it—fearlessly.

DECISIONS, DECISIONS

"There are known knowns, there are things we know we know. There are known unknowns. That is to say there are things we know we don't know. But there are also unknown unknowns. Things we don't know we don't know."

—**DONALD RUMSFELD**

Like it or not, we have to keep making decisions. Should I wear this or that? Should I buy this or that car? Take this or that apartment? Go to this movie or that one? Go out or stay at home? Should the meat be well-done, medium, or rare? Blue cheese or Thousand Island dressing? Smooth or chunky? Small, medium, or large? The list of questions—and answers—goes on and on. Now is the time to ask the right questions—lots of them. At the O. J. Simpson trial, Johnny Cochran didn't ask the jury, is this man guilty? Instead, he asked if there was hanky-panky in the Los Angeles Police Department. It is a matter of interpretation whether this was the right question. What we do know is that if you ask the right questions, you may alter the course of your personal future.

THINK AHEAD

Deciding to change your career, embark on a new venture, or just change jobs is a major undertaking. It means thinking ahead and anticipating where you want to be in the short term. Don't worry so much about the long-term future, because you will probably change your mind and change jobs several times. Most people do. Just remember, you are in charge. You are willing to exchange your time for someone's money, but you are not a prisoner. You can leave a job if you are miserable. Being unhappy is a WOMBAT—a waste of money, brains, and time.

PROCRASTINATION IS THE THIEF OF TIME

When graduation day arrives, many students confess that they haven't had time to think about what they want to do next. They must have been thinking about something more important. Now they are in a panic because they have to pay the rent and deal with student loans, car payments, credit card debt, and plenty of other things, too, so it is understandably tempting to accept the first job that is offered. Too many people are miserable because they think they don't have a choice. Of course they do. They have plenty of choices. But first there is some homework to do.

FIRST STEPS

You'd think it would be easy to decide what you want to do. It is relatively easy if you just want a "job" job, like being a dishwasher or deciding you want to spend your entire life making sandwiches.

Thinking about a career is really hard work. The trouble is there are too many choices. Imagine you've decided to write a cookbook with the title *Chicken Dishes of the World*. You'll drown because the subject is way too big. It would be far easier to settle for *Chicken Dishes of Detroit*. I'm kidding, but you know what I mean. Try and narrow your focus and be realistic. Don't fantasize about being a consultant to Thomas Keller. If you can afford to live on air and tap water, consider instead taking a job in his restaurant as an unpaid intern, or apply for an entry-level position in one of his restaurants. This will give you the opportunity to see whether this is a place where you really want to work. It will be terrific if it pans out, but if it doesn't, you have gained invaluable knowledge. You will free your mind to explore other opportunities.

EXPLORE THE POSSIBILITIES AND
ALL THE POSSIBILITIES WITHIN THE POSSIBILITIES

If you are absolutely stumped, spread out every section of the Sunday newspaper and select only the one you can't wait to read: business, style, dining, science, weddings, the arts, real estate, book reviews, national news, etc. Now you have given yourself a few clues about what you genuinely care about and provided yourself with the beginning of a road map.

WRITE YOUR OWN OBITUARY

Whatever it is you want do, I suggest you begin by writing your own obituary and then try to live accordingly so you can be sure of what others will say about you when the last trumpet sounds.

This is what an elderly churchgoing lady decided to do. She knew her end was near, and she was eagerly anticipating it. She had led a good life and believed everyone would say nice things about her at her funeral, which she had planned with great care.

She went to the preacher of her church and said, "This is the dress I want to wear in my casket. I want these hymns to be sung." Handing him a sheet of paper, she said, "These are the words I want you to say. And I want to be buried with a fork in my right hand."

"A fork?" asked the puzzled vicar. "Why do you want a fork?"

"Well," said the old lady, "all my life, I've been going to church suppers and when they are clearing the table after the main course, they always say, 'Keep the fork,' and I've discovered it's because there's always something sweet coming next."

Writing your own obituary could be a useful exercise. It will make you think hard about how you want others to think of you. For example:

> You were a tireless champion in the effort to rid the world of foie gras, caged chickens, endangered fish, and greasy fries. You were president of the League of Abstinence, and your charm and graciousness persuaded Congress to pass legislation to create a nation of fat-free food. You approached your work with boundless energy and total dedication.

See? There you go. Now you know what it is you have always wanted to do.

ANALYZE YOURSELF

Here's another game to play that is inspired by Richard Bolles, author of *What Color Is Your Parachute?* Draw two simple suns, both with spokes sticking out from the center. Think of one sun as negative energy and the other as positive energy.

Along the spokes of the negative sun, write the things you don't want to do or are not good at doing. For instance, you don't want to work in a restaurant, don't want to work late at night, don't want to work indoors, don't want to work in a retail business, don't want to sell anything, don't have a culinary degree . . . keep going. You may end up realizing that you want to be an organic farmer, take to the high seas, get a gig as a chef on a luxury yacht, work on a fish or mushroom farm, or become a beekeeper.

Now, turn to the positive sun and picture yourself in the center of this universe. Think about such things as, Who am I? What can I do? What do I want to do more than anything else? The point is to carefully evaluate what is important to you. Don't worry about everyone else. Focus on you—only you.

Do you really want to spend more time with your family? Do you secretly want a lot of free time so you can go roller blading? Do you want to live near an airport, an arts center, a medical facility, good schools, great restaurants, or rich folk (important if you want to start a catering company)?

Make a copy of the table of contents of this book and try to match your inner desires with one or several of the job areas I have listed. Recognize that new opportunities are constantly appearing in the form of jobs that have never been known before (like starting your own food blog supported by advertising). You may even create a career that is unique to your own extraordinary talents.

QUESTIONS TO ASK YOURSELF (SLOWLY AND HONESTLY)

Do you like working alone, in your pajamas, with only your computer and the purring cat on your lap for company? You could decide to become an impoverished food writer.

Would you prefer to get dressed and go somewhere on a schedule and work with others? Get a job as a cooking-school teacher or work for a public-relations agency that specializes in food.

Do you like to work with your hands? Become a bread baker or a pastry chef.

Are you craving fame or fortune? Get yourself on television anyway you can. Offer to do the grocery shopping for a food celebrity.

Do you like having a lot of responsibility and find it invigorating to make decisions? Become an executive chef.

Do you hate the idea of working every evening and on many holidays? Then don't get a job in a restaurant.

Do you long to travel? It is difficult to land a job as a travel writer, but considerably easier to become a culinary tour guide or

The Monell Center is a nonprofit independent scientific institute dedicated to interdisciplinary basic research on the senses of taste, smell, and chemosensory irritation. In addition to increasing fundamental knowledge about the chemical senses, basic research at Monell relates to significant public health and quality of life issues, including obesity, diabetes, hypertension, pediatric health, occupational safety, environmental pollution, and homeland security. Our appreciation of many of life's pleasures, such as the evocative realms of scent and flavor, also is enhanced through discoveries from Monell. Monell's science connects us intimately to the world around us, helping to improve the human experience.

a cheese buyers or a specialty food market such as Wegmans or Whole Foods—other jobs where you will be expected to make many exploratory trips abroad.

Are you an accountant who loves restaurants? Transfer your skills to the hospitality field.

Do you prefer working with small, delicate utensils, or power tools? If the latter, your future may include ice carving. If you yearn to become a wedding-cake designer, you probably won't be thrilled to be asked to cut up a side of beef.

By eliminating things you don't want to do; you will begin to narrow your focus into things you *do* want to accomplish.

If you are a professional chef with all-around skills, you can consider every possible field: Interested in science? Apply for a food research job at NASA, Starbucks, Yum! Brands, Panera Bread, M&M/Mars, or the Monell Center (see sidebar).

NOW WHAT?

There are a couple of ways to plan your future. One is to decide where you want to live—Alaska or Hawaii, the North Pole, or Cleveland? Settle on a location and then start looking for a job. Or decide what job you are looking for and be prepared to move to wherever the job takes you.

IF YOU DON'T ASK FOR WHAT YOU WANT, THE ANSWER IS ALWAYS NO

If you don't ask, the chances somebody will come along and hand a career to you are pretty close to zero.

ALSO BEAR IN MIND . . .

If you don't even know what you are looking for, you will have a devil of a time finding it, even if it is right under your nose!

TOTTING UP THE BENEFITS

Deciding whether to accept a position should not depend on such factors as whether you will be provided with health care and other benefits. Don't settle for second choice because you are craving security. There is no such thing as security. Princess Diana had a diamond tiara, lived in a palace, and had both medical and dental benefits, but none of these things gave her any measure of security—or happiness.

Of course, I realize the idea of forgoing benefits may not work for you, but if you can earn enough to pay for your own health insurance, it enables you to evaluate a job opening by other criteria, like how much you will enjoy it.

I had a twenty-one-year-old student in one of my classes who was offered a job as the assistant to the chairman of a company that was opening hotels around the world. He spoke five languages, wanted to travel, and was graduating from culinary school with high honors. The position paid a handsome salary, but provided no medical or dental benefits. Instead, he accepted a job in a small town because it came with a brand new car—and generous benefits.

Recommended Books

Bolles, Richard Nelson. *Job-Hunting Tips for the So-Called Handicapped or People Who Have Disabilities: A Supplement to What Color Is Your Parachute?* Berkeley: Ten Speed Press, 1991.

————. *What Color Is Your Parachute? How to Find Your Mission In Life.* Berkeley: Ten Speed Press, 2000.

Hansen, Katharine. *A Foot In The Door: Networking Your Way Into The Hidden Job Market.* Berkeley: Ten Speed Press, 2000.

Kursman, Louise M. *Best Résumés For College Students And New Grads.* 2nd ed. St. Paul: JIST Works, 2006.

Levinson, Harry, ed. *Designing and Managing Your Career.* Cambridge, MA: Harvard Business School Press, 1989.

Stanny, Barbara. *Secrets of Six-Figure Women: Surprising Strategies to Up Your Earnings and Change Your Life.* New York: HarperBusiness, 2004.

Ask someone at the reference desk of your local public library for *The Occupational Outlook Handbook.* It lists all kinds of information you would need to know (including the salary) of just about any occupation you can think of. Visit http://www.bls.gov/oco for more information.

"When I don't know what to do I've found the best advice I can give myself is, 'What the heck.'"

—**MARILYN MONROE**

"Networking is one of the most positive and effective ways to find a job or expand your business. It is the process that leads to building relationships to support your goals. It takes time, planning and follow-up—which means networking is always ongoing. It doesn't stop at the end of a conference or after a chance meeting. Remember too, that networking is different from selling. The object is the relationship: you are not trying to get someone to buy your product or services in twenty seconds or less. The value of networking is reaped over time and pays off in both imaginable and unimaginable ways."

—**BARBARA GULINO**
(http://www.barbargulino.com)
and **JACKIE GORDON**
(http://www.divalicious.biz)

1

restaurants and food service

EATING OUT IS one of our favorite pastimes. For some, perfection means an elegant room with an ambiance of sophistication and luxury. The tables are far apart. The chairs are upholstered (like the guests) in costly fabrics. The flowers are extravagant. The linens are crisp. The crystal sparkles, and the gleaming silver is heavy in your hand. The lighting is soft and flattering. The movement in the room flows evenly, as though an unseen hand were conducting the orchestra while soothing the guests who are quietly eating their meals.

Other people are more at home in crowded bistros and casual neighborhood eateries. There, the brain-hammering noise reverberates; plates are as big as bicycle wheels. It's acceptable for the server to ask, who gets the ribs? or to drop by tableside to ask, how's everything, folks? No one answers because they are too busy eating.

Contrasts of style abound. At the top of the food chain, froths and foams appear and disappear as fast as a rainbow after a summer storm. There will always be a place for the hushed elegance of fine restaurants, but the rules and conventions of dining have changed across a broad swath of the nation. Many restaurant goers are impatient with yesterday's rituals and ceremonies. Today we demand fast, helpful service that is neither stuffy nor intimidating. We look for big flavors, generous servings, prompt attention, and value for our money.

In ever-increasing numbers, we flock to newer restaurants where there are no dress codes and reservations may not be required. We are daring to savor new tastes, marveling at the dazzling decor and freedom of choices when we dine out. Charming new places to eat are populated with young servers wearing cheerful smiles and snowy white aprons tied flatly around slim waists.

From large cities to small towns we are having a glorious time, sharing in the abundance of the good earth, shouting applause and encouragement for the chefs, and spurring them on to new creations to delight us. And in turn, they, like a jam of jazz musicians, play set after set, variation after variation, and inspire each other with flair and imagination.

When the new American cuisine first streaked across the horizon, we caught glimpses of some of its many components, but trying to define it was as difficult as trying to pet a porcupine. What we can see now, as we look back at that birthing, is that the new American cuisine was the mother—and sustainable agriculture the father—of what has now emerged as a sustainable cuisine. It is no accident that this new baby rapidly developed a social conscience. Everywhere, the vibrant buzzwords are *fresh, fresh, fresh,* harmonized with *seasonal, artisanal,* and, of course, *heirloom, organic,* and *local.* There has never been a more exhilarating time to work in a restaurant. And for so many dreaming of working in the food world, that is where they are headed.

THE STRUCTURE OF A RESTAURANT

What follows is a breakdown of the various positions in a typical, very large restaurant.

BACK OF THE HOUSE

Executive chef
Chef de cuisine
Pastry chef
Sous chef
Chef de partie
Line cooks:
    Poissonier (fish cook)
    Saucier (sauce-and-meat cook)
    Entremetier (vegetable cook)

Hot appetizers or grill cook
Garde manger (cold appetizers and soup cook)
Pastry assistant
Baker
Butcher
Prep cook
Dishwasher
Stagiaire (apprentice)

SPECIAL-EVENTS STAFF

Banquet manager
Banquet chef
Banquet maître d'
Banquet waitstaff
Banquet sales staff

FRONT OF THE HOUSE

General manager
Maître d'
Captain
Receptionist/host
Bartender
Sommelier
Waitstaff/servers
Busboys/runners

ADMINISTRATION

Owner/CEO
Assistant to the CEO
Restaurant consultant
Chief financial officer
Controller
Legal consultant
Human resources manager
Public relations manager
Marketing manager
Facilities designer
Director of purchasing
Food and beverage controller

"A cook and a chef are different entities. *Chef* is a title. A chef can be good or bad or everything in between; he or she can be a hotel chef, restaurant chef, TV chef, personal chef, or a corporate chef. *Chef* denotes a job. But when you are a cook that is who you are. It's your spine and your soul. It suffuses all that you touch. When you see the soil bursting with young lettuce, with tomatoes, with light green vines of peas, all the molecules between your glaze and those vegetables are charged with the energy of cooking. The air sparkles."

—**MICHAEL RUHLMAN**,
chef and author

■

"I'm addicted to heat, sweat, fire, blood, and tears. Those are my drugs. When I'm in my restaurant and it's jamming, there's a great buzz and energy that's my stage, my theater, and I'm my happiest."

—**TODD ENGLISH**, chef/owner of
Olives, Fish Club, and many more
restaurants

■

Payroll and benefits manager
Accounts receivable staff
Accounts payable staff
Auditor
Audio/visual consultant for special events
Computer consultant
Web master
Florist
Reservation clerical staff
Facilities manager
Storeroom manager
Maintenance contractor
Security

It takes an astonishing number of specialized staff to operate a large restaurant. In addition to those working in the back (kitchen) and front of the house (dining room), there are numerous independent consultants and contractors. They include art directors; graphic designers; the team at an advertising agency; architects and kitchen planners; legal, union, and restaurant consultants; and a Web master. All these specialists contribute their skills in a multilayered operation. In a small restaurant, the owner/chef and a tiny cadre of staff manage to combine their talents to take on a multitude of tasks.

WHAT EMPLOYERS LOOK FOR

You may think you know where you'd like to work, but you must also consider myriad aspects of the job. First, it helps to know what top chefs and restaurateurs look for when hiring a new kitchen employee.

More than a decade ago, leading chefs in Europe and the United States responded to a thirty-six-question survey organized by ShawGuides. A total of 391 (29 percent of the European and 24 percent of the U.S.) chefs responded. Despite its age, the survey's results are still pertinent today. Each chef was asked to rate ten abilities or qualities that he or she looks for when hiring. The answers:

- Professional demeanor: 93 percent
- Product knowledge: 89 percent
- References: 71 percent
- Accredited training: 62 percent
- Knowledge of cuisine specific to the region: 60 percent

They were also asked to describe personality traits in a new employee. The responses included "passion," "enthusiasm," "high energy level," "eager to learn," "perfectionist," "strong work ethic," "people skills," "humility," "ability to stay calm under pressure," "team player (preferably captain)," "athletic ability," "asks questions," "keeps their mouth shut," "clothes reflect a sense of style," and "gets their foot in the door any way they can."

Other qualities they looked for included "experience in a high-pressure, high-quality restaurant," "well-rounded training from a good culinary school or apprenticeship," "someone I can learn from," "someone I can teach from scratch," "eager to learn, eager to please," "looks me in the eye," "likes chaos, and "management ability."

———

"We must stop confusing efficiency with excellence. You have to be creative if you want to succeed. Honesty and the demand for excellence are prerequisites but you also have to create opportunities for professional growth. This is a requirement of every restaurant.

"We must respect the greatness of hundreds of years of culinary history and not abandon our business to fads and trends. The things that have to do with standards, that have to do with performance, the things that have to do with words like talent, that have to do with all these things, are part of our business. It's what makes it so attractive, so interesting, so sensual, and so organic to all of us who are in it.

"What makes a fine restaurant isn't necessarily the cost of building it, or the abilities of the chef. It is the quality of its management and management's dedication to relentless, precise devotion to detail, the dedication to please the guests and the ability to show those who work there that they are loved and cared for and their work is appreciated. Those who work in restaurants must love restaurants.

"A restaurant is like a mistress. We must work hard at being romantic. Eating must be an event, theater, a seduction, whether it is business or personal. All of life is seduction in which you mustn't hold anything back. . . .

"Restaurants are in the business of pleasure. Any threat to pleasure is a threat to business."

—JOE BAUM, *restaurateur of, among others, the Four Seasons New York, La Fonda del Sol, the Forum of the Twelve Caesars, Tower Suite, Zum Zum, Tavern on the Green, Aurora, the Rainbow Room, and Windows on the World*

———

"More and more young people are attracted to the industry, but it seems that after a few years, most have deserted the kitchens. We have to stop this exodus. The restaurant industry is aware of the difficulties confronting young chefs entering the business. It is the wise young chef who takes the time to see what is going on behind the scenes before applying for a job in the galley."

—**BOB KINKEAD**, chef/owner of Kinkead's restaurant

■

"I learned the foundation of cooking at a professional cooking school, but I also discovered the many directions, choices, and possibilities the culinary business offers—not just restaurant cooking, but wine, hotels, consulting, education, sales, TV, and books. And these opportunities continue to grow. I urge every culinary student to focus on what you would like to do, and seek out the wide-ranging experiences that will get you there.

"There is more to being a chef than cooking. You need to understand payroll, costs, insurance, mechanics, design, and public relations—and then there are the human-resource issues. To run a kitchen well you need to know how to deal with people."

—**ANDREW CARMELLINI**, chef/owner of A Voce

■

When the chefs were asked what aspects of their own culinary education were the most valuable, they said, "good teachers" "studying under top chefs," "learning basic techniques," "eating in many restaurants," "culinary school," "learning to taste," "European training," "reading," "apprenticeship," "learning to make a good sauce," "learning self-discipline," and "gaining a respect for food products."

Finally, when they were asked what advice they would give someone considering a culinary career, they answered, "Get a job in a restaurant before going to school and see if that's what you want to do," "Work only at the top restaurants (for nothing, if necessary)," "Never stop learning or studying," "Make it your life, not your job," "Taste, taste, taste," and "Remember who matters most—the guest."

For more information, visit http://www.careercooking. shawguides.com. For ShawGuides' free job-matching site, go to http://www.chefjobs.com.

GETTING THE JOB

Edward G. Leonard, CMD, AAC, president of the American Culinary Federation, offers this advice for anyone thinking of working in a restaurant as a cook: "The key is to get in the right kitchen from the start. The right kitchen is one that offers many things that will help a student grow and build a solid foundation for the future."

In the right kitchen:

- You are treated with respect.
- You are made to feel like part of the team.
- You are paid fairly for the work you do.
- You receive an introduction to the kitchen brigade and other department managers.
- Your contribution is valued.
- The kitchen is a learning environment for all.
- The kitchen has a philosophy of excellence in all areas.
- There is a culture of teamwork to make the culinary program become the best it can be.
- You receive feedback on your work and guidance as you look to grow.

When interviewing for a job, research the property or chef online. Google him or visit the library. Look for reviews, articles written about or by him or her, special dinners the chef has cooked, and more. Research will give you insight into the person you are considering training under and will tell you if the chef is someone who impacts the industry. You can also learn about the restaurant itself.

Once you have this information, you can then prepare questions for your interview. The questions you ask will show that you have done your homework and care enough to learn about where you want to work and train.

Plan your résumé and build it carefully to ensure a great future. A résumé that shows six to twelve months in various kitchens will not inspire top chefs to hire you. Spending a few months here and there and throwing around big names does not impress a future employer. In other words, there needs to be substance behind your experience. Truly learning all you can from the right kitchen with the right chef takes at least two to four years, depending on the size of the property.

Having a résumé that shows job commitment for at least a solid year or two makes you a more attractive candidate. Believing that you learned all you needed to about a kitchen in just six months can reflect badly on you or suggests you selected a kitchen that offered poor training. If the property is a large hotel, private club, or resort, a two- to three-year tenure during which time you moved up the kitchen brigade shows you are indeed worthwhile both as a student learning the trade and as a worker who has potential.

Your career's evolution must be planned thoughtfully, so select carefully. Choose a place and a chef who will take interest in you and is dedicated to culinary excellence.

Recognize that nothing beats a personal introduction to a company and that all jobs posted on the Internet will get hundreds of responses. Nevertheless, it is wise to check with industry-specific Web sites. For example, the RestaurantU.com job board includes features like the Job Detective, which helps you set the parameters of your search as wide or as narrow as you wish. This site has some valuable information about interviewing techniques, too.

Another highly recommended site is StarChefs online classifieds (http://www.starchefs.com). Bobby Flay of the Mesa Grill in Manhattan says, "I've found some of my best employees through StarChefs. It is a destination for hospitality employment and job opportunities online. You can search for hotel jobs, restaurant jobs, catering jobs, food journalism jobs, resort jobs, chef jobs, and all food service employment occupations in the hospitality industry."

Specific segments of the food industry often maintain their own job listings. Check listings in local newspapers and the back pages of trade magazines for help-wanted positions. Or take out your own ad in the personnel or classified section.

> "To be successful you need to embrace, understand, and follow basic culinary fundamentals, as they are the foundation of our profession. These fundamentals are needed to succeed in both the hot and cold kitchen, as well as in baking and pastry."
>
> —**FRITZ SONNENSCHMIDT**, certified master chef

> "To be successful is important of course, but I'd like to be remembered by my peers as a chef who gave something back to the industry, someone who cooked food that was important, yes, but also someone who brought others along, as others did for me."
>
> —**TOM COLICCHIO**, chef/owner of Craft, Craftbar, Craftsteak, and 'Witchcraft

BACK-OF-THE-HOUSE JOBS

Kitchens are notorious for harsh working conditions and demanding, domineering (and grossly unfair) chefs. Restaurant kitchens and the military are among the few places where not only is the pay low and the hours grueling, but the recruits keep coming in with optimism in their hearts.

Cooks are on their feet for the better part of a day, lifting heavy pots and sacks of potatoes, accumulating blisters and burns as if they were going out of style. They may or may not have health insurance; in older kitchens, workers toil in tight quarters and suffocating heat. There is little fresh air, and the atmosphere is often fraught with tension. Plus, it can be dangerous.

As the hours are long and vacations scarce, there is little or no time to get a life beyond the restaurant. The evening shift is demanding, and tempers flare when even the smallest thing goes wrong. This is high-stress work, and there are few pats on the back. A busy kitchen during the dinner service is a thousand times more tense than a hospital operating room.

Who could possibly want to work in these conditions? Evidently, thousands of eager culinary-school graduates, career changers, and those who just love to cook.

▶ Executive Chef

The executive chef reports to the restaurant's general manager. He (or she) operates more as an executive than as a chef. His role is to supervise every aspect of the kitchen, both culinary and baking and pastry. He is responsible for the efficient functioning of the back-of-the-house operations. He plans all the menus and establishes the menu price of each dish by calculating not only the cost of ingredients, but also the cost in labor. The overhead is also factored into the final tally, so not only must he be an excellent cook, but he also must also be something of a mathematician.

The executive chef makes sure there is an efficient distribution of work and workers. This means he plans the menu so some foods are grilled while others are cooked on top of the stove or roasted in the ovens. He makes decisions about portion control and the final presentation of the food on the plate, taking care to think not only about the form but also the color (so four plates arriving at the table are not all brown or white, but have contrasting brightly

"Sharing great food, simply prepared, is part and parcel of cooking bistro style. I know I'm happiest when sitting down to a good meal with people I know well, where the food is not being worshiped or fawned over, but rather has just taken its natural place in the moment. The message that comes across to the friends gathered at the table is that, yes, delicious food is important, but just as important are the good times involved with sharing that food."

—**GORDON HAMERSLEY**, chef/owner of Hamersley's Bistro in Boston colored accompaniments and garnishes). He balances simple dishes with those designed to appeal to guests with more adventurous tastes; he also offers menu choices for vegetarians and others with dietary restrictions.

The executive chef makes sure all the supplies arrive on time and in top condition, as last minute requests for special deliveries can be extremely costly. He establishes a network of dependable suppliers, sometimes using two vendors for the same ingredient (such as eggs or shrimp), in order to establish price competition. He makes decisions about purchasing new equipment and oversees its installation.

The executive chef makes all the important decisions about hiring, promoting—and firing—all the members of the kitchen staff, from the chefs and cooks to the dishwashers and cleaning crew. He meets regularly with the owner and the chef assigned to banquets. Increasingly, executive chefs are partners or owners of the restaurant (often with several investors). Customarily, he will have many years of experience before rising to this position in the restaurant hierarchy. He may also have earned at least a bachelor's degree and may have attained more formal education at a culinary school, college, or university.

"Some young chefs want to create a dish and sign it for recognition. When I was coming up, it was a work of the many. You couldn't recognize who created a dish. If a young chef works with Jean-Georges Vongerichten, he's not there to put his imprint on the dish. He's there to conform to the style of the house and absorb it for eight or ten years. Ingest the knowledge, regardless of whether you agree with it. Then adjust it to your style.

"It is essential for a student to work in a [professional] kitchen. He can choose a simple diner or a fancy restaurant. Get to work in both the dining room and kitchen. Get a taste of what the world of cooking is. Wash spinach. Peel potatoes. Work long hours and holidays. If you survive that, go to the next step—culinary school or apprenticeship.

"If you can afford to trade knowledge for money, then work in the best possible restaurant for at least a year. Give that commitment to a chef. If I see new, young employees bouncing around, I know they're trying to squeeze me like a lemon and then move on."

—JACQUES PÉPIN,
culinary superstar

MATTERS OF FACT

- Martha Stewart's net worth is estimated to be close to $1 billion. (She is not a chef.)
- Andy Warhol's series of Campbell's Soup paintings were sold at auction for $117 million. The cost of a real can of cream of tomato soup is—considerably less.
- The United States will generate $7.2 trillion dollars in the culinary and hospitality industry over the next five years.

▶ Banquets and Special-Events Chef

A banquet chef may work on the staff of a large restaurant or hotel or for a country club, sports facility, or cruise ship. The position entails consultation with the banquet manager to decide on a menu and the ability to provide eight to eight hundred meals almost simultaneously, depending on the size of the facility. The banquet chef supervises his own staff of chefs and waitstaff, consults with the banquet manager and the food and beverage director about wine service, and, in consultation with the executive chef, is responsible for the financial management of his department.

▶ Chef de Cuisine

The American Culinary Federation describes the chef de cuisine as "In charge of food production in a food-service operation, whether a single unit of a multi-unit operation or a freestanding operation." This means he or she is in charge of the culinary side of the restaurant. The chef de cuisine supervises full-time staff as they produce the food and most often reports to the executive chef. He calls out orders for food as they come in from waiters. He examines every plate before it leaves the kitchen. When needed, he or she can step in for the executive chef.

▶ Sous Chef

Sous chefs report to the chef de cuisine. A sous chef supervises and trains the kitchen staff. He takes responsibility for all the details, large and small, and often plans staff meals, schedules staff working times, and has a hand in placing orders for produce, meat, and other ingredients.

He makes sure that each table's orders are ready simultaneously so the servers can bring them out at the same time. (There are painful moments when three orders may be trashed if the fourth plate is not yet ready to be served. All these dishes will then be prepared again.) The sous chef has usually worked his way up the restaurant hierarchy after gaining experience at several stations.

From Home Cook to Restaurant Cook

by Alison Fong, culinary student

"ACCUSING A [RESTAURANT] COOK of being a home cook is a grave insult," said my cooking teacher. It implies that she does not possess the focus, urgency, foresight, and timing required for the professional kitchen. A home cook might spend an entire day making balsamic-lacquered duck with beet salad and cremini custards, but in a restaurant, a chef tosses off a dish like that while simultaneously preparing fifteen other things. Had my cooking teacher thrown the insult at me back when I was in class, it would have been completely accurate.

But I love to cook. I have always been enthralled with the spell that a little heat and some butter and salt can cast on an egg. That love drew me from office life to cooking school and finally into a position as a cook at an Italian restaurant. And for the first time, I can grasp the enormity of the slur.

On my first day on the job, I followed the sous chef around the kitchen with my little pocket notebook, scribbling down instructions. This was my first paid position at a restaurant. I was to be a line cook, a position given to me because I had worked with the newly appointed chef in another restaurant. Though I was hired as a fish cook, I had worked with fish for all of two days in another restaurant, one week at culinary school, and once at home.

My notebook amused the sous chef. "I used to be like you, I wanted to write down everything as I did in school, but the kitchen doesn't always let you," he offered. Even so, my notebook came in handy when I had to retrieve the vegetables for a lobster dish the following day. I chopped them into the correct shapes, frequently referring to my notes. But when it came to cooking fish on the line, my little book wasn't as helpful. I had to pay attention to a live demonstration.

"Place a pan on high heat until very hot," instructed the sous chef. "Add oil. Look for ripples in the oil to shimmy across the pan so that the halibut doesn't glue itself to the pan. Season the fish now, not earlier, to prevent the fish from weeping. Gently dip a corner of the halibut into the pan. If it doesn't stick, the pan is ready. With one hand, tilt the pan away from you so that any oil splashing will not scald your face. Hold the fish with the other hand, and gently slide the fish into the pan." As he talked, he demonstrated exactly what he explained. Finally, he pressed the sides of the halibut to feel for firmness and then slid a two-pronged fork into its center. Without any resistance from the flesh, the fish was done.

For the first time, I grasped the obvious. Cooking involves all your senses. The sous chef possessed an understanding of food that can only come with concentration and experience. Without a glance at a pan, he knows when the garlic has overcooked by the smell that wafts across the kitchen, that a cook's knife needs sharpening by looking at the cut it makes in the meat.

I learned to make the same five dishes over and over again. I soon began to own my station and arranged thirty ingredients at hand like a memorized jigsaw puzzle for optimal efficiency. I learned to pick the perfect piece of tuna for well-done or rare, and to preheat a pan or two in anticipation of a fish needed on a moment's notice. I am no longer just a home cook.

▶ Line Cook and Chef de Partie

Apart from having the necessary skills, unflagging energy, and the fortitude to withstand burns, cuts, and sore feet, the line cook must be prompt, even-tempered, and willing to follow directions without complaint. He may be delighted to land a coveted job in a high-profile restaurant earning close to minimum wage. In addition to his cooking skills, a line cook may also need the qualification of a culinary degree and the ability to communicate in a language other than his own first tongue. Experience as a line cook may be the bottom rung of the ladder, but it is a vitally important step in the long climb to reach the stars.

A chef de partie is the head of a station—such as fish or meat—in a restaurant so large that there are two or more line cooks on the same station.

A JOB ON THE LINE

by Mat Nugent, culinary student

"Fire twenty-one, thirty-four, ten, eleven, and twenty-seven," screams the chef as he sauces and wipes the order of scallops. I look at the tickets to see what to plate for each table. I have no table twenty-one or thirty-four on my board. A sick feeling overcomes me. I stand motionless and stiff. A bead of sweat drips off my forehead in slow motion. The sound of the chef bellowing in my ear wakes me from my trance. "Where is my food?"

"I don't know."

"Find it. Now!"

Sure, this scenario is nothing new to the experienced line cook, but for the novice, the sound of a screaming chef instills panic, anxiety, and fear. It is my first night on the grill and I'm going down in flames.

What do I need on the grill? I look at the tickets on the front of the line and quickly toss on the fire a chicken and three filets. I cover the meats with pie pans like I have seen others do in the past and reconfirm that I have everything I need to complete all the fired tables. Just then the sound of the ticket machine sounds like an alarm. More orders are coming in. "We've got two ten tops walking in," announces the runner.

"Order five filets—two medium-rare, three well-done, three chicken, four lamb, and five strips—all medium-rare," shouts the sous chef. Numerous profanities enter my head as I dive into my reach-in refrigerator for all the meats. As I begin filling up the grill with protein, I notice that my fire is dwindling away.

The sous chef glares at me. "You better get that fire up quick, the dining room just got flat." I have no idea what he means, but I know it can't be good. (Later, I find out that "flat" means every available seat in the restaurant is filled.) Within minutes, the grill looks like a scene from Satan's Alley; the back half is ghost-white and one of my chickens is on fire. The chef returns and calls for tables.

"Break it down." Relief fills my entire body. I feel like I just ran a marathon at a dead sprint. I walk back into the prep area and gulp down a pitcher of water. The chef appears and says, "It's fun, huh?" I consider this. I lost three steaks, one lamb, and I incinerated a chicken. I am dead tired. The hair on my right arm is scorched and the burn on my right wrist is filled with ash and grease. It's midnight on a Saturday and all I want to do is go home and pass out. But I didn't quit—I stuck it out and held my own. So was that fun? Hell, yeah!

• MATTERS OF FACT •

FISH NAMES HAVE frequently been changed to make them more appealing. After all, who would want to eat something called pout, carp, or croaker? Patagonian toothfish exporters quickly saw the value of calling their catch Chilean sea bass. Mahimahi was once called dolphin. It was a big turnoff, or course. Most people were horrified to think Flipper was on the menu. In fact, mahimahi has more names than almost any other fish—none of them complimentary. This extraordinarily ugly creature is also known as bellyfish, goosefish, and sea devil. Since its name was changed to mahimahi (Hawaiian for "strong-strong"), it has gone from strength to strength. As long as diners never see what it looks like whole, they love it.

▶ Prep Cook

This entry-level job is lower on the totem pole than line cook. A prep cook has a (mostly thankless) job that involves utterly tedious, repetitive tasks, including peeling potatoes and carrots, pitting olives and cherries, squeezing citrus fruits, and the many other vitally important duties that constitute readying ingredients to be cooked or seared. The prep cook is the foot soldier on whom the entire kitchen staff depends. He usually receives minimum wage, but the amount varies depending on whether the facility is unionized.

Working at a Restaurant in Spain

by Cedric Vongerichten

It is already 1:30 in the afternoon, and I can feel the intensity of the sun through the roof of my apartment. It is another dry, hot day in Spain, almost oppressively hot. I got four hours sleep; we finished kind of late yesterday because we had to do a lot of prep for this evening, Saturday night. Also, I went with Pedro and Antonio, some other cooks, for a *cerveza* San Miguel at Chiquita, the local dive. After work you have this rush of adrenaline and it is impossible to go to bed right away.

I take a quick shower, jump on my 125cc Peugeot scooter, and ride for twenty minutes through the narrow, cliff-hugging, cactus-lined roads of Spain's Costa Brava. Once I get to the restaurant, I park in front of the sign that says El Bulli Employees. I make my way into the locker room and get ready. Every day is a battle to see who gets an apron—there are never enough. Today, I win.

It is ten minutes to two. I pass by the storeroom, grab a bottle of water, and get in the kitchen. I say hi to Rosa and Rick, the dishwashers. I situate myself between Pedro and Antonio around the prep table and sharpen my knives.

Alberto, one of the head chefs, arrives, barely says hi, and goes to the white board to write the list of things we have to prepare:

> Cook and clean 20 kg of crab
> Peel and puree 40 kg of carrots
> Avocado rolls 50 items
> Truffle rolls 50 items
> Trim 60 rabbit ears
> De-bone 50 quails
> Quail stock
> Mackerel fumet
> Family meal
> Salmon toro
> Tomato water 4 liters
> Crack fresh coconut 20 kg
> 100 slices of cactus
> Filet 60 baby red snapper

By the look of things, today is going to be a long day. There is not even time to read the entire list, let alone translate it from Catalan to French, my mother tongue. Chef Para, who is responsible for the preparation crew, yells something in Catalan. I watch what everyone else is doing in order to follow. We start with cleaning crabs.

Para switches off the regular lights and plugs in the black lights. Chef Ferran Adria uses black lights in the crab-cleaning process because it helps us to distinguish inedible tissue (such as cartilage) from the crab meat;

it's a great technique. The prep cooks align on both sides of the table, armed with toothpicks to start the long process of crab picking. I want to explain to Para that my hands are allergic to shellfish—not the rest of me, just my hands. It's sort of weird. I try in English, then in French; I can see Para getting annoyed. I want to say that I need latex gloves, but it's not worth it. I give up and go back to work. I'll just have to live with crab blisters tonight.

The day goes on, with tons of prep and a break at 6:00 for family meal. I have about twenty minutes to relax and to eat my only meal of the day. Then it's back to prep.

At some point in the evening, Alberto comes in the prep room in a fury, screaming. I follow the other prep cooks rushing through the main kitchen.

The chefs de partie and sous chefs are so in the weeds they'll take help from anyone; even me. I get to put together the dishes. Jose gives me the cooked fish, vegetables, and sauces, and I assemble the plates and place them on the pick-up table. Nothing too complicated, nothing I can screw up.

This is my favorite time of the day. I'm in the main kitchen; I'm seeing the food go out. Sometimes I even get to taste it. These five or ten minutes make the crab blisters worth it.

▶ Butcher

The role of the butcher has changed dramatically in the past few years. Traditionally, butchers broke down large carcasses into recognizable cuts of meat, but nowadays this work has been taken over by meat-processing plants. This means the role of contemporary butchers has become more specialized. In-house restaurant butchers may be responsible for dividing pieces of meats, poultry, and even fish into portion-size cuts ready for cooking. This might involve dividing a beef tenderloin into single servings or cutting a whole fish into fillets.

The skills in butchery include manual dexterity, accuracy, physical strength, and the fortitude to work on one's feet for several hours at a time. A butcher must have a fundamental understanding of meat muscle structure and cooking methods.

Recommended Books

North American Meat Processors Association. *The Meat Buyer's Guide.*

Picard, Martin. *Au Pied de Cochon.* Montreal: Restaurant Au Pied de Cochon, 2006.

Rozin, Elizabeth. *The Primal Cheeseburger.* New York: Penguin Books, 1994.

Sinclair, Upton. *The Jungle.* Belmont, CA: Wadsworth, 2004.

Witherspoon, Kimberly, and Peter Meehan, eds. *How I Learned to Cook: Culinary Educators from the World's Greatest Chefs.* New York: Bloomsbury, 2007.

Web sites

American Association of Meat Processors, http://www.aamp.com

American Meat Science Association, http://www.meatscience.org

Meat and Poultry: the industry's information site, http://www.meatpoultry.com

National Meat Association, http://www.nmaonline.org

North American Meat Processors Association, http://www.namp.com

$\mathcal{M}$AKING BEEF MANTI

by Nathaniel Auchter, culinary student

WHEN I WAS an intern at Zaytinya, I noticed a woman who was working on a single project for the entire day. When I asked what she was doing, and why it was taking so long, I was told that she was making manti. I had an opportunity to try this beef manti, which consists of ground beef with spices, wrapped in a pasta dough. It was fabulous, particularly when covered in paprika butter and yogurt sauce. The trick, however, is that these manti are about the size of a thumbnail. In order to prepare enough for Friday or Saturday night, or really any night (it's a hot seller), the prep cook must work from the time she arrives in the morning until she leaves at the end of the shift. She spends her entire day rolling dough, cutting squares, filling them with the ground beef, and then wrapping them into tiny little purses.

• RECIPE FOR SUCCESS •

$\mathcal{A}$N INTERVIEW WITH BRUCE AIDELLS

by Marguerite Thomas

BRUCE AIDELLS EARNED a PhD in biology at the University of California, Santa Cruz, in 1974. Ultimately, he exchanged his lab coat for a chef's toque. In 1983 he founded Aidells Sausage Company and quickly earned a reputation as an innovator in the gourmet sausage business. He soon became a frequent guest on the Food Network and had his own cooking segment on San Francisco's *Evening* magazine. He has appeared on *Martha Stewart Living*, *NBC Today*, *Home Cooking*, *Al Roker on the Road*, and on four episodes of *Paul James Home Grown Cooking*.

MARGUERITE THOMAS: Just how did sausages become a part of your life in the first place?

BRUCE AIDELLS: It certainly wasn't planned! My first attempt to make sausage was in England. I was there working on a postdoc in cancer research, and I was inspired by Julia Child's sausage making in *Mastering the Art of French Cooking*.

MT: Volume I or II?

BA: Volume II, the one that has a big section on charcuterie. I'd brought a little meat grinder over to England with me from the States. I spent hours adapting it to English electrical current, then

continued

"Regular supermarket pork is almost like tofu on four legs because it is so lean."

—JOSH OZERSKY, meat expert

continued from page 28

stayed up all night feeding the meat into the itty bitty little grinder, then trying to stuff it into the casings. It was not a pleasant experience.

MT: But you obviously weren't turned off the process forever. What made you decide to give sausage making another try?

BA: I was back in the Bay Area, and it was evident that the research lab where I was working was in eminent danger of closing down. I just happened to run into a guy who said he was opening a delicatessen that he was going to name Picnique. I asked him if he needed any pâtés and sausages for the shop, and he said yes, so I started making them. At about the time the lab actually did shut down, I went to a Julia Child cooking demonstration and ran into a woman who was going there too. It turned out she was in the process of opening a place called Poulet.

MT: Another deli?

BA: Well, it had some take-out gourmet foods and a few little tables. It was over in Gourmet Gulch, right near Chez Panisse. In fact it's just celebrated its twenty-fifth birthday. Anyway, I asked if she needed a chef, and she hired me.

MT: So what was it that made you think you could convert sausages into mortgage payments?

BA: For one thing, the timing was good. This was the early 1980s, when everyone was into Louisiana-style cooking, and everything was blackened—remember those days? So that's why I was making andouille. Besides, I was really good at making sausage.

MT: What characteristics does a good sausage maker have?

BA: You have to have a very large understanding of and knowledge about spices. And I also liked trying lots of different cuisines. I think you need those things. Then, mostly through trial and error, you develop your own recipes.

MT: When you decided to expand the enterprise, did you develop a business plan?

BA: No, I didn't even know I had a business.

In 2002, Bruce Aidells left the company to pursue his writing career. He has written numerous magazine articles and eleven cookbooks, including *The Complete Meat Cookbook* and *Bruce Aidell's Complete Sausage Book.*

"Understand, when you eat meat, that something did die. You have an obligation to value it—not just the sirloin but also all those wonderful tough little bits."

—**ANTHONY BOURDAIN**, restaurateur and author of *Kitchen Confidential*

∎

"The most moist, flavorful meat is concealed under a thick slab of crisp fat that would make a cardiologist blanch.

"Asking a critic to name his favorite book is like asking a butcher to name his favorite pig."

—**BRYAN MILLER**, former *New York Times* restaurant critic

∎

▶ Dishwasher

Everyone loves a fairy tale: a poor boy who grows up in a log cabin or on the wrong side of the tracks can be elected president of the United States. When he was twelve, the future president of the Culinary Institute of America began his career as a dishwasher. So did John Doherty, who is now executive chef at the Waldorf Astoria, one of the world's most luxurious hotels with annual food sales of $55 million.

A job as a dishwasher may mean scrubbing a pot as large as a witch's cauldron and simultaneously being responsible for fragile crystal glasses, delicate bone china, and valuable silver. New technologies may eventually eliminate the need for the physical presence of a live person in the dishwashing area, but for now the job provides much-needed employment for entry-level applicants. In some socially responsible companies, the job of scraping the dishes and organizing the flatware and glasses into the correct machine may be available to those who may be marginally mentally handicapped but able to perform their duties reliably and show up on time.

• RECIPE FOR SUCCESS •

Anselmo Ruiz, chef de cuisine at Cafe Ba Ba Beeba in Chicago

WHAT IF YOU can't afford to go to culinary school, can't speak English, and are only fourteen years old with no formal education. Can you still become a successful chef? Chef Anselmo Ruiz is proof positive that it is indeed possible. All it took was hard work, the opportunity and an extraordinary amount of perseverance. Ruiz came to the United States from his home in Jalisco, Mexico, in 1983. The eighth of twelve children, he was fourteen when he crossed the border with his older brother to join six siblings who had preceded them to Chicago. He immediately got a job as a dishwasher at one of Chicago's top restaurants thanks to a brother who was working there as a janitor and a fake ID that said he was twenty-one.

When he finished his dishwashing duties, he wandered into the kitchen and offered to assist wherever he could without pay. After six months, the executive chef recognized a spark in the boy and decided to let him try his hand at cleaning fish.

After a few months as prep cook, Anselmo was promoted to the soufflé station, then to the line, and later was appointed to the position of sous chef.

After performing his duties as sous chef for six years, he was elevated to chef de cuisine. His job has taken him to cities in Spain and to Paris, Lyon, San Francisco, and New York and given him the opportunity to work with many of the world's most celebrated chefs. It has also enabled him to raise a family and to help take care of loved ones who are still in Mexico.

Chef Ruiz has become an American citizen, and he and his wife are raising two daughters who talk about becoming chefs one day. He still works for the company that gave him his start in the restaurant business and now takes pride in helping others realize their goals, too.

Recommended Books

The American Culinary Federation. *So, You Want to Be a Chef*. Hoboken, NJ: Wiley, 2008.
This definitive text on the professional-cooking-career ladder in America explains the disciplines and attributes needed to excel as a chef.

On Becoming a Professional Chef is based on American Culinary Federation standards for the professional development of cooks and chefs with strategies and timeframes for achieving success within the hospitality/food-service industry. Topics include the role of the modern chef; passion for food, cooking, and people; culinary learning models for students; profession certification; and culinary competitions to hone skills.

Boulud, Daniel. *Letters to a Young Chef*. New York: Basic Books, 2003.

Brefere, Lisa M., et al. *So You Want to Be a Chef? Your Guide to Culinary Careers*. Hoboken: Wiley, 2005.

Brenner, Leslie. *The Fourth Star: Dispatches from Inside Daniel Boulud's Celebrated New York Restaurant*. Clarkson Potter/Publishers, 2002.

Buford, Bill. *Heat: An Amateur's Adventures as Kitchen Slave, Line Cook, Pasta-Maker, and Apprentice to a Dante-Quoting Butcher in Tuscany*. New York: Knopf, 2006.

The Culinary Institute of America. *The Professional Chef*.

Dornenburg, Andrew, and Karen Page. *Culinary Artistry*. Hoboken, NJ: Wiley, 1996.

Becoming a Chef. Hoboken: Wiley, 2003.

Labensky, Sarah R. *On Cooking: Techniques from Expert Chefs*. Upper Saddle River, NJ: Prentice Hall, 2002.

Maccioni, Sirio, and Peter Elliott. *Sirio: The Story of My Life and Le Cirque*. Hoboken: Wiley, 2004.

Pépin, Jacques. *The Apprentice: My Life in the Kitchen*. Boston: Houghton Mifflin, 2003.

Web sites

Food Arts magazine, http://www.foodarts.com
Nation's Restaurant News, http://www.nrn.com

▶ Pastry Chef

The pastry chef's day usually begins earlier than others in the kitchen. He or she mixes batter and dough, freezes ice cream and sorbets, and generally assembles all the elements for the desserts. It's the pastry chef's job to train her staff.

Pastry chefs have become rock stars of the culinary world. Recruiters show up at their door armed with promises to put their name on their own stand-alone dessert menu. Occasionally, they are even offered a partnership in the enterprise and a share in the profits. Pastry chefs are writing cookbooks, appearing on television, and finding time to invent new creations to delight the eye and the palate.

ℭAKE DESIGNER

by Anne E. McBride

 FROM CAKE DECORATOR in a bakery to cake designer commanding thousands of dollars for a cake, the field of cake decorating has evolved spectacularly over the past twenty-five years. Modern cake designers, as demonstrated by people like Sylvia Weinstock, Ron Ben-Israel, and Toba Garrett, have taken their industry to many levels above what was once considered to be the norm. For cake designers, everything on a cake has to be edible, even if some parts will not be eaten.

Getting Started

A pastry chef in a bakery does what is generally known as cake decorating, or cake finishing, explains Toba Garrett. In such a position, you will be splitting a cake before leveling it and filling it with preserves or citrus creams, then covering it smoothly with a butter-cream icing. If you work in a fast-paced environment, you will have limited time to pipe borders, so you will perhaps only pipe butter-cream roses on top of the cake and add a simple inscription. It's a repetitive process. If you are a baker for a supermarket, you might need even fewer skills, as the cakes might be split and filled for you, and plastic scenery might be used to adorn the cake. You do not need a professional pastry degree for such jobs, but it is helpful to take some cake decorating classes that will give you the basic and intermediate skills you will use over and over again. The salary for these positions starts at twelve to twenty dollars an hour, with time and a half on Saturdays and double pay on Sundays. These are typically unionized positions with benefits, but with remarkably few opportunities to indulge in creativity.

In a more upscale supermarket such as Whole Foods or a local mid- to high-end caterer that commands higher prices for their cakes, you will need a much broader range of skills. Garrett says that in such positions you not only have to be able to ice cakes very smoothly with butter cream, but also use rolled fondant to produce very complex and lush borders, along with tridimensional flowers in chocolate, marzipan, or gum paste. You may also need to be skilled in fine piping, brushed embroidery, and drapery with fondant. Positions like

continued

- Fashions change. Today's wedding cake designers (most, anyway) no longer look with favor to the tacky plastic bride and groom figures standing stiffly on the top layer. Pedestals and pillars have been jettisoned and decorations of fresh flowers have gained favor. Now, five or even six cake layers are placed one on top of another, each composed of a different symphony of flavors.

- Donald Trump, the arbiter of refined taste, selected for his most recent marriage, "An orange Grand Marnier chiffon wedding cake—five-foot-high, seven-tiered, 200 pounds, 32 inches in diameter, covered with approximately 3,000 white icing roses, and filled with Grand Marnier butter cream." It did not have the traditional bride and groom figures on top. Each wedding guest received an individual chocolate sponge cake—about the size of a cupcake, filled with chocolate truffles, with a perfect rose on top—that looked just like the top tier. The cost of the cake was . . . not made public.

- Krispy Kreme tells us, "Doughnuts can be created into a stunning make-believe wedding cake when festooned with cascading ribbons and real (or almost real, certainly life-like) flowers." Thoughtful brides are handing out boxes containing two-for-the-road doughnuts to their departing-but-still-hungry-after-the-reception guests. The doughnut favors are two dollars per box plus fifty dollars

continued from page 31

these form a well-known category, and will make a good impression on your résumé. You will also be more challenged.

As for cake designers, Garrett says that they are true artists who are skilled in all mediums of pastry and decorating. While they often have fine-art backgrounds, a degree in this field is not entirely necessary in order to be successful.

Typically, cake designers start by sketching a design and sending it to their client. These sketches may be revised until all issues are resolved. Garrett says that clients who purchase cakes from designers are usually looking for art more than for a cake; she likens the process to purchasing a designer dress.

Custom-made cakes range in price between twenty-five hundred and fifty thousand dollars. The higher the price, the more lofty are the expectations of the client.

Most of the cake designers' commissions come from word of mouth, as well as through their Web site and sometimes from people who see the designers' cakes in a magazine. You will need to build your reputation, as this is how you will get referrals for cakes. Garrett advises making cakes free of charge for charities. This will give you a lot of visibility. And while legally you should not bake commercially in your home kitchen, you should not commit yourself to renting commercial space until you have too much work to handle at home.

The key to establishing a strong reputation is to have a good business sense and the ability to recognize the length of time it takes to produce excellent cakes, which can be a week or more. It is essential to remember the taste of the cake is as important as its spectacular effect.

Your work might vary from creating a ten-tier wedding cake to three hundred individual ones, which is the most challenging category of cake decorating.

Regardless of the level at which you wish to practice this profession, you will need to build your skills. Accordingly, the prices you (or your company) will charge for each serving of cake will depend on the level of work involved; prices can vary from one dollar a slice for a basic cake to thirty dollars a person for a well-established designer. You will not start calling yourself a designer until you earn it: "Your colleagues and customers will tell you when you have earned the skills to call yourself a cake designer," says Garrett. "There's no set time. You need to be published in magazines to gain the respect that goes with that name."

1. You can improve your skills by taking classes in floral design, drawing, or sketching. Until relatively recently, the Wilton Company provided the only training available for cake decorators, so Toba Garrett decided to teach cake decorating at the Institute of Culinary Education in New York City. "Prospective cake decorators also need to know how to bake the cake," she advises.

2. Starting by selling decorated cookies is a good way to build a consumer base, particularly if you can sell to stores like Starbucks and Dean and DeLuca. "Having an everyday business helps support your specialty business," Garrett says. "If you are looking to support your business, you need to do more traditional baked goods." Publishing a book of your work also helps build your reputation. "Become your own public-relations firm," she adds.

3. "It's a business you have to be married to," Garrett cautions. "No one can be you. Your clients want your signature on the products. You can't take vacations."

to have them passed out by a Krispy Kreme representative.

- The average cost of a wedding is twenty to twenty-five thousand dollars. Prices range astronomically higher—and plummet to much lower.

- Four to six million people are married each year. The most popular months for a wedding are May through October.

- The average number of wedding guests is 189.

- Americans spend close to $2 billion on wedding cakes.

Source: Associates for Wedding Professionals International

• RARE JOB •
FOOD ARTIST

YOU NEED ONLY to step into a gallery, craft shop, or museum to discover that artists have been working for centuries to turn food into art in the form of still-life paintings, jewelry, china, decorative eggs, and serving dishes. Jewelers, potters, glass blowers, and craftspeople use every media from clay to precious metals and gemstones to render food into images to admire and to use. Food is a subject for everything from greeting cards to shopping bags, handbags, and Christmas tree ornaments. Food professionals may use their knowledge to design and manufacture kitchen equipment, teapots, and elegant, useful tools for cooks.

POTATO BREAD AND sourdough, whole-grain bread and brioche, pepper bread and bread flecked with sun-dried tomatoes, olives, herbs, and seeds—all of these bread varieties are appearing on restaurant tables. Many restaurants buy bread from a local wholesale bakery, but others have bakers to create signature house breads and skinny breadsticks as long as your arm.

• RECIPE FOR SUCCESS •

ꙅYLVIA WEINSTOCK

SYLVIA WEINSTOCK'S CAKES are legendary. They are masterpieces of visual design and culinary art that are made to order for almost any taste. Weinstock set the standard for others to admire and has created wedding cakes for Charlie Sheen, Cyndi Lauper, Whitney Houston, Alec Baldwin, Kim Bassinger, Eddie Murphy, Mariah Carey, Billy Joel, and Jane Fonda, to name a few.

"When I started in this cake business, a bride had the option of buying a beautiful but not a fresh buttery delicious cake, or a delicious cake but not one that was particularly beautiful," she recalls. "The challenge was to create both—delicious and beautiful."

She says she was fortunate to learn pastry essentials from a fine pastry chef, and to be encouraged by her friend William Greenberg to design pretty floral cakes. It did not hurt that her first client was Donald Bruce White, a premier caterer in New York who promoted her work.

Weinstock now has seventeen employees who share her passion at what she calls a destination shop for brides and other cake lovers in Soho. She uses only the finest ingredients and customizes cakes for every customer. "One is indeed fortunate to wake up each day knowing a challenge exists. Creation is a joy and so, too, is pleasing your clients," she says. Visit her on the Web at http://www.sylviaweinstock.com.

For More Information

The Bread Bakers Guild of America, a nonprofit organization for artisan bread bakers.
http://www.bbga.org

The field of skilled bakers and pastry chefs is wide open and rapidly expanding. Culinary schools everywhere are applauding the increasing enrollment in these programs. The French Culinary Institute in New York offers a course in artisanal bread baking and has seen classes increase 121 percent from five years ago.
http://www.frenchculinary.com

L'Acadamie de Cuisine at the Academy of Culinary and Pastry Arts offers over one thousand classes for kitchen rookies, seasoned home cooks, and everyone in between.

Visit their Web site to find courses designed just for you. http://www.lacademie.com

The Culinary Institute of America has one of the finest baking and pastry degree programs in the world. http://www.ciachef.edu

ShawGuides provides an invaluable directory of cooking schools throughout the world. http://www.shawguides.com

Recommended Books

Boyle, Tish, and Timothy Moriarty. *Grande Finales: A Neoclassical View of Plated Desserts.* Hoboken, NJ: Wiley, 2000.

Culinary Institute of America Staff. *Baking and Pastry: Mastering the Art and Craft.* Hoboken, NJ: Wiley, 2004.

Garrett, Toba. *The Well-Decorated Cake.* New York: Sterling, 2003.

MacLauchlan, Andrew. *The Making of a Pastry Chef: Recipes and Inspirations from America's Best Pastry Chefs.* Hoboken, NJ: Wiley, 1999.

Peters, Colette. *Cakes to Dream On: A Master Class in Decorating.* Hoboken, NJ: Wiley, 2004.

Sokol, Gail. *About Professional Baking: The Essentials.* Thomson Delmor Learning Books, 2006.

Weinstock, Sylvia. *Sweet Celebrations: The Art of Decorating Beautiful Cakes.* New York: Simon and Schuster, 1999.

Web Sites

The pastry and baking forum of the e-Gullet Society for Culinary Arts and Letters, http://www.egullet.org

Cake Craft and Decoration, http://www.cake-craft.com

National Confectioners Association job bank, http://jobs.ecandy.com

Real Baking with Rose Levy Beranbaum, http://www.realbakingwithrose.com

Chocolatier magazine, http://www.chocolatiermagazine.com

Pastry Art and Design magazine, http://www.pastryartanddesign.com

The Worlds of Flavor Baking and Pastry Arts Invitational Retreat at the Culinary Institute of America at Greystone, in Napa Valley, http://www.ciachef.edu

World Pastry Forum, http://www.worldpastryforum.com

• RARE JOB •

℮UPCAKE CREATOR

HOSTESS MAKES 400 million cupcakes a year. They are not anything like those at the Menino Bakery, where John and Nancy Menino bake "art" cupcakes in every guise from dairy-free vegan to dark, delicious chocolate. "They have to taste fabulous, or why bother," says John.

Cupcakes are now turning up at cocktail parties (served with champagne, of course) and for breakfast, baked in a coffee mug. A small part of their appeal is the "I can't believe I ate the whole thing" good/bad element that allows us to subscribe to the appealing ability to sin and repent, simultaneously. There are also many books on cupcakes, including Clare Crespo's *Hey There, Cupcake! 35 Yummy Fun Cupcake Recipes for All Occasions.*

▶ Master Chef

The next time you hear someone in the news described as a master chef, realize that a few marketing people throw that term around without fully understanding the true dimensions of the designation. In reality, the title must be earned by passing a series of difficult tests. It's not an easy road, but those who reach this milestone say it's worth the years of effort and education.

Currently, there are only fifty-nine master chefs and thirteen master pastry chefs certified in the United States. In 2005 only one chef passed the grueling examination at the Culinary Institute of America (CIA), conducted under the auspices of the American Culinary Federation (ACF). Frank Vollkommer, a lecturing instructor at the CIA in Hyde Park, New York, passed the final part of a ten-day examination that he had begun the previous year.

ACF-certified master chef (CMC) and certified master pastry chef (CMPC) are the highest and most demanding levels of cooking achievement in the U.S. food-service industry. The program began in 1981 with five chefs becoming masters, and the next year the World Association of Cooks Societies recognized ACF's master-chef program. Several other nations also bestow master status upon their countrymen chefs. Only one woman has been certified as a U.S. master chef. She is former Culinary Institute of America instructor and Culinary Olympics gold medalist Lyde Buchtenkirch-Biscardi.

Candidates for ACF's certified-master-chef exam must have been previously certified as an executive chef or executive pastry chef. The master-chef examination requires exacting familiarity and proficiency with a broad range of cooking and pastry styles and techniques, and tests a chef's knowledge of international and American regional cuisines.

"Becoming a certified master pastry chef has been a lifetime goal, and I am proud to join such a distinguished group," Volkommer says. "I urge my peers to undertake this challenge in order to grow as professionals and ultimately enrich our industry."

ꞘNTERVIEWS BY ANNE E. MCBRIDE

François Payard, owners of Payard's Patissesier Bistro in New York City.

ANNE E. MCBRIDE: What advice do you have for someone looking to follow in your footsteps?

FRANÇOIS PAYARD: The first thing to do if you want to follow in my footsteps, before going to school, is to spend a few days in the field, to see if it suits you. Do an internship, even if it means peeling carrots all day. Then, if you're really serious about your commitment for the profession, visit schools and find one that fits your schedule, if you work for example.

AM: What are the advantages of a formal education?

FP: Remember that a school does not give a profession; it gives foundations. It teaches you what at work no one has time to show you, exposes you to a large variety of products, etc. School gave me the theory of pastry, and then I developed the practice. A teacher has time to show and explain, while at work you only have time to execute. A pastry shop gives you practice, repetition, work, and production skills. Work and school combine; it takes both to succeed.

AM: What do you look for when you're hiring a new pastry cook?

FP: When I hire someone, I look at them in the eyes rather than on paper. I look for people ready to invest himself or herself, someone committed rather than someone who thinks he or she has a longer résumé than me.

AM: What special skills does it take to become a top pastry chef?

FP: I don't think that being a good pastry chef requires a unique talent. It's just a passion. Be sure that when you don't know how to make something, you practice. Some people might have artistic talent, but you have to repeat what you do, keep practicing. Practice writing out of a pastry bag every day, for example. You'll get better and better every time.

continued

continued from page 38

Jacques Torres, Jacques Torres Chocolate, New York

ANNE E. MCBRIDE: What is the best training to follow to become a chocolatier?

JACQUES TORRES: Education trains your mind. Practice trains your hands. You have to be willing to make lots of mistakes and that will undoubtedly lead to many discoveries. Work in the best quality places—start where you want to end up.

AM: What advice do you have for someone looking to follow your footsteps?

JT: Work hard, stay late, arrive early, never compromise on quality, try to learn from the people who are already in the profession and are having success, ask questions, listen to the answers.

You must have passion for this business. You can't learn to have passion. You either have it or you don't. Don't get into this business unless you have that passion. If you do, then the long hours and hard work won't matter to you. Always stay positive. Your mind has great power. If you continually think positive thoughts, you will be more likely to succeed. Never let those around you know when you're stressed or tired. Take control of your emotions by focusing on the good.

Rose Levy Beranbaum, author of The Cake Bible, The Bread Bible, *and many other award-winning cookbooks*

ANNE E. MCBRIDE: What advice do you have for someone just starting out?

ROSE LEVY BERANBAUM: Learn from the best. Travel and taste as much as possible before your life and work tie you down and make it more difficult. Develop a firsthand acquaintance with the essential ingredients of your trade. For example, try different types of flour or sugar in a cake and do a "blind" side-by-side tasting. Keep a baking diary. Weigh ingredients and keep careful notes. Use the best and freshest ingredients and you'll find there's no need for over-complexity. Be generous with your ideas. After all, creativity is a bottomless well of inspiration.

- Many American believe that chocolate has a positive influence on their psychological and physical well-being—52 percent say chocolate boosts morale and 46 percent say it revitalizes them. The new advertising message suggests it is heart-healthy (especially on Valentine's Day).

- When people say they'd kill for a chocolate bar, they don't actually mean what they say. Strictly speaking, an addict may kill for a fix, but chocoholics experience a craving—not an addiction.

- Nearly half of all Americans, 46 percent, eat chocolate at least once a week. How can chocolate makers increase chocolate consumption? They are flavoring dark chocolate with ingredients such as hot chili peppers, saffron, and grappa. Milk chocolate is now being flavored with everything from violets to rose petals.

- The Swiss eat twenty-five pounds of chocolate a year.

- The Lindt chocolate company has annual sales of $2.1 billion.

- The Barry Callebaut company has annual sales of $3.5 billion.

- Laughing gas makes chocolate taste more chocolaty. Attendees at the Institute of Food Technologists' annual conference were startled to receive the information from U.K. scientists that nitrous oxide, pumped under pressure into liquid chocolate, produces a more intense cocoa flavor. The testers also found that the gas causes the chocolate to melt more rapidly in the mouth. "Bubbles are undervalued as a food ingredient," reported the lead researcher, Leshavan Niranjan. Clearly, this kind of research will be no laughing matter to the candy men. Going to work can sometimes be a barrel of fun.

FRONT-OF-THE-HOUSE JOBS

▶ General Manager

The general manager shoulders the responsibility for all aspects of the restaurant. This means he or she oversees how the dining room looks, inspects the tables when they are set, makes sure the waitstaff is well turned out and groomed, and checks, double checks, and checks again that the reservation book is correctly maintained. The general manager is also responsible for training the front-of-the-house staff—or at least for making sure they are trained by someone on his staff.

If something goes the teensiest bit wrong, he will turn cartwheels to soothe even the most demanding (and possibly inebriated) guests. Complimentary drinks or appetizers will often mollify a long wait for a table, and an inconvenience caused by the restaurant or its staff may be recompensed with a deluge of desserts.

There are two qualifications for the job: experience—and a terrific personality. The person who pays attention to details and responds to the needs of *all* the workers and *all* the guests and *all* those with whom he comes into contact every minute of every day, is the one who gets the top job—and keeps it. He can expect to receive a large annual bonus if he works in a profitable restaurant.

▶ Maître d'

The person filling the maître d' job (pronounced "may-ter-dee"—an abbreviation for maître d'hotel, which freely translates into master of the universe) decides the seating arrangements. This does not always mean seating a favored guest at the table with the best view, but rather the table that is served by the most skilled waitstaff (and they are often one and the same!). He dots the room with decorative guests and, if motivated to do so, is able to find a table where none was to be had moments earlier. It's his job to keep the tables turning with new customers, without anyone feeling rushed or ignored. This is a difficult dance to master. He may issue a word of warning to a newly arriving guest, advising him of the already seated ex-spouse. He watches every table and every movement of each member of the staff and steps in to take charge of any small hiccups before they escalate into full-scale disturbances. He also takes care of last-minute cancellations and does all he can to keep the tables turning and the guests happy. The maître d' is a salaried member of the staff who expects a gratuity only if he performs extraordinary service.

▶ Captain and Waitstaff

The captain supervises the staff. There may be several captains in a large dining room, and to them fall the minute-by-minute decisions. Under the supervision of the general manager or maître d' the captain might train the staff. He or she also keeps an eye on the food coming from the kitchen and makes sure all the plates arrive at the table at the same instant.

Guests want to be served, not merely fed. This may be disheartening to toilers in the hot kitchen, but more people go to restaurants because the service is good than because the food is fabulous.

Many diners think waiters are transient folk who would much prefer to be occupying themselves with more desirable work, but as the status of chefs has become more elevated, the role of the server is increasingly held in higher esteem, too. As has been the case in Europe for decades, now many people are choosing to become professional servers instead of waiting tables to finance their preferred career.

Runners and busboys aid the waiters, the former by bringing food to the table and the latter by clearing the dishes. They rely on tips to provide even a bare-bones living.

Every now and again there is anguished talk about elevating the public's perception of waiters by offering a decent salary, medical insurance, and paid vacations. As sensible as this proposal seems on the surface, it continues to face implacable opposition from almost everyone. Management claims that if the extra costs were added to the check, the public would be shocked at the total cost of the meal. By separating the food and beverage costs from the tip, the first part is mandatory, and the gratuity appears to be discretionary, though it rarely is in practice. You might think that the restaurant industry, which has 120 million employees, generates $440 billion in annual sales, and forms the "cornerstone" of the American economy, could figure a way out of this quagmire. Not so far.

Many waiters don't want to change the system. In some exalted palaces of gastronomy, particularly those with grand-banquet facilities, they can count on a very large "gratuity" indeed (up to and even occasionally exceeding one thousand dollars a week).

A few culinary schools offer training for waitstaff and those working in what is known as the front of the house, but by far the majority receive their training on the job.

The servers gather together before the doors to the restaurant are opened and receive instructions about the night's special dishes and the "steps of service." These steps may include anything from an explanation of the components and preparation of a dish to a scripted response to the eternal question: where's the men's room?

Most of all, a waiter must be focused, organized, know the menu, remain calm, and never seem obtrusive. Good service equates with discreet service at fine restaurants and with fast, competent service elsewhere. Regardless of the type of restaurant, the waitstaff should be pleasant and businesslike—a balance not always easy to strike, but one a good captain works toward. As has been observed, you can train a nice person to be efficient, but no amount of training can teach a person how to be simply *nice*.

▶ Dining Coach

There is a Victorian saying, "Every meal is a lesson learned." It is at the dining table where we first learn not only what to do, but perhaps more importantly, what not to do. Manners, it turns out, are as important to the pursuit of living as the culture of dining. Knowing exactly how to behave at the table was as important to cavemen as it is in today's corporate dining room. In order to become a fully accepted member of a group, or to be recruited as a team player, it is essential that everyone abide by the same rules and minds their manners.

There are many kinds of behavior that we consider bad manners. Bad behavior often results in the offender being permanently expelled from the group. What may be tolerated but not applauded at home is often unacceptable in public. Learning how to behave when in other countries is crucial to the negotiation of contracts of all kinds. It therefore is essential to learn:

- How to behave in the company of others, i.e. no cell phones; oppressive perfume, or repellent aftershave lotion; no reading materials; no kissing, holding hands, or other overt touching/feeling; and overall no boorishness of any kind, particularly the kind that could become the subject of a *Saturday Night Live* skit.
- How to dine at a formal dining table, including how not to address the waitstaff.
- How to select the correct silver and crystal, and the correct use of the napkin.
- How to be mannerly when in the company of people from countries other than one's own.
- How to offer and respond to a toast.
- How not to spit out food that is offensive to you.
- How to request the check and be grateful to the host, who (thank goodness) graciously beats you to it.

Business is booming for etiquette coaches. Those climbing corporate ladders are recognizing how important it is for them and their significant others to at least appear to be "cultured." A hiring decision may rest on what and how a prospective employee behaved during an interview conducted over dinner.

Pamela J. Holland, coauthor of *Help! Was That a Career Limiting Move?* and CEO of Brody Communications, a Philadelphia-based company that provides dining etiquette training to corporate clients, says, "I think this renewed interest in civility and manners is a reaction to young entrepreneurs who arrived in the workplace wearing sandals and a T-shirt." Pauline Winick and Dale Webb, founders of the Protocol Center in Miami, observe, "Regardless of one's place in the work hierarchy, it is hard to argue against good manners. If you are competing for a job or promotion against others with the same level of competency you must have the social skills, too, so you can always clobber your rivals."

According to an article by Michael Bateman in London's the *Independent on Sunday*, there are several ways for hosts to let dinner guests know it's time to leave. "A Frenchman may ask if you'd like something, a fruit juice perhaps. In Japan, if the guests fail to take the hint, the host and hostess may leave the room and not come back. That usually does the trick."

To become a dining coach you must carefully study *Miss Manners' Guide to Excruciatingly Correct Behavior* by Judith Martin. She will guide you to the correct way to extract a sliver of green leafy food from between your teeth.

It is sound advice for us all not to order the fried eggs, sausage, hash browns and a fizzy drink for breakfast if the host has requested half a grapefruit and a pot of herbal tea. We are counseled not to reach onto the plate of the prospective boss without his express permission, not to pick up your steak with your hands and gnaw the bone, not to dip your bread in the gravy, not to hold your fork like a shovel, not to use chopsticks for the first time when being interviewed for a job. And never, ever wear a lobster bib. Finally, it is even more important to grasp the unwritten rules than the more obvious ones.

For More Information

Books

Fischer, John W. *At Your Service: A Hands-On Guide to the Professional Dining Room.* Hoboken, NJ: Wylie, 2005.

Meyer, Danny. *Setting the Table: The Transforming Power of Hospitality in Business.* New York: HarperCollins, 2006.

Web sites where restaurant people assemble to bellow and blog:

http://www.bitterwaitress.com

http://www.chef2chef.net

http://discuss.washingtonpost.com

http://members.tripod.com/castlenet/now.htm

http://www.ontherail.com

"The most intelligent thing a waiter can do is to offer his services. Not, 'Is your meal okay?' but an open-ended invitation. 'Is there anything I can do for you?'"

—SIRIO MACCIONE

http://www.shamelessrestaurants.com
http://www.stainedapron.com
http://www.tip20.com
http://www.waiterrant.blogspot.com
http://www.webfoodpros.com

• MATTERS OF FACT •

- Research shows that men tip more if the server is female and women tip more if the server is male. A single guest usually goes for 20 percent. At a table for five or more when the check is split, the tip is usually close to 13.2 percent. The larger the party, the greater is the likelihood of a reduced tip (unless the amount has been agreed upon in advance). Many restaurants automatically add a gratuity to tables of six or eight people or more. For very large parties the gratuity is included in the contract signed in advance by the host.

- Apparently, it makes little difference whether the server "advises" the guest to select the baby back ribs or the scallops, whether he provides his name, or if he asks, "Who gets the lobster." But the tip will be significantly reduced if the waiter kneels to take an order, touches a guest on any part of their anatomy, or decorates the check with a smiley face.

- A Cornell University study revealed that professional conduct and prompt attention do little to guarantee a big tip from the vast majority of restaurant goers. Instead, the tip is influenced more by the size of the bill and the fear of disappointing the server than by recognition of good service. If this shocking news is true, then it follows that the management's notion that good service is an incentive for a hefty tip is invalid.

- In most other "civilized" countries, France included, service is included in the check so no one need engage in arithmetical speculation.

- There are twenty-three thousand restaurants in Manhattan.

▶ Busboys and Runners

The job of bussing seems to appeal more to men than women for no apparent reason. The busboy sets and clears the table. He may carry some orders to the table and is usually the person who keeps the water glasses filled. In some restaurants, he receives a share of the waitstaff's pooled gratuities, in which each staff member's share is allocated on a "points earned" basis; the higher the position, the more points are earned, and the higher the share in tips. An extra point or two may be given to busboys who are particularly helpful or have been working in their position for a long time.

$\mathcal{B}$ARTENDER

MARTHA STEWART HAS described Master Bartender Dale DeGroff as "the Billy Graham of the holy spirits." She is right, as always.

Dale DeGroff is to cocktails as a hand is to a glove. They fit. For twelve years, Dale ruled the luminous Promenade Bar at the Rainbow Room in Manhattan. He says, "I fell in love with bars because of the uninhibited, disordered, and surprising way life unfolds at the bar. The only logical progression in my life has been the wealth of characters that have crossed my path. I don't know how Muhammad Ali felt the first time he climbed into a ring, or how Louis Armstrong felt the first time he picked up a trumpet, but for me, I knew I was standing in a very familiar and cozy place when I was standing behind a bar for the first time. I knew I was home."

Dale took a journey back in time to hone his craft. He used only freshly squeezed juices and natural ingredients and figured out how to achieve just the right balance of sweet and sour, strong and weak. He searched for out-of-print recipes for cocktails everywhere he could find them, in garage sales and rare book collections. He experimented with hundreds of recipes, adjusting them to the modern palate and today's larger portions. (The modern palate doesn't have as sweet a tooth as once it did.)

He soon discovered something that bakers have long known: he couldn't simply increase the quantities and hope to get the same result as when he mixed drinks individually. He had to adjust and balance the ratio of acidic fruits to various other components of the cocktail to achieve the results he was seeking.

Dale urges bartenders to attend cooking school in order to get a feeling and respect for composing the many elements and flavors of the ingredients that make up a good recipe. He also encourages an understanding of the importance of using correct techniques. He says, "Watch how chefs use their tools. Collect your own specialty tools and treat them with respect."

When asked where he got started, Dale answers, "I learned about cocktails much the same way I learned to tend bar—through research and experience and talking to connoisseurs. My fellow bartenders taught me about life, and my mentor, the great restaurateur Joe Baum, sparked my curiosity to find out what makes a great cocktail."

"Hospitality is a team sport. If you don't get along with others, you are in the wrong business. Even if you are an owner, the only way your goals can be accomplished is by working with those who respect you and are willing to make every effort to fulfill your objectives."

—**ALAN STILLMAN**, CEO of the Smith and Wollensky Restaurant Group

For More Information
DeGroff, Dale. *The Craft of the Cocktail: Everything You Need to Know to Be a Master Bartender, with 500 Recipes.* New York: Clarkson Potter. 2002.

▶ Sommelier

This splendid job requires much more than the ability to schmooze with the guests. A top sommelier recommends appropriate wines, at appropriate cost, and discusses food pairings with both the knowledgeable and the novice. He must constantly learn about new wineries and new wines and read, study, and taste wines to develop and keep his own palate as finely tuned as a violin. On top of this, he is responsible for ordering all the wine for the restaurant and knowing how best to store it. In many restaurants, the sommelier holds seminars for the waitstaff to increase their knowledge of wine to better serve the customers.

Nicolas Bonnot, sommelier at Taillevent in Paris, says, "To succeed at this profession you must be able to read a client in seconds. When you arrive at a table to take an order, you must immediately determine what he wants and how much he wishes to spend. You must understand why the client is here. If he is here with his wife, or with his mistress, he will have a very different manner. The sommelier must be patient, available, and attentive. It requires psychology, and a great deal of technique. He must be a professional who knows his trade. And he must not want to give lessons. That's the most important thing—he must know how to listen to the client."

Sommeliers are trained, not born. There are numerous programs that qualify them to work all over the world. If you can find a job working for a seasoned sommelier at a restaurant with a good wine program, you will learn a lot.

▶ Restaurant Owner

A typical restaurant owner does everything possible to ensure that his guests have a lovely time. He knows what is going on in the kitchen, in the dining room, in the refrigerator, and on the stove.

A successful restaurateur opens the door and immediately knows whether the temperature of the room is within a degree or two of the comfort zone. He knows if the soup needs more salt. Over the years it has become customary for the owner or chef/owner to leave his kitchen or his counting house and chat with the guests. He smiles upon his favorite customers and extends a cordial welcome to new ones. He dispenses favors like a bee humming over a field of flowers, distributing pollen to the most exotic blooms and saving the sting for the youngest waiter. Former *New York Times* restaurant critic Bryan Miller compared the passage of one uncomfortable owner on such a mission with that of "a long-tailed cat in a roomful of rocking chairs."

The guests seem, for the most part, to welcome a nod from such a grand personage. Some diners in fact feel slighted if the chef they saw on the TV just the other evening doesn't lean his hand on the back of their chair for even a fleeting moment. (This urge to roam around the room is unique to restaurants. You certainly don't expect the bank manager to roam among his depositors asking if they are enjoying the newly minted dollar bills his tellers have dispensed, nor will he offer to reveal just how they are made.)

• **RECIPE FOR SUCCESS** •

$\mathcal{D}$ANNY MEYER

EVERYONE LOVES DANNY Meyer, owner of restaurants in New York City that are regularly voted number one by the Zagat Survey for food and service. They include Gramercy Tavern, Union Square Café, Blue Smoke, Tabla, Eleven Madison, and the Modern at the Museum of Modern Art. He is a prince among men and a giant in the restaurant world.

He said, "In 1965, I took my first family journey to France, and I was forced by my parents to keep a diary. One day's entry highlighted my fascination with the wonderful quiche lorraine I had eaten in a private home in Nancy. In another, I wrote about loving *fraises des bois* with crème fraîche.

"Back at home, it had become my household responsibility to feed my family's pet dog, a neurotic French poodle named Ratatouille. Third-grade friends looked at me with disbelief when I tried to explain the meaning of his name. I enjoyed slipping Rata my leftovers of things like steak tartare, spicy tacos, Milwaukee braunschweiger, and kosher salami because it was important to me that he could enjoy my favorite foods in addition to his foul-smelling Alpo. Once I even tried feeding him peanut butter. He ate it, but it took him at least ten minutes to quit smacking his tongue and get it down the hatch.

In retrospect, Ratatouille was my first regular customer. It made me happy to please him with good food. I may not have known it then, but that's about all it takes to be a successful restaurateur.

For More Information

Meyer, Danny. *Setting the Table: The Transforming Power of Hospitality in Business.* New York: HarperCollins Publishers, 2006.

$\mathcal{T}$HE SILVER DINER

by Ype Von Hengst, vice president of culinary operations

WHEN MY BUSINESS partner, Robert Giamo, and I wanted to start an American-family-cuisine restaurant that bridges the gap between white tablecloth restaurants and fast food, the old-time diner was the perfect answer. We went on the road and spent a year visiting more than five hundred diner-style restaurants in big and small towns across America hoping to understand the timeless appeal of this American icon.

What has made diners so successful for over one hundred years? Of course, diners are known for their unique roadside architecture and generous helpings of home-style food, but the heart of what brings customers back to the diner again and again is the people. It's the folks who serve you and make you feel welcome that make a diner feel like a home away from home.

We opened the first Silver Diner in 1988, and today we have seventeen locations. Starting your own fast-casual restaurant concept is not for everyone, although if you have passion for food and people, becoming a restaurant owner might be the right career path for you.

The Silver Diner is a typical American diner—with a twist. I started the Silver Diner in response to feedback from consumers who showed they were looking for a restaurant that would provide good food and good value in a family-friendly environment—not the usual mediocre food and poor quality service many family restaurants offered.

Now, managing seventeen restaurants takes a great deal of talent, but first on the list is that you must have people skills. When you are a restaurant owner, everything you do is done for people—your guests and your staff—and you need to be able to relate to them and their personal needs. I spend a lot of my time at work speaking with my managers and staff members to make sure that they are happy with their jobs. This is important to me.

The hospitality industry is a service-oriented industry, and above all else, you must always remember to provide great service. Your guests are looking for a consistent product and this includes all aspects of the restaurant, from the knowledge of the waitstaff, to the quality of the ingredients used in the kitchen. We are always working to ensure that we are offering our guests consistent quality that goes over and beyond what they would normally expect from a diner.

Being a restaurant operator also involves a great deal of work with consultants to help you design an atmosphere that your guests will enjoy. The goal is to create surroundings that will welcome visitors and keep them coming back to your restaurant again in the future. However, it is important to keep in mind that the dining room needs to match your product and service; otherwise your guests will find the experience frustrating.

Getting Started

Above all, opening your own restaurant requires a great deal of drive. It is not an easy proposition, and many restaurants close within their first two years. Being a restaurant operator takes patience, and background in the hospitality industry. Before opening your own place, I would encourage anyone thinking about the idea to spend at least five years working in a restaurant.

In addition to having a core understanding of culinary skills, it is important to know how to organize a menu. The menu needs to match the concept, and the needs of your guests. Don't put a steak on your menu for $19.95 when the average check is only $9.00. Your customer is not looking for steak, and it will only hurt your food cost when it does not sell. Product knowledge is also a very important skill, because to manage your food cost and maximize profitability, you must be able to recognize the difference between a good deal and a product of inferior quality.

Long before you open your doors, spend some time in the neighborhood where you would like to open your establishment. What is the clientele like? What types of restaurants already exist in the locality? When are they busy? It is critical for your restaurant to meet the needs of your community, and market research is an important part of ensuring your success.

Keys to success:

1. Work in the industry before you attempt to start your business. Every restaurant concept operates on a unique business model, and diners are no different. Being open twenty-four hours a day for breakfast, lunch, dinner, and late night, they operate very differently from a fine-dining white tablecloth restaurant. Look for a restaurant that matches the type of environment that you would like to emulate, and then get a job there. Stay close to the management, and learn some of the tricks of the trade before you attempt to open your own place.

2. When you hire management personnel, look for the right people who will believe in the brand and will represent you in all your units. If yours is a casual concept, people need to smile and be hands-on, and you need to hire the right people who fit that image of your concept.

3. Include both your guests and your staff in the decision-making process. No one knows your customers better than your waitstaff, so before you change some aspect of service, ask for their opinions. Collectively, you will come up with a better idea for how to conduct your business. If you make decisions only from the top down, rest assured that you will fail.

4. Constantly be in touch with what competing concepts are doing. The food-service industry is extremely competitive, and the world is always changing. As an operator, you need to stay on top of trends in everything from the food to the atmosphere to the service. It is critical that you follow the trends of the market, and that you constantly look at how you can do things differently—and better.

5. Opening a restaurant is like designing a new menu. Look for the ideas; don't look for actual recipes. Come up with your own unique concept, and then put it in a unique package that will appeal to consumers.

For more information, go to http://www.silverdiner.com.

▶ Restaurant Consultant

This is a role that can be filled only by a food professional with many years of experience in the industry. Such a person can help start a restaurant or may be called when one is struggling. Being a restaurant consultant is the epitome of multitasking, according to Restaurant Report, a free weekly e-mail newsletter. The job entails, but is not limited to, one or more of the following areas:

- Feasibility studies
- Marketing research and planning
- Real-estate negotiations
- Concept planning and development
- Financial and legal support
- Construction and/or interior design
- Purveyor management
- Accounting and cost control
- Reservation sales systems
- Group sales promotion
- Employee recruitment and retention programs
- Staff training and development
- Graded operational audits
- Advertising, public relations, and marketing services

It may take several specialists working as a team to fulfill all these tasks, and no one person can do it all. A skillful consultant knows who to bring in to help a restaurant as needed. For example, a financial expert, will not be advising a client about waitstaff training and a computer systems adviser won't know the first thing about how to write a menu. A top consultant can identify what is needed and who needs to do it.

WATCHING THE FINANCES

Are you a financial person with a yearning to get involved in the universe of food? It may seem quite mad to contemplate a marriage between your analytical, mathematical mind and the typical restaurateur who thrives on high risk and extreme flights of fantasy, but it is this very attraction of opposite temperaments that can result in a profitable enterprise. The chef may have the ability to create dazzling dishes, but he is dependant on the banker to provide the funds to buy the best ingredients. As one industry expert tells us, "Revenue management is the practice of selling the right vodka or the right free-range roasted chicken at the right price at the right time to the right customer."

The person making such judgments may be the restaurant's chief financial officer or the purchasing agent. He or she may try to negotiate the price of shrimp based on annual anticipated consumption or accept delivery only on an as-needed basis.

Financial management within the hospitality industry includes jobs in accounting, payroll, real estate, contract and union negotiation, budget forecasting, public relations, marketing, advertising, and charitable donations. It is an invaluable asset for a chief financial officer to have an understanding of food preparation to add to other management and business expertise.

• MATTERS OF FACT •

- Estimates for the cost of the average start-up for a small new restaurant range from $250,000 to $500,000. A more formal restaurant can cost many millions.

- Among those who tempt fate by launching a restaurant, 26 percent are doomed to fail within the first year, 19 percent in the second, and 14 percent face disaster in the third year of epic struggle. Together, the dreadful total comes to a failure rate of 59 percent. This number may be higher in some areas than others.

- Poor management and lack of expertise account for more than half of all new-restaurant failures.

- Restaurant start-ups basically reflect the population of each state. California leads the country in both population and restaurant start-ups, followed by Texas, Florida, and New York. The other states in the top ten for restaurant start-ups are Illinois, Pennsylvania, Ohio, Georgia, North Carolina, and New Jersey. Where are the fewest start-ups? Vermont, the District of Columbia, and Wyoming rank in the last three spots when it comes to start-ups. But even last-place Wyoming recently issued seventy-eight new restaurant business licenses.

- Among the start-up costs of opening a new restaurant are the real estate deposit, architect and design fees, construction costs, utilities, insurance, garbage removal, furniture and fixtures, permits and licenses, legal fees, stocking the wine cellar, purchase of tabletop accessories (silverware, glasses, etc.), staff salaries, menu design and production, and a few other little things like vacuum cleaners and dishwashing detergent.

THE ANATOMY OF A CATASTROPHE

When a restaurant business slows down, as a result of a hiccup in the economy or during a sluggish tourist season, it becomes tempting to accept the "wrong" guests. I don't mean "wrong" in terms of good and decent folk, in a more specific way. For example, encouraging happy families to vacation in a Las Vegas casino may not be as profitable as enticing those who are known as high rollers.

When the seats are filled with those whose images are antithetical to the philosophy of the restaurant, it begins a downward spiral. The desired regulars stop coming. Prices are lowered to accommodate the less-affluent guests. The check average drops along with the tips for the increasingly restive waitstaff. The quality of the food slips. The chef leaves. Service suffers. Creditors come knocking at the door. The doors close.

▶ Purchasing

The purchasing department maintains cost control over every purchase. Depending on the size of the operation, it may be a chef who performs this task, or a specialist in financial matters.

Everyone knows that the idea of "fresh" is subjective, but to make sure the food is sold before it expires, pricing systems must be balanced with projected need and a host of other market forces. For example, a fish may be bought for a specific dollar amount, but after the head, tail, and bones are discarded the resulting edible remains may be more meager in one species of fish than in another.

The purchasing agent may be limited to buying ingredients, or he may also be responsible for buying everything from the flowers on the table to the silver polish.

To get started in this field it is essential to obtain a degree in business, management, and/or accounting, and to develop a sixth sense about what the future may have in store as far as demand and market fluctuations. The ability to make fast decisions coupled with the flexibility to turn on a dime is essential. Equally important is the capability to work with purveyors and wholesalers who handle the supplies. A savvy purchasing agent builds relationships and demands the best.

BRAND-NAME AND CELEBRITY CHEFS

Becoming a brand is not the same thing as being famous or evolving into a celebrity chef. In the marketplace, branding defines a company, a product, and even a chef. While branding may follow celebrity status, it very often precedes it.

It was Paul Bocuse who pioneered the concept of the brand-name chef. It all began at his restaurant, Bocuse d'Or in Cologne, outside Lyon, France. He was awarded the first of his three Michelin stars in 1958 and his fame and name eventually became attached to restaurants in Australia, Hong Kong, and Tokyo, and (briefly) the United States. He endorsed a line of fancy foods and brand-name champagne. He created signature dishes for the president of France: salmon in a pastry crust with scallop mousse and sauce *choron*, followed by *poulet de Bresse* in a creamy sauce of morels and spinach. His restaurant guests were respectful and as aged and distinguished as the wine. Every meal prepared by Bocuse was concluded with a murmured chorus of well-bred "amens." It has been said that Bocuse is our culinary Elvis (albeit rather more elegant).

Many changes have occurred since the biggest names in the business stood at the front of the house and greeted customers. Restaurateurs such as Henri Soulé (Le Pavillon), Warner LeRoy (Maxwell's Plum, Tavern on the Green, and the Russian Tea Room), and Sirio Maccione (Le Cirque) ruled the restaurant universe. They have given way to chef/owners. What goes on the plate has now become as important as who is seated in the dining room. It is now the chefs who stride across the world stage.

Celebrity chefs like André Soltner of Lutèce brought classic French food to New York City. Jean-Louis Palladin brought civilized food to Washington. It was Alice Waters, the originator of California cuisine and the conscience of American cooking, who wrote to President Clinton suggesting, "It would be a splendid idea to plant an organic vegetable garden on the White House lawn." She didn't receive a reply.

Sometimes, the name of the restaurant is more commercially important than the name of chef. For instance, the Four Seasons restaurant in New York City has greater celebrity than the name of its former chef: Seppi Rengli. The name Le Cirque once had more immediate name recognition than that of its former executive chef, Daniel Boulud. Guests at Disney's restaurants are more interested in Mickey Mouse than the name of the chef.

Our current crop of household names includes television personalities and innovative scientist/chefs, such as Ferran Adria of Spain, who produce jaw-dropping cuisine. Chef Adria began his pilgrimage to the pinnacle of haute cuisine as a dishwasher. He is now the dazzling innovator-in-residence at El Bulli, a restaurant discovered only with great difficulty on a remote stretch of beach on the Catalan coast. Weary diners may be refreshed by a tiny sip of a cocktail composed of frozen gin with an astonishing hot fizz of lemon—a prelude to dinner in twenty or more tiny courses composed of such fare as a soft-boiled quail egg with a crispy caramel crust, a polenta of frozen powdered Parmesan cheese, and almond ice cream on a swirl of garlic oil and balsamic vinegar.

Other chefs are quickly joining the parade of culinary fantasy. Heston Blumenthal of the three-Michelin-starred Fat Duck restaurant outside London claims to be a self-taught chef. He worked as a trainee architect, cameraman, and photocopier salesman before getting into the kitchen, where he specializes in bringing science into the cooking process. He says, "This is a place to be creative, to have time and space to work uninterrupted. It's not about reducing cooking to a test-tube experiment. Using a distillation device, we can take a rosemary leaf, put it in a vacuum where it will boil at only forty degrees centigrade. The flavor in the resulting vapor will be uncooked, so we are able to taste herbs like rosemary raw instead of cooked." It has been reliably reported that his snail porridge and mustard ice cream both taste very good indeed.

Avant cuisine is well regarded in Chicago, too. Chef Grant Achatz is not only inventing an entirely new way to cook food, but he also has wildly inventive ideas about presenting it. He serves a "burnt orange" course that consists of orange, picholine olives, and avocado from a long, thin, flexible wire prong called the antenna. "Bacon" is a whimsy of bacon, apple, and butterscotch that arrives at the table on a tension-based wire device known as the bow. These exciting, eclectic innovators are rethinking the very essence of food.

We gather together to adore chefs such as Thomas Keller, Eric Ripert, Lydia Bastianich, Lydia Shire, Patrick O'Connell, Jean-Georges Vongerichten, Daniel Boulud, Rick Bayless, Charlie Trotter, Rick Tramonto and Gale Gand, Marcus Samuelson, Mario Batali, Ming Tsai, Nobu Matsuhisa, Masa Takayama, and Nancy Silverton. They attract the investors who nurture and nourish them with multimillion restaurant design concepts.

Recommended Books

Blumenthal, Heston. *In Search of Perfection: Reinventing Kitchen Classics*. New York: Bloomsbury, 2006.

Martí Escayol, Maria Antònia. *Plaer de la xocolata: la història i la cultura de la xocolata a Catalunya / Maria Antònia Martí Escayal; prò leg de Ferran Adrià*, 2004.

CHEFS AS HUMANITARIANS

As chefs achieve levels of celebrity, they very often feel the need to give back to the community that supports them. This is a natural impulse for men and women who work in a field that, by definition, offers sustenance. And so, it's no surprise that chefs are very generous people.

Cosmologists know that when a bright star explodes, it scatters seeds that give birth to new universes. That is the vision behind Share Our Strength (SOS), the hunger relief and antipoverty organization founded by Bill Shore in 1987. This humanitarian organization has become one of the largest in the United States, but, says Shore, "size and rate of growth are not the point. Impact is. And the reason for that impact is the new way we've engaged people; not by asking them for money, but by asking them to contribute of themselves, through their skills, talents, and passionate interests, thereby connecting them to their communities in ways money never could."

Share Our Strength is about *sharing strength.* It helps culinary communities organize fundraisers in their city or region. So far, more than more than $55 million has been raised and distributed to 450 groups that work to end hunger and poverty by helping people in need. SOS has inspired hundreds of humanitarians who have become leaders in their own communities in the fight against hunger and poverty. Chefs continue to be deeply committed to sharing their personal skills by participating in a series of food and wine tastings and seated dinners and brunches that take place annually across North America.

Second Harvest is also among the nation's largest and most respected nonprofit organizations. Its workers and volunteers collect food from restaurants; caterers, and processing companies that otherwise would be wasted. Last year it distributed two billion pounds of food to more than fifty thousand local charitable agencies. These, in turn, operate ninety-four thousand hunger programs, including soup kitchens and school meals for poor children. This single organization provides emergency food assistance to 23 million Americans every year, and every year the numbers of those applying for help increase.

The United States Department of Agriculture estimates that 10 percent of Americans rely on the nonprofit distribution chain for their food. More restaurants and food-service companies would redistribute surplus food if the state and federal safety restrictions were less rigid. Perfectly edible food is dumped as garbage because companies fear legal action if a consumer claims to have been harmed from eating it.

Liberty Richter, the marketer and importer of specialty foods, and *The Gourmet Retailer* trade magazine sponsors the Gourmet Gala, the industry 's leading charitable event that brings together more than fifteen hundred buyers and suppliers during an elegant evening of fine dining. This is just one among many events, large and small, that encourage us all to ask what we can do to help.

Food-related outreach programs welcome volunteers, and there are full and part-time employment positions for staff members, too.

For More Information

A few among many food banks include the following and can be found on the Internet:

http://nutrition.tufts.edu

Share Our Strength, info@strength.org

Bread for the World, http://www.bread.org

Center on Hunger, Poverty and Nutrition, Tufts University http://nutrition.tufts.edu

Children's Defense Fund, http://www.childrensdefensefund.org

City Harvest, http://www.cityharvest.org

Food for the Hungry, http://www.fh.org

Food Research and Action Center, http://www.frac.org

Foodchain, http://www.foodchain.org.uk

God's Love We Deliver, http://www.godslovewedeliver.org

Meals on Wheels, http://www.mealsonwheels.com

Second Harvest National Food Bank Network, http://www.secondharvest.org

• MATTERS OF FACT •

- In 2005, 35 million low-income Americans—about one-third of them children—lived in households that cannot consistently afford enough to eat.

- 26 million American receive food stamps. Food stamps provide $1.05 per meal.

- Started by Iron Chefs Cat Cora and Bobby Flay, Chefs for Humanity is a grass-roots coalition of chefs and culinary professionals (including some famous names) whose objective is to raise money for hunger relief.

- The U.S. Census Bureau survey of households reports that 11.9 percent of all U.S. households are "food insecure" due to financial need. Of the 13.5 million households that are food insecure, 4.4 million suffered from food insecurity that was so severe that the USDA's very conservative measure classified them as "hungry." These figures have been increasing every year since 1994.

- Even with valiant salvage and retrieval efforts by government agencies and many relief organizations, mountains of food are wasted. Tim Jones, a professor of applied anthropology at the University of Arizona, has spent the past ten years tracking food waste from households, farms, stores, and restaurants. He estimates $100 billion in edible food are wasted every year in the United States.

- A total of 12 percent of American crops, valued at $20 billion, goes unharvested due to difficulty in predicting demand.

- Retailers, including restaurants, throw away 35 million tons a year, valued at $30 billion.

- Households dump $43 billion worth of food a year, or about 14 percent of what they buy.

- American households throw away 1.28 pounds of food a day, 27 percent of which consists of vegetables. (Apparently we dutifully buy vegetables but much prefer pizza.)

- The Tufts University Center on Hunger, Poverty and Nutrition Policy provides evidence from recent research about child nutrition. It reports: "In addition to having a detrimental effect on the cognitive development of children, under nutrition results in lost knowledge, brainpower, and productivity for the nation."

Food-Service Job Opportunities

by Phillip S. Cooke

CULINARY SCHOOLS AND universities offering degrees in hospitality management do a disservice to the food-service industry by narrowly focusing on potential career opportunities, usually citing only restaurants or hotels as possible venues for employment. In fact, job opportunities stretch to the furthermost horizon. Whether an individual is interested in becoming a chef, eventually moving up the ladder to sous chef, chef de cuisine, and executive chef, or has a goal of entering front-of-the-house management, there are stable, well-paid positions in a number of fields, all offering advancement and a proper balance of job to life that is becoming increasingly important to those now entering the workplace.

There was a time, thirty years ago and earlier, when there was a definite stigma attached to working in the noncommercial sector of the food-service industry. Employee feeding offered dimly lit cafeterias with battleship-gray walls and steam-table food that became increasingly unappetizing the longer it remained. With a captive market, little imagination went into either the decor or food. But then, a funny thing happened on the way to the cafeteria. Office buildings, banks, plants, and manufacturing facilities suddenly found themselves surrounded by chains and other restaurants. Employees could now walk across the street to catch lunch in well-lit, pleasant surroundings, ordering foods that matched their lifestyles at reasonable prices. Visionaries such as Richard Ysmael at Motorola, Neil Reyer at Chase Manhattan Bank, and Kay Stammers at Eastman Kodak quickly responded and said, almost in unison, It's time for a change! In came bright colors, attractive dining areas, foods cooked in small batches to order, innovative salad bars, sandwich stations, dessert bars, theme days, and just about everything imaginable borrowed from their commercial brethren.

Almost every segment of the industry quickly joined the revolution. Colleges first added fast-food and pizza-chain outlets to their student unions, then adapted decor and menus that echoed the commercial market to their dining halls. A young genius by the name of Michael Berry created a totally new approach to college and university feeding that became the template for all educational institutions. Hospitals moved quickly to upgrade patient food service. Queenie Towers Hospital in St. Louis shocked the entire food-service industry when it offered cocktail and wine service (doctor approval needed) to their daily menus. And Helen Doherty at Massachusetts General Hospital modeled her food service so closely to her commercial counterparts that it was virtually indistinguishable from dining in an upscale restaurant.

The result of all of this activity was that young people, for the first time, were attracted to work in the noncommercial food service. And, best of all, it fit their new penchant for working a normal eight-hour day with holidays and weekends usually free.

Today we have an explosion of opportunities in this area. Whole new categories of food service have opened. With an aging population, retirement centers are blossoming across the landscape, with upscale townhouses, apartments, and assisted-living complexes that resemble four-star hotels. These offer such amenities as dining rooms, coffee shops, and even cocktail lounges. In fact, the next wave will almost certainly see the entrance of major hotel chains into this burgeoning market.

Museum food service, once confined to snack bars and vending machines, has progressed to the point where the art may now be the secondary reason for visiting. The Des Moines Art Center, one of the nation's best small museums, is consistently listed as having one of the finest restaurants in the city. The Art Institute in Chicago boasts some of the best food and best catering services in the Midwest. The venerable Metropolitan Museum in New York created satellite dining opportunities throughout the museum, and the recently restored and expanded Museum of Modern Art has brought aboard Danny Meyer, one of the city's most celebrated restaurateurs, to shepherd its fine-dining establishment.

The more adventuresome may even want to look beyond these parameters. Spas are sprouting like dandelions. Country clubs have done an outstanding job in recent years of elevating their dining rooms and other food service to meet the rising expectations of their increasingly sophisticated and well-traveled members. Cruise ships offering meals twenty-four hours a day now relentlessly ply the seas and oceans of the planet. And sports arenas and racetracks now offer every imaginable type of food service, from the ever-popular hot dog to fine dining in luxurious surroundings. Levy Brothers, the Chicago-based restaurant and catering company, operates all the food service at Churchill Downs in Louisville, and has introduced a new stratum of culinary excellence and service to the sport of kings.

For those who enjoy life on a more intimate scale, there are bed and breakfasts scattered over hill and dale, and personal chefs are much in demand for fortunate individuals who can afford to be nurtured.

For those inclined toward a more regimented lifestyle, there are even food-service opportunities in prisons, army bases, officers' clubs, and the mess halls of the four service academies in the United States and abroad.

In short, there are unbounded opportunities for anyone and everyone interested in food service, whether working alone, for an entrepreneurial organization, or under the aegis of a major corporation such as Aramark, Sodhexo, or the Compass Group. I urge any person considering a career in the food-service industry to open his or her mind to the many types of positions that wait to be discovered, and to remember that, today, every segment of the food service industry offers unique and rewarding possibilities.

For More Information

> http://www.careersinfood.com describes itself as the number-one employment site for the food-and-beverage-manufacturing industry.
>
> http://www.foodmanagementsearch.com lists a wide variety of career opportunities.
>
> http://www.foodservice.com offers a variety of services, including employment listings, company listings, trade show information, discussion forums, classified ads, daily market prices, food-service books, industry news, editorials, and an eMarketplace.
>
> Foodservice Educators Network International (FENI) partners with food-service educators to advance their professional growth. The organization publishes *Chef Educator Today*, a quarterly magazine. http://www.feni.org

- The food-service industry has moved to the forefront of the country's economy as the nation's largest private-sector employer, second only to the federal government. Currently there are 554,000 commercial food-service businesses operating in the United States with a staggering $400 billion in annual sales.
- The Metropolitan Museum in New York City serves 500,000 diners a year.
- Dr. Tim Ryan, President of the Culinary Institute of America in Hyde Park, New York, predicts the food-service industry will continue to grow at an annual rate of 3 to 5 percent over the next several years.
- Food service encompasses everything from start-up services, such as delivering homemade sandwiches to an office or bringing healthy little meals for toddlers in kindergarten.

• RARE JOBS •

BARBARA DALE-AVANT, an employee of Atlantic Food's cooked-egg division in Hemingway, South Carolina, holds the record for number of hard-boiled eggs peeled per minute. Her best total was forty-eight, which means that she dawdled away exactly one and one-quarter seconds on each egg. And her boss, Wilbur Ivey, is not a man to tolerate bits of shell among the eggs, which are shipped to East Coast restaurants. To get these perfect results, he is willing to allow three seconds per egg, but that's only when peelers are first starting to peel on the job.

"A real clumsy person couldn't do this," remarked one of Avant's peelers. Another confided that the members of the six-woman team (who together once peeled ten thousand eggs in an eight-hour shift,) sometimes throw eggs at each other recreationally, although Mr. Ivey does not entirely approve. On the other hand, he is clearly no spoilsport, as he is credited with devising the initiation rite for new egg-peelers: he slips a raw egg into a recruit's first batch.

HOWARD HILLMAN MADE omelets. He made omelets at conventions, at parties, and wherever two or three or many more people were gathered together all over the country. There was a time when Howard Hillman was making omelets everywhere you went. He made tomato-and-cheese omelets, mushroom omelets, banana-nut omelets, omelets of every kind, large and small, with or without crowd participation. Howard Hillman became the omelet emperor of the Western Hemisphere. He had a skill that many others possess. The difference between Howard Hillman and everyone else is that he took his talent and marketed the dickens out of it.

► Pizza Chef

In the beginning, pizza was a simple affair: a fourteen-inch round of hand-twirled dough topped with sausage, pepperoni, cheese, anchovies (on second thought, hold the anchovies), and tomato sauce. Today, pizza can be anything from three-inches in size to three feet.

Once it took forty minutes to melt the cheese into strings-falling-down-your-chin perfection. Now it takes less than four minutes to prepare in laser-operated ovens. The industry talks contemplatively of speeding up the process to mere seconds. Now cooks make breakfast pizza with eggs, bacon, sausage, and hash browns and ice-cream-sundae pizzas topped with split bananas, raspberry sauce, whipped cream, grated chocolate, chopped nuts, and of course a cheery maraschino cherry on the top. Some of the finds we have stumbled across lately include:

- The southwestern burrito pizza, with lime-marinated chicken breast, black beans, mild chilies, grated aged cheddar cheese, green tomato salsa, and sour cream.
- Pizza topped with prosciutto, caramelized onions, artichoke hearts, fresh figs, and grated Parmesan cheese.
- Pizza topped with duck sausage, sliced duck breast with rosemary, grilled eggplant, and goat cheese.
- Tortilla pizza topped with blackened ostrich meat, papaya, and sun-dried vinaigrette.
- When imported caviar was readily available, Wolfgang Puck prepared his famous pizza with smoked salmon and sevruga caviar.
- A chef from a famous culinary school made a thin crust pizza using triangles of red, black, and golden caviar separated with chopped egg whites and yolks with a raw quail egg poised at the epicenter of the "pie."

• MATTERS OF FACT •

- Americans eat approximately one hundred acres of pizza each day, or about 350 slices per second.
- Pizza is an over $30 *billion* per year industry. There are approximately sixty-nine thousand pizzerias in the United States. Approximately 3 billion pizzas are sold in the U.S. each year.
- Pizzerias represent 17 percent of all restaurants.
- According to an American Dairy Association random sampling survey, pizza is America's fourth most craved food, behind cheese, chocolate, and ice cream.
- Pizza accounts for more than 10 percent of all food-service sales.
- 93 percent of Americans eat at least one pizza per month.
- 66.66 percent of Americans order pizza for a casual evening with friends.
- Each man, woman, and child in America eats an average of forty-six slices (twenty-three pounds) of pizza per year.
- Italian food ranks as the most popular ethnic food in America.
- According to a recent Gallop Poll, children between the ages of three and eleven prefer pizza to all other food groups for lunch and dinner.

● The National Hot Dog and Sausage Council reports that Americans spent more than $3.9 billion on hot dogs and sausages in the supermarket last year.

● The All American Hot Dog Company will sell you the equipment you need (plus a supply of Sabrett dogs) for $2,499. Visit http://www.allamericanhotdog.com/nyc.htm for more information.

▶ Pizza Deliverer

Pizza delivery people have made the following discoveries; none of which constitute what could be described as good news:

- Women tip better than men.
- The longer the driveway, the smaller the tip.
- The best tippers own older model cars. Those with new cars have spent all their cash on their vehicles.
- Most pizza is ordered during TV newscasts and while the weather forecast is broadcast.
- 3.2 million pizzas were ordered on Super Bowl Sunday last year from Domino's and Pizza Hut combined.
- Unconfirmed rumors reveal when dialing a toll-free eight hundred number to access a pizza chain from anywhere in the country, the telephone operator (who may be located on a distant continent) "reads" your address, locates the nearest pizza parlor within seven to eleven seconds, and speeds your order to your door. The pizza is cooked en route to your couch.

• WORDS FROM THE WISE •

WHEN THE COOK asked Yogi Berra whether he wanted his pizza cut into six or eight slices, he answered, "Six. No way am I hungry enough to eat eight."

▶ Hot-Dog Vender

The biggest markets are in baseball stadiums. The best of the best hot dog vendors can hit average sales of 150 to 200 dogs a game and earn something approximating thirty thousand dollars a year while catching an occasional glimpse of the action on the field.

▶ Firehouse Chef

Some of the hottest restaurants in town do not charge more than a few dollars a person for dinner. They also do not accept checks, credit cards, reservations, or customers who do not work on the premises. And all the chefs are volunteers. Firemen chefs are blazing new trails of culinary improvisation. As might be expected, the flavor of firehouse fare varies from city to city, from firehouse to firehouse, and even from chef to chef within each station.

▶ Boutique Chef

Movie houses, furniture stores, beauty parlors, and retail operations are employing cooks and chefs. Enterprising cooks are also preparing exquisite morsels for customers at gyms and health clubs, Internet cafés, the Laundromat, and wherever people cluster. Opportunities for opening a food kiosk or larger facility are also opening up in shopping malls. Chefs are also employed by places of religious worship. Check a denomination near you.

▶ Airline Chef

There is a renewed role for chefs preparing food for first-class passengers on international flights and catering at VIP airport lounges. Even regular carriers such as Delta are serving meals on flights lasting longer than three hours. Airport food malls are thriving as airlines have surrendered their food service to others who are willing to seize the day.

▶ Private Plane Chef

There are airfields for private planes all over the country. You could offer your professional services catering boxed lunches for passengers and crews traveling short and long distances.

CONTRACT DINING

A growing segment of the food-service industry is contract dining. Independent companies contract to run kitchens and dining rooms wherever they are needed, from corporations to hotels and the military. Job opportunities at these companies are enormous. To satisfy the needs of clients, they need cooks, purchasers, dining-room managers, accountants, and waitstaff. And this only skims the surface!

The Compass Group is a London-based firm that provides contract-dining services at forty thousand locations in ninety-eight countries around the world. It is one of the largest food-service companies in the world with $21 billion in annual sales. Its U.S. headquarters are in Charlotte, North Carolina. Visit http://compassext.hire.com for more info.

The Aramark Corporation is another successful contract company. It has won innumerable awards for its food and facilities management of health-care facilities, grade schools, college campuses, parks, and resorts. It serves forty-eight major league sports teams and provides the food for twenty thousand guests each year at the Grammy Awards. The company was named one of America's most admired companies in 2005 by *Fortune* magazine. Since 1998 it has consistently ranked among the top three most respected companies in the food industry. It is headquartered in Philadelphia and has nearly three hundred thousand employees serving clients in twenty countries. Visit the careers section of their Web site at http://www.aramark.com/careers_home.asp.

SYSCO (an acronym for Systems and Services Company) is based in Houston, Texas. It is the largest food-service marketing and distribution organization in North America. The company provides food, equipment, and related services to approximately 420,000 health care, educational, lodging, and restaurant establishments. It generated sales of $30 billion for calendar year 2004, employs more than forty-seven thousand associates, and has operations located throughout the United States and Canada. The company makes up an estimated 14 percent of North America's food-service market, and has expanded its international food market with the acquisition of the International Food Group, Inc., a supplier to chain restaurants in Latin America, Europe, Asia, and the Middle East.

▶ Personal Chef

The role of personal chef was virtually unknown a few years ago. Today, more than seven thousand chefs are registered as active members of the American Personal Chef Association. Industry leaders estimate this number will swell to more than twenty-five thousand within the next ten years. They will be serving nearly three hundred thousand clients and contributing nearly $1.2 billion to the U.S. economy.

A personal chef plans menus, shops for food, and cooks it in a clients' home. He may pack it in neatly labeled containers with heating directions, store it in the refrigerator or freezer, and then leave the kitchen in pristine condition. He or she customarily is employed by several clients.

A personal chef should not be confused with a private chef, who works for one family or one entity. A private chef may live on the property and be on call day and night. A personal chef lives in his own home, chooses his clients, decides which hours he will work, and sets the fees he will charge for his services.

The market for the services of a personal chef includes everyone from single people who work long days and may not know how to cook (or don't want to learn) or can't take the time to shop for more than the bare essentials to couples who relish the idea of having their meals ready to eat when they are. Other potential customers include those who need a helping hand, either temporarily or permanently. This might include new parents and moms and dads who want to spend time with their children when they get home from work or older people who want to stay in their own home but may not be able to handle the chores of shopping and cooking. Then, of course, there are the remaining millions who have figured out that it is less costly to have the refrigerator stocked with only the foods that will actually be eaten. There will be no wasted foods, no midnight temptations, and no time spent on shopping, meal preparation, or dishwashing. This is the kind of enlightened thinking that is spurring the personal chef business.

GETTING STARTED AS A PERSONAL CHEF

This is a business that can be started with virtually no capital. The client pays for the food, plus a fee that may be set by the chef or calculated on an hourly basis. The client pays the chef to buy any essential cooking equipment that is then kept in the client's home, as well as any storage containers that are needed.

ADVERTISING

Advertise your services on a computer-prepared flier with a simple list of services. Keep the information updated frequently. Distribute your information to those who you can reasonably hope will want to use your services; patients who are waiting in the offices of doctors who specialize in delivering babies, law offices where working late is a way of life, and gyms and health clubs whose clients yearn for simple, fresh food, fast. You will have little difficulty thinking of other sites where you can match your preferred cooking style to your clients' wishes.

FEES

Personal-chef earnings are all over the lot. Some make as much as eighty thousand dollars a year. Set your fees according to your needs, not your perception of your client's ability (or inability) to pay. If you charge too little, it is difficult to increase the rate for your services after a few months and you will find yourself feeling resentful if you think you are not being paid enough. If you charge too much, the level of expectation on the part of the client opens the door to perhaps unrealistic expectations. Your job performance is constantly on the line and perceived luxuries—such as your services—are the first to be chopped out of the client's budget if he decides to cut back on nonessential expenses.

CONTRACT TALKS

Once a contact has been made, the chef arranges to meet the client in her home. He discusses the foods the client likes and makes a note of preferences, dislikes, and allergies. A formal contract is signed that specifies how many meals are to be prepared each week and whether the client is anticipating a dessert or only a main course. The more precise details that are worked out ahead of time, the less chance there is for misunderstanding. Put everything in writing; you won't be sorry you took the extra time.

BILLING AND PAYMENT

The method of billing should be established during the contract negotiations. After the initial meeting, some personal chefs may cook in the client's kitchen for several weeks without actually running into the homeowner or the family.

Many personal chefs make arrangements for the client to leave a check on the kitchen counter. The client may prefer to pay for groceries directly to the store(s) from which they have been purchased, or to be provided with sales receipts that will be used to reimburse the chef. Alternatively, clients may agree to provide the chef with a credit card for food purchases.

TIME OFF

Try to maintain a relationship with other personal chefs so there is always a dependable person to substitute for you in an emergency or when you want to take a few days off. The fastest way to incur the wrath of a client or lose her forever is to leave her in the lurch. Get to know other chefs through local caterers, restaurants, and by word of mouth.

CREDENTIALS

Plans were recently finalized by the American Culinary Federation to increase the levels of professionalism by instituting certification testing for personal chefs. Though many personal chefs have attended professional cooking schools or previously worked in restaurants, others are just good home cooks who have the ability to listen to their clients' needs and know how to organize their time and money efficiently. Obtaining certification credentials can bring credibility when soliciting a new client, but it isn't necessary.

WHAT'S MORE?

It is wise to keep a waiting list of new clients. You never know when a client will terminate your service, and a lost client means immediate lost income.

Always try to think of what you can add to improve your service. It costs close to nothing to leave a little gift on the kitchen counter—like a jug of homemade lemonade, a batch of cookies, or a bowl of cherries. These little touches result in a loyal customer.

The successful chef gets almost all his clients from personal referrals. This is very much a word-of-mouth business.

For More Information

The American Personal Chef Association has led the way for this emerging industry by establishing a number of services, including the valuable Find a Personal Chef in Your Neighborhood referral network. The organization maintains forums for members to exchange information, menus, recipes, and advice for fellow chefs. It also serves as a support group, offering group insurance and tax and business advice for members, in addition to recipes and guidance for both the beginner and experienced chefs alike. Their Web site is http://www.peronalchef.com.

• **MATTERS OF FACT** •

- In most states, the Safe Food Handlers card or food sanitation certification is important and renewable in three-year increments upon completion of a daylong course. The classes cost fifty dollars and are given at local community colleges. Call your local health department's environmental protection division to find a class near you. This will reassure clients that you are serious about your job.

- Most local departments of health do not permit personal chefs to cook in their own kitchen and carry the food to the home of the client. Check with yours.

- It is wise to get insurance coverage. For American Personal Chef Association members, flat-fee coverage is available, at the time of this writing, for $600 annually. This is for $2 million of general liability insurance coverage and $300,000 fire coverage for any city in the country. (If the same coverage were quoted on a city-by-city basis for personal chefs operating in New York City and surrounding areas, it would cost closer to $2,500 a year.) The insurance is available through K and K Insurance (http://www.kandkinsurance.com).

ℋOW I BECAME A PERSONAL CHEF

by Candy Wallace, founder of the American Personal Chef Association

MY GRANDMOTHER OFTEN told me, "If you don't see what you want, create it yourself."

I started cooking in my grandmother's restaurant as a kid, and inherited her respect for seasonal foods and her commitment to two central ideas: keep it simple and keep it fresh. Cooking is the joyous part of the industry, but the hours, nights, weekends, and holidays that I had to work in food service left me searching for a way to cook for a living on my own terms. I earned a college degree and worked in the corporate world while continuing to cook profession- ally. I was employed as a marketing vice president during the week and cooked in a French restaurant on weekends. I had the benefit of a broad range of experiences before I decided to blend the two disciplines.

Finally, I decided to open a business cooking for time-pressed clients who wanted to dine out—at home. My sense was that busy people would welcome the opportunity to have custom- designed, palate-specific meals that were prepared in their own kitchens and stored for their future enjoyment. I developed a business where I was paid to do what I love: shop and cook.

I have been a working personal chef for more than twelve years and have been teaching, training, and men- toring others who want to own and operate their own successful businesses for more than ten years through the American Personal Chef Institute (APCI) and the American Personal Chef Association (APCA), which I founded to support and mentor the individuals trained through the institute.

So far, the APCI and APCA have trained, assisted, and supported more than five thousand individuals. My staff and I have helped set up and operate innumerable successful personal-chef businesses. We make cer- tain each personal chef is clear about what level of service they intend to offer, and to whom, and then advise them on how to find their roster of clients. We show personal chefs how to plan menus that not only include a full range of tastes and textures, but also efficient shopping and cooking times in order to reach profitabil- ity quickly.

Many of our members are self-taught passionate home cooks, while others are professional chefs. What you need to remember about this industry is that no two personal chef businesses should look alike, and no two clients are the same. A personal chef must find clients whose food tastes match with the chef's skills, whether this means cooking comfort food, a regimented diet for a diabetic, or highly sophisticated food for an epicure.

Recommended Book

Wallace, Candy, and Greg Forte. *The Professional Personal Chef: The Business of Doing Business as a Personal Chef.* Hoboken, NJ: Wiley, 2006.

▶ Private Chef

Private chefs are full-time employees of one client. They may prepare one to three meals a day (or none at all but remain on call). Many private chefs live in the client's home or on their property.

The best part of being a private chef is the freedom to cook great food for a few discerning people, such as a (wealthy) small family or even one individual. The chef may be asked to prepare (but not serve) food for a small dinner party or even large groups attending special events in the client's home.

The private chef may receive extraordinary perks from their client. For example, working for a pop star could mean free tickets to concerts; a chef for a tennis player may travel the world on the circuit. Cooking for a family may include travel to lovely vacation homes in exotic parts of the world.

The salary for a private chef constitutes only a portion of the chef's income, as housing and health benefits are often provided along with Social Security coverage. The client may also provide a car so the chef can get to the food and wine stores. (He may also be asked to drop off the dry cleaning, pick up the children, take the dog to the vet, and run other errands. How the chef responds to these requests often spells the difference between harmony in the household—or seething hostility.)

Anyone considering this career option should try to nail down the parameters of the position before agreeing to start work. You may not be able to get a written contract, but you will be rewarded if you press for a clear description of the duties you will be expected to perform and the hours you will be working. Being summoned to prepare bacon and eggs in the middle of the night for clients' partying children may not be something you are thrilled to do.

The upside and downside of this otherwise attractive career option is the same: it all boils down to a matter of chemistry between employer and employee; this is among the most personal of food services.

For More Information

http://www.culturalvision.net/html/private_chef.html
Order a Chef, http://www.orderachef.com
http://www.privatechefsinc.com/contact.html
Private Chefs FAQs,
http://www.culinaryagency.com/faq.html

Private Chef Service
http://www.wasatchresortcatering.com/privatechef.htm
StarChef job finder, http://www.starchefsjobfinder.com/
js-jobinfo

► Butler

Has the thought crossed your mind that you may like to be a butler? Check the Internet to find professional schools for learning the trade. Begin with http://www.butlerbureau.com.

Recommended Book
Richman, Phyllis. *The Butter Did It : A Gastronomic Tale of Love and Murder*. Thorndike, ME: Thorndike Press, 1997.

► Corporate-Dining-Room Chef

To a client, an invitation to an executive dining room may be more coveted than one to the finest restaurant in the city. One of the most pressing reasons for the private dining room, at least to the moguls of the money world, is discretion. Mergers, international transactions, and negotiations involving vast sums need to be conducted in secrecy, and if tycoon A is seen at a restaurant with oil minister B or banker C, tremors may reverberate all the way to the stock market. "Even within the confines of the exclusive dining room, I've seen men draw their chairs away from the table and confer in whispers," says one chef, speaking on condition of anonymity.

In principle, executive dining rooms are used mainly for weekday lunches, though some are humming for the occasional breakfast or dinner meeting, as well as for cocktail parties and receptions. Depending on company policy, the room may be used by one exalted chief executive officer or by several partners of a firm.

The talents of a corporate dining chef soar to the highest level of professionalism. The job requires up-to-date knowledge of contemporary food. Meat–and-potato menus are seldom seen. Instead, the food more closely resembles that of an elegant restaurant, often with heart-healthy options available.

For the chef, there are several advantages to working in a private corporate dining room. There is almost total freedom to create market-driven menus in which the cost of ingredients is rarely questioned. The hours are mostly regular and predictable, with plenty of advance notice to prepare for special events. The salary is often remarkably good and includes benefits, and the chef is, for the most part, her own boss.

These jobs are highly coveted, but once you identify which corporations, banks, and financial institutions have private dining rooms, submit your résumé. Be ready to pounce should an opening arise.

Applicants will probably need seven or more years of experience working in a restaurant or food-service kitchen in addition to a culinary degree.

For More Information

Check chef headhunter sites on the Internet and look at job listings in Food Arts and other restaurant trade magazines.

▶ Country-Club or Lodge Chef

There are more than fourteen thousand private clubs employing 256,000 people in the United States. They encompass city clubs, country clubs, golf clubs, sailing clubs, fraternal, college, and military clubs, fishing lodges, religious and special interest retreats, and resorts. The club chef customarily works ten-hour days, five to six days a week, though there is no such thing as regular hours for most club managers and chefs. You schedule your time according to the activities of the club and leave when it is quiet.

Things have changed in many clubs in recent years. In order to attract and maintain an exclusive membership, many have raised the bar on food quality. No more squishy white bread, overcooked chicken, canned asparagus, and prepared-from-a-box mashed potatoes and gravy. No more commercially prepared, sweetened iced tea. The top country clubs are attracting top chefs from the best restaurants in the nation. Ditto for waitstaff, bartenders, dining room managers, and other kitchen jobs.

Lovely environments and facilities abound. Club management can offer you a professional income and health benefits. You might find an ideal location anywhere in the world.

Many executive chefs receive some form of performance bonus ranging from 5 to 15 percent of their base salary, and they may be rewarded with a holiday bonus, too. Other perks can include use of the golf, tennis, swimming, and other facilities, staff meals, and fees paid for continuing professional development such as the opportunity to attend the annual Club Managers Association of America conference.

For More Information

Hospitality Guild Private Club Management, http://hospitalityguild.com/careers.com

The Club Managers Association of America provides its membership at more than three thousand country, athletic, yacht, and military clubs with professional-development study courses, certification diplomas, networking opportunities, and industry-related publications. http://www.cmaa.org

▶ Bed-and-Breakfast Owner

There are more than twenty thousand licensed inns and B and Bs in the United States, according to the Professional Association of Innkeepers International. The technical difference between an inn and a B and B is that an inn may serve lunch and dinner as well as breakfast, whereas most B and Bs serve only breakfast. B and Bs owned and operated by culinary professionals can greatly enhance income, guest satisfaction, prestige, and room occupancy rates by offering cocktails and hors d'oeuvres, dinner, and/or desserts. Creative breakfasts may be served to the local community as well as guests, although a special license may be required to offer this additional service.

The idea of opening a bed and breakfast can be an appealing alternative to commuting to an unrewarding job. You will be able to work at home in a location you love. But there are downsides, too. You are constantly on call, and having strangers staying in your home is not always as delightful as it may seem. Some visitors are inconsiderate when it comes to noise, arguing loudly, or playing music when you and your other guests want to sleep. Thoughtless folk may drop a wet towel on an armchair or dump it on the dresser you so lovingly restored. Some may leave the room in an unimaginably terrible condition with reminders of their brief visit left in the form of stained carpets, broken fixtures, and stolen objects. It is astonishing how much willful damage troublesome tourists and their previously undisclosed pets can make in a single night.

You may also find yourself spending far more time marketing your property than you had anticipated. Unless all or most of the rooms are filled all the time, you could find yourself on the wrong end of a balance sheet. The financial problems are compounded when guests make a reservation and fail to show up or, even worse, skip out without paying for the room. Damage requiring repairs can be doubly costly because the room becomes unavailable for another guest.

Despite these undeniable risks, the pleasures will customarily far outweigh the pains. Many guests return every year and become part of an interesting extended family. Besides, there are ways to avoid problems and avert misunderstandings before they arise. Prospective bed-and-breakfast buyers are strongly urged to talk to experienced owners who will share their stories and become invaluable sources of information.

There are several ways to get started. For instance, you can buy an existing bed and breakfast along with its furnishings, future bookings, and reputation, or you can find a house or other property that has the potential to be a great bed and breakfast or inn. You could even start a bed and breakfast in your current home.

It's not a bad idea to get your feet wet by offering to take over for bed-and-breakfast owners who want to take a vacation. Ask other owners for advice on writing a business plan and where to find out about permits and insurance.

For More Information

The Bed and Breakfast Institute of Learning in Napa, California, has a three-day workshop.
http://www.bbinnstitute.com

The INNexperience Internship program has locations across the country and offers five-day sessions.
http://www.innsitter.bugsteppcom/generic/14.html

Smith, Michael. *The Inn Chef Cookbook: Creative Ingredients, Sensational Flavors*. East Meadow, NY: Callawind, 1999.

▶ Yacht Chef

Do you think you would like to cook aboard a yacht? Dana Minuta has done so and has some good advice for those who yearn for the open sea. First, she says, you must like the crew you sign on with. Unlike other jobs, your coworkers become your family, and you are with them twenty-four hours a day. And, at sea, these are the people to whom you trust your life.

Captains generally ask prospective chefs to cook a meal, and it is not uncommon for the captain to throw in a last-minute monkey wrench. For instance, you may be asked to hold the meal for an hour, or adjust the menu to accommodate a guest's allergy. This is not a form of hazing, explains Minuta. This is what guests really do, and the captain is testing your ability to adapt.

Plan to begin work right away. It is not the nature of such a transient industry to give two weeks' notice. Pack your bags lightly. The crew quarters on a yacht do not offer much living or sleeping space.

To be a successful chef on a private yacht, it is not enough to possess excellent culinary skills. You must be versatile, extremely well organized, always willing to please, and be able to cook in a galley that is seldom horizontal. When a guest is paying upwards of twenty thousand dollars for a one-week charter, the word *no* is not part of a crewmember's vocabulary.

On yachts up to 130 feet, a chef is a one-man show. There's no sous chef, no saucier, no garde-manger, no pâtissier, no dishwasher— you are on your own. From planning the menus to choosing the wines, from breakfast to midnight snacks, you are on the clock.

It is not uncommon to have six guests onboard who require three different menus due to dietary restrictions or food aversions. It is the chef's job to happily respond to each request and execute each meal flawlessly.

Provisioning a yacht can be quite a task. There are no purveyors from which a chef orders. Supermarkets, farmers' markets, and specialty shops are a yacht chef's suppliers. On provisioning days, says Minuta, she never spends fewer than six hours shopping. The looks from other shoppers are quite comical when they see a yacht chef approaching a checkout with three carts filled to the brim. After all, it takes a lot of food to cook for the hungry guests and crew.

Stocking a yacht for a week takes practice. Spoilage and space can be great antagonists. Generally speaking, the yacht will dock somewhere around midweek to allow the chef to restock fresh fish and fruits and vegetables. Good communication with the captain is essential in this matter.

This may all sound like very intense work, and it is. The good news is that the average yacht is only chartered for fifteen to twenty weeks out of the year. The rest of the time is spent maintaining the boat and cooking for the crew, often in gorgeous locations.

The best way for someone new to the industry to find employment is to work with a crew agent, says Minuta. In the United

States, Fort Lauderdale, Florida, is one of the best places to find a crew placement agency in the winter. During the summer months, try Newport, Rhode Island, on the East Coast. On the West Coast, Seattle and San Diego are good bets.

Another way to secure a job in the industry is to walk the docks. As the season opens, crews are busy showing their yachts to brokers, and at night it is one big party—a good time to get to know the crews.

Crew Agencies on the Web
http://www.crewfinders.com
http://www.crewunlimited.com
http://www.elitecrewintl.com

• MATTERS OF FACT •

- In 1890, when New York Yacht Club Commodore Elbridge Gerry went on a two-week cruise aboard his 173-foot yacht, *Electra*, the champagne bills were reportedly larger than those for coal, the crew's wages, and yacht maintenance combined.

- The south of France is the center of yachting. It is the ultimate place to show off a $200 million vessel. The general rule is: "Never spend more than 10 percent of your wealth on your boat. It will cost $4 to $5 million a year to operate a 245-foot yacht with one or two heliports, a main dining room that may seat as many as seventy guests, and an afterdeck to accommodate a cocktail party for a hundred visitors. Charter costs for such vessels hover in the region of $70,000 a day or $850,000 a week (meals included). The view of oceans of seawater is complimentary.

- It is anticipated that the guests and temporary host will leave a gratuity for the staff.

- The chef's salary is tax-free assuming the ship sails beyond the three-mile coast of the United States. The cabin and onboard food are also provided.

- Microsoft cofounder Paul Allen's *Octopus* is the world's largest privately owned yacht. It has two helicopters, seven boats, and a remote-controlled vehicle for crawling on the ocean floor. Paul Allen is the only private individual to simultaneously own three yachts measuring sixty meters (about 197 feet) and up.

For More Information
Dana, Richard Henry. *Two Years before the Mast*. New York: Heritage Press, 1941.
Kretschmer, John. *Flirting with Mermaids*. Dobbs Ferry, NY: Sheridan House, 1999.

Philbrick, Nathaniel. *In the Heart of the Sea*. New York: Viking, 2000.

Thompson, Jennifer Trainer and Elizabeth Wheeler. *Feasts Afloat: 150 Recipes for Great Meals from Small Spaces*. Berkeley: Ten Speed Press, 1990.

Wouk, Herman. *Don't Stop the Carnival*. New York: Doubleday, 1965.

▶ Cruise-Ship Lecturer

If you like to travel and have knowledge about the ports of call you might be interested in exploring the possibilities of becoming a part-time lecturer or full-time employee of a luxury cruise ship.

The talks to the passengers customarily last about forty-five minutes with another few minutes of questions from the audience. Topics could include the food and culture of the region, and you may also offer cooking classes. The lecture may be repeated three or more times during the voyage; the rest of the time is your own to soak up the sun, read a book, or make new friends. You may also be invited to bring a guest to share your cabin/stateroom.

If you know the region well, you may also be invited to become a tour guide. Some cruise lines provide a small honorarium, others actually bill you fifty dollars a day to cover their costs, and you may be responsible for getting yourself to the dock, but once there you will be living high on the hog with all meals and accommodations complimentary (though you must buy your own booze).

For more information, contact cruise lines directly. Princess Cruises, Queen Elizabeth 2, and Crystal Cruises hire guest speakers, as do Royal Viking, Silver Seas, and Radisson. Or contact a booking agency such as Sixth Star (http://www.sixthstar.com), which describes the role as follows:

> A Destination Speaker's responsibility is to give a series of original presentations illustrating the culture and history of the ports of call on a given cruise itinerary. For instance, a Speaker on a cruise to Mexico may discuss the Mexican-American War, foreign policy between the United States and Mexico, or the culture of the country. The talks should not be a reiteration of what to see-and-do in Puerto Vallarta. Rather, they should provide the guests with insight into the ports that one would not be able to find in an average guidebook.

► Cruise-Ship Chef

The Cruise Line International Association (CLIA) claims their industry is the most exciting growth category in the entire leisure market, with revenues growing at an annual rate of 8.4 percent since 1980. The CLIA suggests the enormous variety of ships offer an experience for every pocketbook and everyone who reserves a berth needs to eat. Celebrity chefs and dazzling restaurants have become part of the enticing packages. Indeed, fine dining is listed as being among the top reasons for choosing one shipping line over another.

The chef is responsible for the quality of the preparation and presentation of the food and must also maintain the highest standards of food safety. He or she oversees multiple restaurants and sometimes other food-service options such as deck and cabin service. The chef is also responsible for the crew's meals.

These jobs are a lot of work, but a lot of fun, too. You will be able to check out any number of ports of call and will get to know a lot of people, who on some ships may come from many different countries.

Most high-level chef positions on cruise ships require a degree from a professional cooking school, a minimum of five years of experience working as a sous chef, plus three years in another food preparation position.

Maintaining tight controls over a large inventory and purchasing at several ports on the voyage can be a headache. For example, if you shopped for a typical seven-day cruise, you would buy 9,000 pounds of beef, 7,000 pounds of veal, 2,500 pounds of bacon, 4,000 pounds of potatoes, 250 gallons of cream, and 3,000 pounds of butter (and possibly some seasickness remedies, too).

For More Information
http://www.crewfinders.com
http://www.cruisejobline.com
http://www.yachtingcrews.com

► Spa Chef

The term *spa food* used to call to mind a few sad lettuce leaves seasoned with a squirt of lemon juice, but today that salad is likely to be gathered from an adjoining garden, dressed with a fragrant extra virgin olive oil, garnished with edible flowers, and presented like a still-life painting.

Each top spa across the country has its own unique character and focus. Southern California's Golden Door gained international attention for its elegant, personalized service. Executive Chef Michel Stroot's innovative cooking style, based on vegetarian principles, has influenced dining trends, both here and abroad. "More than half of our produce comes from our own organic gardens," he says. "For health reasons, we do not use butter or red meat, and we do not serve fried foods." Stroot refers to these forbidden foods as "aggressive foods." "People who eat a lot of aggressive foods tend to be aggressive themselves," he observes. An admirer of Asian cuisine, Stroot relies on brown rice, homemade stocks, seasonal produce (preferably homegrown), citrus, and organic herbs and spices to compose his menu. "Eating should be a happy experience. A nurturing experience," he says. "I believe in food that is fresh and light and simple. This is an idea that translates into pleasurable minimalism."

Spa food is based on the freshest ingredients, seasoned delicately to bring out their natural goodness. Frying and sautéing are taboo; instead, the ingredients are steamed, grilled, roasted, or gently poached. Reduced stocks or vegetable purées are used to thicken sauces. Taste comes from fresh herbs and other flavor accents, seldom from salt. The coffee is decaffeinated, but freshly ground and properly brewed.

The influence of ethnic cuisines is apparent in the Japanese minimalist approach to both presentation and ingredients. David Barrocas, director of food and beverage at the Stowe Resort and Spa in Stowe, Vermont, says there is no reason to "say *no* to all meat. Game meats, such as venison and antelope, can be quite lean. And you don't need to nix other meats like beef, as long as you choose lean cuts and reduce portion sizes."

Even so, at almost all spas, the emphasis is on whole grains, fish, and plenty of fresh fruits and vegetables. Portions are small but beautifully presented, and the emphasis is on true, pure flavors. Mineral water is downed in large quantities and herbal teas are greatly in evidence.

Michel Nischan has long been a crusader for sustainability in fishing and farming. He is an advocate of pasture-fed beef and lamb and foods that are raised humanely and grown responsibly. "I never intended the pursuit of healthful, organic cooking to be my lifelong endeavor, much less my passion," he wrote in his first book, *Taste Pure and Simple*." But I am passionate about it: passionate about achieving balance in every meal, about eating what is ripe and best in its season, and about enjoying the pure pleasure of eating simply and eating well."

In his book, he gives this advice to chefs:

- Don't use substitutes: No creamless cream sauces, no butterless hollandaise, no tempeh chicken breasts.
- Don't preach. The holier than-thou attitudes of health-food restaurants turn people off.
- Guests want the sausage and bacon on their breakfast plates. Don't take away every pleasure. Think about the whole experience and cut back on other foods.
- I am not a hopeless romantic who believes that one day all hamburgers will be coming from grass-fed cows. It's not going to happen. But we should applaud changes in that direction. The more that well-being and sustainability become profitable, the more business is going to say, "This is a good model. Let's figure out an even better way to do it." So I believe the future is going to be "doing well by doing good." It's going to happen.
- I think the public has moved to a point where they really do want natural foods. This point is proved when you look at the reality that organic foods are the only expanding segment of the retail grocery market.

For More Information

Nischan, Michel, with Mary Goodbody. *Homegrown Pure and Simple: Great Healthy Food from Garden to Table*. New York: Chronicle Books, 2005.

Nischan, Michel, with Mary Goodbody. *Taste Pure and Simple: Irresistible Recipes for Good Food and Good Health*. New York: Chronicle Books, 2003.

Stroot, Michel. *The Golden Door Cooks Light & Easy: Delicious Recipes from America's Premier Spa*. Layton, UT: Gibbs Smith, 2003.

The International Spa Association, a networking and educational organization, has twenty-five hundred members in seventy-three countries. http://www.experienceispa.com

▶ Hospital Chef

Hospital food has long had a terrible reputation, but this is changing as hospitals compete for patients who are well enough to consider the food they are eating, such as those undergoing

- The spa business is booming: it is the fastest growing area of the resort-hotel sector. In 1990 there were an estimated 1,274 spas. That number has rapidly increased to more than twelve thousand, with annual sales hovering around $4.5 billion.
- More than 45 million people spent time at health spas last year. The figures are increasing.

• MATTERS OF FACT •

*T*HE TOTAL ALLOWANCE to cover three meals a day in the federal penitentiary $2.52.

elective surgery. Chefs offer upscale salads and healthy menus both for patients and staff and for visitors in the cafeterias.

The food facilities have become a profit center for some hospitals. Ray Potter, executive chef at Houston's St. Luke's Episcopal Hospital, has his name on the menu. His recipe for low-fat, low-calorie jalapeño cornbread is featured on the hospital Web site and his full-size cardboard likeness in chef's whites is a permanent fixture in the patient admittance office. Outsiders choose the hospital as a place to eat, even when they are not visiting a loved one. They become voluntary in- and outpatients.

At Memorial Sloan-Kettering Cancer Center in Manhattan, a staff of ten cooks and two executive chefs produce 1,300 room service–style patient trays, 3,500 retail meals, and 750 catered meals daily. Entry-level cooks are hired from two-year community colleges or culinary schools. "Degreed graduates from colleges such as the CIA or Johnson and Wales with five years' experience join as executive chefs," says food and nutrition director Sharon Cox.

Many hiring managers, such as Cox, recruit experienced candidates mainly from hotels and country clubs with large batch-cooking environments, but others hire from restaurants.

Given broad government and industry regulations, extensive training for new hires is often conducted by the care facility. Food-service companies such as Sodexho and Morrison offer additional orientation before offering a specific assignment. These companies provide ongoing chef training.

What culinary skills lead to success in this field? Strong interpersonal and organizational skills and a willingness to work on multidisciplinary teams are important. A sincere interest in sharing knowledge about healthful cooking is also a plus.

The upscale VIP private-care unit is a fast-growing phenomenon at many medical centers. Rack of lamb is a popular staple, and lobster is among regular luxuries. Chefs are getting a foothold in modernized hospital kitchens and have finally tossed out all (or almost all) the familiar, wobbly red and green gelatin.

Salaries for chefs working in health services vary by the location and size of the medical center. Most benefits packages are worth about 30 percent of the base salary. A typical plan may include health insurance, life insurance, paid vacations, and retirement benefits. But also bear in mind, like other branches of food service, executive chefs are responsible for budgets and are expected to break even or turn a profit on retail operations. Acute-care medical centers face serious financial crunches, especially in city and country health systems where many patients without medical insurance are treated—and fed without fees.

▶ Retirement-Home Chef

Brooksby Village in Massachusetts is a retirement community for nearly one thousand residents and is a good example of how dining services in similar facilities are changing. "We want our residents to feel like they are eating out in a restaurant," explained Paul Coco, director of dining services. "We have stepped away from having residents circle what they want on a piece of paper to having waitstaff take orders and place them, electronically. The dining experience is very important to our residents. For example, the Harvest Grille and Cider House are situated in a building called the Clubhouse. Harvest Grille is a two hundred–seat, buffet-style restaurant offering rotisserie foods and a carving station. Cider House is a pub with a full bar that seats fifty people. In addition to alcoholic beverages, patrons can dine on pizza and bistro-type fare. Cider House features a stone fireplace, an outdoor terrace, and a big-screen television."

The advantage of working in a retirement community, rather than a medical center, is that there is a relatively stable number of healthy guests, and quite wealthy folk, too, who look for variety and innovative menus, thus challenging the chef to do his best work for an appreciative, mostly captive clientele.

Health and other benefits, sometimes including free lodging, may be included in the salary package of an executive chef working in upscale retirement communities.

BRUNCH FOR THE BEREAVED

Chefs welcome the opportunity to cater a wedding breakfast. Everyone is upbeat, lovely young people laugh and frolic, and the food is contemporary and irresistibly enticing. Brunch for the bereaved is an entirely different proposition. The congregants tend to be terribly gloomy, somber, and tearful. Even so, there is nothing like a morning funeral to sharpen the appetite, and restaurants that fail to seize the opportunity to offer sustenance to melancholy mourners miss many a boat. Woody Allen once noted, "My grandfather had a wonderful funeral. It was held in a big hall with accordion players. On the buffet table there was a replica of the deceased rendered in chopped liver."

• RARE JOB •
ℒAST MEALS

NO MATTER HOW well Brian Price cooked his steaks he could never count on repeat customers; as a cook in the Huntsville, Texas, Wall Unit, he prepared the last meals for over two hundred inmates between 1991 and 2003. Price, who upon arrival at the prison was assigned to kitchen duty due to his teenage experience at a local pizza kitchen, made his first last meal for Lawrence Buxton in 1991, volunteering to take the job when no other prisoners would. Although reluctant at first to associate himself with any part of the executions conducted in the prison, he volunteered to make all subsequent last meals throughout his time at the jail. He understood the importance of the last meal as the last conveyor of earthly comfort to the condemned. Price was eventually released and no longer prepares meals for the condemned, but he has published a compilation of his signature recipes called *Meals to Die For.*

▶ Military Chef

Experienced chefs are responsible for the food service for senior officers, VIPs, and visiting dignitaries in Washington, D.C., and on military bases throughout the world. The chef may be asked to prepare breakfast, lunch, or dinner for visiting members of Congress—even perhaps for the president.

At all large military bases, the executive chefs are of the highest caliber, both at home and overseas. Protocol calls for host officers to invite their ranking counterparts to meals at the officer's club. Executive chef positions in the military are appointed after acquiring at least fifteen years of culinary experience as a certified chef. Prior military service is not required, but is a big plus if you have it. It is essential to have previous documented experience as a cooking instructor, as training other chefs is an important part of the job. This means that certification by the American Culinary Federation is a must for most applicants seeking executive chef appointments in the U.S. Navy, Marines, Army, and Air Force.

For More Information

The Military Hospitality Alliance is a Web site where worldwide personnel discuss scholarships, daily issues, education, benefits, and issues of mutual interest.
http://www.mhaifsea.com

For more information on becoming a military chef, visit http://www.prochef.com

▶ Arctic Chef

The following is an actual posting for a chef position by the British Antarctic Survey Natural Environment Research Council (http://www.antarctica.ac.uk):

Antarctica is the coldest and most isolated continent in the world. It's also the most exhilarating, providing a unique and spectacular setting for our vital scientific research.

The successful chef candidate must have proven experience in kitchen management, including inventory control and producing quality menus for up to 100 people. You'll also have basic computer literacy, good communication skills and the ability to work under pressure with limited time and resources. You must be willing to make a commitment for 18 months. Annual salary 23,000 British pounds [approximately 45,000 U.S. dollars]. Qualification in food hygiene required. [A thick skin and thermal underwear would be useful, too.]

COOKING IN PUBLIC-SCHOOL KITCHENS

There are nearly 50 million students enrolled in elementary and secondary schools in the United States. The vast majority are offered pretty horrible food. School food has become a battlefield for the bellies of students. The lines are drawn between giant food processors, school boards, and parents.

Nonetheless, schools all across the country offer hot lunches and many serve breakfast, too. Schools need cooks, dieticians, and supervisors capable of planning menus and ordering the food. And many school cafeterias serve far better food than they used to, so there are challenges for caring professionals.

The American Beverage Association announced its new school vending policy: In elementary schools, only bottled water and 100 percent fruit juices are available. Middle schools will have only nutritious and lower-calorie beverages. No high-calorie soft drinks and no high-calorie juice drinks with only 5 percent fruit juice. High schools are allowed a variety of beverage choices, but no more than 50 percent of them may be soft drinks. Fast-food franchises operating in schools are under intense scrutiny.

When one influential organization has the courage to take a first step, others will surely follow. Chefs are joining the chorus of advocacy for better food for growing children. "We are facing a national epidemic of childhood obesity," says Alice Waters, the award-winning restaurateur and political activist, and one can hear both sadness and outrage in her voice. "I'm not interested in preaching to the converted. We need to reach kids in the public schools, right now, while they are young, with good food in the lunchroom as part of their everyday lives."

Waters is best known for Chez Panisse, her Berkeley, California, restaurant. It was the original melting pot for the American organic-cooking revolution. She has watched her passion for supporting local farmers' markets grow into a unanimously-passed, school board-approved pilot program that may soon impact every child in her hometown, and in other areas across the nation. She has had a profound impact on the nation as she spread the word about the original Edible Schoolyard program, in which she encouraged a school's principal and the students to transform a barren plot of urban land into a thriving garden.

Alice Waters explains, "The Berkeley School Lunch Initiative helps kids of all ages experience food directly. This means that kindergartners might learn how to count with peas, eighth graders could apply scientific laws to a garden's irrigation system, and high school sophomores could discover Morocco by preparing and eating a vegetable-laden couscous (bursting with fresh ingredients, of course)."

Is this a model for public schools everywhere? "I never imagined a school lunch program could become a part of an academic curriculum," Waters says modestly. "But I kept pounding on the door. And, you know what? The door opened."

The vision of the Berkeley School Lunch Initiative is to revolutionize school lunch by giving it a central place in the academic curriculum and to:

- Provide healthy, freshly prepared meals for all students from kindergarten through high school, every school day.
- Support local and sustainable farms.
- Establish composting and recycling programs.
- Integrate food into classroom lesson plans, teaching students about the connections between sustenance and their academic subjects.
- Engage kids in the hands-on educational experience of growing, cooking, and sharing food.
- When these steps are taken, school lunches may well be reformed. And everyone will benefit. There are limitless opportunities to initiate school-food programs for every age group from daycare and special education facilities to private and public schools and colleges.

For More Information

Partners in the Berkeley School Lunch initiative include:

Chez Panisse Foundation,
http://www.chezpanissefoundation.org

Center for Ecoliteracy, http://www.ecoliteracy.org

Children's Hospital Oakland, http://www.chori.org

Berkeley Unified School District,
http://www.co.berkeley.ca.us/aboutberkeley/busd.html

College-Dining-Hall Chef

Northeastern University's new Stetson West dining hall is an example of the new and vastly improved food services on college campuses. Pizza ovens, sushi bars, stir-fried foods, pasta stations, grilling stations, Mexican, Indian, regional American, vegetarian, vegan, and organically grown foods from local farmers are among the new menu options enticing students to eat well rather that relying on breakfast cereals, junk food, and instant noodles.

Colleges everywhere are spending millions of dollars to attract more students. Not incidentally, new meal plans that commit students to buying their food on campus are adding big bucks to school revenues.

Alice Waters, along with her daughter, Fanny, led the charge at Yale University, where Fanny was a student, to alter its food service so it included sustainable and organic foods. Their efforts have borne great results spurring Harvard, MIT, and other universities to join the initiative to make available more healthful food alternatives for students and faculty.

Dining-hall services that have traditionally borne the brunt of jokes have acquired a new respect. The new dining hall at MIT is open twenty-four hours a day and has a chef on hand to cook food made to order. The enterprise is so successful that it is attracting students from all over the campus. At Smith College, the café in the new campus center serves made-to-order salads and sandwiches, freshly baked muffins and scones, and gourmet coffee. It is dedicated to one of the college's favorite alums, Julia Child.

These changes at colleges and universities mean there are job opportunities for trained cooks who want the challenge of running a large kitchen. An added perk is that at many colleges chefs are invited to attend degree courses for token tuition fees.

Caterer

Do you love throwing parties? Do you read cookbooks and food magazines the way other people read newspapers? Are you already planning parties for friends, colleagues, and family without getting paid for it? You may even have gone so far as to investigate attending cooking school. Catering might just be the perfect job for you.

The $5 billion catering business has enjoyed a 20 percent increase in sales in the last decade. Hotels, restaurants, country clubs, charter yachts, and even airlines represent catering opportunities. By becoming a chef in a private home or an executive dining room, supervising catering for special events for department stores, galleries, schools, public relations firms, or running take-out counters in supermarkets and specialty shops, caterers can create their own job opportunities.

Most hotels have a catering department that handles their banquet rooms. An entry-level position will give you the opportunity to meet prospective customers and build a client base of your own. This also provides you with the opportunity to get an inside look at how in-house catering works.

Caterer Denise Vivaldo says, "If you plan to open a small operation, you will probably find it easy to handle parties for five to fifty people (buffet, not sit-down) with just one assistant. Most large catering companies don't like taking on parties for fewer than thirty guests, nor will they consider last-minute jobs. You may be ideally situated to handle small jobs on short notice and keep costs competitive by using your client's kitchen."

If you have a specialty—beautiful custom-designed cupcakes or mini cheesecakes, for example—consider baking them on a large

---

• **RECIPE FOR SUCCESS** •

$\mathcal{B}$OUTIQUE-STYLE CATERING

by Chef David James Robinson, www.bezalelgables.com

 DO YOU CRAVE variety and challenges? If you can listen, collaborate, and conjure your client's dreams into edible realities; if you can cater to their appetites, whims, and egos, then catering is the right arm of food service for you.

I started out as an advertising executive at a trendy Manhattan ad agency in Soho. I was an extremely passionate home cook who spent a lot of my weekends throwing lavish dinner parties for friends. I was good at advertising, but fairly certain I had just fallen into it, as opposed to actually choosing my vocation.

On September 11, I watched from my window as the World Trade Center towers fell. It was a pivotal moment and added substantially to the old-fashioned midlife crisis I was having. I gave up advertising and trained to be a professional chef at the Culinary Institute of America in Hyde Park, New York.

While I chose food as a profession, I fell into catering because someone asked me to cater a party. The guest list was glamorous, the money was good, and the party was accidentally a great success. Most important of all, I found the work deeply satisfying. I figured I could work as a line cook for an hourly wage or own my own company, develop recipes, and cater for a living.

Formal culinary training is not always necessary for success in catering. I would put my money on an experienced, inventive home cook any day. What culinary training does help with is knowing what's possible and what type of foods will hold well. In most instances, doing individual soufflés for four hundred guests isn't practical. When restaurant chefs tell me they did two hundred covers in a night, I know that they have three staggered seatings. When we do two hundred covers, everyone is eating at once and we're working out of a tent with a garden hose for water.

When you consider catering, you have to ask yourself, Does the food have to be as awful as it usually is? My answer is no. We set out every day to prove that it can be an amazing accompaniment to celebration. My company, Bezalel Gables Fine Catering and Events, is a boutique-style catering company that creates luxuriously handcrafted food from the Hudson Valley and Berkshire Mountains. We make just about everything from scratch: our stocks, our mozzarella, and our sauces. We smoke our own salmon. We grow many of our own herbs and even bake our own crackers. Our company is the antithesis of the rubber-chicken dinner.

A full 20 percent of my job is cooking, and the other 80 percent is trying to create a menu—and an event—that succeeds in fulfilling a client's wishes and then selling them on it and exceeding their expectations. In an unusual move for catering, we do a custom menu for each event. We've created menus of foods from Uganda, Brazil, and the American South. It's never boring. I get to research recipes that I wouldn't be naturally drawn to. I'm terrifically curious and I get paid for satisfying my curiosity. Plus, I love the fact that I have a certain amount of creative control, in collaboration with my clients.

For a birthday party we threw for the author of this book, we scanned the titles of her many cookbooks and made them into "badges" for all the guests to wear as they arrived. Her birthday cake was a genoise white cake with lemon-curd filling. It was made in the shape of a stack of her books with the book covers reproduced in full color on the rolled fondant icing. Edible pastiage flowers were used as decorations. We brought a bouquet of roses marking every year that was being celebrated and made a four-hour program of her favorite music. The tablecloths were color coordinated to the palate of her English country garden and the martini bar included the English Rose: a rose-infused martini with candied rose petals! It was a truly fabulous event.

scale. Take samples to local restaurants, gourmet take-out shops, and upscale coffee houses. Be aware that health department regulations will require you to produce food in a commercial kitchen, so talk to large caterers, schools, churches, or local businesses with kitchens about renting space.

Consider catering special events. This requires marketing, so you will have to make up a promotional package that describes your services. Include descriptions, photographs, and a video of your brilliant presentations, great staff, and fantastic food. Send these out to anyone connected to special events in your area. The Convention and Visitors Bureau or office of the mayor may help guide you to potential clients who are holding local conferences.

By renting you can get into the business of catering without incurring too large an investment. You can rent just about anything, including tables, chairs, place settings, flatware, stemware, coffee urns, linens, lighting, tents, dance floors—even revolving ceiling mirror balls. Just be sure to work with businesses that are reliable and have well-maintained inventories and timely deliveries.

Always check with your local municipality to find out what, if any, health department certificates you may need. Start small and use your friends as guinea pigs, or help out a worthwhile nonprofit group and see whether catering is right for you.

• **RECIPE FOR SUCCESS** •

ABIGAIL KIRSCH

"IF YOU WANT to get married, find a job in a catering kitchen. We have consummated at least ten marriages within our kitchen staff," says caterer Abigail Kirsch. But there's more to catering than spouse hunting. When addressing culinary students, Kirsch says if you love to throw parties, event planning may be the perfect job.

"You can be an innovator; designer of super, cutting-edge menus; create unusual dining scenes; be an ace at logistics; create diagrams; and understand party flow," she says. "On top of all that you have to be the supreme psychiatrist, working with and between the client and your staff."

She also suggests that if you love to food shop, you might want to get a job as a purchasing agent for a catering company. "There are so many products to choose from, nationally and internationally. You could be talking to a fruit farmer in Chile and a few minutes later speak to a truffle supplier in France or Italy," she says.

"This career is a very detail-oriented and time-critical position, but it is as exciting as the person wants it to be," Kirsch concludes.

Recommended Book

The Culinary Institute of America and Bruce Mattel.
   Catering: A Guide to Managing a Successful Business Operation. Hoboken, NJ: Wiley, 2008.
Kirsch, Abigail, with David Nussbaum. *Invitation to Dinner: Abigail Kirsch's Guide to Elegant Entertaining and Delicious Dinners at Home.* New York: Doubleday, 1998.

For More Information

Catersource magazine is the leading industry resource that delivers critical products, news, and educational information to professional caterers. http://www.catersource.com

The Conrad N. Hilton College of Hotel and Restaurant Management at the University of Houston

The International Caterers Association offers advice and support services to on-premises and-off premises caterers and promotes catering as an important branch of food service. http://www.icacater.org

The National Association of Catering Executives (NACE), http://www.cateringresearch.org. NACE's career site has partnered with Brainhunter.com to provide a comprehensive job-networking source. You can search and apply for hundreds of targeted jobs with employers from around the world, as well as manage your résumé and job applications online. According to material in its Web site, "NACE encourages the professional development of caterers through voluntary participation in its certification program. Achievement of the Certified Professional Catering Executive (CPCE) designation demonstrates expertise in catering earned by taking a comprehensive examination that covers all aspects of professional catering. The three-section exam was developed in collaboration with the Educational Institute, a nonprofit foundation of the American Hotel and Motel Association."

Roman, Michael. *Catering: The Art, Science, and Mystery.* CaterSource, Inc. 2001.

Vivaldo, Denise. *How to Start a Home-Based Catering Business.* Guilford, CT: The Globe Pequot Press, 2003.
Do It For Less! Parties. Food Fanatics, Inc., 2005.

ASSOCIATION MANAGEMENT
by Daniel D. Maye

It may seem strange at first to suggest to an individual with a culinary/hospitality degree that association management may be a plausible career decision. Today, however, with the list of culinary and hospitality associations growing ever longer, and with the demand for knowledgeable executives to serve as staff, the field is rich with opportunities.

It takes a certain type of person to master the management skills necessary to work with associations. If, as the Bible says, no man may serve two masters, consider that, at any given time, an association executive may report to as many as fifteen or twenty "masters," better known as a board of directors. Patience, diplomacy, the ability to multitask, excellent verbal and writing skills, and a good sense of humor are all needed to successfully swim in these shoals!

But the rewards are also many: the chance to work with dedicated, passionate volunteers who lead an association and the satisfaction of implementing programs that create membership growth, financial stability, and, ultimately, a position of influence within the industry.

No matter where a person's interests may lie, an association exists that is tailored to that individual's needs. And, as the food-service/hospitality industry continues to evolve, new associations will be created to fill new niches. Certainly, with the growing importance of technology within all segments of the industry, we may expect to see new associations devoted to very specific disciplines.

To list the major associations serving the industry is a dizzying prospect. The National Restaurant Association is a mammoth Washington-based organization with the primary function of lobbying the federal government in the interests of the food-service industry as a whole.

The Society for Foodservice Management represents the non-commercial corporate food-service universe. The National Association of College and University Food Service serves both self-managed and contract food service at institutions of higher learning.

Two associations, the American Society for Healthcare Food Service Administrators and Healthcare Foodservice Management, represent hospitals and healthcare facilities across the United States. The American Dietetic Association accredits dietitians and offers educational programming to its members. The American

School Food Service Association has as its members public-school food-service directors.

There is an association for research chefs named, appropriately, the Research Chefs Association. There is a brand-new association for chefs who develop new products for chain restaurants. And there is the Council of Independent Restaurants of America, another association that represents the interests of independent restaurateurs and chefs. Women who work in the industry have their own association named Women Chefs and Restaurateurs. And, not to be overlooked, is the venerable American Culinary Federation, which is the accrediting organization for practicing chefs in America. Two other groups that have excellent representation by their associations are those food-service executives working in country clubs (the Club Managers' Association), and those who work in catering (the National Association of Catering Executives). This listing is in no way meant to be comprehensive, but is intended to give a quick snapshot of representational organizations that closely parallel the interests of those whose primary training has been in the culinary and hospitality field.

Other associations may also be of interest. The International Association of Culinary Professionals represents cooking school proprietors and teachers, culinary school faculty, consultants, journalists and others working in the food-service media, and a broad spectrum of food-service professionals whose primary vocation fits within the parameters of the organization. The American Cheese Society's members are entrepreneurial artisanal cheese makers. The organic produce growers now have their own association. The American Meat Board, the American Lamb Council, and the Pork Producers Council represent farmers and producers of America's meat supply, and there is an association for the seafood industry, as well as ancillary associations for each individual species of fish and crustacean both wild and farmed. There is a board for eggs and an institute for frozen foods. There is a board for strawberries and a council for blueberries, and an association, no doubt, for every other type of fruit and vegetable grown in America. Indeed, there is an umbrella association called appropriately the United Fresh Fruit and Vegetable Association. Consider that there is even an association for dry peas and lentils for proof that the list is inexhaustible.

The true purpose of this brief overview, as indicated at the outset, is to alert those who have formally trained for careers in food service and hospitality to the myriad opportunities that exist in association management—a field that relatively few consider when staking out a future in the industry. Individuals who are first coming into the industry after graduation or those who have labored long and who may now be bored or burned out, may wish to make a course correction and gravitate to this hitherto unexplored field of endeavor. It is a field that promises a challenging and interesting life. Knowledge of food preparation and menu planning is essential for an association manager who is responsible for meal planning during conferences.

For More Information

The Culinary Institute of America, in association with the American Culinary Federation, offers ProChef certification. It is the only certification program for chefs that validates specific skills in culinary arts, personnel management, and financial administration. The multi-tiered certification programs are designed to validate the achievements of culinary professionals throughout all stages of a career from journeyman cook to executive chef by providing the necessary culinary skills and techniques to ensure advancement. The program also offers mentoring from professionals who help young chefs map a career path for themselves. http://www.prochef.com

The School of Hospitality Business at Michigan State University offers a variety of degree programs in the business and hospitality industries. The Undergraduate School of Hospitality Business offers a business-based curriculum in the hospitality industry; the Michael L. Minor master of science in food-service management offers a graduate program; and the business-executive programs offer membership in the Club Managers Association of America/Business Management Institute and certification in meeting management. http://www.bus.msu.edu/shb

Le Cordon Bleu offers a master of international meetings industry management degree that is the only program of its kind. It can be accessed online from anywhere in the world. Sound knowledge, strong decision-making capability, and team skills built in the program will have graduates a step ahead of the changes occurring on a global scale. Delivered entirely online through one of Australia's finest universities, it has been developed in conjunction with Le Cordon Bleu and the International Congress and Convention Association (ICCAA).
http://www.lecordonbleu.com.au/FAQ_MIMIM.pdf

GRAPE ADVOCATE

by Jim Howard

MOST INTELLIGENT PEOPLE fail to see how working as a criminal defense trial lawyer is the perfect training to promote grapes. But there's actually a strong link between the two. Getting a jury to find your client not guilty often means finding a compelling a story about how fate, bum luck, and bad police work has led to an unjust criminal charge. Getting jaded New York magazine writers to write about a product that has changed little in the past ten thousand years requires telling a compelling story about, well, whatever you can think of that is new, exciting, and of interest to their readers. Still, I did not set out to represent the California Table Grape Commission. I set out to be a lawyer.

One year when my wife and I were living in Iowa, I made Thanksgiving dinner for a dozen people, including a newspaper editor who was impressed with the meal. When the job as restaurant critic for the paper came open, this editor figured I knew food and suggested I throw my name into the mix.

After writing an essay and competing in an anonymous reviewing contest, I landed the job. Suddenly, I was being paid to eat and my legal career was doomed. A few years later, we ended up in Fresno, California, where I worked as a restaurant critic, but the pickings became slim once the chain restaurants moved in. One day, I received a call from the California Table Grape Commission.

Frankly, I'd never heard of the commission. I didn't know what a commodity group was and I could only guess at exactly what they meant by the term *table grape*. Incredibly, the job requirements turned out to be an ideal fit with my varied background—food, writing, reporting, photography, and law.

The back story to my current world is intriguing. The California legislature created the commission in 1967 to increase demand for fresh California grapes. As the person in charge of domestic promotion, I still write—I just switched from stories and reviews to news releases, brochures, and speeches. The complex issues facing a billion-dollar agricultural industry requires the strategic thinking I'd learned in law school and I soon discovered that the best way to get magazine editors to write about your product is to take them to dinner. Once again, I was being paid to eat.

2

retail jobs

HEN WE TALK about retail jobs in the food business, we're talking about entrepreneurs. Think of Starbucks and Ben and Jerry. These companies started small, grew, and grew some more. Through smart marketing and a dedication to producing a quality product, a modest idea turned into a big deal. Not all entrepreneurs strike it as rich as these companies—and not all need to or want to. But many are successful enough to make a positive impact.

The National Dialogue on Entrepreneurship defines an entrepreneur as an individual who owns a business. People are typically driven to start businesses by two motivating factors: discontent and anxiety at a traditional job. The anxiety factor remains all too familiar to many who decide to open a retail business, yet despite the difficulties, countless small businesses thrive, provide employment for thousands, and generate flowing rivers of pleasure for millions of grateful customers.

The Food Institute estimates there are more than 128,000 retail-food outlets nationwide. This includes groceries, delis, health-food stores, convenience stores, produce markets, farmers' markets, cheese shops, bakeries, ice cream parlors, fudge purveyors, and, of course, specialty food shops. In addition, packaged and fresh foods are appearing in bookstores, gift stores, movie houses, and even gas stations.

Private enterprisers can also hope to sell their specialty food to one or more of the nation's 31,830 supermarkets or to one of the 136,000 restaurants. Your product doesn't have to compete in all marketplaces. A very thin slice of the pie—even a few crumbs—can provide you with a comfortable living.

Each facet of the food business is a potential opportunity to market your food, and if you can't get your foot in the door of a bricks-and-mortar building, you can try to sell it on the Internet. It is interesting to note that many brilliant, new artisanal businesses are flourishing as a result of global electronics!

FOR MORE INFORMATION

Entrepreneur is a monthly magazine for readers seeking advice on how to improve their business. Free newsletters are available on topics including starting a business, growing a business, franchise news, sales and marketing, and e-business. Other publications include start-up guides to food service, the retail business, mail order, and more. http://www.entrepreneur.com

The Entrepreneurship Institute is a national nonprofit organization. Its Web site has information about education programs and networking opportunities and offers additional guidance to its members. http://www.tei.net

The Service Corps of Retired Executives (SCORE) Association is a nonprofit dedicated to entrepreneur education and the formation, growth, and success of small businesses nationwide. It is a resource partner of the Small Business Administration. SCORE Association volunteers serve as "counselors to America's small businesses." Working and retired executives and business owners donate their time and expertise as volunteer business counselors and provide confidential counseling and mentoring free of charge. Courses offered in most large U.S. cities cover topics including how to start and manage a small business, writing business plans, e-commerce, import/export, and keeping good employees. http://www.score.org

$\mathcal{S}$OUP PEDDLER

by David J. Ansel, the Soup Peddler

A SCANT THREE years and four months ago, an idea occurred to me while sitting on a porch swing at a magical house in South Austin, Texas. What if I could make a living cooking food and taking it to people's homes? At my wits end trying to figure out anything I could do for a living instead of being a mediocre computer programmer, I figured it was worth a try.

Though I had no culinary training, I had dabbled with cooking dinners for large groups and had started spending a little time at the local restaurant-supply store. I espied some little white buckets that would be perfect for taking food to folks' houses. But what would fit best in those buckets? What is the most form-fitting food in the history of the universe? What was the only thing I knew how to cook halfway decently? Soup!

Once I had the menu taken care of, I had to set my thoughts toward the delivery mechanism. Well, I figured I would probably have to spend a lot of time in a car, which I don't really like. I much prefer to bike, so I decided to deliver soup around my neighborhood by bicycle.

I needed a name for the business. I retreated to the porch swing, where I get most of my best thinking done. Soup Subscription Service for Savory Soul Sustenance? Probably not. The Soup Man. Eh. Need something cute. How about Soup Peddler? Soup Pedaler? Which spelling to use? I'll use peddler, just in case this thing gets too big for bicycles.

I sent out an e-mail to my friends and neighbors describing the service. Sunday afternoon, I'll bring you a bucket of soup on my bike. Seventeen generous customers took me up on the offer. I went out and bought an eighty-dollar pot and made gumbo in my own kitchen (not entirely legal but I had to start somewhere). Three short years later, my staff of soup makers, peddlers, and I have cooked and distributed ten thousand gallons of dozens of different varieties of soup to the porches of Austinites over the course of an eight-month soup season. We work out of a commercial kitchen. I have been featured in such disparate media as the *Christian Science Monitor* and *Punk Planet*. I have become the Ferris Bueller of Austin, liked and respected by hipsters, soccer moms, and tattooed punks equally. I have been referred to as an "American folk hero."

How did this happen? The task of describing the breadth and depth of the entrepreneurial effort is nearly impossible. Boot camp for the Army? Nothing. Swimming the English Channel? Yawn. Raising a child? Yeah, sorta. Spending an eternity pushing a boulder up a hill? You're starting to get there. Of course, most of those comparison cases have their rewards, and entrepreneurship does, too. Most of them change you on such a deep level that you never look at the world or the people around you the same way again. The same goes for starting your own business. It takes every ounce of your soul, and the risk is that you'll be left a desiccated shell of a human being with nothing to show for your efforts. The potential reward is huge, though, not the least of which is having your destiny under your own control as much as is humanly possible.

David Ansel's book is *The Soup Peddler's Slow and Difficult Soups: Recipes & Reveries.* Berkeley: Ten Speed Press, 2005.

SPECIALTY FOODS

The category of specialty foods encompasses the more unusual foods and new ideas, such as Four Star Provisions Original Roasted Raspberry Chipotle Sauce or Strawberry and Lavender Jam. It is in the small companies where dreams are created and with enough toil, tenacity, and adequate financing, numerous struggling entrepreneurial companies expand and prosper.

Many cottage industries—as these small companies are often called—follow a similar pattern. An entrepreneur has an idea for a product—a chocolate sauce perhaps or a flavored vinegar or a ready-to-eat snack food. The enterprise begins as a hobby, and the creation is given as a gift to friends, who beg for more. Suddenly, the item is seen as a way to make a little extra income. The local specialty food store is persuaded to put a few jars of homemade preserves on the shelf and with a spot of luck the neighborhood newspaper may run an article about it. The product, in the vernacular, flies off the shelf and the store wants more. The pot of gold is glimpsed, and the opportunities seem limitless.

Off goes the entrepreneur to exhibit at the Fancy Food Show held three times a year in New York City, San Francisco, and Chicago and sponsored by the National Association for the Specialty Food Trade (NASFT). But no one places an order. Hardly anyone even looks at the display. Gloom, doom, and depression descend—but not for long. The invention is terrific—perhaps it's the packaging that is at fault. So a designer is hired who swallows up a big chunk of capital to develop a fancy logo and a smart label for the jar. An expert must also be hired to conduct the nutrient analysis. A bar code must be glued onto the jar, too. Invoices, stationery, and many labels and other forms must be printed at considerable expense.

Suddenly, the amateur begins to feel like a pro. Orders pour in from big retail stores. One wants 124 cases—immediately. Now quite extended and often undercapitalized, the entrepreneur hires more people to fill the jars and spends more money to ship them in a box rigid enough to prevent breakage in transit. Insurance is needed. Zoning laws must be obeyed. Health inspectors show up at the door.

Sales increase, but so does the paperwork: the orders and the billing, accounts receivable, and accounts payable pile up. Some customers pay late, others go out of business and never pay at all. But there is so much work to do that it becomes imperative to hire even more staff.

By now, the profit margin is precariously thin and getting thinner. There are times the payroll can barely be met. The originator of the product, the inventive dreamer who was once stirring the sauce or baking the cookies and delivering them in the family car, finds more and more time is spent away from the kitchen, traveling to promote the product and trying to land more orders.

The entrepreneur who started a small business is caught up in all the problems of big business, but often without much depth of experience. Entrepreneurship almost always means learning on the job—and all too often learning from mistakes.

All this is not to say that small business is inevitably doomed. That would be far from the truth. Hundreds and indeed thousands of cottage industries are alive and well and generating ideas for the foods and cooking equipment we will be enjoying well into the future. But it's wise to explore the hazards before embarking on a perilous journey. In the end it will be worth all the headaches if you learn how to cope with the many facets of the specialty food business before embarking on your own enterprise. There is a logical chain of events that must precede making a product available to the retail market.

The manufacturer of the product sets a wholesale price and determines sales policies These policies may concern shipping costs, returns, in-store sampling, advertising allowances, and donations to charities.

The wholesaler is responsible for the local, national, or international distribution of the product. Sales are made at trade shows, via the Internet, through catalogs, or by commissioned sales representatives.

The retailer negotiates the "deal," including obtaining free freight or a freight allowance (i.e., discount), extended billing terms, and free products for in-store sampling. He may also ask for display aids. The retailer sets the selling price of the product.

GETTING STARTED

It isn't necessary to reinvent the wheel when you write a business plan. By the same token, you don't have to have an MBA (although it can't hurt). There are several publications available to guide you through the process of building a comprehensive business plan. Among the best is a piece of software called BizPlan Builder 8, which offers downloadable business-plan formats recognized by banks, lenders, investors, and the Small Business Administration. You can find it at Amazon.com and other retailers.

A business plan should be comprehensive and clear. It will act as a blueprint for your business and be a helpful reference as you chart your entrepreneurial waters. This is the time to be honest with yourself about the prospects for success.

Banks and other financial institutions usually require business plans if you apply for a loan. A good business plan can open doors and be the first step to establishing a long-term relationship with a bank.

For More Information

The National Association for the Specialty Food Trade (NASFT) is a not-for-profit business trade association established in 1952 to foster trade, commerce, and interest in the specialty food industry. It is an international organization composed of domestic and foreign manufactures, importers, distributors, brokers, retailers, restaurateurs, caterers, and others in the specialty food business. Long known for its breadth and *the* quality of its practical, business-building online guides, workbooks, and self-study courses. Many of the materials are free and they are regularly updated.

NASFT has sponsored trade shows since 1954. They are considered to be the premier marketplace for reaching the specialty food trade. Referred to as the Fancy Food Shows, they attract between 19,000 and 32,000 attendees, including owners of specialty food stores; those working in wine, gift, and department stores; supermarket personnel; restaurant people; mail order representatives, and people from other related businesses. These attendees come to buy products from more than one thousand exhibitors from around the world, presenting more than fifty thousand specialty foods. The Food Marketing Institute Show, All Things Organic, United Produce Expo and Conference, and U.S. Food Export Showcase have joined the Fancy Food Show to make it five shows in one. Many of the exhibitors are entrepreneurs who created their own recipes and started their own companies.

For more information on the Fancy Food Show and for daily e-news about the food industry, go to http://www.specialtyfood.com.

Publications of Interest

Source: Northeast Center for Food Entrepreneurship
Title: *The Pros and Cons of Starting a Specialty Food Business and Steps to Start a Specialty Food Business*
Description: The food business start-up steps outlined include: the product, business planning, labels, market decisions, and production.
http://www.nysaes.cornell.edu/necfe/

Source: North Central Regional Extension
Title: *Selling Food Products: A Business from Your Home* (PDF)
Description: Outlines what you need to consider when starting a food business with particular emphasis on food safety.
http://www.extension.iastate.edu.Publications/NCR259.pdf.

Source: Rutgers Cooperative Extension
Title: *So You Want to Be a Food Manufacturer . . .*
Description: Reviews the basics and includes a resource section of books, food-industry directories, and trade magazines.
http://www.rcre.rutgers.edu/pubs/

Source: Food Ventures (a nonprofit community development corporation to support specialty food producers in Southeast Ohio)
Title: *Food Industry Resources and Worksheets*
Description: A thorough guide to developing your product, preparing product for market, accessing markets, worksheets, and resources.
http://www.acenetworks.org/frames/fvaabout.htm

Source: University of Georgia Cooperative Extension Service
Title: *Food Product Development*
Description: A comprehensive guide featuring a step-by-step system and worksheets for developing food products.
http://www.caes.uga.edu/extension

Source: Virginia State University Cooperative Extension
Title: *Starting a Food Processing Business*
Description: Outlines food business start-up steps from thinking about a business to product development, using a food processing facility, and creating a professional image.
http://www.ext.vt.edu

Source: Western Massachusetts Food Processing Center
Title: *Complete Solutions for Food Producers and Entrepreneurs*
Description: Provides technical assistance, workshops, and resources to help start or expand a food business.
http://www.fccdc.org

Specialty Food magazine delivers actionable information that retailers, distributors, and other professionals can put to work to improve their business. The free magazine gives new product information, identifies trends, profiles retailers, and provides practical business insight from industry experts. It reaches more than twenty-nine thousand buyers. http://www.specialtyfoodmagazine.com

Fancy Food and Culinary Products magazine, now in its twentieth year of publication, is distributed to twenty-three thousand retailers. It includes articles on marketing, upcoming holidays and events that can promote sales, and new foods and other products from suppliers around the world. http://www.foodinfonet.com

Gourmet Retailer addresses the interests of specialty food and housewares stores. It includes material ranging from staff training to trends in prepared foods. http://www.gourmetretailer.com

The Food Marketing Institute (FMI) conducts programs in research, education, industry relations, and public affairs on behalf of its fifteen hundred member companies; food retailers, and wholesalers in the United States and around the world. FMI's U.S. membership is composed of large multistore chains, regional firms, and independent supermarkets. Its international membership includes two hundred companies from fifty countries. http://www.fmi.org

SO, YOU WANT TO OWN A RETAIL MARKET?

If you have an idea for a specialty food store, an ice cream parlor, a coffee shop, or any other small retail shop, the Institute of Culinary Education (http://www.iceculinary.com) offers a course that will help you to evaluate and develop your idea into a real business. From concept and niche marketing to controlling costs and making money, you will learn to navigate the pitfalls of opening a business. Subjects discussed include:

■ Developing a business plan
■ Adding a café, catering, or party planning to an existing business
■ Finding a location and understanding the lease
■ Designing the business
■ Figuring out the money aspect—financial benchmarks
■ Controlling revenue and inventory
■ Looking for investors

- Hiring the best and training for service
- Advertising and promotion
- Selling psychology

• **RECIPE FOR SUCCESS** •

$\mathcal{T}$HE SELLER

by Jonathan King, founder of Stonewall Kitchen

MY PASSION IS horticulture. I love bountiful gardens and I'm happiest at the moment when everything is ripe and ready to pick. I like making jams, herb vinegars, pickles, and sauces. I used to give them away to friends at a greenhouse where I was employed during the day. I was a waiter at night.

One day it occurred to me that I could sell my stuff at the local farmers' market. I needed some extra money. I was twenty-three and struggling to pay off my student loans. The seed money to start my business was five dollars, which allowed me to open up a folding three-foot-long table to display my wares: Raspberry Peach Champagne Jam, Wild Maine Blueberry Jam, Roasted Garlic and Onion Jam, and Maple Chipolte Grill Sauce. It proved to be a roaring success.

The first day at the market I made two hundred dollars. I was grinning from ear to ear. I could earn the entire monthly debt in one day! Each week I got busier and busier. I was racing around selling at several farmers' markets, craft shows, Junior League, and other benefits—anywhere I could get my foot in the door. The *Boston Globe* wrote an article about me. After three years, Stonewall Kitchen was a $1 million business.

About that time, a woman I know suggested I start selling wholesale. I didn't know a thing about that side of this business, but she advised me on the logistics. I exhibited at the Fancy Food Show and set up a booth that looked just like it did in the farmers' market: lots of burlap, apple bins, and a Smith and Hawken kind of umbrella. The look seemed to work. Orders came pouring in. Now we've got more than six thousand wholesale accounts.

In the beginning I'd been using just plain old Bell canning jars, but I decided it was time to make a change. I talked to a glass designer about creating a distinctive jar. We came up with what are now our trademark square jars with green lids. We kept the design

continued

continued from page 103

of the original labels that I wrote by hand. Our goal was to create a package that conveyed our philosophy of sophisticated simplicity.

I've always thought packaging is important. The big problem with producing our own jars was that I had to commit to buying eighty thousand all at once. Before long we found five hundred thousand jars lasted only two months. More of our customers recognize the jars than remember the name of the company. (It was named for the graceful stone walls that surrounded the original New England farm where the company was born.) We grew out of a small kitchen in New Hampshire and moved to a renovated barn in Kittery, Maine. Now our headquarters are in York, on the Maine coast. We're pretty far from anywhere, so we find it is more practical and certainly a lot more fun to design and make almost everything to sell ourselves and employ a full team of designers.

My partner, Jim Stott, knew nothing about photography, but now he is the full-time photographer. He takes all the pictures for our catalog, Web site, and our latest cookbooks.

Getting Started

My advice for anyone embarking on a new career is, Don't be afraid to take a risk. I started out with a degree in child psychology. I didn't have a business plan. I've never had one. I followed my passion. It's passion that drives a successful business—not concentrating on the bottom line. Yes, we've developed and matured. We are now a $40 million company. We have more than 350 employees, eight stores, and a restaurant in York. We have 170 varieties of jams and jellies, condiments and sauces, chutneys and vinegars, kitchen tools, table linens, furniture, gift baskets, and gifts for the home and garden. We plan to continue expanding in the Northeast.

This seems like incredibly rapid growth since we started in 1991, but I'd advise people to try not to grow too quickly. If you have a product you love, stick to one thing and grow it slowly. Word of mouth is your best advertising. Top quality is your badge of honor.

For more information, visit http://www.stonewallkitchen.com.

RETAIL SHOP OWNER ELAINE YANNUZZI (THE BUYER)

ELAINE YANNUZZI WAS one of the most success-ful specialty store owners on the East Coast. She founded Expression unLTD in Warren, New Jersey. At the time there was a wildly enthusiastic interest in what was quaintly known as "goo-er-may." It was fueled by Julia Child, who reigned supreme on public television. The golden girls of *The Silver Palate* were gaining attention, Martha Stewart was looming on the horizon, and dozens and dozens of small kitchen stores were popping up everywhere. Many offered cooking classes, French mustard, Italian olive oil, Belgian chocolates, freshly roasted coffee beans, and imported cookies.

Expression unLTD was different. It made tons of money. When the thriving business was sold, a few million dollars flowed into Elaine's bank account. How did she achieve so much success? She had nerves of steel.

When she walked along the aisles of the Fancy Food Show in NYC, vendors prayed Elaine might stop at their booth. When she did, she was utterly charming. She would taste the vendor's olive oil, pro-nounce it excellent, and then pulled out her own order form. "I'll take 66 cases," she'd say. Fairly swooning with joy, the vendor beamed. He didn't see the freight train coming.

Next, she'd stop at the booth of a Stilton cheese wholesaler. "How much do you have in stock?" she'd ask sweetly. "We're expecting a new shipment next week," might be the answer. "Then I guess you'll be wanting to get rid of your old inventory?" she'd muse. "Hmm," he'd be puzzled, wondering where this conversation was going. Then she'd pounce: "As it is nearing its expiration date, I'll take seventy-eight wheels at a 60 percent discount." (Stilton cheese lasts almost forever so the customer is more likely to expire before the cheese does.)

The cheese seller would be unable to breathe for a moment, but after making a quick calculation and arriving at the conclusion it would be good to make a quick, even if small profit, he'd swallow hard, and agree. "Free freight." She'd observe Mary Poppins–like primness as she entered the order on her form. Gulp. "And I'll need a sampling allowance . . . and an advertising allowance . . . and 120 day billing.

continued

continued from page 105

Thus she had bought a huge quantity of cheese at a price that was, to put a good face on it, pretty close to grand larceny. When the delivery truck disgorged all the mountains of Stilton, she put an ad in the local paper. (Because she was a regular advertiser, the ad was billed to her at a deeply discounted price.) "Stilton Cheese," The ad would say. "Regularly $15 a pound. Special sale only $8.95." The customers lined up to buy it—and all sixty-six cases of olive oil that had been "negotiated" on similar terms.

The person who said life was all about buying and selling took a page out of Elaine Yannuzzi's book. (Note: Elaine remains a close personal friend, though I've never learned to negotiate a deal of any kind with anything like her consummate skill!)

SAY CHEESE

It's fair to say that the new American cuisine was based on charismatic goat cheese. We are still eating our way through mountains of it. It is served warm with a flourish of baby lettuces. It is rolled in fruitwood ash and floated upon a sea-green virgin oil. It is sliced into medallions and garnished with nasturtium petals. Goat cheese is turning up in omelets. It is topping fancy pizzas. It is crumbled into pricey salads and molded onto crisp baguette slices to accompany super-cool chardonnays.

It is Terrance Brennan, of Picoline and Artisanal restaurants in Manhattan, to whom we should give thanks for the mounting interest in cheese. He inaugurated what is almost certainly the most extensive cheese selection for diners to enjoy. His master cheese connoisseur, Max McCalman, keeps a watchful eye over the vast selection, ensuring each is served to guests in the best possible condition.

As we embrace our love affair with artisanal cheeses, more opportunities are opening for jobs in every facet of cheese production and cheese retailing.

Recommended Books

Fletcher, Janet. *The Cheese Course*. San Francisco: Chronicle Books, 2000.

Jenkins, Steven. *Cheese Primer*. New York: Workman, 1996.

Kaufelt, Rob. *The Murray's Cheese Handbook*. New York: Broadway Books, 2006.

Lambert, Paula. *The Cheese Lover's Cookbook and Guide: Over 150 Recipes with Instruction on How to Buy, Store and Serve All Your Favorite Cheeses.*

Lambert shares the vast knowledge she's gained in two decades running the successful Mozzarella Company.

McCalman, Max. *Cheese: A Connoisseur's Guide to the World's Best*. New York: Clarkson Potter, 2005.

Nantet, Bernard. *Cheeses of the World: An Illustrated Guide for Gourmets.*

Robuchon, Joel. *French Cheeses: The Visual Guide to More Than 350 Cheeses from Every Region of France.*

Teubner, Christian. *The Cheese Bible.*

Werlin, Laura. *The New American Cheese.*

• **RECIPE FOR SUCCESS** •

CHEESE GURU ROB KAUFELT

by Denise Purcell, managing editor of Specialty Food *magazine*

MURRAY'S CHEESE HAS been a Greenwich Village landmark since 1940, when Murray Greenberg, a wholesaler of butter and eggs, opened it. Rob Kaufelt, a neighborhood resident who frequented the shop and had a background in food retailing, purchased the store in 1990, moved it to a vacant meat market nearby, and built it into a New York institution. As cheese came back into vogue following the low-fat craze of the early 1990s, Kaufelt was instrumental in introducing a curious public to then-unheard-of varieties.

Murray's Cheese remained in its new location for nearly fifteen years, though "we ran out of space in 1999," notes Kaufelt. He began the daunting search for Manhattan real estate, with an eye toward a wholesale space to expand his business. In the meantime, he opened a second counter at Grand Central Station's new European-style market.

Shortly thereafter, the landlord at 254 Bleeker Street approached Kaufelt about acquiring his property. Kaufelt purchased the residential building with a total of six thousand square feet of retail space in June 2003 and subdivided the space to bring in Amy's Bread and Wild Edibles, neighboring retailers at Grand Central. The expanded Murray's Cheese opened in November 2004.

Murray's selections include cheeses from Vermont's Jasper Hill, Sprout Creek in Poughkeepsie, New York, and Sally Jackson from Washington State, among myriad others.

In addition to retail sales, which have nearly doubled since the move, the wholesale arm has in recent years grown to 150 clients nationwide, including the upper echelon of New York restaurants such as Alain Ducasse, Chanterelle, Jean Georges, and Per Se.

The most cutting-edge and impressive feature of Murray's is the five authentic cheese caves based on traditional European design.

continued

continued from page 107

Affinage, or the art of aging, long a tradition in Europe, has become a buzzword among American cheese purveyors as a way to provide optimum storage and aging of inventory until it reaches its peak. Murray's is among the first retailers in the U.S. to replicate traditional aging caves. (In Manhattan, Artisanal Cheese Center operates a ten-thousand-square-foot affinage center, opened in 2003, for wholesale and mail-order business.)

A French *affiney* consulted on the construction of the aging caves. Each contains vaulted ceilings and is made of natural materials. To provide an ideal environment for cheese maturation, proper ventilation, temperature, and humidity is individually controlled in each cave. A glass panel on the sidewalk offers a view of the aging cheese, enticing passersby to enter the store.

The Cheese Course

The inclusion of an educational facility was a must for Kaufelt, and he planned to initiate a series of classes to address consumers' growing quest for food knowledge. A staff of food professionals, historians, authors, and farmers teaches the cheese course program, which offers between four and six classes each month. Response has been positive. "Almost every class is already sold out," says Kaufelt, who teaches Cheese 101: Ask the Big Cheese once a month. Other recent classes include The Mystery of the Caves, Weird Cheese, Sweet and Savory: Dessert Pairings with Cheese, Beer and Cheese Pairing: Cows Don't Eat Grapes, and Chutneys, Fruit Pastes and Fruit-Based Cheese Accompaniments.

THE NEW BREAD

A few years ago all the great bread was baked in France. In the United States artisanal bread bakers were a rare breed. Now, when we go to the supermarket we can choose among potato bread and sourdough, whole-grain and semolina, pepper bread and bread flecked with sun-dried tomatoes, olives, herbs, and seeds—and all of these breads are also appearing in boutique bakeries and in bountiful baskets handed around to guests in restaurants.

Some chefs are baking their own signature breads. Irresistibly, the appetite is seduced with a choice of grainy yellow cornbread, muffins, fresh from the oven. On upscale tables, too, are feather-light, lily-white biscuits; sweet muffins with carrots and cranberries, or raisins and walnuts; and hot scones flecked with melting morsels of white and dark chocolate. Soft focaccia, buttery brioches, crusty baguettes, crackling croissants, and hearty, healthy seven-grain breads are also available. Bread has become the icing on the cake.

$\mathcal{A}$MY'S BREAD

 WHEN AMY SCHERBER changed careers, she also eventually changed the lives of the 130 men and women who now work in her New York City wholesale bakery and three thriving retail store–cafés, all open for breakfast, lunch, and late-night sweet pastry treats. In these cafés, she sells her signature breads: fennel semolina with golden raisins, potato and onion dill bread, French baguettes (baked twice a day), and focaccias, as well as fourteen different sandwiches for lunch, pizzas, brownies, muffins, cookies, layer cakes, and applesauce doughnuts.

Amy has traveled a dedicated path in pursuit of her own expression of excellence. After graduating from St. Olaf College in Minnesota, her first step was a conventional one. She took a job in marketing. She stuck it out in the corporate world for three years before abandoning her financial security and enrolling in the New York Restaurant School in New York City. Her enthusiasm for cooking and baking developed alongside her spirit of entrepreneurship.

Eager to learn all she could from some of the most respected leaders in the field, she worked both as a line cook and pastry cook at David Bouley's restaurant before deciding she should move to France to study the traditional methods and techniques of artisanal bread baking. She apprenticed in three bakeries before returning to the United States and began to bake breads at New York's Mondrian restaurant. The contacts she made during this time proved invaluable. Today she delivers her fresh-baked breads and rolls to more than two hundred restaurants and stores throughout the city.

In the summer of 1992, she opened a small storefront on Ninth Avenue in Hell's Kitchen (this is a real neighborhood, not a description of her workplace) and from there, she opened two more stores. Every day, her three retail stores showcase her work and bring her more loyal customers and wholesale accounts. Customers can see that the standard of quality is maintained day after day and throughout the year.

Each step Amy has taken has proved to be one more stride in a continuum of preparation. She didn't engage a publicist. She says, "My goal is simply to always be available." This policy has resulted in an extraordinary profusion of feature stories in magazines and newspapers and on television. Her involvement in the food industry has also proved both enriching and beneficial to her career. She currently serves on the board of Bread Bakers of America and was elected to the board of directors of Women Chefs and Restaurateurs. She has received numerous awards, including being named among "the five top bakeries in the U.S. that have changed the world of bread." by *Bon Appétit* magazine in 2006. Honors and acclaim continue to come her way.

Looking back at her still-evolving career, Amy urges today's students to study at the French Culinary Institute in Manhattan, the San Francisco Baking Institute, the Culinary Institute of America, or other prominent professional cooking schools specializing in bread baking and pastry. More than 50 percent of her employees have attended a cooking school. She says, "It may no longer be necessary to go to France to learn the traditional methods and techniques of bread baking. In fact, it's probably even more useful to study in your own country where you are working with American rather than European flours, butter, and fresh herbs. The recipes you are using are written in English, which is more helpful than wrestling with the nuances of a foreign language.

continued

continued from page 109

"It helps to go to school even for a relatively short six-month course," she continues. "Even so there is still a lot to learn. It takes three or four years to develop a depth of knowledge about bread and an intuitive understanding that changes in the weather result in variations in the ingredients. It is essential to use the best organic products and long fermentation to achieve a depth of flavor and intensity of taste."

Amy's advice is to be willing and enthusiastic to learn everything you can. This includes jumping at the opportunity to work in the middle of the night, shaping bread, scoring the risen dough, and keeping an eye on the browning process. At Amy's Bread, consistent quality is achieved by concentrating on small batches of hand-shaped, hearth-baked loaves that develop crisp crusts and chewy crumbs that have been memorably described as "huggable edibles."

Amy's decision to change careers was supported by her parents, who agreed with her resolve not to care too much about financial matters. Her advice to beginning bakers and entrepreneurs is, "Roll up your sleeves. Spend your own money to attend seminars. Be committed and invested. Accept the idea of being an entry-level employee. Be willing, flexible, and enthusiastic. It is far more important to follow your heart and be willing to do whatever it takes to reach your objective. Don't spend all your life in one field. Take risks. The rewards will follow."

THE MARKETPLACE: WHERE RETAIL SHINES

Successful retail businesses have the potential to grow into large businesses, and when they do, they employ many people. Some of the most successful are in the natural-food sector, while others cater to shoppers just looking for good, high-quality food and great service. Below are some of the most impressive.

Shoppers love going to Wegmans because it's not just a trip to the grocery store, but also a getaway to what the company likes to call a "global food village." The stores in New York, New Jersey, Pennsylvania, and Virginia, have the feel of European markets, with displays of fresh-baked artisan breads, wheels of cheese, fresh fish, and produce from local farms.

Wegmans employees travel to Europe and Asia to learn first-hand about the latest food trends. Those trips lead to new and varied choices in ready-to-eat foods as well as new product lines. The company has seventy-three hundred private-label products among the sixty thousand products it sells. It has its own commercial bakery and meat-processing center to ensure quality and freshness. It is among the hundred largest privately owned companies in America, with more than thirty-two thousand employees and over $3 billion in annual sales, and consistently recognized as one of the top one hundred companies to work for in America.

Renowned French pastry chef Pierre Hermé was recruited to develop desserts for Wegmans. At some locations, executive chefs with advanced culinary training and restaurant experience create the prepared foods. The message to culinary professionals from its chairman, Robert Wegman, is "We've always believed that the path to great customer service begins with treating our own employees right. If our people feel valued and supported, they will give their best to our customers."

The original Whole Foods Market opened in 1980 with a staff of nineteen people. Back then there were fewer than half a dozen natural-food supermarkets in the United States. At the time of this writing, Whole Foods has grown to 194 stores with thirty-nine thousand employees. Within five years, the company plans to more than double its sales nationwide and have revenues of $10 billion. Employment opportunities are available in Whole Foods in various departments, including specialty foods, prepared foods, in-store dining facilities, catering, bakery and confectionary departments, grocery, deli, cheese, meat, poultry, seafood, and produce purchasing. Career-development programs consisting of twelve- to twenty-six-week courses are offered to employees looking for leadership positions in the company.

As interest in healthful eating, sustainable agriculture, and organic food continues to grow, markets such as Whole Foods will offer growth opportunities for a host of products—and full and part-time employment.

Trader Joe's has expanded to more than two hundred stores since its inception. In each unit there is a captain (manager) and first mate (assistant manager). This is the team that leads the store crew. Each store is staffed with several full-time crew members, known as novitiates. Specialists and merchants round out the supervisory ranks. Employees and their dependents at Trader Joe's receive a full package of benefits, but what really sets this company apart from its competition is its retirement plan. Trader Joe's contributes 15.4 percent of each employee's gross income every year to his or her retirement account. This account earns tax-free income until retirement day arrives. Employees are not required to contribute a single cent, and most staff members get to wear funky Hawaiian shirts throughout their working years. The company is described as being "unique in the retail market. It doesn't have a direct competitor because it

- The average supermarket carries thirty thousand items.
- Supermarkets nationwide employ 3.4 million employees and generated $457.4 billion last year.
- The Panera Bread Company opened its twelve hundredth retail bakery/café and racked up $2 million in annual sales per store. (By way of comparison, Starbucks produces $750,000 per store, Chipotle $1.4 million, McDonald's $1.85 million, and Wendy's $1.3 million.)

is smaller and more specialized than a conventional store, but larger and more varied than a convenience store," says one writer. "With Trader Joe's, you're going to go in there and say, 'Wow, look at all this stuff I can buy.'"

Dean and DeLuca was a pioneer among specialty food stores. It operates Manhattan locations in SoHo, Rockefeller Plaza, and in the Paramount Hotel. Dean and DeLuca espresso bars have been opened in New York and Washington, D.C., along with the main store in Washington's Georgetown district. The company has even expanded into Japan. This is a great place to learn every phase of the specialty food business before taking the plunge and opening your own business.

Zabar's, located on Broadway and Eightieth Street in Manhattan, is famous for its bagels and smoked fish. It has attracted a loyal following since its founding in 1934. Its closest competitor is Zingerman's, which is fast becoming America's best-known deli.

Paul Saginaw and Ari Weinzweig opened Zingerman's in March 1982 in an historic building near the Ann Arbor Farmers' market in Michigan. They began their business with a staff of two, a small selection of great-tasting specialty foods, a number of traditional Jewish dishes, and a relatively short sandwich menu. Today the company serves thousands of made-to-order sandwiches with ingredients like corned beef and pastrami; free-range chicken and turkey, homemade chopped liver, and chicken salad. It also stocks a huge array of farmhouse cheeses, estate-bottled olive oils, varietal vinegars, smoked fish, salami, gelatos of many flavors, and innumerable other specialty foods. The company restaurant claims it serves "really good American food" including southern-style barbecue, all-natural dry-aged steaks from Niman Ranch, five kinds of oysters, and six kinds of macaroni and cheese (in addition to whatever else the chef whips up). Zingerman's is what is described as "a happening place."

Citarella founder is Joseph Gurrera. The son of a fishmonger, as a small boy he worked side by side with his father. At the age of twenty-eight he left the store and bought the Citarella Fish Market on the Upper West Side of Manhattan. It was a tiny shop, barely twelve feet wide. Now he has several fish-focused locations and generates annual revenues soaring to well over $100 million. In other words, his stores have gone gourmet.

Citarella, Zingerman's, Zabar's, Dean and DeLuca, Trader Joe's, Whole Foods, Wegmans, and other less renowned beautiful markets and specialty food stores around the country offer an extraordinarily wide range of employment opportunities for culinary professionals. Just walk through any of these businesses and imagine yourself working with the foods you most love. These businesses need cooks, bakers, purchasers, produce experts, nutritionists, and many other food professionals. Working for any one of them has a lot of pluses. The hours are regular. Health benefits, paid vacations, opportunities for advancement, and many other perks are offered at well-paying jobs in this sector of the food universe. (Some even provide day care for the employees' children.) As a food professional, you can find a job simply by asking for an interview. Send a cover letter and your résumé to the human relations manager. If you don't know her name, pick up the phone and ask or access the Web site of the company and click on employment opportunities.

▶ Sandwich-Shop Owner

Almost every culture does the same thing with food, but they do it differently. They all enclose small amounts of protein or vegetables in outer wrappings in order to make them go further, but the choice of covering makes each variation distinctive. Some people like to insert their burgers between two halves of a bun or their pastrami between two slices of rye. Others prefer to wrap their food in lettuce leaves, cabbage leaves, grape leaves, banana leaves, palm fronds, or cornhusks. Morsels of food are enclosed in plain pastry, puff pastry, wet noodles, or paper—rice paper, parchment paper, even newspaper.

A bewildering variety of meats, fish, cheese, vegetables, nuts, and fruits turn up inside blintzes, buns, burritos, cannelloni, chimichangas, crêpes, dumplings, egg rolls, empanadas, fajitas, knishes, kreplach, quesadillas, ravioli, spring rolls, strudels, tortellini, turnovers, and wontons. And an entire fortune can be contained inside one single cookie.

The business of making sandwiches is growing rapidly. A proprietor of a small operation in a busy location can literally make a fortune providing healthy, hearty, homemade sandwiches for the lunch crowd.

HOME COOKING AWAY FROM HOME

Judie Byrd is a stay-at-home mom who loves to cook. She owns the Culinary School of Fort Worth and in her spare time founded Super

Suppers, a rapidly expanding chain of nearly one hundred retail stores. What is she selling? Recipes and ingredients to make into meals on the premises. Customers buy twelve entrées and come to the store to assemble them under the watchful eyes of cooking teachers. The finished food is frozen and reheated in the customers' home kitchens. There's no shopping and no clean up. Good idea? Great idea! This is a contemporary cooking version of quilting bees.

▶ Ice-Cream Namer

Abby Ellin never imagined her big breakthrough as a writer would be a two-word masterpiece: Karamel Sutra, a new Ben and Jerry flavor. She had beaten out 4,250 people who send in flavor-name suggestions by e-mail every year. She remembers the day the creators of the flavor Chubby Hubby were celebrated with a parade of one hundred motorcycles through her hometown of York, Pennsylvania. Hoping perhaps for something along the lines of a Karamel Sutra Weekend in Central Park, instead she received six pints of ice cream packed in dry ice, a scooper, and a fleece vest imprinted with the Ben and Jerry logo. "Clearly," she commented, "the success won't make me rich, but most people don't get to see their handiwork in a freezer at the local deli, and my friends think I'm cool."

When it comes to food names, Ben and Jerry takes the prize for originality. The company employs a "primal ice cream therapist" whose task it is to dream up new flavors. This is no laughing matter. When the chocolate chip cookie dough flavor was launched in 1991, it was a breakthrough in the ice cream business. Wavy Gravy and Cherry Garcia launched the enterprise into the stratosphere, which just proves what Ben and Jerry said: "The '90s are the '60s standing on your head and we are all the same person trying to shake hands with ourselves." *Ah-so!*

▶ Truffle Salters

Ron Post and Ilyse Rathet, co-owners of Ritrovo, an importing company, dreamed up truffle salt, a more purist approach to truffle derivatives. For every hundred-gram jar of truffle salt, they select forty grams of black summer truffles from Abruzzi, air-dry them, crush them, and combine them with Italian sea salt. The

ROBERT HEISS, OWNER of Culinary Specialties and Coffee Gallery, is a specialty food retailer based in Northampton, Massachusetts. He offers some advice:

- Be passionate about what you do. Build a business that reflects your passion.
- Positioning is critical. Know who you are and what business you are in. Be very specific and focused so your customers will have no question as to why they buy from you. Don't try to be all things to all people
- Set a pace for your business that is comfortable to you. Your positioning will help dictate whether you like to sell small quantities to a lot of people, or if you prefer to spend more time with fewer customers who buy more.
- Be consistent. Your product line, the type of employees you hire, and your hours of operation should all reflect your position in the marketplace.

mixture does contain truffle essence, so its aroma skews more closely to real truffle than any truffle oil, truffle butter, or truffle honey. It's a lot cheaper than buying truffles by the pound.

SPECIALTY FOOD STORES

Entrepreneurs with grit in their bones are able to make a decent living by selling just one product or a combination of three or four products. For example, olive oil and olives, nuts and dried fruits, salts and peppers from around the world, dried herbs and seasonings, and sauces. Success hinges on the depth of each product line, the design of the store, and the charm of the store owner (remember the Soup Nazi?).

There are individuals making a living by selling just one item with several line extensions. For example, a store in Manhattan sells only hummus, others sell only tofu, French fries, or puddings. There is likely a market for the things you love to eat among others who share your cravings.

▶ Vegetable Arranger

Pascal Passariello makes a wonderful vegetable bouquet (Le Bouquet du Potager) that includes peppers, artichokes, green beans, carrots, garlic flowers, and more. To create the effect of flower-like stems, Pascal improvises by spearing each pepper with a floral stick. She rubber bands a handful of green beans together, then conceals the band with raffia and spears the bundle with a dowel or floral stick. Carrots are individually wrapped with floral tape, then bundled together and floral-taped to a floral stick. One tip, though: because the vegetables are so heavy, you may want to arrange them in a vase rather than in your hand. Pascal's business, Veranda Flowers, can be found online at http://www.verandafleurs.com.

SPECIALTY FOODS BY MAIL AND INTERNET

Mail-order food has come a long way since the 1970s, when an order from a so-called gourmet food catalog consisted of, more often than not, a huge gift basket filled with foil-wrapped processed cheeses in various flavors, salami full of preservatives and artificial flavorings, canned pâté, and impressively large but totally tasteless fruits.

Now, when the holidays come around, practically everyone with a mailbox or and e-mail address is deluged with catalogs and Web offers for foods that run the gamut from glorious artisanal cheeses and olive oils to caviar and black and white truffles. Deciding what kinds of foods to include in the catalog and how to describe them can be a fascinating job for someone who loves food and can condense the selling copy into a few action-oriented words. Internet food sales are expected to grow to $17.4 billion in 2008, up from $3.7 billion in 2005, says Bryan Eisenberg, head of Future Now, a Web-consulting firm.

$\mathcal{D}$EBORAH OLSEN,

manager of C. J. Olson Cherries

 OLSEN HAS EXPERIENCED the delight of finding a letter from Prince Albert in her mailbox. It was sent from the Palais de Monaco and read, "It was a nice surprise to receive again a beautiful and delicious basket of your new crops of cherries." She also once received a thank-you note from Julia Child, saying, "Your beautiful cherries just arrived—what an absolutely delicious gift from you. I will most certainly enjoy them, and if my friends are lucky, I might share a few! These are the best ever!"

Says Olsen, "My advice to anyone starting out in this business is think everything out carefully. There are many hidden costs. You have to consider not only the costs of ingredients, but all the time involved, the overhead, packaging, transportation, and marketing. You need insurance against product liability. Take the time to talk to others who are established in your particular specialty. There are different challenges to selling fresh fruit from baked pies. Go to trade shows. Join professional organizations. Expand your thinking. Find additional suppliers for your product. Visit your competitors and be on friendly terms with them so you can help each other. Share the costs of building or leasing a commercial kitchen and warehouse space close to where you live. Learn how to make decisions—immediately.

"I knew I wanted to do this since I was fourteen. I grew up among traditional farm people in the Santa Clara Valley. I spent summers selling cherries and picking apricots. I remember playing with my girlfriend in her family swimming pool, only to get a frantic call from my Grandma Rosie to get over to the farm stand as fast as possible. It may have been summer vacation for other kids, but in our family, summer—especially summer weekends—meant work, and everyone pitched in to help.

"During the off-season, I spent a lot of time in Grandma Rosie's kitchen learning to cook. I really loved to cook and my delight led to a BS degree in food and nutrition at Long Beach State University. I dreamed of going on to one of the large cooking schools in Paris and finally, I acted on the dream. I attended La Varenne, where I received a culinary diploma and with the diploma, a totally different exciting world opened for me.

"I continued working on the farm during summers, but spent the next eight winters in France working as a *stagiare*, or apprentice, including periods of time at three-star restaurants and working with the famous Michel Guerard at his hotel, spa, and restaurant in Eugenie-les-Bains in the French Pyrenees. He taught me how to combine good nutrition with intriguing dishes. I have also studied confectionery. I remember making chocolate-cherry truffles when I was studying with Chef Patrick Perfendie in his restaurant outside Paris and getting more chocolate on my apron than on the platter!

"For the past few years, I have devoted most of my time to managing and expanding our business, developing recipes for foods that we can sell by mail, and finding new ways to create our gift baskets. Even though I live in the middle of Silicone Valley, I am not tech-oriented so this was a hindrance in the beginning, but I found some help and now it is becoming a big part of our business. Mail-order sales keep increasing, too."

Check out the C. J. Olson Cherries Web site at http://www.cjolsoncherries.com.

$\mathcal{D}$'ARTAGNAN:

Right Place, Right Time, Right Product Line

ARIANE DAGUIN AND George Faison met in 1979 when both were students living in the International House at New York's Columbia University. Ariane had come to New York from the village of Auch in the Gascony region of France, where seven generations of her family had worked in the food industry. She grew up helping out in the kitchen of her father, André Daguin, an internationally known chef and owner of Hôtel de France, a Michelin-starred restaurant. And though George, a native Texan, had a very different history with food ("I came from an area where you didn't buy game birds, you shot them," he says), he had the same passion for French food. He had recently spent six months eating and drinking his way through France.

The two became fast friends. Daguin's epicurean pedigree eventually won out over her journalistic aspirations, and she went to work for Trois Petits Cochons, New York's well-known French pâté company. Faison soon joined her there part-time while he finished his MBA, and together they learned the specialty food business.

They launched their own company and named it D'Artagnan for the young Gascon hero from Alexander Dumas's *The Three Musketeers*. The business launched in September 1984 on fifteen thousand dollars of borrowed money, a small refrigeration space, a leased truck, and an exclusive contract to sell foie gras and ducks from Commonwealth Enterprises. Today, D'Artagnan is the largest specialty meat distributor in the country, with revenues of over $40 million. It still specializes in foie gras, duck products, pâté (twelve different types), and such specialty foods as wild-boar *saucisson*, marinated duck breasts, and duck prosciutto. (The company's cassoulet ingredients are marvelous!) It has also evolved into the purveyor that many high-level restaurants, gourmet stores, cruise ships, airlines and even supermarkets turn to when they need fresh (never frozen) rabbit, lamb, quail, and organic turkey for Thanksgiving dinner. The company now has a wild mushroom line, and is always the first to provide sought-after seasonal vegetables such as ramps and white asparagus.

George Faison says that starting the business was hard. "The first year was sweat equity—no salary. It took us five years to get back to the salaries we were making at our last jobs." But Faison and Daguin knew they were onto something

In 2005, Daguin bought out her long-time partner, and she is now the sole proprietor. D'Artagnan can be found at http://www.dartagnan.com.

▶ Gift Basketry: It's What's Inside that Counts

There is an art to making gift baskets both for mail order delivery and in-store sales. A food professional knows not only which foods go well together, but also how to make them look attractive. Cherie Reagor, president of the Basket Connection, has produced seven videos, covering every aspect of assembly and design to market and sales. She also provides a series of marketing tools to help the gift basket entrepreneur get started. She offers two-day workshops focusing on design, product buying, theming, pricing, and shipping. She can be found online at http://www.cheriereagor.com.

Lisa Sexton sells customized gift baskets under her company name, the Perfect Gift. She has found a niche for herself by designing customized gift baskets for each recipient. Many of her baskets are food-oriented. For instance, an Italian lover's basket contains a cookbook, pastas, oils, white truffles, and Italian specialty foods along with coffee beans, a coffee grinder, and perhaps even an espresso pot and demitasse cups; the spa basket has a bath pillow, teas, bottled water, and anything to tie into the theme and the person's preferences. The company was recently cited by *Gift Basket Review* magazine as one of the top one hundred businesses with growths of 300 percent or more in a year.

For More Information

The Web site http://www.festivities-pub.com provides a wealth of useful information about getting into the business of gift basketry.

3

art and design

ART AND DESIGN sell everything we touch. We are delighted (or appalled) by the interior design of hotel lobbies, the contours of a restaurant bar, the curve of a wine glass, and the innovative artistry of a wine label. We buy more in a well-designed supermarket, and often choose our food on the basis of the attractiveness of its packaging. The hospitality industry has embraced beauty in everything from the textures of fabrics to the decorative plates that display the creative talents of the most accomplished pastry chefs. We no longer bow before the captains of conformity.

When the Four Seasons restaurant opened in New York City in 1959, it became the inspiration for the modern American restaurant. It was one of the purest examples of an abstraction transformed into vibrant reality. The planning for the restaurant consumed two and a half years and cost four and a half million dollars—a mighty heap of money in the 1950s. (At that time the average price of a car was twenty-two hundred dollars, gasoline was thirty cents a gallon, and the average annual income was $5,565.)

Philip Johnson, the architect for New York's famed Seagram Building, designed the restaurant. It was the first time that architects and graphic artists and designers of the stature of Mies van der Rohe and Eero Saarinen were invited to join a restaurant planning team. Their work has endured and can still be admired today.

The Four Seasons introduced dozens of other innovations that have permanently changed the way we now view restaurants; at first dubious New Yorkers scoffed at the idea of hanging Miro and Chagall paintings on the walls of a mere restaurant. Skeptics predicted the fine crystal would be smashed in the dishwasher. (It wasn't because a special low-water pressure machine was perfected.) They warned the silver spoons would be stolen. (A few did disappear, but they were a precious few. The loss was considered part of the advertising budget.)

Now, art and design are essential signature elements that contribute to the success of grand restaurants, bustling bistros, and comfortable family cafés. The same elements also touch other areas of the food business. The emphasis on fine art is seen in food styling and prop styling. Design plays a role in choosing accessories for gourmet markets and even in packaging for fast-food restaurants.

Art and design are major elements in all sorts of advertising and marketing. The way that books, magazines, newspaper pages, and Web sites look is the handiwork of art directors or other design professionals. In short, the possibilities are endless for anyone with a good eye, an abiding interest in food, and the dedication to break into the field.

▶ Designer/Art Director

The art director is a trained specialist in color, texture, form, and function. The designer creates the look and feel of magazines, newspapers, cookbooks, menus, Web sites, mail-order catalogs, food packaging, and advertising. The designer also creates the look and feel of restaurants, supermarkets, and specialty food stores. For a restaurant, for example, he or she may select or even design everything from the plates and glasses to the waitstaff uniforms. He chooses the color and the pattern of the carpeting and adjusts the intensity of the lighting in the dining room and bar.

The art director must pay attention to a client's needs and be diplomatic. The client may have firm (but terribly wrong-headed) ideas about creating a visual image that will effectively sell his product or service. A successful restaurant art director understands food and can draw on this knowledge and passion to guide a client along the path to success.

The art director and graphic designer translate a concept into its final form through the use of type, illustration, and photography. Both are problem solvers with considerable communication skills matched with extensive technical abilities. Very often, clients fall into the category of those who know what they like only when they "see it."

MILTON GLASER

UNDER THE STEADY rain of goods and services that we know as consumer culture, the graphic designer is the invisible force in nearly every transaction between producer and purchaser. His is the persuasive hand responsible for the design that says to the buyer, *Look at me, remember me, trust me, want me, and buy me—now*!

Everyone who knows his work agrees that Milton Glaser is the preeminent genius of graphic design whose inspiration and innovative ideas have influenced countless admirers. He created the iconic "I ♥ New York" logo and gave it as a gift to the city. This is just one of the innumerable delights and senses of enchantment he brings to our daily lives.

Milton Glaser's portfolio includes a complete redesign of the 379-unit Grand Union supermarket chain, where he introduced the much-admired prototype of islands of cheeses, oases of fresh fish with their own recipe cards, and breathtaking displays of harvests of vibrant fruits and vegetables. "I particularly like supermarkets," he says. "I'm interested in food and the supermarket is a complex form. You're dealing with a lot of issues: a sense of value, visual information, passage, interaction with the community, and social desire. You can create, through the use of space, light, and color, a place where people are transformed emotionally. This means changing things from an existing condition to a preferred one."

Glaser was a cofounder of *New York* magazine, where he wrote a restaurant review column called the Underground Gourmet. At the other end of the spectrum, he shaped the interior design for the Rainbow Room and both incarnations of the Windows on the World restaurants. He muses, "I love the social effect of restaurants: the fact that for a brief moment you feel better there than anywhere else."

Milton Glaser was educated in New York City at the High School of Music and Art and at the Cooper Union. Armed with a Fulbright Scholarship, he studied at the Academy of Fine Arts in Bologna, Italy, and has taught at the School of Visual Arts in Manhattan since 1961.

GETTING STARTED

A degree in fine arts is usually required to obtain an entry-level position in a design studio. Business courses are an asset, too. An entry-level job offers the opportunity to work under the guidance of more senior staff. During this training period, a new employee will learn about budgets, how to identify the nuts and bolts of producing a product, and how to traffic jobs so a busy design department hums along.

A junior, or beginning, assistant must possess many talents, including the ability to be creative, listen attentively to a client's objectives, and to work within budget and time limitations. He then must be able to communicate ideas effectively. He should have the skill to translate abstract ideas into visual images and to sketch ideas on paper or computer. He must possess an understanding of technical knowledge that will impact costs and also have the ability and enthusiasm to create original solutions for a client. An employee with artistic ability and extensive food knowledge and restaurant experience is an invaluable member of a design team or architectural company that specializes in restaurant concepts.

For More Information

The Art Directors Club of New York (http://www.adcny.org) is a not-for-profit organization of leading creative executives in advertising, graphic design, and interactive media.

• RECIPE FOR SUCCESS •

EXHIBITION CURATOR

by Darra Goldstein

PUTTING TOGETHER A museum or gallery exhibition relating to food is a wonderful way to deepen your knowledge and share your food passion with the public. The possibilities for venues are nearly endless and include small private galleries, fine arts museums, natural history or science museums, living history museums, historic houses, even libraries. Excellent exhibitions have been held on such varied topics as chocolate (at Chicago's Field Museum); accoutrements for serving coffee, tea and chocolate in early America (New York's Metropolitan Museum of Art); nineteenth-century cast-iron stoves (the Albany Institute of History and Art); cutlery (the Cooper-Hewitt National Design Museum in New York); rice (UCLA Fowler Museum of Cultural History); and images of food and dining (Edith C. Blum Art Institute at Bard College in Annandale-on-Hudson, New York), to name only a few. Food exhibitions can be comprehensive, extending through several rooms, or they can be limited to a single display case to draw attention to food as part of a larger exhibition on a different topic. A museum with an excellent graphic-arts collection might never have considered mounting an exhibition of posters relating to food in tourism and commerce. A library might have an extraordinary menu collection that begs to be interpreted and shown.

The immediate difficulty for someone interested in curatorial work is that in most cases a track record is necessary. Putting together an exhibition is not the same as writing a first cookbook and sending it off to an agent or publisher. Because exhibitions are expensive, museums tend to be cautious. The larger museums generally rely on their own curatorial staff, though they occasionally seek guest curators. It is therefore best to begin with a local museum and offer a modest proposal rather than an overly ambitious one. For instance, if you live near a regional maritime museum, you might scour their holdings (including archives) for material relating to the sea trade in food, or to the seafarers' diet. If you are knowledgeable about herbs, you could research period gardens and offer to create a kitchen garden for a local historic house. If you are adept at hearth cooking, you could offer to give demonstrations, using authentic techniques, at an ethnographic museum.

Any exhibition, whether large or small, must have a solid concept that is clearly laid out in a proposal. Who is your audience? What are you trying to convey? Will the proposed show further public knowledge in an important way? How will it differ from previous exhibitions that have been held elsewhere? Most importantly, will the exhibition highlight and promote the objects in the museum's collection?

Curatorial skills include excellent organization and the ability to research a topic in depth. If you are unsure about proposing an exhibition that you've designed on your own, a good way to start is by approaching a curator in the museum or gallery that interests you and offering to consult on a special project.

Compensation in the museum world is usually not very high; most curators work for love of the objects rather than for monetary gain. Curators are highly trained professionals who have usually attended graduate school in art history or museum studies. If you are interested in this type of career, you might simply volunteer at a museum to gain familiarity with its workings, or find out whether an internship program is available. Learn all about the museum's collections, make yourself indispensable, and then propose a small show relating to food.

For a listing of graduate programs in museum studies, visit http://www.gradschools.com/programs/museum_studies.html. For a listing of specialized food museums throughout the world, go to http://foodhistorynews.com.

Food Photographer Jim Scherzi

"A FOOD PHOTOGRAPHER tries to capture the essence of a pear, a head of garlic, a completed dish, or the noisy vibrancy or hushed luxury inside a restaurant. Each person sees things differently and translates an impression into a unique style," says famed food photographer James M. Scherzi (jim@scherziphoto.com). He says he knew he wanted to be a photographer since he was seven or eight years old and is still fascinated with the art of his craft. He didn't set out to be a food photographer specifically, but gravitated into the field because it constantly presents new and different challenges. He says, "I like being around food people. I love food and I love to cook."

His advice is, "Follow your passion. You have to develop your own ideas. In order to stay ahead of the trends in photography read everything you can, particularly food and home magazines like *Architectural Digest* and *Metropolitan Home*, and subscribe to many food publications. I watch TV to keep up with new styles. In this field you are listening and learning twenty-four hours a day. You are always looking for something new. You are never off the clock. Something new is always out there and your job is to make sure you see it.

"When I get a commission, I do as much research as I possibly can. Sometimes I end up knowing what will work better than the clients do and I have to persuade them that I know how to get them the maximum amount of attention. There are stumbling blocks in every job and our business is not to take the easiest route. There are times though, when against my better judgment, I have to be agreeable and agree to do just what the client wants.

"Being a food photographer is like making bread. It's a lot of work, but it is so rewarding when you know you have produced something good. My role is to stop the reader long enough to capture his attention and make him want to read the copy and buy the product."

Food photography is a wildly diverse field and while it sounds glamorous, like any field, it requires a lot of training, discipline, and hard work. With the recent changeover from primarily film to primarily digital photography, food photographers need to be adaptive and technically savvy, as well as possessing a good eye. A little luck never hurts, either.

Some photographers get jobs by developing relationships with nearby magazines, newspapers, or advertising agencies. Others rely on a rep, a person who may handle several photographers, get them jobs, and discuss rates. Fees are almost always set by the day, called a day rate.

Getting Started

Photographers who specialize in food often shoot other things, too. What they know is how to take a memorable photograph, whether using film, or more commonly, digital technology. Many study the craft at art school or a community college. Some have been taking photos all their lives simply because they love it. They start their professional career by assisting an established photographer. The assistant may find herself carrying equipment from the studio to a shooting location, keeping track of cameras and other things, and even picking up lunch, but the experience and contacts are invaluable.

Look into high-level photography courses, practice your craft wherever possible, and contact established photographers you admire and ask about interning or trailing. Put together a professional-looking portfolio and Web site and shop yourself to local ad agencies and PR firms.

▶ Food Stylist

A food photographer who shoots finished dishes and other food relies on a food stylist to prepare the food. Rarely is this a job for the person who wrote the recipe. Cooking is one thing, preparing food for photography is quite another. Styling food so that it will look good in photos requires considerable skill, knowledge of foods, and the patience of a saint.

For advertising purposes, the law demands that photographs must show the food exactly as it looks when it is sold. The advertiser must not mislead the public by photographing food in a way that would make it impossible to reproduce at home. Marbles can't be dumped in the soup so the vegetables rise to the surface making it appear full of peas, beans, and carrots. Delicious-looking thick, golden brown motor oil cannot be substituted for real maple syrup to pour on the pancakes. But these restrictions don't apply to foods or decorations used as background images.

In pursuit of perfection, a food stylist may slice several pounds of Swiss cheese in order to find one geometrically perfect slice. It is the stylist's artistry in combination with the photographer's skill that makes a professional photograph outstanding and arouses the desire of the consumer to get her hands on the food—immediately.

The task of the food stylist is to make food look irresistible for the cameras. He or she works with photographers to produce ads for magazines, newspapers, and television commercials, and creates gorgeous-looking meals for Hollywood movies and in-store produce videos. Stylists are also called in to prepare photos for cookbooks and beauty shots for television shows.

Like photographers, stylists charge by the day. In large cities, these day rates can be significant. Very often, stylists and photographers team up to offer clients a complete package. These alliances are usually casual partnerships that wax and wane like the jobs themselves.

GETTING STARTED

No officially sanctioned licensing is required to become a food stylist, but having a solid cooking foundation is important, and a degree from a professional cooking school is invaluable. To keep current with the new technologies, food stylists attend art and photography classes. Another way to break into the field is to intern with an established stylist. These jobs are hard to come by, but wonderfully interesting work will come your way once you become established in the field.

For More Information

The Association of Stylists and Coordinators, http://www.stylistsasc.com

Food on Film in Minneapolis has a three-day workshop for food stylists every other year in the spring. http://www.foodonfilm.com

The Mississippi University for Women offers a one-week food-styling program for college credit. http://www.muw.edu

---

• **RECIPE FOR SUCCESS** •

FOOD STYLIST DELORES CUSTER

AS A LONGTIME and well-established food stylist, Dolores Custer's work is widely admired. Her own experience speaks to the many opportunities that are available in the field. She has worked with food magazines, advertising agencies, and public-relations firms. Her talents are in demand for television, feature films, and food companies. She says, "The best thing that a beginner can do is to assist good food stylists. Put together a portfolio of your work to promote yourself and apply for an intern or junior assistant position with an established professional."

Custer agrees that most stylists must pay their dues. There is a lot to learn and the best way is to assist someone who is good at it. She also says it's important to live where the work is and develop an adaptable freelance personality.

"One of the things I like best about the freelance world of food styling is that there are no typical days," says Custer. "Each day is different from the next. We shoot in every conceivable environment and work with many different foods. One day we may prepare a picnic for a TV commercial and the next day we are spreading the client's frosting on a single cupcake."

Delores Custer teaches food styling at the New School in NYC and the Culinary Institute of America campus in Hyde Park, New York (http://www.ciachef.edu).

Prop Stylist

Both food stylists and food photographers very often work with prop stylists. These are the people who provide everything other than the food for a photo or film.

For anyone who loves to shop, landing a job as a prop stylist is like receiving manna from heaven. Working with a client, art director, photographer, and food stylist, the prop person is responsible for setting the scene for a photograph. This involves not only searching for the china or handcrafted pottery on which the food is photographed, but also the table cloth, napkins, knives, forks, spoons, glasses, vases, flowers, and candlesticks. Like food stylists and food photographers, experienced prop stylists earn very respectable day rates. The work can be physically demanding, and the stylist will find him- or herself running from showroom to store in search of the perfect prop. While many manufacturers and stores happily lend items for credit, most prop (and food) stylists collect an inventory of their own plates, linens, vases, flatware, and glasses, too.

Tabletop Buyer

Lavish sums are spent not only on what food goes on a restaurant plate, but also on the plate itself. Lois Bloom and Patricia Boyer write a monthly column with photographs of the latest tabletop accessories for *Food Arts* magazine. They are the pioneers of tabletop consultants. They scour china, silver, and glassware showrooms; study design catalogs; and arm themselves with knowledge about the size, shape, color, and price of everything from the perfect blue glass plate on which to serve the smoked salmon, to the ideal rustic pottery casserole for the cassoulet, to the perfect lavender-colored plate on which to display the chocolate cake, to the pristine white pot for the mint tea.

When hired to work with a restaurant, the tabletop buyer shows the chef, restaurateur, or designer several samples from which to choose. The final selection will often be coordinated with other design elements. Tabletop consultants customarily have a roster of several restaurants and learn to understand the taste, whims, and idiosyncrasies of each chef/restaurateur. Some daring chefs present their food on twigs and wires, in test tubes, and via other wildly creative forms. Working with sculptors and jewelers, they invent new ways to serve—and eat—their food. It is essential for tabletop consultants to keep up with rapidly changing food trends and take note that some avant-garde chefs serve food unconventionally.

To get your foot in the door of this field, assemble a portfolio of photographed real or proposed table settings along with sources and costs, and be prepared to pound the pavement to sell your services. Try to intern or assist established food stylists or prop stylists to learn the business. This is a dream job for anyone who likes to spend their days shopping—and returning rejects to the showrooms or manufacturers, where you will need to develop relationships, too.

▶ Uniform Designer

You might question the connection between uniform design and cooking, but it is surprising to discover how often students who are enrolled in professional culinary schools express an interest in this endeavor and in other aspects of art and design. Clearly, a love of food seeks its expression in many creative ways.

White shirt, black bow tie, and black pants with a tightly tied white apron have long been the uniform for a bistro server, but nowadays waitstaff uniforms for more formal restaurants are inspired by fashion designers. The colors may reflect the color palettes used by the restaurants' architects. The new designers don't want the guests to feel that the waiters and sommeliers are better dressed than they are (though truth be told, sometimes that is the case).

Fabrics for staff uniforms are tested for durability and stain resistance. Teflon coatings are used to help preserve the life of the materials. Each new employee is fitted with his own uniform because smart restaurateurs know the happiness of the staff and their appearance is critical to set the scene appropriately. Job seekers may have a degree in costume design from New York University's Tisch School of Arts or other fashion-design schools across the country.

Uniform designers are presented with unique challenges. They must calculate the cost of producing the uniforms in washable materials or the considerably more expensive fabrics that require dry cleaning.

▶ Menu Designer

The menu reveals the soul of the restaurant. It serves two purposes: to indicate what food is available and its price. If a guest innocently thinks she is making up her own mind about what she wants to eat, she should think again. She may be guided into choosing what *the chef* wants her to eat. One of the ways to steer diners toward the dishes that produce the highest profit is a subtle technique known as motion. In theory, every menu has a sweet spot, the place where the eye falls first. A graphic designer can lead the eye to a specific destination.

On the classic magazine-style or two-fold menu, the dominant space is on the upper-right-hand side. On one-page menus, the sweet spot is in the center. Conversely, if the owner wants to hide a popular but less profitable dish, the lower left is the place to put it. Other attention-getting techniques include boxing the item; underlining, circling, or shading it; lengthening the description; and enlarging the type size, which can be done so subtly that it is only observed subliminally.

The wordsmithing of the menu is also important and is usually the responsibility of the chef or someone on his or her staff who is good with descriptive words. Calling a chicken "roasted" rather than "roast" adds another $ or $$. And everyone understands that the concept of "fresh" is a subjective idea. Is a carrot "fresh" if it has traveled across the country or even from another continent? No matter. The menu designers' task is to entice and increase the sense of anticipation for the diner. Would you prefer to order Fish 'n' Chips or Wild Alaskan Herb-Rubbed Sea Salmon with Tiny Sautéed Fingerling Potatoes?

Menu writers should have a working knowledge of graphic design and the ability to spell correctly. A restaurant owner may assign the task of creating a menu to the executive chef, who works with anyone who can turn out a computer-generated list of the evening's dishes. An artistic menu adds immeasurably to the pleasure (and cost) of dining in a fine restaurant.

KITCHEN DESIGN

Restaurant kitchens require careful attention to every detail, particularly when they become an open stage for a performance by the chef and his corps de cuisine. Currently, many high-end restaurants offer guests the opportunity to reserve the kitchen table, which is strategically placed to provide diners with a panoramic view of the cooks in action. For this privilege, they pay a premium. The setting had better look good—and, it usually does indeed. Another reason today's restaurant kitchens tend to look stylish, sleek, and inviting is because so many are open kitchens, with the "fourth wall" open to the diners. Even kitchens that are not constructed to be open kitchens need to pass muster since a growing number of chefs offer guests kitchen tours upon request.

After extensive consultation with the client, the highly qualified kitchen design team creates detailed drawings, a structural model, computer simulations of traffic patterns, or a full-scale prototype. Most designers use computer-aided design (CAD) tools to create and better visualize the final product. Computer models allow ease and flexibility in exploring a greater range of design alternatives, and thus reduce design costs and cut the time it takes to arrive at a concept that conforms to federal, state, and local authorities' safety regulations and building codes.

Not surprisingly, commercial kitchen design focuses on function. This means the plan will evolve from who the guests are and how many guests will be served and the style of the food, which can range from simple assemblies to vastly complicated fabrications.

The design for a kitchen in a university that will serve hundreds of hurried students is entirely different from a high-end restaurant kitchen.

Kitchen-design consultants are usually expected to draw up specifications that are used for competitive bidding among contractors. This means subsequently providing the client with a schedule for completion and a budget.

GETTING STARTED

As with many jobs, the best way to gain experience as a kitchen designer is to apply for work with a kitchen design company. A college degree in design, architecture, or business (or a combination) is extremely helpful in order to rise to a senior position in a design company. You should have good math skills, whether you apply them to making accurate measurements or to understanding budget and time constraints.

Designers must be able to work as part of a cohesive team that constantly faces new challenges. The expected never happens; it is always the surprise glitch that requires well-reasoned thinking to come up with a timely and practical solution, as when the owner of a fine restaurant realized in the final few days before opening that it had failed to allocate space for a ladies' room. A culinary degree and some restaurant experience are invaluable because only a person who has worked in a commercial kitchen fully understands how the system operates at maximum efficiency.

The ability to withstand heat from clients and contractors is highly desirable. So too is a thorough understanding of structural engineering. This ensures that a heavy piece of equipment, such as a commercial stove, will not crash through the ceiling of a floor below, nor will a leaking pipe cause a costly problem. This said, it's a fact that lawyers are among kitchen designers' best friends. They draw up watertight contracts. It's helpful to know there are lawyers who specialize in legal and union issues for the hospitality industry.

For More Information

Hannington College of Design, Chicago IL

International Academy of Design and Technology, Tampa, FL

Kazarian, Edward A. *Foodservice Facilities Planning.* New York: Van Nostrand Reinhold, 1989.

Kitchen Design School: Brooks College, Long Beach CA

▶ Residential (Home) Kitchen Designer

One of those often-repeated truisms is the more the kitchen costs, the less it is used. It is not unusual for a home kitchen to cost a great deal more than fifty thousand dollars. Whether it actually functions efficiently depends on its design.

A skilled kitchen designer is usually a cook as well. She understands the most practical way to organize the workspace. For example, the designer makes sure the refrigerator door opens in the right direction and the sink is correctly positioned in relationship to the cooking surfaces and the dishwasher.

Kitchen design involves far more than shopping for attractive cabinets and choosing the stove, refrigerator, and faucets. Knowledge of the most energy-efficient appliances is as important as choosing the easiest-to-clean flooring and the most attractive lighting. A highly polished granite counter and a stainless-steel refrigerator are hard to keep clean.

Clients may yearn for professional-cooking equipment until they realize commercial sub-zero freezers may be as noisy as a city bus and fridges with glass doors require an artistic arrangement of the contents. A homeowner may covet a fire-engine-red cast-iron stove, but the conscientious kitchen designer will explain that such a luxury appliance requires so much energy that it is not the most efficient way to reheat a frozen pizza.

Cobalt blue, harvest yellow, avocado green, or other one-time fashionable colors will date a kitchen and reduce the resale value of a home. According to appliance retailer P. C. Richard and Son, "Five years ago, consumers often bought a hodge-podge of appliances because they liked a particular brand. Now they fall for the styling. They want the cabinetry handles and the front panels to match, and the contours and the ergonomics have to go together." The kitchen designer keeps an eye on fashion trends, studies the customer's real eating habits, and ferrets out idealized good intentions.

GETTING STARTED

Nearly a third of designers are self-employed. This is almost five times the proportion for similar occupations. Many have backgrounds in interior design and may be certified master kitchen and bathroom designers (CMKBD). Many concentrate on specific areas. For example, some designers concentrate on creating models of efficiency in tiny kitchens in studio apartments, while others choose to work in mansions in the suburbs or to specialize in Mediterranean-style or Colonial period homes.

Kitchen designers must be able to communicate clearly with both the client and the contractors. They must be detail-oriented, organized, comfortable working under pressure, and able to complete the work in the allotted time or explain delays. In addition, the most successful have studied CAD software so that they can provide clients with blueprints of the proposed design and be able to alter them to accommodate the client's wishes.

Designers must listen to the client and point out disadvantages as well as positive reasons for choices. They should select the most important appliance (like the stove) first and then choose the other equipment to coordinate with it. And of course, designers must pay close attention to budgets.

National Kitchen and Bath Association,
http://www.nkba.org/student

International Interior Design Association (IIDA),
http://iida.org

National Kitchen and Bath Association (NKBA)

Several kitchen design schools offer two-year courses.
Search the Internet to find one near you.

4

publishing, television, the internet, radio, and all things media

WHAT AN ENORMOUS subject this is! In this chapter we address books, magazines, newspapers, television, radio, and the Internet—all forms of media that communicate with the public about food. Cookbooks and magazines are filled with food writing and recipes; most newspapers publish food articles and recipes, too; and the Internet has both in various forms of polish and reliability. TV and radio shows promote cooking techniques, cooking contests, and the personalities behind the food.

▶ Food Writer

So you want to be a food writer? This is good news. It means you have put your hand on the door. Now push it open and consider all your options. You must decide whether you want to be a newspaper columnist or write for a consumer magazine like *Cook's Illustrated* or *Gourmet* or a trade journal, such as *Nation's Restaurant News, Pizza Today, The Progressive Grocer*, or *Chef: The Professional Magazine for Chefs*.

Perhaps you'd like to compose profiles of famous chefs or write press releases for restaurants or commodities boards. You might dream of being a world traveler who rhapsodizes about food in far away places. Do you yearn to become a restaurant reviewer or write a cookbook? These are just a few among many destinations to consider.

Many food writers are specialists: Jane and Michael Stern write about the kind of food found at roadside cafés and diners. Jeffrey Steingarten writes lengthy, scholarly analysis on such subjects as the salt consumption of the Yanomamo Indians living in Brazil. He is a wonderfully entertaining and informative writer who found a permanent home at *Vogue*, of all places. Mark Kurlansky writes books with such titles as *Cod: A Biography of the Fish That Changed the World* and *Salt: A World History.* Calvin Trillin writes about food in every publication under the sun from the *New Yorker* and the *Nation* to *Modern Maturity.* He has the one thing every food writer needs: the talent to see what others see, but make his view distinctively different from others. Even the unwelcome sight of Brussels sprouts at a buffet in a London restaurant provoked his ire. Turning to his wife, Alice, he said, "The English have a lot to answer for." Calvin Trillin has the rare ability to engage and inform his readers and make them chuckle, too.

Publishing is not an easy field to get into. The competition is ferocious. You don't have to be as good as the next person—you have to be a whole lot better. But have courage. Remember, even the greatest writers had to find a way to wriggle their toe through a seemingly closed door. And there is always something new to explore.

Our views on what to eat and when and where to eat it are constantly shifting. The task of the writer is to ferret out all these interesting highways and byways and report on the findings to a reader. For a skilled writer, this means writing not to millions of readers, but to the one single reader who the author has in mind.

Food writers must constantly ask questions. Why do people eat Jell-O? Why have cheap bourbon sales plummeted while the cost of expensive vodka has soared? Who types the Ms on the M&Ms? Why does the crime rate plummet on Thanksgiving Day? Answer: Everyone is at home eating turkey and gravy.

If you passionately want to be a food writer—and you must be passionate about this—you will find a magazine that will provide a home for your work. But this will happen only if you suggest a topic that will interest the specific demographic profile of its subscribers.

IN ADDITION TO being a foreign correspondent and Washington bureau chief, the late R. W. "Johnny" Apple Jr. of the *New York Times* transformed himself into a prolific food columnist. He needed no new credentials. He just added his interest in food to his ability to write well. He said, "If you're going to write about food you have to travel, you have to eat, otherwise you are forced into the position of sounding like where you live is the center of the universe, and that's not healthy. It's no more healthy than writing about foreign affairs while sitting in Washington, D.C., never getting other perspectives, or writing about presidential campaigns and never getting off the plane and talking to people. I write about food the way I write about foreign policy."

▶ Magazine Writer

Close to six thousand magazines are published regularly, and new opportunities are always opening up. To get an idea of the numerous possible outlets for your work, go to a magazine stand at a busy airport or a bookseller with an extensive magazine section. Splurge. Buy as many publications as you can afford and study each one to see if your ideas will fit its editorial philosophy. The *New Yorker* may publish a profile of a famous person, report on a current event such the bee colony collapse disorder, or explore the issues pertaining to bird flu or mad cow disease. The *New Yorker* also publishes occasional double issues devoted to feature stories about food, but the company is only interested in recipes if they come in the form of a cartoon.

The *Atlantic* and the online magazine *Slate* publish food articles, and so do *Esquire, GQ*, and many other consumer magazines. *Newsweek* and *Time* report on health issues and happenings in the food world. It is your task as a food writer to figure out *which* magazine is likely to be interested in *what* subject.

Look at the ads in magazines; they provide reliable clues about the income level and degree of sophistication of the readers. Check the publications' Web sites because they may contain instructions for submitting a query letter. (If not, call the magazine and ask an editorial assistant if there is a writer's guide available.)

Gourmet, Bon Appétit, Food and Wine, Cook's Illustrated, Saveur, Cooking Light, and other food magazines may seem like obvious places for your work, but the terrible truth is that it is difficult to break into this exalted territory. Salaried staff writers and those who swim in the pool of favored contributors write many of the articles so there is little room left for talented freelancers.

There are many other opportunities to get into print, though. You could write recipes for a supermarket (Wegmans supermarket chain publishes a terrific food magazine, as do many others), suggest a dining column for a winery newsletter, submit your material to a culinary Web site, or start your own blog.

To find new venues for your material, read everything you can lay your hands on. You'll find prospects in the most unlikely places. Write an article for a dentistry publication exploring the reasons why our teeth are getting smaller. (They are, but very slowly over the course of centuries.) Explore the reasons why steaks are getting bigger and submit it to *Esquire* magazine. Uncover the reasons why there are an increasing number of vegetarians and submit your theory to the *Vegetarian Times*, or write about vegetarian athletes for *Sports Illustrated* and explore the history and politics of eating for a general-interest magazine.

Women's magazines such as *Family Circle, Woman's Day, Ladies' Home Journal, Redbook, Parenting,* and *Child* have cut back the space formerly allotted to their food sections. Surveys reveal that few readers have the time or enthusiasm to devote to making dinner. It is one thing to enjoy cooking as a hobby, but quite another to find the energy to cook every night. Several new magazines such as *Real Simple* concentrate on recipes that call for fresh ingredients that can be combined with store-bought packaged foods.

Specialty magazines like those that concentrate on gardening, sports, and health issues are interested in food-related articles that appeal to their clearly defined market. Other niche markets are travel magazines and age-related publications that focus on every decade from infancy to old age. Look, too, at industry-specific magazines such as those devoted to coffee and tea retailing, military clubs, and mushroom growing.

Then there are city and regional magazines like *New York, Time Out, New Orleans, Texas Monthly, Southern Living, Canadian Living,* and *Hudson Valley Table.* These publications accept articles that are tightly focused on the locality. They publish stories about local farmers, local restaurants, and local gourmet shops.

Health, Body and Soul, Men's Fitness, Men's Health, Woman's Health, Prevention, Allure, Glamour, Shape, Chatelaine, Cooking Light, Eating Well, Better Homes and Gardens, Elle, Bride's Parents, Muscle and Fitness, Runner's World, Self, and *Vegetarian Times* all cater to clearly identified readers. And don't overlook such possibilities as *Reader's Digest*, which has a worldwide paid circulation of about 19 million—and that staggering number extends to an estimated 85 million who read but don't subscribe to the magazine. *Consumer Reports, Glamour, Ebony, Better Homes and Gardens*, and *Martha Stewart Living* are among literally hundreds of magazines that offer hope and, occasionally, employment, too.

GETTING STARTED

Many top food writers have a journalism or liberal-arts degree. Some have also attended a professional cooking school, though it is not absolutely essential to earn formal culinary credentials to become a food writer. You just need to have terrific writing skills and something interesting to say.

Several magazines offer temporary positions for interns. Send a carefully worded letter to the editor to apply for one of them. Once there you may find yourself doing utterly boring work, but you may also gather some terrific experience and have the opportunity to do some copyediting, fact checking—or even writing! The downside is that while there is rarely any real money attached to this enterprise, you will be expected to show up on time, be decently dressed, remain cheerful at all times, and not beg for food. Internships can provide you with college credit, and you may receive a letter of commendation. When applying for an internship, send your résumé and copies, not originals, of articles you have written for writing class, a school newspaper, or any other publication.

Ultimately, the only way to get started is to get started. It isn't enough to say you'd like to be a food writer if you've never actually got around to writing anything. Focus on an idea. Write the headline. Write the introduction. Write the conclusion. Write the stuff that goes in the middle. Rewrite the middle part. Rewrite the conclusion—and then the introduction. Rethink the title. Do this exercise six, seven, or eight or more times and then you'll be able to get started for real.

Once you have an idea, send a query letter to the magazine that is most appropriate for your subject matter. Keep the query short. Make absolutely, positively sure you haven't made any spelling mistakes or grammatical errors! Never use an exclamation mark. It implies the reader is too feeble-minded to understand your meaning. Double exclamation points are triply wrong.

QUERY LETTER

Whatever you do, don't write the article first and hope you will be able to find a place to publish it later. It'll surely be dumped. The possibility of getting it right, according to the likes and dislikes of an editor, are about as difficult to calculate as trying to guess her Social Security number.

Address a query letter to the food editor of the magazine or the articles editor (not the editor in chief or the publisher). Introduce yourself. State your idea in one or two concise sentences. Describe your qualifications—briefly. Allow yourself at least a week to write the letter. It is the only opportunity you get to make the sale. Remember the busy editor will view it as junk mail so it must be arresting to capture her attention.

Send your query letter either by e-mail or regular mail. Don't fax it, or it will get lost. Don't ever telephone an editor to propose an article. She will be in the middle of doing something and will not welcome the interruption. She'll just tell you to buzz off.

KEYS TO SUCCESS

- Every magazine has its own range of topics and style of dealing with them. It is essential to study each publication carefully before sending a query letter to the appropriate editor.
- Don't send more than one idea at a time, or they will all, almost certainly, be rejected. Don't become suicidal if your idea is rejected—or more likely, simply ignored. Editors receive more query letters than you can imagine, and there simply isn't time to respond to every one.
- Before writing your article, gather as much research as you can. If you have only five facts, you will have to use all of them. If you have fifty facts you can select the best.
- When you think you have finished the article, read it—slowly—into a tape recorder as though you are speaking on the radio. Rewind and listen *very* attentively to the rhythm of your words. You'll be surprised how many changes you will want to make. Examine every word to make sure it fits as comfortably as a pair of old shoes. If you think it is perfect, think again. Nothing is ever perfect.

- Learn to tell time. The editor does not have the time or patience to remind you when your article is due. If it is late, you will probably be forever banished from her list of favored freelancers.
- Be agreeable about making changes even if it means grinding your teeth into stumps.

Writing class

by Carol Penn-Romine, student in the professional food writing course at the Institute of Culinary Education

 "IT'S LONELY OUT in space," laments David Bowie in "Space Oddity." For freelance writers, that's where we are, adrift in the ether, without the company of anyone who truly understands our lot in life. Our family and friends love us, but unless they're all writers, they don't know what it feels like to slug away at this profession all alone. We writers are a suspect lot anyway, making obscure references, cracking obtuse jokes, and scribbling notes no one else can understand. How do they know we're pondering the structure of an article or where to place that odd paragraph? As far as they're concerned, we could be daydreaming about chocolate soufflés, or sex—or both.

We need to have our batteries recharged periodically, and taking a writing class gives us that recharge in at least three vital ways. Most obvious is the study of the subject itself. No matter how long we've been writing or how much we've studied the craft, we'll learn at least one thing we didn't know. It may be something that's not even on the class schedule.

When I signed up for a professional food writing class at the Institute of Culinary Education, my teacher encouraged me to write humorous essays. I've written them all my life, but seldom have I tried to publish one. I've always been too focused on paying the bills, buying the cat food, and writing informative prose. But during our class, she saw that what flowed most naturally from me was humor. She confirmed there is a market for it and she nudged me in that direction.

Which brings us to the second benefit of signing up for a writing class: the relationship you build with the instructor can be surprisingly helpful. Some are more approachable than others, but if you hit it off with your teacher, you'll have an ally in your corner who can help

continued

"Writing is not a contest. Every writer is starting from a different point and is bound for a different destination. Yet many writers are paralyzed by the thought that they are competing with everybody else who is trying to write and presumably doing it better. This can often happen in a writing class. Inexperienced students are chilled to find themselves in the same class with students whose byline has appeared in the college newspaper. But writing for the college paper is no great credential; I've often found that the hares who write for the paper are overtaken by tortoises who move studiously toward the goal of mastering the craft. The same fear cripples freelance writers, who see the work of other writers appearing in magazines while their own keeps returning in the mail. Forget the competition and go at your own pace. Your only contest is with yourself."

—**WILLIAM ZINSSER**,
author of *On Writing Well: The Classic Guide to Writing Nonfiction*

continued from page 143

you weather the bad times and celebrate the good ones—and whack you upside the head when you need it.

Toward the end of his life, I had the good fortune to take a writing class with Peter Taylor, the storyteller whose elegant explorations of the changing Old South won him a Pulitzer Prize. One day he mused, "You know, my friends used to be my teachers. Now my friends are my students." I was honored to know that this esteemed author felt we were equals. We feed and we are fed by one another, regardless of our age.

Third, and perhaps most important, are the friendships you build with your fellow classmates. "I've already got all the friends I need," is one of the saddest, most misguided assertions I've ever heard. You can never have too many friends, and in a writing class, you aren't just building friendships, you're building professional relationships. Among the friends you make in a writing class you'll find a variety of ages, education levels, and professional and life experiences. While you will learn from some, you'll find yourself reaching out to help those who haven't traveled as far along the path as you have.

Networking also enables you to share ideas. Some writers are concerned that if they discuss their ideas with others, they'll lose them to someone faster and hungrier. I don't subscribe to this attitude. Rather, I believe in the generosity of spirit, and that the more you give, the more you receive. Often those who network find a painful interest in common, such as alcoholism, divorce, or disease. Contrarily, establishing a network of writing support comes out of a positive, joyous impulse—the urge to write. When we find others who share our passion for the written word, we should celebrate our good fortune. If we're going to drift in outer space, let's bring along some likeminded folks.

Personally, I can't assign a dollar value to all the benefits I've received from the writing classes I've taken. Their worth is far greater than their cost. Just don't tell the IRS.

For More Information

There are three excellent sources of comprehensive information about periodicals, whether in the field of consumer and trade magazines or professional journals:

Magazines for Libraries

Ulrich's International Periodicals Directory

The Standard Periodical Directory

Writer's Market (http://www.writersmarket.com) provides listings of magazines and fees they pay to authors.

Jennifer Stewart has excellent free online advice for writers: The Write Way is a weekly e-zine with advice on how to improve your writing. When you subscribe, you'll also receive two e-books. Scroll down to see why you need this material, whether you're writing for profit or pleasure. Each week, in the Write Way, you'll find tips on how to avoid common errors in writing as well as a feature article on one aspect of writing for the Web, a short vocabulary quiz to improve your word power, and a humorous look at different types of writing. http://www.write101.com

The Symposium for Professional Food Writers is a popular conference for professional food writers and editors only. It is limited to 90 attendees and customarily held in the spring at The Greenbrier, WhiteSulphur Springs, West Virginia. A team of successful writers leads discussions and workshops. http://www.greenbrier.com/site/foodwriters.aspx

---

ℬECOMING A FOOD WRITER

by Dianne Jacob, author of Will Write for Food: The Complete Guide to Writing Cookbooks, Restaurant Reviews, Articles, Memoir, Fiction, and More, *and coauthor of* Grilled Pizzas and Piadinas

 A RECIPE FOR fettuccine with prosciutto, cream, and nutmeg. The history of tea. A first-person adventure in Chinatowns around the world. Where to get the best deli sandwiches. A dictionary of food terms. Food writing wanders over dozens of subjects. The storytellers and their craft are what bring it together. You might have many reasons to write about food:

- Perhaps you'd like to tell your life story and pass down recipes to family members.
- You're a caterer or chef whose customers have asked for recipes.
- You might be fascinated by the history of a certain food and want to research it.
- You'd like to write a cookbook based on experience or knowledge you've developed.
- You love to travel, and want to capture the cuisine of a country and people.

Whatever motivates you, food writing has requirements that make it irresistible: you like food, and you get to eat and write about it. What's better than that?

continued

continued from page 145

Food writers might write cookbooks, create their own Web sites, or write for magazines, newspapers, or corporations. They start with a passion for food and an ability to write. The best are enthusiastic researchers, great storytellers, fearless about going after the information they need, and extremely detail-oriented, particularly when it comes to recipe writing.

There is no one set of requirements, though, because food writing covers so many different skill sets. If you are already in the food world or write professionally, you're halfway there. Otherwise, take classes, read, travel, or intern to build up your credibility and skills.

Getting Started

It's difficult to make food writing an entire career, just as it's difficult to be a full-time novelist. Many food writers supplement their work by teaching cooking classes, catering, writing corporate copy, and doing jobs that might be unrelated but pay well. To play it safe, many approach food writing as a side job, to work on like a novel: something done on nights and weekends.

Successful food writers are fundamentally good writers. If you're already a published writer, if friends love the e-mails you send when you travel, or they love your stories, food writing might come more easily to you.

Recipe writing, however, mimics technical writing more than narrative. It's extremely precise, detail oriented, and instructs the reader how to perform a task. Even so, cookbooks have introductory text and headnotes that draw readers in and tell stories. Recipe writing is a large piece of food writing, but not the whole story.

People always wonder if it's essential to have a degree from a culinary school or to have worked at a restaurant. The answer is no, but it helps. If you have neither, take cooking classes and build up your skills and knowledge by reading food magazines and reference books.

Many authors move into food writing from other careers. Those particularly suited might be chefs, newspaper reporters, teachers, caterers, recipe contest prizewinners, and cooking school students.

Some people have romantic ideas about food writing, and think it means free travel, free dining in fine restaurants, and free food delivered to the door. Sadly, this is fantasy, not reality. Travel writers, more often than not, pay their own expenses and hope to make them up in fees paid for stories. Restaurant reviewers are anonymous if they're any good, and therefore pay for their meals. Some publications reimburse, but many do not, although they pay (usually a pittance) for the article.

- Good writing is the essence. *Saveur* magazine Editor in Chief Colman Andrews says, "If you're not capable of being a good writer, you can't be a good food writer. It's about clarity of expression, style, voice, accuracy, knowledge of structure and rhythm of language. The idea that food writing is a separate discipline is false."

- Food writing should not have too many adjectives, clichés, and flowery metaphors. It also avoids overuse of the word "I." Many first-time writers start by putting their own experiences and memories down on paper, and that's perfectly legitimate. As they develop as writers, the first person becomes minimized.

- Many writers succeed by developing expertise and then writing about it. If you are an expert on Turkish food, for example, you'd do well to follow that path as a writer.

- The best food writers are persistent and have a thick skin. That's what it takes to get published. Editors, agents, and other gatekeepers drown under story and book proposals. Inquiring about yours, in a polite manner, is part of the job, as is understanding that rejection by one doesn't mean rejection by another.

Recommended Books

Allen, Gary. *Resource Guide for Food Writers*, http://www.foodbooks.com.

Herbst, Sharon Tyler. *The New Food Lover's Companion: Comprehensive Definitions of Nearly 6,000 Food, Drink, and Culinary Terms*. Barron's Cooking Guide, 2003.

Jacob, Dianne. *Will Write for Food*. New York: Marlowe and Company, 2005.

Kamp, David. *The United States of Arugula*. New York: Broadway Books, 2006.

Ostmann, Barbara Gibbs, and Jane Baker. *The Recipe Writer's Handbook*. Hoboken, NJ: Wiley, 2001.

Smith, Andrew F., ed. *The Oxford Encyclopedia of Food and Drink in America*. New York: Oxford University Press, 2004.

Steingarten, Jeffrey. *It Must've Been Something I Ate*. New York: Knopf, 2002.

Stern, Jane and Michael. *Roadfood*. New York: Broadway Books, 2002.

Trillin, Calvin. *Third Helpings: A Sequel to American Fried*. New York: Penguin, 1984.

Alice, Let's Eat. Boston: Ticknor and Fields, 1983.

Truss, Lynne. *Eats, Shoots and Leaves: The Zero Tolerance Approach to Punctuation*. New York: Gotham Books, 2004.

Professional Organizations

American Society of Journalists and Authors (ASJA), http://www.asja.org. ASJA Contracts Watch offers a free service that updates writers about the latest negotiations in print and electronic publishing.

Authors Guild, http://www.authorsguild.org

The International Association Culinary Professionals (IACP) is a not-for-profit professional association that provides continuing education and development for its members who are engaged in the areas of culinary education, communication, or in the preparation of food and drink. The worldwide membership of nearly four thousand encompasses over thirty-five countries and is literally a who's who of the world of food. The organization has an annual conference in April where you can meet many of the important people in the food media. http://www.iacp.com

International Food, Wine and Travel Writers Association, http://www.ifwtwa.org

National Writers Union, http://www.nwu.org. Ask the organization for their Freelance Writers' Guide. It is an extremely useful compilation of information.

The Symposium for Professional Food Writers is a popular conference for professional food writers and editors. It is limited to ninety attendees and customarily held in the spring at the Greenbrier in White Sulphur Springs, West Virginia. A team of successful writers leads discussions and workshops. http://www.greenbrier.com/site/foodwriters.aspx

Web sites

If you have hunted without success for a food book, or cookbook you will almost surely find it at

---

"We have three hundred thousand loyal customers who know it is often cumbersome and time-consuming to search for a certain title or type of book at a large chain bookstore. We take much of the work out of selecting a book. I look at what readers are asking for and give them the best of the best—at the best possible price."

—**PAT ADRIAN**, former editorial director of the Good Cook Book Club. For more information visit http://www.bookspan.com.

http://www.alibris.com

Chowhound, to gather and exchange information,
chowhound.com

E-gullet Society for Culinary Arts and Letters,
http://www.egullet.org

Jessica's Biscuit, an online cookbook store,
http://www.ecookbooks.com

http://www.thinkexist.com

• RECIPE FOR SUCCESS •

FREELANCE WRITING AS A BUSINESS

by Cynthia Glover

 MAKING A LIVING as a freelance writer has always been a dicey business, but these days, given the budgetary constraints of newspapers, magazines, and book publishers, it is especially difficult. One answer is to look beyond traditional definitions of freelance writing to explore new ideas and markets.

A survey conducted by the International Association of Culinary Professionals a few years ago revealed that many of its members earn less than twelve thousand dollars per year. Very few earn more than fifty or sixty thousand dollars, or what can be considered a decent salary.

I started writing about food ten years ago, when I decided to take a sabbatical from a freelance corporate copywriting practice. A friend asked if I wanted to do some work for *Baltimore* magazine. Shortly thereafter I became the magazine's restaurant reviewer. Ultimately, I became its food and wine editor, a largely ceremonial position that didn't pay anything but did put me on the masthead and gave me first crack at writing features. I started writing for other magazines, too, and became known as a regional expert on the culinary scene. But I wasn't earning much money.

A friend recommended me to the travel section of the *New York Times*, but I quickly realized that writing for such publications, while exciting, still doesn't go too far toward paying the bills. The typical fees paid for most travel articles don't come anywhere close to covering the costs of the kind of trip it takes to get into a national publication. At the same time, many publications ban writers from subsidizing the trip through press junkets. Many who write for major travel sections have other jobs that actually support them. For them, such newspaper assignments provide the gravy, not the meat and potatoes, of life.

Two years ago, I quit restaurant reviewing, but continued writing articles for magazines and newspapers on farming, food, and travel. Newspapers in particular just chew up ideas. I ended up with a terrific pile of clips, but I felt worn out, and still didn't have much money to show for it.

That's when I decided to found Smart Works, a marketing company that handles advertising, graphic design, publicity, and media placement for culinary and other clients. I wanted to combine my old skills as a

continued

continued from page 149

corporate marketing writer with the connections and reputation developed in ten years of food writing. The Harbor Court Hotel in Baltimore and Cabot Creamery in Vermont were among my first clients. I still write for magazines and newspapers, and I'm testing out the possibilities of balancing editorial and corporate writing.

My advice to a freelance writer is to see yourself as a business. Decide how you are going to define profit and loss, both in terms of money and energy. Freelancing requires constant evaluation of the marketplace, looking beyond the obvious kinds of work, and developing a real sense of what's important to you. To succeed you really must branch out, do many different things, and upgrade the skill sets that can improve your income.

On a basic level, freelancers don't know what to charge for their services because they are accustomed to taking what has been offered. I have an hourly rate. When I submit a proposal, I determine how many hours it will take to complete this job and I use this measure to calculate the total cost. It's important to be realistic about whether the pay is commensurate with the work.

• MATTERS OF FACT •

- Freelance food writers may be paid by the word, with rate ranging from two cents a word to considerably more, depending on the renown of the writer and the circulation and the solvency of the publication. Zero is the sum customarily paid (grudgingly) by scholarly journals. Dazzling five or six figure payments are (occasionally) remitted by a high-profile publication.

- The writer signs a contract specifying the target word count and delivery date for the article and spelling out the rights of both author and publisher. Three months after the article is published, the author usually has the right to reuse the material. If an article or recipes are to be included in book form, the original publisher will request permission to reprint and pay the author an additional (small) fee.

- If the original publisher posts your work on the Internet, it is unlikely you will receive any additional compensation. This is a matter of considerable concern to writers, but there has so far been no satisfactory resolution of the matter.

- Many cookbooks have a shelf life somewhere between milk and yogurt.

MEMOIR WRITING

I've discovered memoirs fall into distinct genres, such as exotic locations, histories, and, lately—sex. Ethel G. Hofman wrote a beautiful journal titled *Mackerel at Midnight: Growing Up Jewish on a Remote Scottish Island.* The Shetlands Isles are so far north they are almost out of this world, as is her recipe for Coggly Woggly that would warm many a chilly morning.

Irish food is gaining attention, but on the whole there have been relatively few diarists from the British Isles since Samuel Pepys, who was born in London in 1633, the fifth of eleven children. He wisely observed, "A good dinner and feasting reconciles everybody." He didn't add that it also prompts far too many authors to relive their childhood meals.

Nigel Slater wrote *Toast*, a memoir in which he reminisced about his mom, who burned the toast regularly. He also remembered the family trifle: a traditional English pudding made with canned fruit cocktail, Jell-O, cooking sherry, leftover cake, and custard. He wrote, "Christmas stood or fell according to the noise the trifle made when the first spoonful was lifted out. The resulting noise, a sort of squelch-fart, was like a message from God. A silent trifle was a bad omen." Now that's great writing.

Such fond memories surely paved the way for the success of Fat Duck, London's hottest restaurant where guests can sup on snail porridge, sardines on toast sorbet, and bacon-and-egg ice cream. "How cool is that?" as Rachael Ray might ask.

Madhur Jaffrey remembers her childhood in India. Paul Kovi, former ringmaster at the Four Seasons restaurant in Manhattan, recalled *Transylvanian Cuisine*. *Ant Egg Soup* describes life in Laos and Cambodia. Peter Mayle's *A Year in Provence* went platinum. Frances Mayes's *Under the Tuscan Sun* blazed the way for countless others to chronicle their life stories. Michael Redclift, a social historian and ecology scholar, makes a valiant leap for immorality with his tome, *Chewing Gum*, which traces how one of the world's most useless products gave rise to a Mayan revolution in the Yucatan jungle.

The ever-erudite Calvin Trillin put Kansas City on the gastronomic map. "The most remarkable thing about my mother is that for thirty years she served the family nothing but leftovers. The original meal has never been found," he observes. His first and perhaps best book is *American Fried*.

Amanda Hesser carved an engrossing food diary about her enchanted romance with Mr. Latte. Betty Fussell describes *My Kitchen Wars*, in which she details the collapse of her marriage while skillfully weaving the thread of food preparation throughout the narrative.

Love, marriage, and food rightfully belong on the same page, but what about sex? It's hard to understand why a restaurant critic, who goes to absurd lengths to render herself incognito, would be willing to bare all her indiscretions and sexual liaisons, but Gael Greene, the former powerful restaurant reviewer for *New York* magazine, lays out her extraordinarily athletic love life in her porno-chic *Insatiable: Tales from a Life of Delicious Excess*. She brazenly puts forth the astonishing proposition that food and sex are inextricably intertwined. Who knew? Ruth Reichl tells it like it was in *Tender at the Bone* with talk of sex and tales about her mother.

Paul Levy, a renowned raconteur who describes his Kentucky childhood in *Finger Lickin' Good*, suggests that all autobiographers have a problem conjuring with the truth. He says, "Memoir writing gives us a chance to play God and re-create our own families."

Alan Richman's *Fork It Over: The Intrepid Adventures of a Professional Eater* chronicles his brilliant career as a wonderfully witty restaurant critic. In *The Debt to Pleasure*, John Lanchester reveals his philosophy about more or less everything from the erotica of distaste to the psychology of the menu. Michael Pollan has moved on from *The Botany of Desire* to contemplate *The Omnivore's Dilemma: A Natural History of Four Meals*. These books constitute essential reading.

And here come chef whisperers who trod their path through dark Satanic kitchens before ascending to the highest rungs leading to haute. Sirio, the haughtiest haute of them all, coauthored his biography, titled simply *Sirio*. He was preceded by George Lang, Jacques Pépin, and many illustrious others.

Chroniclers have detailed the lives of M. F. K. Fisher, James Beard, Julia Child, and undoubtedly many more memories of Italian mothers and grandmothers' kitchens will continue to pour forth, but in case you might have missed them, two of my favorite memorable memoirs are *Epitaph for a Peach* by David Maas Masimoto and *Meal Observed* by Andrew Todhunter, whose reflections on Taillevent in Paris will caress the palate in your mind, as will Georgeanne Brenner's *A Pig in Provençe*.

HOW TO INTERVIEW AND PROFILE A CELEBRITY CHEF

Interviewing is a complex skill. Don't ask questions with answers you could have found in advance. Try instead to think of questions no one else has asked. But if you are not certain the information you have is right, ask for confirmation. Facts need to be verified. It is okay to go back and check, but not too often. (You should have been listening carefully in the first place.)

Study the pros to learn how to be a better interviewer. Don't ask confrontational questions like, "Do you think the recently fired chef is a jerk?" Instead, lead off questions with, "What were your impressions of . . ." or "Many people are saying . . ." or "What can you say to people who think . . ." or "Do you think it is possible that . . ." Like a good waiter, you have to learn when to wait; when the subject of your interview is about to say something else but is hesitating to reveal something important, just wait. The tension of silence may cause him to blurt out something interesting.

Don't quote anonymous sources. This is the bailiwick of political reporters. If you print false information purposefully or even accidentally, you can be sued. You can also be in serious trouble if you reveal anything that is clearly intended to be off the record, even if the subject of the interview has not specifically said it is privileged information.

Your job is not to provide your opinion or share your experience. The profile is not about you. It is the writer's job is to present the subject's story accurately. A playwright puts words in the actors' mouths. An interviewer puts another person's words on the page in the rhythm and cadence in which they were spoken.

If there is a question that may anger the person being interviewed, save it for last. It's like nibbling around the edges before taking the last bite. Everyone has an agenda. Determine your own agenda first.

NEWSLETTERS

If you study newsletters, you will quickly recognize the ones that are most effective in conveying their message and what moves readers to subscribe to them. This is a category of publishing often overlooked by would-be food writers.

There are nearly ten thousand newsletter listings on the Internet. Among the best food-specific ones are:

- *Simple Cooking* showcases John Thorne's stylistic prose in the food newsletter that he publishes with his wife Matt Lewis Thorne. www.outlawcook.com
- *The Art of Eating* carries Edward Behr's in-depth articles on major food and wine topics with emphasis on traditional artisanal methods on primarily French and Italian tables. http://www.artofeating.com
- Sandra L. Oliver's *Food History News* prints news, essays, book reviews, a reader's exchange, and a calendar of events, all pertaining to the food history of North America. http://www.Foodhistorynews.com

COOKBOOKS

Despite ample evidence to the contrary, the myth persists that all cookbooks sell. The grim truth is few authors earn back their advances and rumors abound that the sale of seventy-five hundred copies is considered to be an industry average. Nevertheless, hundreds of cookbooks are published every year; 432 cookbooks were submitted to the International Association of Culinary Professionals for cookbook awards in 2007, and that represents a mere fraction of the number produced.

Part of the difficulty a cookbook author faces is getting the book to stand out from its competitors. There is no other industry that produces so many versions of what is essentially the same product every year. Every cookbook must be positioned differently in the marketplace—a situation analogous to Kellogg launching 432 new breakfast cereals every year and trying to persuade consumers to sample each one.

Many otherwise sensible people have the quaint idea they could easily write a cookbook if only they had the time. Having possession of a collection of recipes is not sufficient reason to think they could be turned into a marketable cookbook; there is a craft to writing one, and it is an art. Some wryly suggest if you really want a cookbook, it is easier and faster to go out and buy one—and it's cheaper, too.

It may come as a surprise to realize that fashions in cookbooks are as fleeting as fashions in clothing. When Alfred A. Knopf published Julia Child's *Mastering the Art of French Cooking* with Simone Beck and Louisette Bertholle (an updated edition was published in 1983), it lit the fire of a burning interest in French cuisine. In the intervening thirty or forty years, cooking styles have come and gone, each with its own crop of must-have cookbooks. Despite this wide-ranging body of work, Americans recently seem most intrigued by cookbooks that tell them how to cook and how to do it quickly—preferably in thirty minutes or less. Keep an eye on the television cooking programs, food magazines, and newspaper food sections; they provide clues to recognizing where the market for cookbooks is headed.

GETTING STARTED

The first step is to choose a good (saleable) subject. The acquisitions (buying) editor at the publishing house has to convince the money people that your book will sell.

Assume you have chosen a great subject for a cookbook—let's say salads. If a previous book on salads had brisk sales, the editor is far more likely to look favorably on your proposal than if you are offering up an entirely new concept such as eel cookery of the Netherlands. The next step requires some research to define the market and evaluate the competition. You may be astounded to discover that in publishing, originality is not always a virtue and imitation is not always a vice.

Some ideas are too big for one book. For example, *Chicken Dishes of the World* might not be as attractive as *Fifteen-Minute Chicken Recipes*. It's best to keep the title to as few words as possible so the buyer can instantly grasp what you are selling. A great title is *How to Cook Everything*, by Mark Bittman. These few words

"Testing recipes for others makes a good portion of my living, and my clients find my services invaluable. These people are very busy cookbook novices who need an assured, objective hand to hone their recipes. My authors include professional restaurant chefs and bakers who are running a full-time business, celebrities writing cookbooks between television or concert appearances, editors who have collected recipes from home cooks writing in a variety of styles that need synchronization and non-American food writers whose books need testing with U.S. ingredients and kitchenware in order to work. I could make this list longer and give many more reasons why outside testing is often the only way to go. However, I am under deadline to finish testing 150 recipes for a celebrity chef and I have to get back to the kitchen."

—**RICK RODGERS**, cookbook doctor

■

immediately get the idea across. If you can't make your idea clear in three or four words, you have a problem. Of course, all rules have delightful exceptions, and among the most memorable are James Trager's delicious *The Enriched, Fortified, Concentrated, Country-Fresh, Lip-Smacking, Finger-Licking, International, Unexpurgated Foodbook.*

Writing a cookbook is a long-term project even for those who love their subject. Unless you plan to self-publish, writing a cookbook begins with crafting a proposal, finding an agent to represent you, and then finalizing the contract once a publishing house buys it. Quite a small book requires a huge amount of work, usually a minimum of a year to write and another year for the publishing house to produce it into a finished book. Some books take a lifetime.

KEYS TO SUCCESS

- Organize your time. Make a road map for yourself. Before writing a single word, decide what will be on every page and establish check-off dates to complete chapters of the book. Don't set off on your journey without knowing where you are going. By plotting the route, you will eventually save yourself a huge amount of time and anxiety.
- Listen to the advice of your literary agent and editor, who almost certainly know the marketplace better than most authors. Don't insist on doing something that may doom your book to the remainder table.
- The energy of the author can sell many more books than the efforts of the publisher. Plan to devote a considerable amount of time to marketing your cookbook through personal appearances, cooking demonstrations, and media interviews.
- Create your own Web site or blog. It needn't be elaborate, but it establishes a home base where you can be reached.

$\mathcal{C}$OOKBOOK COLLABORATOR

by David Joachim dsj@fast.net

THINK OF THE most successful cookbooks ever published: *The Joy of Cooking, Mastering the Art of French Cooking, The Silver Palate Cookbook*. These best-selling books all had multiple authors. While writers often describe what they do as a solitary act, you may find that collaborating on a cookbook gives you better results.

Cookbook collaborations work in a variety of ways. On one side of the spectrum, coauthors share similar interests and work hand in glove throughout the entire project. On the other side, a chef or expert provides the content and the writer puts that content into an appropriate form. Most collaborations fall somewhere in between these two extremes.

Whether you're a writer, chef, or a combination of the two, the first all-important step is to find the right collaborator. "A book is a creative project," says Melanie Barnard (melaniebarnard@aol.com), who has coauthored with Brooke Dojny on more than a dozen cookbooks, including *A Flash in the Pan*. "The key thing is an intrinsic, hard-to-find chemistry," she says. "You either click or you don't." An agent or editor can help make a good match. Or contact professionals in your neighborhood—those who teach cooking classes or whose names you see in magazine articles. Here are some tips to keep in mind when considering potential collaborators:

If you are a writer ask yourself:
- Does this chef have enough good material for a book?
- Will the amount of the advance be enough to pay for my services?
- Can I work harmoniously with this person?

If you are the chef:
- Does the writer understand what kind of book I want?
- Can the writer convey my style, voice, and creativity?
- Can I work harmoniously with this person?

Get It in writing

Plan to invest a day or so on the preliminaries—talking, sharing a meal together, reviewing each other's work. Before taking one more step, get a signed agreement. "There must be a collaboration agreement before one word of the book—or even the proposal—is written," advises Jane Dystel, president of Dystel and Goderich Literary Management, who represented this book and the work of dozens of successful chefs and writers.

A collaboration agreement is not a book contract with a publisher. Rather, it is a sort of prenuptial agreement between those producing the book, and it's the second most important part of the process after the personal chemistry. Agents usually handle the nitty-gritty of agreements. "If there are two agents," says Dystel,

continued

continued from page 157

"the agents will negotiate between them for the collaboration agreement, but the chef's agent will usually sell the book proposal to the publisher."

A good agreement will clearly delineate duties for each party, a work schedule, and details of compensation. For instance, how much will the writer be paid for writing the proposal? I've charged proposal fees ranging from five hundred to six thousand dollars, depending on the length and depth of the proposal. Judge your fee based on the amount of work required. The agreement should also answer sticky questions like, who owns the proposal if the book doesn't sell?

What happens if the collaboration turns sour before the book is complete? Are both parties jointly or individually responsible for book expenses like photography, the index, and publicity? Who holds the copyright to the work? How will each person be paid for and credited on the book?

When considering payment, "Keep in mind the financial realities of the book," counsels Rick Rodgers (rick@rickrodgers.com), who has collaborated on more than fifteen cookbooks and authored more than twenty others, including, most recently, *The Carefree Cook*. "Let's suppose a restaurant chef is lucky and gets a one-hundred-thousand-dollar advance," says Rodgers. "He takes about thirty thousand dollars off for the photography and will eventually pay about a third of the advance in taxes. Figure he now has forty thousand dollars to split with the collaborating writer. You have to ask yourself, Can I write, edit, and/or test 150 chef recipes for twenty thousand dollars? The answer may be no, because in the above scenario, you (as the writer and recipe tester) will also take off a third for taxes and about five thousand dollars for groceries. That leaves you with only eight or nine thousand dollars for six to eight months of your time. If you consider that many advances don't come close to a celebrity chef's hundred thousand dollars, and the agent's fee will average 15 percent of the advance, a careful calculation of the split between collaborators becomes even more important."

Make sure that you will be fairly compensated for your end of the deal. On some projects, the writer is paid a flat work-for-hire fee for the service. Other times the writer gets a percentage of the book advance and royalties. Percentages may even fluctuate throughout stages of writing and sales. For the book *Fresh Choices*, I received 100 percent of the advance and my coauthor Rochelle Davis will receive 100 percent of the royalties until we are evenly compensated. After that, future royalties will be split 50-50. Many authors cite a 50-50 split of advance and royalties, but deals vary considerably. "In most of my deals, the writer gets about 40 percent," says Dystel. "Generally, the more money the writer gets, the less credit he or she gets."

It's helpful to think about what means more to you: a big paycheck or your name on the cover. "I used to say that the only place I care where my name appears is on the check!" quips Mary Goodbody, a seasoned food writer who has collaborated and/or worked on more than fifty books, including *Taste: Pure and Simple*, cowritten with chef Michel Nischan. "But over the years, I've moved from the acknowledgements page to the cover," she says. If you do get cover credit, be prepared to discuss whose name comes first, how big, where the names are printed, and whether the names are connected by the word *with* or *and*. These may seem like trifling matters, but they connote a different level of collaboration between the authors.

Sometimes, you don't know who worked on the cookbook because the collaborator is not named. Rick Rodgers has worked behind the scenes on several chef cookbooks and prefers that anonymity. "I'm not a big *and* or *with* person," he says. "A client's ego can sometimes be a little delicate. I find it psychologically advantageous to let the chef be the star. After all, whose book is the public buying?" Decide on a per-project basis whether it's best to have your name on the cover or not.

The collaboration agreement should protect your interests when you get a book contract with a publisher. Then you can get down to the interesting work of putting the book together. In the chef-and-writer scenario, the chef typically provides the recipes, stories, voice, and signature personality. The writer magically channels these elements into the recipe headnotes, sidebars, chapter text, and introduction. "The best collaborations have been when I am standing next to the chef and they're cooking," says Rodgers. "That's when the little secrets and stories come out. It's my job to ask, why did you put that duck breast in a cold pan?"

Keep in mind that if you are a writer collaborating with a big-name chef, you won't be the one on TV, talking with reporters, and doing book signings. But you may be paid well and get some recognition for your work. If you are the big-name chef, know that you'll have to spend time working closely with the writer to get the best results.

Either way, having a coauthor can help to make big book project less daunting and make good use of each person's expertise. It can also save time if you've got other pots on the fire. "Many of my books are companion books to television shows," said Julia Child. "*Baking with Julia* was written by Dorie Greenspan, while I was taping the show. Dorie was right there watching me measure things out. Without a collaborator, we couldn't have done the book at all because there wasn't the time."

Be on the lookout for collaborative opportunities that may call for your unique skills. You never know when a collaborative project will pop up, and what it may lead to. "For *Mastering the Art of French Cooking*," said Julia, "I collaborated with French colleagues who needed someone who spoke English to help write the book."

Keep an open mind, and you may find a successful collaboration changes you life.

Five Ways To Find A Collaborator

Whether you are a chef who needs a writer or a writer who needs work, you may benefit from collaborating on a project. Here's how to find a good coauthor.

- Look at chef cookbooks. Check bylines and acknowledgements in your favorite cookbooks for leads on potential writers or other collaborators.
- Contact someone who has collaborated before. A colleague who has coauthored a book can offer valuable insight.
- Check with writers' organizations. Post a job (or scan for one) on the National Writers Union job list. Or use the writer referral service at the American Society of Journalists and Authors.
- Ask agents and editors. Schedule brief appointments at professional conferences to pinpoint the right person.
- Make direct contact. If you see book potential in a chef's or other expert's work, contact them directly and ask if they would like to collaborate on a cookbook.

David Joachim has written, edited, or collaborated on more than twenty-five cookbooks. With Rochelle Davis, founder of Generation Green, a nonprofit organization that focuses on food policy and children's health, he cowrote *Fresh Choices: Easy Recipes for Pure Food When You Can't Buy 100% Organic. His most recent book is* the *Food Substitutions Bible: More than 5,000 substitutions for Ingredients, Equipment and Techniques.*

SINGLE-SUBJECT COOKBOOKS

Books on single subjects often have a good long life. A clearly defined single-subject book that is moderately priced will often outsell a general topic. Apple pie, potato salad, and Christmas cookies are excellent topics.

If you have a passion, you might think about a single-subject book. There is always room for a new take on such topics as pies or barbecue or tomatoes or chocolate or fish or pasta or whole grains and greens.

From time to time there is considerable interest in such subjects as microwaves, slow cookers, pressure cookers, ice cream machines, pasta machines, and bread machines. Small recipe booklets that also describe how to use the appliance may be written specifically for the manufacturer and packaged in the box in which it is sold. When a new product appears on the market, contact the manufacturer immediately to offer your services to write recipes and other support materials.

ℱOOD WRITER AND FOOD HISTORIAN

by Betty Fussell

A LONG TIME ago and for a very long time, I led, as a writer, a double life. My respectable job was to write literary criticism for academic journals while teaching Shakespeare and the history of English literature during the college term. My underground job was to write travel articles for newspapers and magazines during the summer. The best part about the moonlighting job was discovering that the easiest way to write about travel was to write about food. Food by definition was fun, but I had no idea that food would take over my life.

My first two books came out within a year of each other and they neatly summarized my double life. *Mabel*, a biography of Mabel Normand published in 1982, was the culmination of ten years of research into the history of early Hollywood and silent movies. I chose to write about Normand because she expressed a new vision of the American girl—a bathing beauty, an athlete, and a comedienne shaped entirely by the movies. The following year, I published *Masters of American Cookery*. It took a close look at the work of M. F. K. Fisher, James Beard, Craig Claiborne, and Julia Child and considered their collective wisdom. Since I'd spent most of my adult life feeding other people, I thought I surely knew something about the subject without resorting to libraries, but it hadn't occurred to me that the history of food was a subject as worthy of study as the history of drama, literature, or any other art or craft.

While I was undecided whether to follow up *Mabel* with a biography of Jean Harlow or maybe Carole Lombard, I kept on cooking and reading and interviewing because I'd gotten hooked on the question of whether there was such a thing as American cookery, and if so, what it was and where it had come from. Also, as an American, I wanted to know about myself. Without noticing, I was continuing to be a travel writer, but I was doing it in my own country instead of Europe, hopping from Vermont to Charlestown to New Orleans to Santa Fe to Seattle to Milwaukee, combining what I had learned from journalism with what I had learned as an academic historian, blending together my bifurcated writing styles.

When asked what I was doing, I'd say "I'm a food historian," and people would squint and say, "What's that?" It was a good question and the truth was I had backed into the subject of food almost by accident, but once inside, I was delighted I'd taken the bait because I relished the combination of talking to people, cooking, writing, eating, exploring, discovering—without end. To me, that was an extraordinary discovery. The history of food, I saw, was the history of mankind, and you could take it anywhere and everywhere you wanted to on the immense grid of past and present.

Over the past decade, to my real surprise, that is just what happened. Even as I write this, foods are being mapped, surveyed, and classified into a multiplicity of culinary sites by people with a great variety of motives but a common cause of exploration. Food writing, food history, and food studies have swelled from a few rivulets of gastronomic essays to a snowmelt of personal memoirs to a tsunami of academic treatises. Food, thank God, has joined the pantheon of subjects that matter, like sex, death, movies, and how best to live in a world we are constantly destroying. Like someone you love—man, woman, or child—the subject of food is inexhaustible and infinitely rewarding because it links all of our individual and shared pasts to our communal present.

Recommended Books

de Silva, Cara, ed. *In Memory's Kitchen: A Legacy From the Women of Terezin.* Translation by Bianca Steiner Brown, foreword by Michael Berenbaum. Northvale, NJ: Aronson, 1996.

An extraordinary, haunting, brilliant book.

Fussell, Betty. *The Story of Corn.* University of New Mexico Press, 2004

Hofman, Ethel G. *Mackerel At Midnight: Growing Up Jewish on a Remote Scottish Island.* Camino Books, 2005.

A memoir that will delight and enthrall every reader who may not have even the remotest connection to the title.

Nathan, Joan. *The Flavor of Jerusalem.* New York: Little, Brown, 1975. Among the distinguished authors who have drawn on their life experiences to write extraordinarily excellent books are Joan Nathan, whose meticulous research and gift of speaking—and more importantly, listening—to others has resulted in several groundbreaking books including this award-winning title.

Visser, Margaret. *Much Depends on Dinner.* Collier Books, 1986.

A particularly valuable book to include in your personal library.

For More Information

Advice on Research and Writing is a collection of advice about how to do research and how to communicate effectively, primarily for computer scientists, but there are some items of interest to all. www-2.cs.cmu.edu/afs/cs.cmu.edu/user/mleone/web/how-to.html

Citation Style for Research Papers from B. Davis Schwartz Memorial Library, Long Island University, C. W. Post Campus, is a colorful presentation of the various bibliographic styles. http://www.liu.edu/cwis/cwp/library/workshop/citation.htm

Literary Marketplace, the ultimate insider's guide to the U.S. book publishing industry, covering every conceivable aspect of the business, is available in most libraries. http://www.literarymarketplace.com

Publishers Weekly magazine, http://www.publishersweekly.com

Purdue University's Online Writing Lab (OWL) has handouts available on topics including general writing concerns, avoiding plagiarism, research and documenting sources; English as a second language, and professional writing. http://owl.english.purdue.edu/

Resources on Writing—many print references on writing are gathered by the Survival Skills and Ethics Program of the University of Pittsburgh. http://www.survival.pitt.edu/library/biblio/writing.asp

Roget's Internet Thesaurus, http://thesaurus.reference.com/

Strunk, William, Jr, and E. B. White. *The Elements of Style.* 4th ed. Boston: Allyn and Bacon, 2000.

The University of Wisconsin's Madison Writing Center Writer's Handbook has access to information on grammar and style, documentation, academic writing, reviews, and more. http://www.wisc.edu/writing/Handbook/index.html

• MATTERS OF FACT •

- Approximately 40 million cookbooks are sold every year in the United States.
- One in every four books purchased in the U.S. is a cookbook. More than four hundred cookbooks are published every year; down from 702 in 1987, but they are still the perennial number-three selling category in Barnes & Noble stores.
- The typical cookbook buyer purchases one to four cookbooks a year.
- In 1994 Oprah Winfrey's former private weight-loss chef sold 5.4 million copies of her book, *In the Kitchen with Rosie.* This book holds the all-time record for sales in a single year by a single author, though Rachael Ray is likely to eclipse this record.
- More than 30 million copies of *The Better Homes and Gardens Cookbook* have been sold since it was first published in 1930.
- More than 25 percent of all cookbooks are sold through book clubs like the Good Cook Book Club, which has more than three hundred thousand members, or Jessica's Biscuit (named for the owners' dog), another popular club.
- Close to 30 percent of all cookbooks purchased are given as gifts. Please note, if you are writing a book on dieting, you cannot give it as a gift (even politely to your best friend).
- A first-time unknown author may receive an advance as low as seventy-five hundred dollars, although it could be considerably more.
- Elizabeth Schneider's' brilliant cookbook, *Vegetables from Amaranth to Zucchini: The Essential Reference* was named book of the year by both the James Beard Foundation and the International Association of Culinary Professionals. This dual recognition is incredibly rare and her book deserves the highest honors.

▶ Literary Agent

A literary agent represents the author of a book to publishers and ensures that every publishing transaction a writer makes is fair. It is as important to find the right literary agent who will represent your work conscientiously, as it is to find the right publisher to produce your work respectfully. A small group of literary agents devote most of their energies to cookbooks. Most work on the East or West coasts, where the large publishing houses are located.

A good agent knows the editors personally and knows which ones are most likely to be interested in your subject. The most experienced agents have worked with cookbook editors for many years and know where to submit a proposal. Many editors only consider proposals submitted by an agent.

The bad news is that it is almost as difficult to find an agent as it is to find a publisher. An agent won't waste her or his time trying to sell a proposal unless she or he thinks it will find a home.

Usually, an agent asks the author to sign a contract stipulating the agency will receive a commission for the agent's services, which means they will take a percentage of the funds advanced to the author and book royalties. (This is generally in the 15 percent range.)

Other than access to publishers—which is critically important—the agent negotiates the author's contract. Most contain standard, boilerplate stuff, and are not open to further discussion. Among the areas that are up for debate are the amount of money given to the author as an advance, delivery dates, and royalty scales. If these terms sound unfamiliar, you need an agent.

The author receives payments at stages; the first is typically received when the contract is signed and the next is paid at different points in the publication process. All are contingent on the author meeting the terms of the contract. Usually, there are no more than three payments, and this schedule is a kind of insurance for the publisher, who wants to make sure the author won't complain too loudly or actually refuse to make any of the editor's suggested changes.

The agent also negotiates the vexing question of who pays for certain things such as photography. Sometimes the publisher advances the cost of photography, but the fees may be deducted from the authors' future earnings. Occasionally, the agent is able to persuade the publisher to pay for the index, though frequently this is a cost billed to the author.

The author is always responsible for obtaining written permission to quote from another writer's work and will be required to pay any fees that are incurred. Even dead authors are entitled to payments, remitted to their estate.

Lisa Ekus-Saffir, who is an agent for numerous cookbook authors, says, "Having representation tells an editor that your book project has been vetted by a professional who thinks highly enough of you to take it on. Agents offer third-party endorsement and respect in the industry. I review inquiries within four weeks of receiving them and I turn down better than 50 percent. Why? First, the material must be well written, well presented, and it must interest me. Sometimes it's a good proposal but conflicts with another client and project I'm already representing. But often I receive proposals that are incomplete, poorly researched, or on a subject that's been done to death. If I'm intrigued with a concept and feel it's viable, I will work with an author to create a solid proposal package." The Lisa Ekus Group, LLC, (http://www.lisaekus.com) specializes in culinary public relations, media training, and representing authors as a literary agent.

To get started as a literary agent, apply for a position with an agency that is representing the kind of books that appeal to you. Many authors thank their agent on the acknowledgement pages of their books and so with just a little detective work you can easily track them down.

▶ **Cookbook Editor**

A good editor has the curiosity, energy, and ability to bring out the best in another person's work. Few writers are good editors and the process of editing and writing are collaborative ventures. The editor performs a role every bit as important as a lawyer for the accused.

A cookbook editor first makes the judgment about the salability of a proposal based on the sales history of books in a similar genre, the name recognition of the author, and the perceived ability of the author to come up with the goods. The editor must decide if the author has the skill to write the material, organize it sensibly, deliver it according to the terms of the contract, and promote the book.

Once a project is taken onboard, the editor helps shape it and then reviews the manuscript for its content, style, structure, and pacing. The voice of the author is respected by the most conscientious of editors and trampled upon by an intrusive, insensitive one.

A great editor can make the material soar; her work is not limited to editing. She (and in the cookbook arena it is often woman) decides which photographer to commission, works with the art director to create the design of the book, and with the sales staff and the publicity and marketing people.

If the editor is displeased with the manuscript, she has the option of asking the author to make requested changes, assigning the manuscript to a "book doctor" to heal the affliction (in which case the consultation fee is charged to the author), or canceling the contract. In the last case, the author may be required to repay the fees that have been advanced. This is the worst possible scenario, but it does happen occasionally. The best way to ensure both the author and the editor are happy is to establish good lines of communication from day one.

When the editor is satisfied with all aspects of the manuscript, she sends it to the production department, where it is copyedited, proofread, and prepped for printing. The final step before the book is printed is to decide how many copies to print. The publisher determines the specific quantity after consultation with the sales experts.

To get started as an editor, apply for a position as an editorial assistant in a publishing house. To find the name of the publishers who specialize in cookbooks, visit your local bookstore and study the cookbook section. Publishers' catalogs are also available on the Internet.

▶ Copy Editor, Fact Checker, Proofreader, and Indexer

The task of a copy editor is to quietly set about correcting all the authors' egregious errors, appalling typographical errors, questionable punctuation, and idiosyncratic grammar. She points out contradictions, inconsistencies, ridiculous claims, questionable statistics, and the accuracy of quotations and alleged facts. She makes sure all the headings are uniform, the page references are correct, and generally nit-picks her way through the copy. She asks impossible-to-answer questions and generally turns sloppy writing into sparkling material for which the author customarily takes full credit without offering a single word of thanks.

The copy editor is an invaluable, though often unrecognized, member of the editorial team. Often an accomplished cook, a skillful cookbook copy editor recognizes missing ingredients in recipes and questions the author if the quantity of an ingredient appears to be incorrect.

A fact checker double-checks all the alleged facts and holds the author accountable for verifying the accuracy (and provenance) of every statement of fact that is asserted or implied in the manuscript. Often, the copy editor is also the fact checker.

The proofreader is the last person to read the typeset book before it begins its journey to the printer. His or her job is to pay attention and make sure there are no ghastly mistakes, repetitions, or problems, such as referring the reader to an incorrect page number. A parallel obligation is to make sure no one ends up with egg on their face. This is a great job for a person with extensive culinary knowledge and a keen editorial eye.

The indexer scours the edited manuscript to create a reasonable and comprehensive index. These days, software helps indexers create their lists, but it still requires someone with an understanding of recipes and cooking. For instance, the indexer decides how the reader will best find all the recipes for chicken, as well as all that include the word *tomato* in their titles. Anyone who uses cookbooks knows how valuable a well-crafted index can be.

Recommended Books
Desaulniers, Marcel. *I'm Dreaming of a Chocolate Christmas.*
   Hoboken, NJ: Wiley, 2007
Death by Chocolate.
Desserts to Die For.
An Alphabet of Sweets.

INDEPENDENT BOOK SELLERS

With the proliferation of large chain bookstores such as Barnes and Noble and Borders and the growth of the Internet book-selling Web sites such as amazon.com and allbookstores.com, independent bookstores are becoming more endangered. A few brave owners remain, which is good news for cookbook authors. Independent bookstores love cookbook authors. They draw people into the store with cooking demos. And their books tend to sell well in this setting.

In the estimation of many food professionals and cookbook collectors, the best independent cookbook store in the United States is Kitchen Arts and Letters in New York City. Kitchen Arts and

THE TRUE MEASURE of the commercial success of a cookbook is the length of time it continues to sell. The only syndicated service that offers a complete picture of the publishing industry is http://www.ipsos-insight.com, which reported the decline from 45.8 million cookbooks sold in 2000 to 38.9 million the following year. Some publishing authorities predict the slide will continue as fewer people cook at home and more rely on the Internet to find their recipes. Even so, sales of cookbooks are astonishingly high, particularly those that make ideal gifts during the Christmas season.

Letters sells more copies of distinguished, scholarly books than any other enterprise. This destination cookbook store stands squarely at the epicenter of delight on the route of all cookbook lovers, and contains thousands of current and rare books.

CULINARY BOOKSELLER

by Nach Waxman

HOW DOES ONE get to be a bookseller? In just the way most people end up finding their careers—by indirection, by false starts, by making decisions that may have seemed to be good ideas at the time but less so later on, by rebounding, by accumulating knowledge and experience, and, of course, by plain luck. The combination of unpredictable events and unfathomable choices that bring us to what we become in our lives is somewhat like the way that the random combing of our parents' genes helped direct our physical makeup. For many people, both processes turn out, surprisingly, to stimulate growth in new directions, to promote vigor and opportunities for innovation. It appears that what is indeterminate in the ways that we are shaped and in the ways that we have developed proves quite often to be very much to our benefit.

My particular story begins with entering college at Cornell, where I first concentrated in chemistry. Chemistry was supplanted in barely more than a semester by a new love: anthropology. That was a rather more protracted affair, which ran out of steam at Harvard nearly eight years later. Adrift, I found myself in New York, casting about, hardly encouraged by those who informed me that in the real world, my fine record and my impressive education had me pegged as little more than unskilled labor.

Publishing, a career counselor informed me, was a good soft landing place for those whose academic balloons had sprung a leak and were falling irreversibly toward earth. Fine, I said. I had grown up with books and loved to write, so why not?

First, I went to work writing for, then editing, encyclopedias. A few years later I entered the world of trade books, those general interest publications sold in bookstores. Over time I acquired and edited every sort of nonfiction, from archeology to biography, natural history, and deep-sea fishing. That was good and often interesting, but something in me made me certain that I really didn't want to keep working for others, but, for better or worse, to be my own boss, to pilot my own vessel. Unable to visualize that vessel with any precision, nor ready to give it a specific name, I stayed on in publishing for more than a dozen years, scratching my head, talking to friends, barking up innumerable wrong trees, until after silent adventures too harrowing and far too embarrassing to recount (innkeeping in rural Vermont was one starry-eyed, derivative notion, not quite as self-destructive as many of the others), I had to admit that books still had me in their firm but nurturing grip.

In time I came to realize that I would start a bookstore—not itself a tremendously original idea, but here is where it began to get exciting. I knew enough about myself to realize that mastery of a single subject, rather than dabbling in many, was my way of going at things. So starting not just a bookstore but a specialized one, it was clear, was the way to go. Sports? Health? History? The occult? No, there was one love in my life that rivaled books, and that was food. It struck me that from the time I had started cooking in my off-campus apartment at college, to my graduate school summer job as a private chef for a family on an island off the coast of Maine, to writing and submitting recipes to general magazines, to editing a number of cookbooks in my nonfiction publishing mix, I had been grazing absently at the margins of a captivating field; I was right on the edge of blue-grass heaven and never even knew it.

But that wasn't all. The more I thought about it the more I recognized that this could be a really good business. I saw that the food industry was a huge one, with perhaps a third of our population engaged in the activities that feed the rest of us: chefs, restaurateurs, caterers, those who grow food, those who process and package it, and those who ship it and sell it. And there are others, too: people who wait tables in restaurants and work in bakeries; who write and publish about food; who teach about it; who explore its scientific, historical, and social dimensions; and, of course, the millions who prepare it in their home kitchens and serve it, daily, to their families.

The subject is immense, but interestingly, when, in 1983, I opened Kitchen Arts and Letters in New York City, there were fewer than a dozen such shops in the entire world. There are barely more than that today. Clearly nothing is ever as big as one imagines it can be. We all get cold noses in winter; it has not been shown that there are fortunes to be made in nose-warmers. But with a professional base, backed up by a great sprawling constituency of motivated home

continued

continued from page 169

cooks, I have a good, solid business; it's one that attracts only cus-tomers who are really interested in what we have to offer; one in which people are willing to spend more and not confine their spending to cer-tain seasons of the year; one that draws those who know a lot about our subjects—often a lot more than we know—and therefore from whom we learn much every day; one that is known to its users as a great good place where their colleagues come to exchange news and gossip, discuss methods and ingredients, and perhaps even learn about jobs.

It is also a place in which I can satisfy my need for mastery, sur-rounding myself with not just cookbooks, but also books on food sci-ence, on cooking creativity, on restaurant business and economics, on food in literature and the arts, on collecting kitchen antiques, on agri-culture, on the sociology and anthropology of food, on wine and wine-makers, on the lives of those who have worked in food, and on the rich, entertaining history of cooking and gastronomy. And all of that is offered in current books, as well as in older ones, no longer in print, and in many languages, and at many levels, from manuals and guides for beginners to scholarly works for those who do rich and original thinking. We carry all of these.

It is quite wonderful; a world of good, hard knowledge contained within the covers of somewhere around fifteen thousand books, a repository to be shared by my staff, our customers, and me. This excit-ing store offers me an untold intellectual bounty, day in, day out, year in, year out. It also offers me a living and the opportunity to do reward-ing practical work.

This is not some utopian library, but a business; a business that has to keep records, pay taxes, restock its shelves, unpack boxes, open mail, write checks, ship parcels, and perform a hundred other activities that make it clear that heaven does indeed rest on pillars of earth. But whatever it is, whatever it has become, it all began with directionless exploration, with barely-informed hunches, with growing awareness of personal prejudices and temptations, with dead ends, with much floun-dering, and with more than a few times of doubt. There was no plan for this place, for this career, no formula, no inevitability, but it all fell into place at last, bringing with it rewards and satisfactions beyond any dream or fantasy I could ever have imagined.

Kitchen Arts and Letters is the country's largest store devoted completely to books on food and wine with more than fifteen thousand cooking titles in English and foreign languages and access to thousands of out-of-print titles. It helps food professionals, scholars, and the food publishing community, as well as the general public, to discover books old and new that represent serious contributions to the world of food and wine. Kitchen Arts and Letters is located at 1435 Lexington Avenue, New York, NY 10128; for more information, visit http://www.kitchenartsandletters.com.

▶ Cookbook Reviewer

In a perfect world, all cookbooks would provide clear and accurate information, but all too often a well-known author receives glowing reviews but scant attention is paid to the accuracy of the recipes. On the other hand, little-known authors who have worked hard to make their recipes perfect may get little critical attention. Since even short reviews can have a significant impact on a book's sales, a good reviewer must take the job very seriously.

A conscientious critic may decide not to write a review if he knows nothing about the book's subject. Obviously, it wouldn't be ethical for a vegetarian to comment on *Meat 'n Potatoes* (a cookbook written by William Rice). It is the subject of endless controversy whether a reviewer who knows nothing about Thai cooking is entitled to review a cookbook about the cuisine of that country. And if a reviewer is an authority on the food of Afghanistan, she *must* resist the wholly understandable desire to impress the reader with her own infinitely superior knowledge. A good reviewer tests four or five recipes; an even better reviewer tests many more—and reads the entire text—before writing a critique of a cookbook.

GETTING STARTED

A reviewer must read many cookbooks in order to acquire a frame of reference for judging the merits of a new publication. It is also important to become familiar with an author's previous works. An author can write a brilliant first book, and when the second and third books appear he is described as "prolific." If he writes too many books, he becomes "a hack" (unless he is a famous food writer who makes frequent TV appearances, in which case he is known as a genius).

The reader may not agree with your opinion of a cookbook, but it will be credible if you briefly explain the criteria you brought to bear in making your own unbiased judgment. The reviewer who fully understands the subject is able to write quickly and with authority. Reviewing cookbooks for a newspaper is demanding work, requiring the critic to compile literally hundreds of opinions every year.

One way to begin a career in this field is by writing for a food Web site. However, this may mean you will have to buy your own copy of the book until you have established a credible byline. Publishers send complimentary copies of their books only to professional book reviewers and industry leaders.

KEYS TO SUCCESS

- Practice being nice while being constructive.
- Read the preface and introduction of the book. Often the author will spell out the purpose of the book and the logic behind the organization of the material.
- Study the index. A good index provides a reliable road map to the material in the book.
- If the title implies the recipes can be made in fifteen minutes, does this include one and a half hours of baking time? If the recipes are made with just a few ingredients, are there hidden caveats within this assurance?
- Tell the reader if the book, despite its possible claims to the contrary, may fundamentally have been written for a food professional. A professional can look at a photograph and know how to prepare the dish; a recreational cook will need detailed directions and comprehensible terminology.
- Comment on the design of the book, the quality of the photography, and the paper—and the cost. Some assert a cookbook should not be heavier to lift than a coffee table.
- Studiously avoid reading the opinion of other reviewers before rendering your own.

▶ Recipe Writer

Most cookbook writers are recipe writers, but this is not always so. Some authors hire professionals to help them write the recipes for their books. Chefs, cooking teachers, and others may find themselves having to write recipes for publication. Doing so takes attention to detail. To achieve success, a recipe must be written with impeccable accuracy and unambiguous clarity. If the recipe is flawed the publishing house could be deluged with outraged letters from readers. Even one or two letters could convince an editor your recipes may not be trustworthy. If the quantities of ingredients are incorrect or the instructions are not understood, the home cook loses time and money.

Recipe writing is a serious business, but one that affords its practitioners plenty of opportunities to display their literary skills. Those who excel maintain a following of devoted admirers. Renowned cookbook writers don't need to invent dazzling new dishes; they simply have to strike that exquisite balance between explaining what they have in mind and inspiring the anticipation of pleasure.

We should remember that neither Julia Child nor James Beard wrote original or innovative recipes. It was their unique style and dependable instructions that brought them respect and recognition.

The most skilled recipe writers lead the cook to an understanding of a culinary concept by adding little helpful hints along the way. For instance, you can offer an occasional reassurance such as, "Don't worry, it will thicken when it cools." You might also want to offer several variations that can be made on basic themes.

You'd think it would be a piece of cake to write a good recipe, but every publication has its own style for recipe writing; these stylistic differences distinguish one from another. It saves a heap of trouble to follow the preferred format of the specific newspaper or magazine. There are some rules that apply to all publications:

- List the number of servings.
- List the ingredients in the order in which they are used in the recipe.
- Use precise amounts or quantities (size, tablespoons, or cups). Do not list dry ingredients for baking by weight for the consumer market. Only professionals use scales to weigh ingredients.
- List substitutes for hard-to-find ingredients (or better yet, don't suggest hard-to-find ingredients).
- Try to use a whole can or package of food. For example, if a standard-sized can of beans is fourteen ounces, don't specify 12 ounces if you can help it.

- Specify the size or capacity of pots and pans.
- Provide temperature, cooking time, and instructions, about variable factors that indicate doneness.
- Indicate the steps in a recipe that can be prepared ahead of time.
- Indicate accompaniments and serving suggestions.

• WORDS FROM THE WISE •

THE INTERNATIONAL ASSOCIATION of Culinary Professionals Ethical Guidelines booklet describes the following methods of attributing recipes:

- When a recipe has been obtained from another source (a friend's family heirloom recipe, a restaurant chef, a cookbook, etc.): You may make some minor changes, but the recipe remains fairly intact (even if completely reworded to suit a different format). In these cases, the source should be credited: "This recipe is from John X of Restaurant Y." Or, if appropriate, you can credit the source in the recipe title: "John X's Peach Pie." If the recipe is from a cookbook, you must obtain permission from the publisher.
- When you have made some changes in a recipe from another source, but the original essence still remains, indicate that "this recipe is *adapted from* or *based on* a recipe from John X."
- When you have changed a recipe considerably, but still want to indicate derivation from the original, you can indicate that "this recipe is *loosely adapted from* or *inspired by* a recipe by John X."
- When a recipe is so subsßtantially changed that it no longer resembles the source recipes (a soup made with fish instead of meat, for example), you can print it without credit or mention of the original idea if you like.
- When you have looked at several versions of a traditional, standard dish that is in the classic repertoire (Irish stew or angel food cake, for example), you can print your own tested version without credit unless you have borrowed heavily from an identifiable source.
- When you have adapted a recipe from an old cookbook or historic source and changed the ingredients for today's taste, the source should be credited. This adds resonance to your recipe.

Note: Permission to reprint anything, whether a recipe or a quote, must be obtained in writing. It is not enough to have an oral agreement. If you are in any doubt whether or not to credit a source, let your conscience be your guide and allow caution to take precedence over indecision. Occasionally, the original author or publisher requests a fee (usually a fairly modest one), but more often permissions are given generously.

▶ Recipe Developer and Recipe Tester

You can make a career out of developing recipes if you have a passion for food, a love of science, and a creative flair. Put most simply, a recipe developer creates new recipes, explains recipe developer Jane L. Baker. Baker worked for several years in the test kitchens of Borden developing recipes and from there went on to become a food editor for a newspaper. Now she is marketing director for the Cherry Marketing Institute and supervises the creation of cherry recipes, often using freelance recipe developers.

As a full-time employee of a food company or magazine or as a freelancer, you might develop recipes for package labels, recipe brochures, cookbooks, magazine or newspaper stories, advertisements, or press releases. Your career could center on consumer recipes or large-quantity recipes for the food-service industry.

A recipe developer usually has a food-related degree in food science, nutrition, or commercial foods, says Baker. The degree should include basic science courses, especially chemistry. Courses in communications and/or writing are useful.

Although the terms *recipe developer* and *recipe tester* are used interchangeably, a recipe tester is someone who tests the recipe after it has been developed to make sure it is written accurately and works well. A tester might have a food degree, though more likely does not.

A recipe is a scientific formula. There are science-based reasons why the cake rises—or falls. You need to know how ingredients interact and be able to think creatively. A broad knowledge of food is important, because you probably will develop a wide range of recipes. No matter what the project, you need to know your target audience—who is the recipe for? That's the first question you should ask before you come up with recipe ideas or concepts.

GETTING STARTED

Recipe developer Baker says the most important factor to getting a position as a recipe developer is experience. "Experiment at home; practice developing recipes, write up a few of your creations to include with your résumé. Next, get creative with your job

"Be as diverse as possible. Know how to work with meat, vegetables, fruits. Also, it is really important to keep abreast of trends. What are the newest convenience foods? What ingredients are popular or may become popular?"

—**MARY JANE LAWS**, a food industry consultant in the Chicago area who has worked in the test kitchens at Quaker Oats and currently works on a variety of freelance recipe-development projects

■

"It's is the only way to get into this field. All the work I have obtained has been from someone I knew professionally who knew someone who was looking for a recipe developer or recipe tester."

—**CAROL HACKER**, a recipe developer and tester in the Cleveland, Ohio, area

■

search. Join networking organizations. Perhaps through your networking or other research, you can find a mentor who is willing to help you break into the field," she says.

"Landing the first job will probably be the most difficult step. Then, if you are successful at that first job, others will follow. A job as a recipe developer has the potential to lead to other career choices." Baker insists her background at college and in the test kitchen has been useful at all stages of her career.

For More Information

Food magazines such as *Cook's Illustrated*, *Cooking Light*, *Better Homes and Gardens*, *Bon Appétit*, *Food and Wine*, *Gourmet*, *Good Housekeeping*, *Sunset*, and many more will give you recipe ideas and help you follow trends.

Visit Web sites such as epicurious.com, allrecipes.com, cooks.com, as well as magazine and supermarket Web sites.

Jane L. Baker and Barbara Gibbs Ostmann have written a highly recommended comprehensive manual titled *The Recipe Writer's Handbook*. The book contains detailed information on the development and writing of recipes. In addition, a basic cookbook will help you find recipes and standard procedures.

The International Association of Culinary Professionals (http://www.iacp.com) is a valuable networking organization. Other possibilities include the American Dietetic Association (http://www.eatright.org), Retail Bakers Association (http://www.rbanet.com), and the Home Baking Association (http://www.homebaking.org).

*B*ECOMING A CULINARY LIBRARIAN

by Barbara Haber

JUST BEFORE GRADUATING from library school in 1968, I went to a job interview at Radcliffe College's Schlesinger Library, affiliated with Harvard University. The library collected solely on the subject of American women, and in addition to books, acquires such primary materials as the unpublished papers of feminists like Betty Friedan and the late Andrea Dworkin. During the interview, as I sat listening to the library director, I found myself gazing at surrounding shelves packed with cookbooks. Without disclosing I was an avid reader and collector of cookbooks, I inquired why they were there and was told that they were a gift to the library and that I should pay no attention to them, for the real work of the library was not cooking but women's history.

Although I never argued, I believed from the start that the two subjects were not mutually exclusive, since women have been responsible for preparing food since the beginning of recorded time. I was hired as curator of books, and soon afterward women's history—and women's studies in general—exploded as a byproduct of the women's liberation movement. Sadly, activists of the day stigmatized cooking as a symbol of women's oppression rather than recognizing it to be the creative and gratifying activity I believed it to be, so the library's cookbooks continued to be ignored.

Since the political winds were blowing in the wrong direction, I had to bide my time before growing the cookbook collection. Eager as I was to do so, I needed some sort of base of support before initiating a radical new direction for the library, and mine was long in coming.

It came finally in 1990, just after Julia Child gave her substantial collection of cookbooks to the library. Radcliffe sent out a press release and the media was soon knocking on our door, intrigued with the notion that a Harvard-related research library saw value in cookbooks. This was also a time when American interest in food in general was growing, and publicity about the library's culinary collection attracted new users. I decided to capitalize on this phenomenon by forming a Radcliffe Culinary Friends group as an avenue for raising money to buy books for the culinary collection. I began to offer public programs featuring food writers on book tours and other noted food celebrities, attracting increasingly larger audiences from Boston and Cambridge.

I also started Chef's First Monday, monthly discussion groups for

continued

continued from page 177

local professional cooks and restaurateurs featuring speakers on relevant subjects such as sustainable agriculture, artisanal bread baking, or the art of tipping. Each wave of publicity about the library's activities in the area of food attracted more followers, some of whom donated significant collections of cookbooks.

I was also given the opportunity to raise funds to endow the cookbook collection. This allowed me to shape it with the aim of acquiring all of the various editions of major historical cookbooks, from the works of La Varenne to *The Joy of Cooking*, and at the same time to add books that would have value as historic artifacts. In the 1980s, for instance, cookbooks were in vogue that advocated cooking everything from scratch in microwave ovens, now used almost exclusively for heating frozen dinners or melting butter. Those interested in the history of kitchen technology will be able to find bygone microwave cookbooks in the library's collection.

Public enthusiasm for the culinary collection did not sit well with most of my library colleagues who boycotted my programs and felt I was diverting attention away from the "real" work of the library—women's history. But I considered their objections invalid and found support among the volunteers I brought into the library and also other research librarians at Harvard who began to buy cookbooks for their collections, many in exotic languages, as food history became a respectable part of traditional academic disciplines.

By the time I left the library at the beginning of 2003, the cookbook and food history collection was being consulted more frequently than any other collection in the library, and the newly appointed director appreciated their value. Just before leaving, I acquired for the library the unpublished papers of Elizabeth David, which joined similar collections of M. F. K. Fisher, Julia Child, and Irma Rombauer.

At the beginning of my career I would never have believed that my love of cookbooks could lead to most of my professional satisfactions. No such job as culinary librarian existed and the opportunity to create it had to be approached with patience, planning, and the ability to rally support in an unfriendly environment. As a result, when young people ask me for career advice, I tell them, Do what interests you, and keep your eyes open for opportunities to change things so that your creative urges can flourish.

Barbara Haber is the author of *From Hardtack to Home Fries: An Uncommon History of American Cooks and Meals*. This is a book that combines women's history and the history of food.

$\mathcal{R}$ARE BOOK COLLECTOR

IT IS THE old and rare cookbooks that are most often treasured by collectors, and those in the know treasure such people as Jan Longone, whose Wine and Food Library has become the foundation for the Longone Center for American Culinary Research at the University of Michigan's William L. Clements Library.

Food Arts magazine reported that Longone, a dealer in rare books, and her wine-savant husband Dan assembled the staggering collection over a period of forty odd years. When it is fully catalogued it will offer an unprecedented roster of categories for interdisciplinary study, among them the history of food advertising; chefs; restaurants, hotels and menus; food and the media; the cooking school movement; food and the arts; appliances and equipment; and industrialization of food production, among many others.

Longone's personal collection of rare books dates from as far back as the 1500s, and includes America's earliest cookbooks, such as Thomas Hariot's *A Briefe and True Report of the New Found Land of Virginia*, published in 1588. The book contains a description of attempts to grow wine grapes on Roanoke Island (the "lost colony"). The library also owns one of five known first editions of that book, as well as the papers (including his restaurant bills) of General Sir Henry Clinton, the British commander in North America during much of the American Revolution. The collection contains originals, facsimiles, and reprints of classic books on wine, food and cooking equipment.

▶ Archivist

"It is not often a curator gets tingles up his spine and tears in his eyes at the same time," said Marvin Taylor, head of the Fales Collection. "This marvelous donation will expand upon and enhance the NYU Libraries' Food Studies collection. Last year we acquired the Cecily Brownstone Collection of American Cookery, containing some twelve thousand books and five thousand pamphlets. This collection will add measurably to our current focus on American, New York City, and Greenwich Village–related material in Food Studies." When food celebrities donate their papers to an institution—for example, Julia Child donated hers to the Schlesinger library—an archivist has the enviable task of annotating the collection. Similarly, landmark restaurants such as the Rainbow Room in Manhattan had an archivist to collect every scrap of newsprint, magazine article, and other printed material from the date of its opening in 1934 and organize it in such a way that it is available for researchers and writers. Food companies celebrating significant anniversaries may also engage the services of an archivist to assemble documents that can be used to compile a commemorative book. Experts are hired to organize collections of menus and other memorabilia to be used in exhibits. The New

York Public Library Rare Books Division has a twenty-six-thousand-piece historical menu collection. If you are a meticulous researcher, brilliant organizer, and careful filer you could suggest compiling an archived collection for a business or long-lived restaurant in your neighborhood.

ℳAGAZINE EDITOR OR PUBLISHER

THE EDITOR DETERMINES the content of the magazine. Magazine editors are the gatekeepers who accept or reject authors' queries and, like real estate agents, are both buyer and seller. They buy a specific number of words from a writer for a specific and already existing space in the magazine and sell the words to the reader. Like real estate, an article must therefore fit appropriately into the neighborhood of the publication. An editor is not at liberty to create an entirely new department to accommodate an essay, no matter how eloquently it is written. Nor can she just tack a few extra pages onto the magazine. The profile of the typical subscriber and the economics of magazine publishing impose strict guidelines for what may or may not be judged as suitable stories.

The mission of the publication may be to cover anything from trendy food and fusion cooking to entertaining with an unlimited budget or traditional family dinners. What works for one magazine will not be acceptable for another. *Fine Cooking* doesn't print chef profiles. *Cooking Light* doesn't do rich chocolate desserts. *Chocolatier* isn't interested in an article on beef stew. When Colman Andrews was at *Saveur* magazine, he explained, "We don't write about the hot young chef in Seattle or Chicago, but we might want to write about his grandmother, because she may have been his inspiration for his love of cooking."

Kristine Kidd, food editor of *Bon Appétit*, says: "Know what the magazine does and does not do. We don't publish articles about cooking with children. Every May is a foreign issue. July is barbecue. *Bon Appétit* is more current than groovy and hot. It is more American regional than international."

Each magazine has it own distinctive voice. The voice encompasses more than vocabulary. It means absorbing the style and rhythm, even the accent, of the publication, much as an actor gets into a new part. The editor also makes sure a writer keeps the reader in mind: an inexperienced reader may not fully comprehend culinary terms like *bake blind*, or *nap with sauce*, or *stand under cold running water*.

One way to get onto a magazine staff is to use your writing skills to secure a job as an editorial assistant in any department. Plan to move into the food area when an opportunity appears. A starting position in the editorial department of a magazine, usually as editorial assistant, commands a low salary though staff writers at a magazine may earn between forty thousand and seventy thousand dollars. Top editors, writers, and critics can expect salaries many times those amounts, but the job entails long hours. Senior staff is often responsible for planning future issues and may suggest writers for specific assignments. The editor may also be involved in planning and attending photo shoots and discussing business matters with the magazine publisher.

Most top editors climbed the editorial ladder, moving from one magazine to another and making vertical moves. Dana Colwin, editor of *Food and Wine*, held managing editor positions at *Mademoiselle* and *Home and Garden* and was an associate editor at *Vogue*. Ruth Reichl was the restaurant critic for both the *New York Times* and *Los Angeles Times* and a book author before moving to *Gourmet* as editor in chief. Martha Holmberg worked as a cookbook author, private chef, and administrative director of La Varenne cooking school in Paris before becoming editor in chief of *Fine Cooking*.

by Christopher Kimball, publisher of Cook's Illustrated

MOLASSES COOKIES. ANADAMA bread. Baking-powder biscuits. Baked beans. Apple pie. Roast of beef. Fresh milk from the cow out back. Potatoes any way you can cook them. These are the foods I grew up with during summers on our small farm in the Green Mountains of Vermont. Marie Briggs was my first cooking teacher. She was the town baker and lived in the Yellow Farmhouse just over the town line. No traveler who stopped on their way into town ever left empty-handed; the most frequent gifts were a generous slice of warm homemade white bread with a thick spread of yellow butter or a just-fried nutmeg doughnut.

Marie began her day before dawn and only sat down for noon dinner and then again in the late afternoon for tea. She was taken out to dinner once a year on Christmas Day. The rest of the time was devoted to hard work: baking, cooking dinners, and feeding farmhands and strangers alike. On rainy days, I might help Marie with a bit of baking. Like any good Vermonter, she never directly told me what to do. She would just stand close and show me the right way to shape a loaf of bread or roll out pie dough without a word spoken. The shame of doing a mediocre job was all the motivation I needed. (Until the late 1960s, the Yellow Farmhouse had no indoor plumbing other than a hand pump in the pantry sink. It did, however, have the best gossip and stories in town told by Floyd Bentley, who was featured in the Norman Rockwell painting *Breaking Home Ties*.)

The lessons of those long summers were the reason I launched *Cook's* magazine in 1980. For farmers, food was fuel. It wasn't a hobby, recreation, or a lifestyle badge of honor. Cooking, at least for me, has always been a means of bringing people together, of doing something for others while performing a basic, necessary function at the same time. When my wife Adrienne moved into our Vermont farmhouse, our neighbor Jean brought over a shaker of salt and a loaf of bread. That's the way old-timers used to welcome you to the neighborhood.

In the late 1970s, food was just starting its long love affair with American culture, dragging itself out of the bleak humdrum of putting food on the table and transforming itself into a glamorous expression of the good life. Chefs were quickly becoming stars. The launch of *Food and Wine* in 1978 was a nod to that trend, as were gourmet ingredients, recipes from afar, and any dish that had an exiting story to tell of a far away place or culture. Putting dinner on the table was not the point. Being knowledgeable about food and looking good while dining at a trendy restaurant was the thing. (A deli owner in Westport, Connecticut, once told me, in response to a query about star chefs and gourmet ingredients, "It's only food!" The point was not that food is unimportant; it was that one should stop talking about it and start enjoying it.)

In that context, I wanted to launch a food magazine that was truly about cooking, not eating. Thanks to processed and fast foods, it was clear that there was a whole new generation of cooks who had learned nothing at their mother's or grandmother's elbow. Most recipes I found in cookbooks or magazines did not work very well. In addition, cookware was changing rapidly; the Cuisinart was a watershed event, one that brought chopping and mincing into every home cook's repertoire); and the availability of ethnic and gourmet ingredients was mushrooming. America was just starting to take a fresh look at the quality of its food supply, with a few brave souls actually producing top-notch ingredients such as Laura Chenel's chèvre or the produce grown by Tom Chino and his family in California.

continued

continued from page 181

In the midst of all those cultural shifts, I wanted to go back to the basics, to test basic cooking techniques so people could indeed understand what they were doing, not just follow instructions by rote. Why do you let meat rest before carving? What is double acting baking powder? Do you still have to proof yeast? And why would anyone in their right mind make croissants at home? (The French don't.)

The first issue of *Cook's* appeared in May 1980 and, with a lot of luck, we managed to pay our bills for three years until, in 1983, the *New Yorker* purchased a controlling interest in the magazine. That was a lifesaver and also an education. At the *New Yorker*, business folks were never allowed in the editorial areas and, one day, when one of my advertising salespeople had wandered onto the infamous twentieth floor (home of the editor, William Shawn) in search of a working soda machine, I received an irate call from the publisher, explaining in no uncertain terms why this was unacceptable. (I was also once called into the office of the publisher, a gentleman who had previously been the chief financial officer. He handed me a yellow Post-it note with a rather large figure written on it. I said nothing until he queried, "Do you know what that money is for?" I begged ignorance. "Well, that' s my monthly alimony payment!" We never did end up talking about magazines.)

Finally, I brought in Swedish partners at the end of 1986, buying out the *New Yorker*, and stayed for an additional three years as publisher and editorial director. After I had left, the magazine was sold back to the owners of the *New Yorker*. It ceased publication, and the subscriber file was merged into *Gourmet*.

The original *Cook's*, the one I had published in the 1980s, did take advertising and I had always felt that ads make it difficult to write and edit for the readers. A travel advertiser wants to see travel editorial before he or she will place an ad. The same holds true for liquor, credit cards, travel, clothing, jewelry, etc. So a magazine that is truly just about cooking will never sell many ads or the editorial has to evolve into a much broader mix of articles than "How to Make Fudgy Brownies" or "The Secrets of Southern Fried Chicken."

So, I set out to relaunch *Cook's*, putting out the magazine that I had always wanted to create. That meant no advertising and a persnickety attention to recipe testing and investigation. My first step was to call the trademark office and buy my lapsed trademark back for a mere $175. (The Swedish owners from the 1980s had forgotten to renew the trademark.) Next, I developed a new prototype (no color; dense with copy) and we launched the premier issue in the spring of 1993. To my great surprise, the new *Cook's* was an instant success. A small mention in the food pages of the *New York Times*, for example, generated fifty-eight hundred subscriptions alone. Today, we stand at eight hundred thousand paid readers per issue.

In the late 1990s, I was pursuing a TV show for public television. The only producer I knew at the time, Geoffrey Drummond (also Julia Child's producer), refused to return my phone calls and for good reason—a bow-tied Yankee with, at best, a very droll sense of humor, did not appear commercially viable. I finally did get a call from a TV producer in Washington who was a *Cook's* fan and also a long-time business associate of Walter Cronkite. He produced the first half-hour show and within a year we were running on public television. (Geoff Drummond became the producer after seeing that first tape.) We have now filmed six seasons—over one hundred shows—and we are the top-rated cooking show on public television. The obvious question is, why?

Neither the magazine nor the television is entertaining in any accepted sense of the word. No bands. No cute humor. No frenzied energy. What we do reasonably well is to explain why recipes fail and then how to make them work. Everybody, and I mean anyone who has ever cooked anything, has one thing in common with all other cooks. Failure. And failure—bad food if you will—is the starting point for everything we do at *Cook's*. It is the common ground between editor and reader or viewer.

The other underlying factor in the success of *Cook's* is pure, run-of-the-mill good luck. For one, men are flooding into the kitchen and they enjoy a nuts-and-bolts approach to cooking. For another, most folks have little cooking experience and therefore the "whys" of cooking are at least as important as the recipes themselves. Finally, we take no advertising, which gives us the freedom to opine on the quality of kitchen appliances and supermarket foods. Is KitchenAid really the best mixer? You can count on *Cook's* to spend weeks finding the answer, or at least the answer that makes the most sense to us.

To work at *Cook's* is quite a different experience than one might have at other food publications. First, all editorial material is produced entirely in-house and we now employ over twenty-five test cooks. Working with outside authors was always difficult, especially for them, since we would ask contributors to go test the recipe another twenty times (after they had spent three weeks on the original version). In addition, our entire editorial philosophy is based on the notion of a group process. So, as we develop a recipe and a story, the entire editorial staff has the opportunity to taste and critique at every point along the way. This does not always mean that we discover the absolute "best" recipe, a claim that is our hallmark. And, to be sure, a group process does sometimes eliminate recipe variations that have a more personal or more charming point of view. The benefit, however, is that one has a much better chance of producing recipes that really work as promised and that appeal to the widest possible audience.

The large, oval table used for editorial meetings expresses this community approach to editorial matters. It is a Harkness table, a piece of furniture that goes to the heart of the educational process at many New England prep schools. The method is simple. Everyone around the table is on the same footing, including the editor. Everyone must participate in meetings, everyone is open to criticism, and nobody can hide in a back row. My role is Socratic—I ask a series of questions, hoping to draw out the flaw in a method or a solution to a problem. And, to be fair, I learn as much as anyone else at those meetings.

I am often asked about the success of *Cook's*, as if it all happened overnight. Throughout the 1980s, I could barely pay my printing bill, it seemed as if we were always on the edge of economic disaster, and the magazine was a long way from my original vision of practical advice for home cooks. Today, I can look back over twenty-five years of publishing and editing *Cook's* and, I admit, feel a great deal of satisfaction. The pleasure is in the nature of the organization, more so than the business success. (That does, I admit, sound like the bank robber who claims that he didn't do it for the money.) Watching young cooks develop their skills and then go on to be editors, television personalities, or terrific recipe developers is, indeed, a pleasure. It's simply a lot of fun to work at *Cook's* because the job requires not only culinary skills and a decent palate, but also intelligence, logic, and hard work.

Over the years I became friendly with Julia Child, as did just about everyone in the food world in Boston. Julia was fond of inviting folks over for dinner and everybody had to cook something. On my first "date," she greeted me at the door with two dozen oysters and asked me to shuck them. After fifteen tortured minutes of miserable failure, Julia looked over my shoulder and said, "Need some help, dearie?"

For most cooks, demonstrating gross incompetence in the presence of the great Julia Child would simply be too much to bear. But Julia understood all too well that cooking, like everything else, isn't about success, it's really about failure. It is the self-confidence to put oneself at risk, even in the most humbling circumstances, in the pursuit of knowledge. President Kennedy was once asked if he was happy being president. He paraphrased Aristotle in his reply: "If you define happiness as using one's education and experience in the pursuit of excellence, then I am a very happy man indeed."

That notion, the pursuit of excellence, sounds lofty, I admit, but Kennedy's words have stayed with me down

continued

continued from page 183

through the years. Doing one's best always includes a fair measure of failure—you just have to keep at it long enough to find success. That is, in a nutshell, what *Cook's* has meant to me personally. We are quite happy to publicly display our failures and our ignorance in pursuit of excellence. (And I have upon many occasions demonstrated my complete lack of publishing skills.) That is our common ground, the one thing that reaches out to our audience and gives them assurance that we are standing elbow to elbow.

Cooking has been glorified, tarted up to appear easy, fun, and entertaining. But that approach is wide of the mark. Through practice, hard work, and experience, cooking allows one to transform simple foods into the foundation for a community no matter how small (cooking for two) or how large (the potluck pork dinner at the firehouse). A good cook is, in fact, what we hope for in our children. We hope that they come to understand the benefits of work, persistence, an appreciation of excellence, and the selflessness to contribute to the well being of others.

And, lest I forget, the food is pretty good too!

WRITE FOR A NEWSPAPER

"When people ask me, how do I get to be a food writer? my answer is, you get there the same way you get to be a metro writer or a sports writer. You go out and report stories. You absolutely have to meet the same standards and requirements as any other journalist at the newspaper. Food journalists have to do all that, but we also have to write stories that don't scare people away from food. You can't just warn people about food-borne illnesses or make them feel guilty for using butter. Our role, sometimes, is to be a port in the storm."

—JEANNE MCMANUS,
the *Washington Post*

Michael Bauer is the executive food-and-wine and restaurant critic of the *San Francisco Chronicle.* In his seventeen years at the newspaper, the staff has increased to seventeen, making it the largest food-and-wine staff of any newspaper in the country. In 2002 he was responsible for starting the wine section, the first free-standing weekly newspaper section of its kind in the country. Much of the content has been syndicated by King Features and is now published in some of the largest newspapers in the country. Bauer was also responsible for launching the highly successful *San Francisco Chronicle Cooking School* that is taught by *Chronicle* staff writers. With Fran Irwin he edited *The San Francisco Chronicle Cookbook,* published in 1997.

Bauer is an exception. Not only is he exceptionally talented, but he is also bucking the trend. Few newspapers publish either the quality or quantity of food stories that the *San Francisco Chronicle* does. Doug Brown, a successful freelance writer from Baltimore, insists this is changing. "Newspapers around the country are dedicating top staffers to the food beat, and they are hungry for well-reported stories with timely angles. . . . [It is no longer all about] 'five things to do with cream of mushroom soup.'"

Though, understandably, the focus of many newspapers is on seasonal recipes, commodity councils such as those for blueberries or pork or beef or catfish contribute many of the articles. Few food sections are enthusiastic about publishing serious stories on subjects such as hunger or declining fish populations. They prefer to cover local food personalities—and for a very good reason: these stories are of interest to their readers.

Warren Belasco, professor of American studies at the University of Maryland and expert on the historical, social, and cultural meanings of food, says, "I see lifestyle journalism (the sort of thing you read in small city newspapers) as a handmaiden to consumer culture, helping people refine their choices, become more expert as consumers and more discriminating."

If you are at a loss about what to write, take a look at any of our major newspapers and you will see the food-related material includes food business news, technology, safety, travel, history, fashion, restaurant and cookbook reviews, even the menu for a sports event or a dinner at the governor's mansion. So you see, food stories can fit in many different sections of the newspaper in addition to the food pages.

GETTING STARTED

Florence Fabricant, the highly regarded food columnist for the *New York Times*, started her career writing a column in the local free newspaper. Her work was seen by those in a position to offer a job. Even if you get paid very little, a huge audience may see your work, and it could lead to other opportunities.

Build a portfolio of your published material. If you want to be a writer, the most important thing to do is write.

Talk to people to provide color to your narrative. Readers are interested in people, particularly celebrity people, and their weight and ever-changing diets. They want to know about new foods, new restaurants, and new places and things to eat, and there is an endless fascination with trends and fads. There is always room in the newspaper for reports on new cooking equipment, and the major newspapers are *sometimes* willing to report on serious issues like . . . snails. (Where oh where have all the escargots gone?)

COOKING CONTESTS

We love food fights. On TV, the Food Network is particularly devoted to cooking contests. It seems to be part of our ancient imprinting to ask, mirror, mirror on the wall, who is the fairest of us all?

We are mesmerized by competitions of all kinds: Super Bowls, Oscars, *Apprentices*, *Survivors*, *Idols*, winners, and losers. How

"In newspaper writing, you have to get to the point quickly, and you have to write for everyone. That includes someone who has no interest in food. At the same time, you're writing for a core audience of food lovers who read the section every week."

—**SHERYL JULIAN**, *Boston Globe*

"An article is your thoughts made tangible; it is like a painting of your thoughts and ideas. It reveals your personality. Whatever you say some will agree and others will think you are a fool, or a fraud or you will become a bitter enemy.

—**ANDY ROONEY**

contestants compete depends a lot on the way they view the world. Joe Namath once observed, "You learn how to be a gracious winner by being an outstanding loser." Richard M. Nixon viewed the rivalry differently. He decided, "It is necessary for me to establish a winner image. Therefore, I have to beat somebody."

Stirring the pot has become the route to success for many ambitious home cooks. A mom in a remote village in the Scottish Highlands just nabbed the coveted title of Golden Spurtle, thus becoming the world's porridge-making champion. Closer to home, we have the New Jersey State Barbecue Championship. There's a bit of booty to be had, but everyone knows it isn't the money that's the big draw, its beating out the competition.

AND THE WINNER IS . . .

The prize money is largely the point for the one hundred finalists who compete for $1 million big bucks in the forty-second annual Pillsbury Bake-Off. Pity the poor judges.

Over fifty-four hundred entries were submitted for a contest staged by another food company. A few suggestions were made for future entrants by a now happily retired judge, who announced, "Today's spelling word, class, will be *morsels.* Some of our contestants simply do not know how to spell this word. Several folks submitted the following attempts: morcels, more sells, morsals, morsles, morsoles, and mosels, among others. And other pupils apparently gave up and just called them 'chips.'

"Choose the name of your dish and its description carefully. These are examples of titles that need a little work: Chocolate Chip Mess, Gooey Squares, and Mean Mountain Mama's Mudslide. . . .

"One competition entry called for 'garden-fresh fish.' (Perhaps it came from a pond in the contestant's backyard?) Another recipe was called Duck Pond Cake. It uses two cake layers, adds a 'lake' of blue-tinted frosting and fills it with plastic ducks. It has areas of green frosting for 'grass,' chocolate morsels for rocks in the lake, bushes are created using pretzel sticks dipped in melted chocolate, and cascades of blue 'water' run down the side of the cake." If only there had been a photo. The judge went on: "Parasol Pie is a lovely idea that combines bottled ranch dressing with lemon Jell-O. The pie is baked in a yummy wheat germ-curry crust." Yummy, indeed.

Contestants are advised to proofread their submissions carefully. The computer spellchecker will catch some things, but not all. Proofreading can help avoid such errors as calling for "fourteen cups of all-purpose baking powder" and instructing readers to "let cool and cry completely on a rack." Try to catch typos such as "concerteated milk" and "everaped milk."

AND THE PRIZE GOES TO

Other segments of the food industry struggle through an awesome deluge of competitors in order to come up with some credible front-runners. Accolades among a recent Specialty Foods category in the Outstanding Gluten-Free Product Line, went to the Soy Crunch Pizza. First Place in the Savory Condiment group went to the Original Bumpy Beer Mustard while, no surprise here, the Olive Oil Factory of Watertown, Connecticut carried off a third-place finish with its Gourmet Rosemary Oyl.

Winners, runners-up, and also-rans were found among those who grew the Biggest and Best Tomato, the Tastiest Grilled Cheese Sandwich in America, or the largest pumpkin in the world. The Greatest Advances in Lipids were awarded for "achievements characterized by dedication, service, innovation within the industry—and passion." Passion? Who'd have guessed passion was part of a lipid equation?

The Soil Association gives an award to the Organic Business Person of the Year. (The organic field is flourishing.) Bartenders receive awards for tending. Waitstaff are conferred with medals for knowing when and how to wait. There are Hospitality Awards, Gold Plates, Silver Spoons, and Peta Proggy Awards. The most recent Proggy went to the Best Cruelty-Free Outdoor Shoe Company that seems to have given leather the boot.

The Unilever Award for Consumer Insight was presented to Smurfit for the development of the Shelf Assured campaign to "satisfy the hidden consumer in the supply chain who makes a critical difference to on-shelf availability of products in a retail store—the Shelf Stacker." Another company demonstrating admirable consumer insight is Young's Bluecrest Seafood Ltd. "Whose product caught the imagination of buyers in the U.S. who were mightily impressed with the 'topless mussels' that were picked for the top prize because of their impressive market penetration." And, at a glittering black tie affair, ASDA Stores Ltd. was flushed with success, upon being awarded a blue ribbon for "Recycling Office Paper into Smart Price Toilet Paper."

The best cooking schools, most remarkable teachers, most provocative journalists, simply stupendous cookbooks, glossiest magazines, most tasteful television shows, and chefs with nerves of steel are all acclaimed and applauded. A galaxy of the best and brightest restaurateurs are regularly revered.

Food-service companies are scooping up awards for vastly improved guest and employee dining facilities. Ivy and Feni awards are conferred upon those who have earned richly deserved recognition. Prime ministers and presidents court charismatic chefs. James Beard has been resurrected (again), and prizes and medals are handed out in his name at the annual mind-boggling, rear-end-numbing, throat-clearing, tear-jerking five-hour ceremonies to all who toil in restaurants north, south, east and west of hither and yon. Every year, only five among all the esteemed and exalted are inducted into membership in the Who's Who of Food and Beverage in America. "They are selected by the James Beard Foundation Awards Committee for their achievements and impact on the food industry." Fewer than two hundred people have been voted into this august gathering, and already some have died and gone to—wherever.

At the International Cherry Pit Spit Competition, in Eau Claire, Michigan, the winner summoned a super spit distance of seventy-two feet, seven and a half inches—that's thirteen and a half inches farther than a pitcher throws a baseball to the plate.

Whether an award is worth the proverbial bucket of spit or a crystal trophy to display to one and all is largely a matter that is seen through the eye of the beholder. Of infinitely greater importance to our daily lives than the three little words *the winner is* are those far bigger words that we all yearn to hear, like *good job*, *well done*, and *thank you*.

▶ Cooking-Contest Judge

This is customarily an honorary appointment. Meaningful money rarely changes hands. The task requires a stomach of steel, the ability to remember what you tasted ten or fifteen tastes ago, the fortitude to withstand reproachful glares from the losers and a plethora or wet kisses from the winners. Skip this job if you can.

▶ Food and Restaurant Critic

Mimi Sheraton was appointed restaurant critic at the *New York Times* in 1976. "*Times* reviewers must visit a restaurant three times," she says, though she often went six or eight times, just to be sure.

Tim and Nina Zagat have been described by the *Financial Times* of London as "One of the great success stories in publishing." The Zagats were attorneys before transforming their informal restaurant surveys for law firms from a hobby into a new career. In addition to restaurants, their familiar narrow burgundy-colored guidebooks now cover family travel, nightlife, theater, movies, music, shopping, golf courses, hotels, and resorts.

Speaking at a Culinary Institute of America commencement, Nina Zagat said, "Our guides' popularity indicates there has been a revolution both in the way Americans eat and their growing power as consumers." Her husband added, "There has been a shift from restaurants telling people what to eat to customers demanding what they want." Today, 250,000 amateur critics help rate restaurants in more than seventy cities around the world. Reportedly, there is something called the "Zagat effect," in which a restaurant, once it has achieved a top rating, continues to do well year after year, regardless of any change in the quality of the food. The Zagats reminded the graduates that the revolution has made this an exciting time to enter the restaurant industry. "The profession now has panache, indeed celebrity. This was unthinkable when I was growing up," said Tim. "How did eating raw fish go from being a fraternity prank to a delicacy?" He advised the students to learn from the critiques. "Use reviews as a window into the perceptions of your restaurant. You will discover something you didn't know."

Restaurant critics learn to live in an atmosphere where their presence—if detected—is met with groveling, cringing servitude, and anxiety embedded with hostile loathing. But being liked is not part of the job. Honesty is. Lately, there have been fewer poisonous reviews than in past years, and markedly fewer critics have shown any inclination to go out of their way to decimate a restaurant with a hail of contemptuous comments. There are exceptions to the kinder, gentler school of thought: restaurant reviewer A. A. Gill recently described an item on the menu of a restaurant that, for decency's sake, shall remain be nameless: He likened the fish and foie-gras dumplings to "fish liver–filled condoms" and called them "vile, with a savor that lingered like a lovelorn drunk and tasted as if your mouth had been used as the swab bin in an animal hospital." That's telling it like it is, by Jove! (Gill subsequently dismissed the chef's furious reaction to his observations with a "boo-hoo.")

It is rare to see a critic frankly deploring the deplorable. André Soltner, the famed former chef from Lutèce, asks: "What is the nicest color, blue or red? Blue is not nicer than red, but a critic may prefer it. The same thing is true with restaurants. A reviewer may simply like one more than another, for no real reason, and give three stars to one and only two stars to another on that basis. And that's not right."

And Jeffrey Steingarten, contemplating his appointment as food critic of *Vogue* magazine, writes, "I realized how inadequate I was to the honor, for I, like everybody I knew, suffered from a set of strong and arbitrary likes and dislikes regarding food. I feared that I was no better than an art critic who becomes nauseated by the color yellow, or suffers from red-green blindness. . . . The nifty thing about being omnivores is that we can take nourishment from an endless variety of sources and easily adapt to a changing food world—crop failures, droughts, herd migrations, restaurant closings, and the like. Cows will starve in a steakhouse and wolves in a salad bar, but not we."

When critics do go out on a limb, though, the First Amendment to the Constitution guarantees the right to express an opinion, and there is not much an aggrieved restaurant owner can do about it.

Despite the fact that many people think being paid to eat in restaurants and then write about the experience would be a dream job, the reality is anything but. By the time William Grimes, former restaurant critic for the *New York Times* left his position, after serving five years on the job, he calculated he had written 438 reviews and devoured twelve hundred meals. "But there are compensations," he hastened to add. After dining at a monstrously costly restaurant, he was relieved that "the tab wasn't coming out of my pocket. Taking pen in hand I affixed my signature to a bill that totaled nearly $1,500 for four diners dinners, tip not included. In one Olympic motion, I had broken all previous records by several hundred dollars. I felt the kind of mad exhilaration that criminals must feel when they've done something terribly, irrevocably wrong."

He also comments, "Learning to eat is a kind of education. It rewards the adventurous. It pays double dividends to thrill seekers who dare to taste a sea urchin; who do not flinch in the face of an andouillette; who, instead of sniffing and picking and probing when something odd turns up on the plate, dive right in, sending off sparks with their forks. We have a name for such people. We call them adults. And when they go out to a restaurant, they are not looking for solace, they're looking for a good meal."

Phyllis Richman, a former critic for the *Washington Post*, says, "Being a restaurant critic is not just a job—it's a lifestyle. It's something you devote your whole body to. You have to eat *what* you eat *when* you have to eat it. It means you eat a lot of bad food—probably more bad food than anybody who cares about food would choose to eat."

Most of the top critics acknowledge they spend a minimum of thirty hours a week eating. The rest of the time is spent writing.

Ruth Reichl, former restaurant critic of the *New York Times* and now editor in chief of *Gourmet*, notes, "The critic's responsibility is to the public. I don't care about restaurants,. I care about readers."

"A restaurant critic is a consumer advocate. His role is to provide the reader with a second-hand experience before going for a first-hand one," says William Rice, who has covered restaurants for the *Chicago Tribune* and many other publications. "What the reader wants to know is if he can anticipate receiving a good meal at an appropriate cost. The more the meal costs, the higher will be the expectations of both the critic and the guest."

An essential fact is that critics should like—or, better still, love—the restaurant business and be knowledgeable about every aspect of it. A guest who has had a poor experience in a restaurant will tell a dozen friends. A restaurant critic expresses an opinion to hundreds or even thousands of readers. Rice adds, "I predict that reviewers will eventually need to be certified—earn a college degree in the subject. Restaurant reputations are too important to be left to the impressions of the uninformed."

FOOD WRITING ON THE INTERNET

Writing for the Internet may never replace the seductive food picture painted by well-written, taste-tempting words that spring from a glossy page. On the other hand, magazines do not have the immediacy or interactive capabilities found on food Web sites.

Epicurious is a media offshoot of publishing giant Condé Nast. The site features a database of more than twelve thousand recipes. Many are original, while others are from Condé Nast publications *Gourmet* and *Bon Appétit*. Users can try the recipes and then share their opinions in the reviews and rating section. The site includes four monthly features designed for the home cook.

Here are some other sites that attract food lovers. Visit them and see if you might like to write for them.

Asian Cuisine. Articles and recipes for exotic Asian cuisine. http://www.asiacuisine.com.sg

Baker Boulanger. An online magazine for bakers. http://www.betterbaking.com

Cook's Illustrated. Selected articles from the magazine filled with hundreds of step-by-step, hand-drawn illustrations of useful cooking techniques. http://www.cooksillustrated.com

Cyberchef. Edited in Paris, the site features interviews with famous chefs, home recipes, cooking tips, menus, and cookbook and restaurant reviews, with a focus on international cuisine. http://www.cyberchefs.net

Delicious magazine. Recipes from top name chefs such as Jamie Oliver, Nigella Lawson, Rick Stein, and others, plus interviews, special offers, and more. http://www.deliciousmagazine.com

Fabulous Foods. Recipes in all categories, all with simple to follow step-by-step cooking instructions. http://www.fabulousfoods.com

Fiery Foods. Recipes for cooking with chili peppers, as well and many barbecue recipes. http://www.fiery-foods.com

Foody. An online magazine covering all aspects of English, Welsh, Scottish, and Irish food and drink. http://www.thefoody.com

Gastronomica. Selected articles from the journal devoted to discussion and reflection on the history, literature, representation, and cultural impact of food. http://www.gastronomica.com

Gourmet Connection. Dedicated to gourmet food, health, shopping, diabetes, fitness, and more. http://www.tgcmagazine.com

Gourmet India. A site that features sections on Indian food recipes, restaurants, food and drink forums, free job postings for chefs, and more. http://www.gourmet-india.com

iChef Recipes. Search thousands of free recipes. Add your own or request a special recipe. http://www.ichef.com

La Cucina Italiana. Features a searchable database of Italian recipes and a glossary.

http://www.italiancookingandliving.com

Leite's Culinaria: Food columnist David Leite offers recipes, articles, columns, tips, restaurant reviews, and resources.
http://www.leitesculinaria.com

Martha Stewart Omnimedia: Recipes and everything Martha.
http://www.marthastewart.com

Sally's Place: Celebrity interviews, news, and daily feature stories on food, restaurants, beverages, and travel.
http://www.sallys-place.com

StarChefs: Secret ingredients, anecdotes, tips, and recipes from famous chefs and cookbook authors.
http://www.starchefs.com

Taste of Home: Recipes and cooking tips from country cooks.
http://www.tasteofhome.com

Useful Web Sites and Blogs to Keep Up with What Is Going On In the Food World
(There are millions more if you find yourself with time on your hands.)

http://usaweekend.com/food/index.html
http://www.ctnow.com/features/food/
http://www.smh.com.au/entertainment/goodliving/luke-mangan/index.html
http://www2.ocregister.com/ocrweb/ocr/section.do?section=WINE_FOOD
http://www.nola.com/tastes/t-p/
http://www.gastropoda.com/
http://www.gastropoda.com (Regina Schrambling is one of the best)
http://www.leitesculinaria.com
http://www.egullet.com
http://www.writersweekly.com
http://www.absolutewrite.com
http://www.writer2writer.com
http://www.writesuccess.com
http://www.mediabistro.com
http://dabblingmum.com
http://netwrite-publish.com

ℐNTERNET PUBLISHER

by David Leite

BY 1998, I'd been an advertising copywriter for ten years, and the decade of frantic schedules and punishing deadlines had taken its toll. An idea for an article had been clanging around in my head for a few years, so I pitched it to the *New York Times*, *Los Angeles Times*, and the *Chicago Sun-Times*. To hell with starting small, I thought.

The piece, which was about my maternal grandmother and the food of the Azores, was accepted by the *Sun-Times* and appeared in the paper's food section in December. Enthralled by the idea of becoming a journalist, I decided a cyber portfolio—where editors far and wide could read my work—was in order. I taught myself Dreamweaver, a program that allows users to create Web sites without needing to know HTML coding. The result was Leite's Culinaria (http://www.leitesculinaria.com), which launched in early 1999 and consisted of a homepage and the lone article about my grandmother.

By early 2000 it wasn't editors but readers who sought me out. Because search engines such as Google and Yahoo! spider sites on a regular basis, my articles and recipes were being included on search engines, in directories, as well as on other food-related sites. I began receiving a steady stream of e-mails from readers who were requesting information on everything from the origins of *pimenta moída*, a Portuguese pepper paste, to the importance of Spam to the U.S. military during World War II. Happy to be of service, I answered each one until it became impossible to keep pace with the avalanche of demands.

Seeing an opportunity to help these readers, as well as to create a formidable presence for myself as a burgeoning food writer, I began contributing directly to the site. I posted my responses to readers' queries, included hard-to-find recipes, and wrote original content. My first column, "Abstinence Makes the Taste Buds Grow Fonder," was chosen for inclusion in the anthology *Best Food Writing 2001*.

Because of the added content, the number of visitors to the site increased dramatically, and I decided to create an e-newsletter that would alert subscribers to new content. It would also include exclusive recipes and information that wouldn't be found on the site.

By 2003, Leite's Culinaria had grown so large and its database of articles was so vast, that when pitching a story idea to a new editor, all I had to do was direct her to the site to read my work. The site eventually attracted other like-minded people who wanted to be a part of the enterprise.

Leite's Culinaria was one of the first Web sites to take advantage of the enthusiasm of online cooks. Years ago we set up a program where each month testers are given recipes from soon-to-be-published and/or recently published cookbooks, and they put them through their paces. Only those recipes that score high enough are added to the site, making Leite's Culinaria a carefully edited, highly selective compendium of recipes and cookbook recommendations.

Today, Leite's Culinaria hosts an average of 1.4 million visitors each year, and more than 6.2 million pages are viewed annually. More importantly it has the ear—and eye—of newspaper, magazine, and book editors. Partly as a result of the site, I've been assigned articles, asked to speak or teach at various writing or Web programs throughout the country, record some of my essays for radio, appear on TV, and write a book. And I was delighted to learn that many of our recipe testers have parlayed their experience with Leite's Culinaria into internships and paid positions in test kitchens at several magazines.

▶ Food-Site Blogger

When she absently entered food terms into an Internet search engine, culinary student Sasha Foppiano got hit with 1,593 pages. As she clicked through the more interesting-looking Web sites, she stumbled across food blogs. She was hooked.

Although each blog has a unique bent, they represent an underground, ever-evolving community of bloggers. These are recipes of the people, by the people, and for the people. With each new posting, fellow bloggers dissect cooking processes and share information. They admire what is beautiful and write endlessly about how good they imagine some dishes must taste. Foppiano was right at home with the bloggers.

In general, the careful philosophies of Escoffier and Carème are secondary to the indulgent pleasures of culinary experimentation for bloggers. And there are errors out there. For example, take terrines. A terrine was, according to various explanations, a chilled block of egg salad layered between wheat bread, pickles, and lettuce; a delicate pineapple panna cotta gelèe; an oversized sushi roll; and a tower of Potatoes Anna. Errata can flow freely, unchecked and even unnoticed, but even errata can educate the best cooks.

Professionals, who may be caterers, restaurateurs, food writers, or entertaining celebrity cooks like Alton Brown, host some blogs. Their sites remain refreshingly experimental, albeit significantly more polished.

On the same night that she discovered food blogs, Foppiano started her own blog. She says she finds satisfaction in being completely anonymous and the fear of failure dissipated as positive feedback flooded her comment banks. She found, as have so many others, that no other forum stimulates creativity and encourages discussion quite the way blogs do.

> ## Food Radio Host

By Sue Zelickson, WCCO AM/CBS Radio

To be part of the food universe as a radio reporter requires you to look at things fairly yet form your own opinions and be aware that your words can influence the decisions made by others. A food reporter must have an extensive knowledge of and interest in food as well as a genuine curiosity about the people who are involved in producing it.

Radio reporting is easier than being a TV reporter, as you don't need to worry about looking like a fashion model. You do need a good voice, though, and you must be prepared to do your homework, checking facts and the background of guests. Having quick recall is essential, and it is important to have a solid grounding in the subject on which you are reporting. You must enjoy eating all kinds of foods and preferably not have allergies, aversions, dietary restrictions, strong dislikes, or prejudices. Also, you must not argue with your guests about their views on controversial issues.

I learned how to be a radio host while on the job at WCCO AM/CBS Radio in Minneapolis, Minnesota, where I work with a program director and producer. We plan the programs together, deciding which guests to interview and preparing a list of questions.

Many guests want to promote their cookbooks or their product and arrive at the radio station with a prepared list of questions for the radio host to ask. I prefer to ask my own questions so I don't

"Coming to media training was the most profitable forty-eight hours I've spent in years. It reaps rewards every time I step in front of a microphone or camera, talk to a producer or journalist, and every time I must dream up yet another enticing angle. It gave me the ability to focus, communicate, and prepare."

—**LYNNE ROSSETTO KASPER**, author and radio host

get a canned answer. To keep the guest on his or her toes, it is important to develop your own style and separate yourself from all the other radio programs. The listeners want information that they can use, not just a lot of idle chatter.

After twenty years as a food reporter, I have learned to talk slowly, chew my food quietly, and choose my words carefully, while enjoying every bite and every experience along the way.

▶ Media Trainer

By Lisa Ekus-Saffir

Authors who are media-trained know how to look and sound good on the television, and this increases their chances ten-fold of being published successfully. Emeril has his "essence," Sara Moulton has her "secrets," and Gale Gand has her "sweet dreams." Aside from their talent and skills, each of these chefs started out with a consistent message point—one that they skillfully crafted and presented with a good dose of passion to captivate a TV audience.

Media training has become hot for authors, spokespersons, and anyone who has something to sell. This applies particularly to chefs. As a media trainer, you'll help food professionals get ready for when the camera rolls by teaching them how to:

- Select and break down recipes for demonstrations
- Create detailed equipment and preparation lists for food escorts and stylists so they'll have everything necessary on hand—and nothing that will bog them down, trip them up, or otherwise cause confusion and delay
- Define and articulate key message points
- Build an effective relationship with their interviewer
- Maximize their television opportunity

There are only a handful of professionals who specialize in culinary media training, although there are numerous media-skills training programs nationwide. Your expertise will be your knowledge of food and the media. Ideally, your background should include experience in public relations and publicity. Editorial and television production experience is a plus. A degree in mass communication is beneficial, as is culinary training.

As a coach and guide, you'll help chefs get comfortable cooking and talking simultaneously, fielding difficult media questions,

"I cannot tell you how invaluable this was for me. . . . I now have a different perception of what makes for good public relations and great public relations."

—JASPER WHITE,
chef, restaurateur, and author

■

dealing with unexpected real-world situations, and learning how to lead rather than be led by the interviewer. Watch as many food programs as possible, learn what works and what doesn't, and understand what makes a chef or culinary personality stand out.

You need to be comfortable both in front of and behind the camera. You need to know how to cook and what recipes appeal to a broad audience. You'll conduct mock media events to help chefs practice with you as host, engaging your clients in what feels like down-to-earth conversation all while they chop, stir, sizzle, and garnish.

At Lisa Ekus Group, LLC, the media training involves either a one- or two-day intensive session, which costs $2,000 or $3,500, respectively. (Food costs, travel, and accommodations are additional expenses.) The company has a professionally equipped kitchen and uses professional-grade camera equipment to tape the media trainee.

Have as much excitement about what you do in your role as a media trainer as the chefs who are seeking your advice have about demonstrating their talents. Always remember that having fun is an essential ingredient for making food work on a national tour or a single television appearance.

Lisa Ekus-Saffir specializes in culinary public relations and media training. She is also a prominent literary agent. Find her on the Web at http://www.lisaekus.com.

WORKING IN TELEVISION

"I loved the training and found it valuable in many ways. Learning what skills are necessary to present a real recipe in unreal time especially helped me. Having a list of clear-cut goals and message points was key!"

—**MOLLIE KATZEN**, author

No one has discovered how to predict the magic that makes one person shine on television and not another. On-air talent is only part of the story. Beyond the celebrity chef there are producers, directors, camera operators, and the crew behind the scenes. As the arena of food-oriented television grows, so do possibilities for employment. Not everyone can be Rachael Ray or Emeril—and not everyone wants to be—but if you have an interest in the medium, there very well may be a job for you.

JULIA CHILD: AMERICA'S FAVORITE TV COOK

by Alex Prud'homme

JULIA CHILD DIED in 2004 at age ninety-two. *Mastering the Art of French Cooking* was first published in 1965. She was then forty-eight and her career had not yet begun. She and her coauthors had worked on the manuscript for ten years. It was a model of clarity, rigor, and accessibility.

She was still working on a book about her life in France with her husband, Paul, when she died. Her last TV cooking series, with Jacques Pépin, was in 1999 when she was eighty-eight. It came with a companion book that she reviewed.

It was her vigorous curiosity and joie de vivre that made Julia so appealing to so many people. And it is one of the things that set her apart from many of today's celebrity chefs and lifestyle entrepreneurs. But she could sometimes show her "flinty" side, too. This was an aspect of her personality that people tend to overlook or ignore, yet it was just as much a part of her as the fun-loving "ham" and "hayseed" that was her television persona. She was not simply a funny tall lady who dropped food on the floor and appeared to swig wine intemperately. (In fact, she was privately irritated by such caricatures.) She was a driven and rigorous technician, a well-trained and hard-working cook who loved French cuisine in part because it had what she called "rules."

She wanted things done right and had an acerbic quality to her personality that was rarely seen in public. She hated the joyless, thin-lipped food police who didn't understand the joy of cooking, eating, and drinking. Pommes Anna was one of her favorite dishes. It consists of thinly sliced potatoes, garlic, Parmesan, and lashings of butter and cream. She said, "If you are worried about using so much butter, substitute more heavy cream."

Julia Child said, "People looked at me and thought, 'Well if she can cook, I certainly can.' If you watch people who are too expert, you think you could never do it. But if you see a sort of normal person cooking, it makes you feel more confident. I had learned to cook at a mature age myself, so I understood that beginners need lots of details. At that time a lot of the recipes were very brief; they'd say put it under the broiler for twenty minutes. Well. I remember the first time I did that. When I came back, the chicken was all burned up. I'm sometimes laughed at for having long, detailed recipes, but if you don't know how to cook, you really want to know how far under the broiler to put the chicken, what to baste it with, and how hot the oven should be."

Her epitaph was that she made millions of people happier. But she also showed them that nothing good comes easily and that pleasure is the reward for hard work.

Recommended Books

Child, Julia, with Alex Prud'homme. *My Life In France*. New York: Random House, 2006.

Shapiro, Laura. *Julia Child*. New York: Viking, 2007.

ODAY, 80 MILLION households can tune in to the Food Network. There are stations in Atlanta, Los Angeles, San Francisco, Chicago, Detroit, and Knoxville. There are viewers in Canada, Australia, New Zealand, Korea, Thailand, Singapore, Philippines, Monaco, Polynesia, and Great Britain.

"Never assume or project that you know everything about food. The learning curve is endless and even Julia Child probably didn't know it all."

—**WESLEY MARTIN**,

culinary producer, food stylist

■

▶ Culinary Television Producer

By Todd Coleman, former culinary producer at the Food Network, current food editor at *Saveur* magazine

Are you a detail-driven foodie who loves to keep up with culinary trends, has a bottomless supply of cooking know-how, tricks, and tips, and has the wherewithal to edit recipes and put out figurative and literal fires?

Lights, camera . . . sauté. The cameras pan, tilt, and zoom in and around the cooking-show star as they cook and talk, encouraging the viewers to chop, stew, and roast in their own kitchens. Broadcasted to millions of people, cooking shows are feats of tremendous preparation, talent, and teamwork. And bringing it all into focus in the shadow of the set is the culinary producer.

With the advent of the Food Network, there has been an explosion of cooking shows, and with that a new world of culinary jobs has opened up for food professionals. Bridging the world of both cooking and TV production, the culinary producer is a chef with a headset, communicating with the star of the show, the producers and director who handle the technical aspects, and the cooks and food stylists who help to mold the food into sizzling, mouthwatering food porn.

TV production is stressful and fast-paced yet exhilarating and rewarding—just like working in a professional kitchen. The old kitchen axiom "make it happen" applies here ten-fold.

Different stages of production require different skill sets. The starting off point is the meticulous preparation process called pre-production or "pre-pro." (It's important to learn and internalize the lingo, as well.)

Pitching show themes kicks off a run of shows. Staying in touch with current food trends in the world of cookbooks and magazines helps to inspire new or relevant ideas, which leads to the conception of compelling episode titles and subjects.

Moving forward, you need to be a fastidious researcher, able to glean and cull important tidbits relating to the history of certain dishes, ingredients, techniques, and anything relevant to the particular theme of the show. The research can turn into talking points, on-screen tips, and smaller, actuated elements of a show like a demo-within-a-demo ingredient explanation that might not have happened without in-depth research.

Writing is a daily part of the job, from rearranging recipes into script form to recipe writing and editing to coming up with Web-based articles that correspond to an episode. Most importantly, you need to work hard to make sure that the needs and instructions from the star of the show and the executive producer are taken care of, followed, and communicated to everyone who is responsible for carrying out certain tasks. Good communication makes everything run smoothly.

Taping requires you to be on your toes. Depending on the style and type of production, you may be working in a studio, in the field in different locations, or in a rented house. You'll need to memorize this mantra: check, check again, and recheck. At the Food Network, studio cooking shows are often taped at a four-a-day clip, so things can go bad fast if everything isn't in order.

Time is money, and if the wrong cut of meat comes out onto the set in between acts, there's going to be trouble. If it takes thirty minutes to run out and shop for it that's a very long time, and you often can't make substitutes as talking points, graphics, and even the theme of the show may be based on that cut of meat. While taping is in full gear, you need to be flexible, aware, constantly fielding and answering questions, and trouble-shooting. You may need to dream up tips and tricks at the last minute to fill in time or rearrange the structure of an act. Above all, you need to know and love food and cooking. If you strive to learn and know as much as possible you will have prepared yourself properly.

GETTING STARTED

A culinary producer needs to be a cook first and foremost. Getting a degree or diploma from a culinary school is the best first step. From there you should try to obtain an internship at the Food Network, either in the production or culinary departments, or alternatively with one of the production companies that produces a lot of the programming that's on the air.

Even if you plan to strengthen your cooking skills by working in restaurants, catering, or as a private chef first, it's very important to meet people in the business, so that you can get in touch with them later—you might not have the opportunity to do an internship later on. Conversely, once you get to know them, there's a good chance that they'll call you down the road when they're hiring. Companies usually hire people that they already know over brand-new applicants.

There are other food jobs whose avenues lead into food TV. Recipe writing and developing, food styling, food writing, and

"The key to being a successful culinary producer is recognizing possible talent. This is a lot more difficult than it appears. It's being able to draw the balance between food knowledge and camera presence. There are those who have fantastic food credentials but lack the necessary charisma to host a show and vice versa. The trick is finding someone who has both, and then nurturing that talent until he/she reaches his/her full potential."

—**GEORGIA DOWNARD**, culinary producer

other media jobs such as editing at a magazine often lead to meeting the right people and gaining the right media-centric skills.

Most of the work in food TV is freelance, as most TV production is done on a job-to-job basis, so it's important to work very hard to get your name and résumé out there. Accept a non-food-related job as production assistant just to get your proverbial foot in the door.

Try every angle to get the job. Guerrilla market yourself by writing to your favorite cooking show star asking them to consider you in an entry-level position. You never know. That's how Sara Moulton got to work on one of Julia Child's shows.

• RECIPE FOR SUCCESS •

GEOFFREY DRUMMOND

GEOFFREY DRUMMOND PRODUCES cooking programs for television. He graduated from Cornell University and attended graduate school at Stanford, but he didn't study television production or the culinary arts at either. Rather, his film career began at Time Life Films as a writer on the TV science series *The World We Live In*; eventually he became its producer.

He next cofounded and was president of Saga Communications Group, an international film and television production company. Saga produced numerous award-winning films, including the cult classic, *My Dinner with André*. Under his own independent banner, Drummond went on to produce television and home-video programs such as Garrison Keller's *The Prairie Home Companion*, Disney's concert series *Going Home*, and the Master Chefs series for PBS. It was while working on Master Chefs that he began his *affaire de cuisine* and subsequent involvement with culinary programming.

For more than twenty-five years, Drummond and his company, À La Carte Communications, has produced and directed commercial, public television, cable, and home-video programs. Many of the country's most respected chefs including Lydia Bastianich, Daniel Boulud, Julia Child, Emeril Lagasse, Jacques Pépin, Nancy Silverton, Charlie Trotter, Jean-Georges Vongerichten, and Alice Waters have become familiar faces to home viewers through programs that Drummond brought to television.

Recommended Books

Corriher, Shirley O. *Cookwise*. New York: William Morrow, 1997.

Davidson, Alan. *The Oxford Companion to Food*. New York: Oxford University Press, 1999.

McGee, Harold. *On Food and Cooking: The Science and Lore of the Kitchen*. New York: Scribner, 2004.

And buy as broad a range of cooking magazines as you can afford.

Web Sites

Baking 911, http://www.baking911.com

Chowhound, http://www.chowhound.com

eGullet Society for Culinary Arts and Letters, http://www.egullet.com

Food Network, http://www.foodnetwork.com

The Food Section, http://www.thefoodsection.com

Mediabistro, http://www.mediabistro.com

PBS, http://www.pbs.org/home/home_cooking.html

Star Chefs, http://www.starchefs.com

―――

"Here are two rules that are posted on the refrigerator door during every one of my shoots. The first I call the 'Jacques Rule,' as it was developed during my stint on Julia and Jacques: Cooking at Home:

- Always keep on hand some of every ingredient in its unprepped, uncooked, untampered-with state. Never shell all the shrimp, string all the snow peas, or bone all the chickens. You can never anticipate what the host will want to do during a scene. If it isn't in the script, it will most likely end up on camera.
- "Never dump anything for any portion of the show before the director wraps the entire show. You may be done with a scene, but not until the show is wrapped are you in the clear. Technical difficulties or bumpy spots on the talent's part may not rear their head until well after a scene has been shot. It is better to face these situations with the backup ingredients you so wisely prepared than make another trip to the supermarket."

—CHRIS STYLER, *culinary producer*

―――

5

promotion and publicity

YOU MAY HAVE the best product, the most carefully researched cookbook, or the most inviting restaurant, but you cannot exist in a vacuum. You need customers, readers, and patrons. This is where promotion and publicity come into play.

Publicity is all about getting the word out. Every business should have a marketing plan—a collection of ideas for making sure the endeavor becomes part of the public's consciousness, either locally or to a wider universe. The marketing plan may include hiring a publicist or public relations (PR) specialist.

People who make promotion and publicity their career generally are forward thinking and creative. It helps, too, if they enjoy socializing and selling their client.

Advertising is just one part of the promotional fabric. Advertising costs tend to be higher than those for public relations, but results are easier to quantify.

Whatever your business is, you need to launch some sort of publicity campaign. We all hope for that best promotion of all: word of mouth. Before that can happen, good PR is essential.

ADVERTISING

Oh, I wish I were an Oscar-Mayer wiener; that is what I'd truly like to be. 'Cause if I were an Oscar-Mayer wiener, everyone would be in love with me.

Your programmed mind supplies the music to advertising messages such as this. The sound effects add to the excitement of commercials, especially commercials aimed at children. Many of those little jingles that you just can't get out of your head are directed to the lucrative under-six-year-old market. Little tots add up to a mighty heap of dough. But plenty of advertising is directed straight at the slightly more mature consumer, too, and a lot of it is for food.

Advertising is only one way food is marketed to the public, but it's the most obvious. Others include marketing, branding, and public relations. Food advertising is a $3.6 billion industry. McDonald's spends nearly $800 million a year on advertising, compared with a mere $1 million spent by the National Cancer Institute to promote fruits and vegetables. Advertisers like Coca-Cola, Frito-Lay, and Taco Bell shelled out $2.4 million for a thirty-second spot during Super Bowl XXXI. Estimates of how much money a fast-food company might sink into a single movie-based advertising campaign go nearly as high as $100 million. Who could ever have imagined that food could be so much fun? One bite of a snack food and you're surfing in California or soaring on your skateboard to a happy land!

Advertisers target every segment of the market, and their aim is spot on. They have figured out that the food of the well-heeled is line-caught, organically-grown, humanely-reared, grass-fed, home-smoked, char-grilled, blackened, pan-seared, wind-dried, sun-dried, oven-roasted, slow-cooked, free-range, artisanal, local, and seasonal. A little lower down the economic ladder, the food is convenient and easy to prepare.

Words such as *hand dipped* and *country fresh* have nice rings to them when you live in a crowded city. Packaging margarine in a mud-colored plastic tub and saying it's country fresh is a nice touch even though in our hearts we surely know it is manufactured from chemicals in a city factory.

We believe what we want to believe, egged on by the advertisers. "Because we care," because it has "the taste of real . . . ," "it's natural," "it's better tasting," and best of all it's "free" (of almost everything—including taste).

This doesn't mean that advertising is inherently bad or obfuscating. Advertisers say they "record, monitor, reflect, re-create, and anticipate the social construct of America's collective consciousness." Many major food companies are eager to respond to consumers' concerns, which means there are plenty of opportunities for food professionals to have their say as to what goes on the air, onto the Internet, and into print.

If you like to sell and are fascinated by market-driven trends and ideas, you might want to try your hand at advertising. There are several avenues from which to approach it. Apply for a job at a traditional agency where you can work your way up as you learn; look into smaller, boutique agencies where your job description may be more diverse; or explore the marketing departments of large companies.

> "The new food professionals must understand marketing and promotion, economics and real estate, health and safety and have the ability to study and interpret trends."
>
> —**RAYMOND SOKOLOV**, journalist

For More Information

Saint Joseph's University's Academy of Food Marketing offers a course of study that emphasizes marketing skills and techniques for those in the food industry. Its offerings include an undergraduate degree in food marketing; a master's degree in food marketing through the Executive Food Marketing program, targeted to professionals employed in the food industry and related fields; international marketing; and a bachelor's of science degree in food marketing. The school's Web site is http://cfm.sju.edu.

PUBLICITY PROFESSIONAL

Those involved in publicity include public relations specialists, publicists, and spokespeople.

Publicity is a more subtle approach to marketing a product or service than advertising. The methods are different, though they have the same objective: to reach the consumer quickly and effectively and to differentiate a product from its competitors.

Anyone can buy advertising space, but its value cannot be compared with having a favorable article in a prestigious publication or a mention on national television. The latter create that all-important buzz. But how can you get this publicity?

The public relations expert must have a thorough understanding of the philosophy of management and knowledge of the guests in order to develop the correct approach to positioning a restaurant or product in the marketplace.

Every new restaurant and retail business begins with a concept that will play a significant role in its marketing plan. The central idea is the same whether you are trying to publicize a trattoria or a bistro, a casual café, a formal restaurant, or a gourmet market selling prepared foods and tabletop items. The thinking process leads to the definition and refinement of a marketing plan, but often the stew becomes richer when a pool of talented people get together to strengthen each other's ideas.

One way to make sure you are on the right track is to walk on the street where you plan to open your business. Look at the people passing by. What are they wearing? What is their average age? Who is driving past? What kind of car is driven? Who occupies the passenger seats? Where are they coming from? Where are they going? How busy is the neighborhood at noon, at the cocktail and dinner hours, and after dark?

These passers by are your best potential customers, but they are not captive. How do you get them to come in the first time? Even more importantly, how do you get them to come back—and come back often?

Metaphorically speaking, in order to stand apart from the competition, don't color the bus yellow. Paint it bright pink and purple, with yellow dots. Exceed the expectations of your customers. How this goal is achieved rests not only on the quality of the food and service, but also the skill and imagination of the public relations, marketing, and advertising talent that is employed by every business. This is where an experienced public relations professional is most helpful. He or she can help the business to position itself. And PR is a business where creativity is a premium. The businesses that survive and thrive are not those with the deepest pockets, but the nimble ones that study a problem and unleash the creativity of a team of eager employees.

Food PR often means thinking outside the box when it comes to promoting a product or restaurant. Creative parties, charity auctions, and celebrity tie-ins are just the beginning. Anything you can envision that would get your client attention in the press is fair game.

PUBLIC RELATIONS THAT WORK

Whether you are the business owner doing your own public relations or a hired public relations pro, start with a mission statement. Define a clear idea of how you want the business to be perceived. This doesn't mean a woolly-headed statement full of clichés or an abstract name that is hard to remember and nobody understands. It is far more understandable to call your restaurant Joe's

Pub than MS22 (for 22 Main Street). If you are promoting your personal chef business, declare yourself as Tom the Personal Chef, not I Have Thyme for You.

Once the concept is clear, it frees you to think up all sorts of promotions that the media will be kind enough to convey to your target market: Offer a free turkey-carving class the week before Thanksgiving, a table-setting demonstration before Christmas, a two-week lobster feast in July, or a harvest festival in the fall. At Easter time, the pastry chef could make hot-cross bunnies or chocolate Bugs Bunnies. Print the desserts on an edible menu. Serve beefsteak tomatoes with a steak knife. Keep records of guests' birthdays. Offer to send a limousine to pick up regular guests if they come back to celebrate their birthday with you next year. On Mother's Day, Mom's dinner is *complimentary* (a nicer word than saying it's *free*). Make a gingerbread house to raffle for charity.

A promotion takes a lot of planning, but it establishes a restaurant or small business in the community and brings in a gratifying amount of business. A festival of oysters provides the opportunity to stage an oyster-and-wine-pairing event (with muscadets, Chablis, and champagnes by the glass). An oyster menu might feature oysters Rockefeller, oyster pan roast, and oyster stew. Announce a contest in which the winners receive a free wedding reception. Persuade other local businesses to contribute the wedding rings, cake, tuxedo rental, and travel arrangements. The publicity all will receive will be incalculable. Or stage a white sale in January when restaurant reservations are scarce—put everything white on sale including white rice, whitefish, chicken breasts, and vanilla ice cream. You will surely get mentioned in the newspaper, and the seats will fill in no time.

GETTING STARTED

Intern with a public relations agency. Use the telephone directory to locate agencies in your area. A phone call will determine if they work with restaurant or other food-related businesses.

To get hired for an internship or rise from an entry-level position, you need to learn how to write press releases, fact sheets, pitch food stories, and be comfortable on the phone. Perhaps most importantly, you must be detail-oriented so you can be counted on to organize events.

Many colleges offer courses on media relations. Take one to learn the right way to make cold calls to food editors, TV producers, and reporters. Here are some tips:

- A successful PR pro knows whom to reach for the best exposure. Different media use different kinds of information. Newspapers may want recipes, magazines look for celebrity, while Web sites want quick tips for easy cooking. Television is the holy grail, and all of the above apply.

- A good tactic is to write an article for a magazine. It's not easy to break into national magazines, but even local magazines get your client's name out. The publicity value is incalculable if you tell your client's story to the right readers.

- Go-getters bring in new clients. All successful PR people very quickly learn the importance of networking.

- Read, watch, listen, and surf the Web to discover what other businesses are doing. Think up new riffs on existing ideas. Giveaways are always popular. Danny Meyer at Blue Smoke in New York City dispensed with toothpicks and instead gives his guests plastic "brush picks" that proved so popular at the barbecue hot spot he is designing similar giveaways for his other restaurants. Wish restaurant in Miami Beach, Florida, gives away electric ice cubes with lights inside. Customers come back for more.

• RECIPE FOR SUCCESS •

by Patti Londre, president of the Londre Company,
a marketing and public relations firm

HAVE YOU EVER heard someone say, "I can't believe I get paid to do this." We hear it a lot in the field of food public relations and marketing, an undeniably fun profession. But to get to the fun, you will walk through fire. If you crave a fast-paced, highly stimulating profession that demands results, look here.

My job is president of a boutique firm that provides corporate and product marketing PR for food, agriculture, nutrition and packaged goods. Our efforts are mostly media-related and involve promotions, events, and creating positive exposure. An explanation of how agencies do this would fill volumes—PR isn't black and white. The sky is the limit as to how to reach consumers about a product and to present its features and benefits so a consumer might want to purchase it. The goal is to make a sale, which is what pays our salaries. Because of that, marketing and public relations pros who make it to the top of this field are highly paid and rarely unemployed for long. In fact, great clients tend to follow really good PR pros, so you can see the attraction.

While getting into this profession can be fairly easy, staying here and becoming a top practitioner doesn't happen overnight. The routes may be creative, yet the roads are long and challenging.

Getting Started

My entry into PR was unconventional, not unusual in this field. With a bachelor's degree in home economics from San Diego State University, I first worked in community relations for a supermarket chain, then in food-service sales for Campbell Soup, but I wanted to be back inside an office environment. Fully believing I could do PR because I had a tiny bit of exposure to others in the field, I landed an agency job. My previous experience gave the impression that I could run their food accounts, but after eighteen months it was evident to them that that was incorrect, and I was terminated. Thus, in 1982, fueled with righteous indignation and not much else, the Londre Company Marketing and Public Relations was founded. A three-year night course in PR at UCLA Extension and membership in the Public Relations Society of America bolstered my skills as I pitched new business, while learning PR via the school of hard knocks.

My agency has grown the painful way, and I can say with great experience that there are no shortcuts to the top, but there are plenty of fast tracks back to the bottom! So when it comes to being a success in this area, never stop learning.

How do I know what to do for my clients? Experience is the answer, and that is why agencies work in account teams. You won't know what to do until you've been in the trenches for years with teammates. Being a team player sounds like a cliché, but you learn from your partners, and you teach your partners.

Keys to Success

Personality traits include persistence, dedication, vision, enthusiasm, curiosity, and patience. Physical traits include stamina and good health. Professional skills and tools include:

- The ability to write. We write all day, every day. Articles, pitch letters, speeches, scripts, correspondence, and Web content, all day long.

- The knack to sell. Pitching is selling. Landing new business is selling. You have to be thick skinned, take rejection from media (and clients) daily, say thank you, and do it again, year after year.

- The ability to communicate clearly. Can you explain how the government new food pyramid works to your grandmother, so she picks it up on the spot? Give it a shot.

- Creativity. Not "new twists on old traditions." Extreme creativity. Not just borrowing ideas, but every day dreaming up new ways of looking at practically everything. Fresh approaches, classic concepts, real contributions.

- Strategic thinking. The ability to see a problem and map out the way to solve it. The ability to figure out what to do. The mind of an engineer.

- Understand finance. There is a myth that PR people are bad with money. In my book, only lousy ones are. We spend our company's money or our client's money. You have to understand the basics of accounting, both in your career, and frankly, in life. Better learn now.

continued

continued from page 211

More Marketing Advice

How are you doing with your marketing plan so far? Are you making headway, or slipping behind? Here's an easy checklist to help you to see how well you're doing—or to provide you a fresh to-do list. Answer yes or no to the following:

1. My agency's Web site is up, current, and every link works.
2. My professional photo was shot in the new millennium.
3. My hit list has received something from me in the past three months.
4. I've attended at least one trade show for new business leads.
5. I've joined one new group and have become involved in a committee.
6. I've asked my current clients and vendors for referrals, and I have made a point to give good referrals to others.
7. I've rechecked and maximized search engines for my Web presence.
8. I have a current brochure or mailer that clearly presents what my business does.
9. I've sought out new areas of value-added skills to add to my capabilities.
10. I've adjusted my attitude from, I've never had to market myself before, to, what can I do today to market my business."

For More Information

The Holmes Report, http://www.holmesreport.com

International Association of Culinary Professionals, Marketing Communicators Section, http://www.iacp.com.

O'Dwyers PR/Marketing Communications Web site, http://www.odwyerpr.com

Ries, Al and Laura. *The Fall of Advertising and the Rise of PR.* New York: Collins, 2004.

University of Los Angeles, California, Extension, Certificate in Public Relations, http://www.uclaextension.edu

Hotel and Restaurant Promotion

*by Andrew Freeman, founder and president of Andrew Free-
man and Company, hospitality and restaurant consultants
(http://www.andrewfreemanandco.com)*

 WHAT A RIDE it's been—working at leg-
endary restaurants such as the Russian Tea
Room, the Rainbow Room, and Windows
on the World. After ten years in the hospitality industry, I landed a
prime position as director of restaurant marketing with a fast-growing company, San Francisco-based Kimpton Hotels and Restaurants. And then came my biggest achievement, the opening of
Andrew Freeman and Company. Who would have thought I would
end up with my own agency?

When I went off to college to pursue my dream of becoming a
Broadway star, I realized that I could make a lot of money by working in restaurants. So I did. As I moved my way up from waiter to
manager, I found I had a real gift of gab and loved to think up ways
of promoting and building the business. I took a career shift and pursued a marketing degree. After graduation and a few great jobs with
advertising agencies, I decided I could couple my passions for food
and sales and marketing and find a job that allowed me to do both.
After several jobs at restaurants, I landed a prime position as director of restaurant marketing with Kimpton.

In the ten years I was with Kimpton, I was promoted several
times and had the great fortune to oversee all the public relations
for the hotels, restaurants, and key executives. I also developed and
maintained key strategic relationships with community/civic
groups, vendors, and charitable partners. In addition to my PR
responsibilities, I handled all the promotions for the new restaurant openings and managed the restaurant marketing program. I
also led the company's Social Responsibility Initiative: Kimpton
Cares, and chaired our Gay and Lesbian Employee Network. And
when I started my own firm, Kimpton was my first client. How's
that for synergy?

Now, for each of our clients, we develop strategic marketing programs that include demographic and psychographic studies, competitive research, and market analysis. Once we have the concepts

continued

continued from page 214

established, we pursue public relations opportunities, advertising, community involvement, and direct sales.

My advice to anyone entering this field is: Have a great product. Keep your costs in line; stay on top of the competition; keep your offerings interesting; listen to your guests, your employees, and to your gut—and be consistent. Make sure you are promoting your business to the right group of people. For instance, if your restaurant is surrounded by hotels, you should be best friends with the concierges—they will send you business.

Getting Started

For a job as an in-house public relations professional, you should have:

- Actual work experience in hotels or restaurants
- A creative spirit that doesn't get offended when your ideas are shot down
- A sense of humor—we are feeding people and giving them places to sleep. We need to ensure that our guests feel a sense of caring, comfort, style, flavor, and fun in everything we do.
- Great writing and verbal skills
- Amazing organization and follow through
- Ongoing culinary education and skill-building. I take courses, eat out a lot, and try to stay up on what's happening and what trends are coming.
- Flexibility and patience

▶ Product Spokesperson

Professional spokespeople represent a product on behalf of their clients. Chefs, cookbook authors, and nutritionists are among the credible experts who are employed to get a message to the public on television, radio, and in print. The spokesperson is required to show up with time to spare, look good if going on TV or streaming video on the Internet, be charming, and make the product so irresistible that the viewer, listener, or reader will be overcome with enthusiasm and rush out to buy it, preferably for the rest of their natural life.

The "talent" (spokesperson) must repeat the message with sincerity a hundred times. The ability to stay on message and deliver predetermined selling points is a skill that is developed and fine-tuned by the most successful spokes-ladies and spokes-gentlemen.

Typically, the brand spokesperson must exhibit the ability to weave adulation about the goods into what appears to be a non-commercial conversation. They must never be seen as selling or being too obvious, but still must mention the product as often as possible within a very limited period of time.

As a spokesperson, you may be asked to provide quotes for a print or audio release. A satellite media tour may be planned for television or radio, with local media enticed to consent to an interview. You may be asked to participate in an online "chat" with the public.

For example, as a spokesperson for the Canned Food Alliance, Jacques Pépin shared his perspectives about upcoming culinary trends and cooking with prepared foods. He noted, "Americans are coming to terms with the food world. In France, people have always had their own sense of flavor. Until the last fifteen years, Americans relied more on what food critics said than their own opinions about food. Now, when they want something easy, people cook with canned and prepared foods without feeling apologetic." Bingo. This is a good observation and a soft sell from an unimpeachable source and helps to promote his book *Fast Food My Way* at the same time. And it lets the listener feel good about doing what she is already doing—eating canned and frozen foods.

Bonnie Tandy Leblang's company, MediaMentor *http://www.bonnietandyleblang.com), offers targeted media outlet analysis, instructional networking, practice pitching ideas, and instructions for creating press mailings. She also covers professional phone and e-mail manners and offers classes on how to get a message heard above all the shouting.

Among other major public relations companies that employ spokespersons in the food arena are the Londre Company, Ketchum Public Relations, Hunter Public Relations, Porter Novelli, and Fleishman Hillard.

Occasionally, a writer can make a marriage of convenience with a potential sponsor, offering perhaps to become a spokesperson for a barbecue sauce or a grill after publishing a book on the subject of grilling, but usually an aspiring spokesperson must become highly visible first and wait to be invited to audition for the role of product pitchperson.

▶ Product Demonstrator

The best part of being a product demonstrator is that you can be any age (over eighteen) and work only when you feel like it—although you won't get rich. It is helpful to have some knowledge of food or the cooking equipment you are demonstrating to the largely distracted shopper as she passes in front of your display table.

A demonstrator may handle any number of products in a variety of venues ranging from a grocery shop to a department store. Work is contracted through research firms, temporary personnel agencies, food processing companies, and equipment manufacturers.

The demonstrator sets up or checks the product display and demonstration area to make sure that the product is attractively presented. He or she explains the product to customers and answers questions while keeping the area neat and tidy. Although demonstrators are not salespersons, they may offer discount coupons, product samples, brochures, and fliers, and provide information to the public about the product in an effort to persuade them to buy it now or later (preferably now, this minute). They must also coax suspicious passersby to taste a morsel of an unfamiliar food that they have prepared. (This is a task that is much more difficult than it might seem.) In other words, they are on the front lines when it comes to product marketing.

Demonstrators are often asked to count the number of their clients' products on the shelves at the beginning and close of day. They keep records of the number of questions received and the number of coupons and samples given away. They also note weather conditions or other information that could be helpful to the store owner or distributor in deciding if the promotional efforts or products are worthwhile, or perhaps if a blizzard or hurricane warning is responsible for slow traffic and minimal sales. Based on their experience, the demonstrator may recommend how to improve the product and provide better service to customers, or tell their employer what is wrong with the product, though such counsel may not automatically prove helpful in obtaining future employment.

The downside of this job, other than fairly low pay, is the obligation to remain standing for several hours at a stretch while enduring minor cuts or burns without complaint. The regrettable truth is the work can get boring during slow shopping periods and customers can be rude or even mean at times.

The employment outlook is frankly astonishing: the number of demonstrators in California alone will soon be near nineteen thousand. There will also be an estimated sixty-three hundred new job openings in the state due to people retiring or leaving the occupation for unspecified reasons.

6

history and culture

FOOD HISTORY AND culture are increasingly popular with many who are interested in the ways the social sciences define our and other cultures. Add to this the growth in niche travel. An understanding of the culinary history of a region can enhance the adventurous traveler's experience. Food historian Sandra Oliver explains, "Every ingredient contains fascinating stories about its origins, uses, and travels over the earth and throughout time. So does every recipe we read, every dish we produce, and every utensil and cooking method we employ.

"Food historians uncover, record, and reproduce these stories, recipes, and dishes," Oliver continues. "They search literary texts and nonfiction works, including old cookbooks, for hints of daily diet and culinary customs to get a clearer picture of what the average person, not just the wealthy and upper classes, ate at any given time and place. They search for new sources studying kitchen inventories, trade and taxation records, photographs, as well as oral histories."

Very often, historians study their subject for the love of it—and then look around for ways to use their knowledge. Food history may be combined with a job in travel, teaching, or writing. Culinary libraries need the help of historians, as do academic journals and publishers. Trend predictors and futurists rely on historical patterns, too, because it is imperative to understand the past in order to comprehend what is happening now and what is likely to occur in the future.

> "Indeed the next best thing to eating a good dish is to read how it is made; and somehow the old cookbook writers learned to write the most appetizing English."
>
> —**WALTER DE LA MARE** (1873–1953), British Poet

• **RECIPE FOR SUCCESS** •

by Francine Segan, food historian and cookbook author

AMONG MY MANY hobbies—flying, skeet shooting, hiking, tennis, and skiing—is creating meals based on cookbooks of the past. I gave a dinner party a few years ago that ended up converting that hobby into a full-time career.

The dinner, given to celebrate a friend's performance with Gwyneth Paltrow in Shakespeare's *As You Like It*, was based on Elizabethan cookery books and included readings of sixteenth-century jokes, puns, and riddles—a regular part of feasts back then. The guests so enjoyed the evening that they encouraged me to write a book on the frivolity of feasting in Shakespeare's time.

Random House liked the idea and contracted to publish my cookbook. *Shakespeare's Kitchen: Renaissance Recipes for the Contemporary Cook* was released two years after that first dinner party. Random House has subsequently published two other books based on my themed dinners, *The Philosopher's Kitchen* and *Movie Menus*.

Thanks to the success of those books, I've had the opportunity to work with dozens of organizations recreating meals of the past. Some examples include:

Elizabethan dinner feasts for theater groups such as Shakespeare and Company in Massachusetts, Princeton Shakespeare Festival, Theater for a New Audience, and Lincoln Center in New York City

A formal Gilded Age–style dinner fundraiser for the Foundling Hospital, an apt theme for an organization founded in the Gilded Age

A luncheon and lecture on the foods of the roaring 1920s for the Norman Rockwell Museum's exhibit of Jazz Age illustrators

A dessert party of sweets from nineteenth-century Viennese cookbooks for the anniversary gala of the Music Ensemble for the Romantic Age

In addition to working with organizations and event planners, I've been invited to lecture on the foods, dining customs, and etiquette of the past for museums, universities, historic homes, theater groups, libraries, and reading groups across the country. I've also had the good luck to share my interest in foods of the past with a wide audience of radio and television viewers.

My experience is, I know, very uncommon. I hope that my good luck serves to motivate anyone with a food passion to try to share it. Start by setting your sights within easy reach, writing for small neighborhood publications, cooking for a local church group, or teaching cooking classes to a group of colleagues from work. Don't put it off. Do something with your hobby. You never know where a hobby can lead.

• RECIPE FOR SUCCESS •

by Andrew F. Smith

I NEVER PLANNED to become a culinary historian and in fact there was no such field until a decade or so ago. My academic training was in international relations and education, and I had assumed that a combination of these two disciplines would be my lifelong career.

Then in the 1980s I read an article about Robert Gibbon Johnson eating a tomato on the courthouse steps of Salem, New Jersey, in 1820, at a time when the tomato was believed to be poisonous. Thousands of people gathered, according to the article, to watch Johnson die. This story raised questions: Why wasn't the tomato eaten earlier? Why did Americans think the tomato was poisonous? I wanted to know more and despite quite a lot of research, I never found definitive answers.

These differences fascinated me enough to drive to Salem and see if I could find out more about this little-known incident in American history. After months of poking around, I concluded that the incident never happened and that many people in America ate tomatoes before 1820. I wrote up my findings and submitted them to *New Jersey History* magazine, and the article was accepted for publication.

I was hooked. If Johnson did not eat the first tomato in America, who did? And how did the tomato become so important in America? These questions led to writing additional articles on tomato history. When these were accepted by history journals I figured that I was on a roll and should write a book on tomato history. I submitted a proposal to a publisher and much to my surprise I received a contract.

continued

continued from page 222

My first book, *The Tomato in America: Early History, Culture and Recipes*, was published in 1994.

When you publish a book, you think differently about yourself— and others think differently about you as well. A few months after it was published I was asked to teach a course in culinary history at the New School. I readily agreed. Other than tomato history, of course, I really didn't know much about culinary history so I spent weeks reading and preparing for the class. I've continued to write and teach culinary history ever since.

Today, there is a broad-based field of culinary history, and I have contributed to the making of it, which gives me great satisfaction. If I had advice it would be to follow your curiosity and be open to opportunities that, if pursued, may change your life.

For More Information

http://www.foodbooks.com/foodlink.htm is an important and extremely useful Web site for everyone who wants to learn about food history. It provides excellent information about libraries with extensive food and cookbook collections and listings of food historians' newsletters. It also lists organizations of food historians, and information about conferences, lectures, and courses. The site will also undertake searches for rare and out of print books. The following information is reprinted from the foodbooks.com Web site:

American Culinary History Center. A large and tasty slice of Americana has found a home in the Longone Center for American Culinary Research at the University of Michigan's William Clements Library.

Campbell Library of the Academy of Food Marketing. This library specializes in works on the food industry. The collection consists of over four thousand books and 275 serial publications.

The Culinary Archives and Museum at Johnson and Wales University in Providence, Rhode Island, is the premier museum devoted to the preservation of the history of the culinary and hospitality industries. Internationally renowned, this collection of over half a million items represents five millenniums of history, often referred to as the Smithsonian Institution of the food service industry.

Culinary Holdings of the New York Public Library. The collection on gastronomy and the history of foods is unusually extensive, and the cookbook collection alone numbers well over sixteen thousand volumes.

Culinary Holdings of the Schlesinger Library. The Schlesinger Library at Radcliffe College includes nearly twelve thousand works in the fields of cookery, gastronomy, domestic management, the history of cooking, and related reference works.

The Culinary Institute of America's Conrad N. Hilton Library houses an outstanding collection of specialized literature in the culinary field. The library has three hundred current periodical titles and more than fifty-two thousand volumes on cooking, baking, food and beverage management, business, history, psychology, communications, computers, and languages. They also maintain a collection of menus, rare books, and videotapes.

Feeding America. Full-text reproductions of seventy-six historic American cookbooks are available on a Web site created by the Michigan State University Libraries. Feeding America: The Historic American Cookbook Project' was a two-year digitization project funded by the Institute of Museum and Library Services. The seventy-six cookbooks featured on the site include some of the most significant works in American culinary history, including a 1798 printing of Amelia Simmons' American Cookery.

Indiana University Bloomington Libraries—the Lilly Library. The Lilly Library's acquisition of Mrs. John T. Gernon's collection of American cookbooks forms the core of the library's collections pertaining to food and drink.

Szathmary Collection at the University of Iowa Libraries. The University of Iowa Libraries have in their collection more than twenty thousand items owned by Chef Louis Szathmary, including books, pamphlets, and manuscripts.

Newsletters

The Cookbook Collectors' Exchange is a growing phenomenon. At forty-eight pages, published bimonthly, this publication is a medium for the exchange of cookbooks and information and related experiences volunteered by collectors and enjoyed by a large audience. To order the latest issue of *The Cookbook Collectors' Exchange*, send $2.00 to: CCE, P.O. Box 32369, San Jose, CA 95152-2369.

Flavor and Fortune is the only Chinese-food magazine published in the U.S. Ken Hom is the honorary chairperson of the institute that sponsors it. The cost is $19.50 per year for this award-winning quarterly that reports about Chinese food culture, history, cookbooks, restaurants, equipment, recipes, and more. Send checks made out to ISACC (Chinese Institute) and mail to P.O. Box 91, Kings Park, NY 11754. For more information contact Jackie Newman at jloveschfd@aol.com.

Food History News is edited and published by Sandra L. Oliver, 1061 Main Road, Islesboro, ME 04848. If you have any interest in the history of food then *Food History News* is a must. http://www.foodhistorynews.com

Recommended Books

Fernánandez-Armesto, Felipe. *Near a Thousand Tables: A History of Food.* New York: The Free Press, 2002.

Sonnenfeld, Albert, trans. *Food: A Culinary History from Antiquity to the Present.* New York: Columbia University Press, 1999.

Tannahill, Reay. *Food in History.* Eyre Methuen, 1973

Toussaint-Samat, Maguelonne. *History of Food.* Blackwell, 1993.

▶ Futurist

In order to predict the future, it is essential to be a historian. A food futurist studies trends rather than isolated happenings in the food world. He looks at logical events in many other parts of society that gradually or suddenly change the way we eat.

A futurist understands that when it comes to food, nothing just happens. Supply and demand are the result of history, geography, politics, and trade agreements. Of equal importance is the influence of the advertisers and special-interest groups. Together they fan the fads and fashions of pop culture.

A food futurist reads dozens of magazines—not only food magazines, but publications like *American Demographics*, the *Economist*, *World Watch*, *Discover*, the *Wall Street Journal*, and, of course, the *Futurist,* a magazine of forecasts, trends, and ideas about the future. The bimonthly magazine has been published since 1967 by the World Future Society and is read by twenty-five thousand members worldwide.

A futurist also studies food trade magazines and Web sites that cover everything from supermarkets to farming. He dines in restaurants and makes notes about who and how many are eating breakfast in fast-food restaurants, (the numbers are increasing) and who is drinking coffee at Starbucks, including the age of the customers and frequency and times they arrive—and leave. Scientific magazines will lead the futurist to suggest that before too long a solution will be found for the problems of allergies and food intolerances.

This kind of in-depth research is useful for those making plans for the future. For example, if the number of single-person households is increasing, it makes sense for food stores to offer a single slice of cheesecake and for restaurants to add a table for communal dining. Moreover, if companies do not insist on business clothes for their employees, it is difficult for a restaurant to insist on jackets and ties and if both parents work away from home, it makes sense to open child-friendly restaurants.

The late Art Siemering, who was a very well-regarded food futurist, offered these guidelines for would-be trend spotters:

- Digest a broad range of cultural content from newspapers, magazines, broadcast media, and the Web. Pull bits and pieces of information together to determine whether they create a pattern. Then analyze the overall result to uncover implications for your specific segment of the vast food industry.
- Make direct observations at every opportunity—as you travel to trade shows, attend seminars, go on consulting assignments, or even take pleasure trips.
- Check out the "glamour districts" of places you visit: Go to the newest restaurants, the most-crowded supermarkets, and the hippest shops. Look for pockets of vibrant activity in college towns and upscale resorts. Trends will seem to jump out at you.

Armed with current-day observations, it becomes possible to predict we will not always have three three-course meals a day. In fact, in some of the hippest restaurants in the world's most cosmopolitan cities, "small plates" are the hottest commodity around.

We may have more frequent smaller meals, smaller portions, with meat no longer occupying the center of the plate. As more foods become shelf-stable, we will have less use for the refrigerator and freezer. We will need only the flip of a lid to flash heat, or flash chill, our foods.

▶ Ethicist

Perhaps no greater ethical question confronts the food world than that of biotechnology. Many thoughtful people have weighed in on the subject of genetic modification, with a consensus yet to be reached. Richard Sherlock, who holds a doctorate degree from Harvard University and is currently professor of philosophy in the department of languages and philosophy at Utah State University, addresses the issue of biotechnology head-on. He declares unequivocally, "Genetically modified foods are here to stay. The process can't be stopped. It can be slowed down but there is no possibility of going back to ground zero.

"Food produced through biotechnology will not harm humans in a physical sense. The U.S. regulatory agencies have instituted rigorous inspection standards. There is no evidence of any adverse consequences. The answer to the question, is it safe? as far we know, is yes.

"But that is not the only question," Dr. Sherlock continues. "Why is the public concerned and what should the response be as there obviously is public concern? The central anxiety is not about the science but a quasireligious belief that may be nontheistic— thinking about the natural way of being. Many consumers believe, largely erroneously, that eating genetically enhanced food is dangerous. One would not want to prejudge what the reactions of a consumer may be to more education. Surely more information would be more, not less, helpful. Few people know what the data is. As a result, pastoral concerns are now being legislated."

Ultimately, science makes bad religion, and religion makes bad science. Faith is by its very nature unquantifiable. Science is only accepted when specific facts can be proved and replicated.

The role of the ethicist in our society will become increasingly important as science and technology continue to exert an ever-more powerful presence in our food supply and distribution system. It will be important for ethicists to weigh in on matters related to clean drinking water, the building and dismantling of dams, plummeting wild fish populations, fish farming, and animal cloning.

"I believe if ever I had to practice cannibalism, I might manage if there was enough tarragon around."

—JAMES BEARD

Food companies will consult ethicists, universities will provide homes for some, and others will become public voices through their writings, speaking engagements, and Web sites.

Recommended Book

Sherlock, Richard, and John D. Morrey, eds. *Ethical Issues in Biotechnology.* Rowman and Littlefield, 2002.

▶ Psychologist

Paul Rozin, professor of psychology at the University of Pennsylvania, suggests:

Freud chose to frame the clash between our biology and society in terms of the mastering and socialization of our sexual impulses. It seems to me that he would have had a stronger case with eating. Although both food and sex are biologically basic, the need for food is more frequent, more compelling, and frankly, more important in both daily life and in the evolution of animals and humans. The process of civilization must tame our desire to promptly consume anything that looks appetizing; we cannot grab an attractive morsel of food that is in someone else's possession, just as we cannot engage in sexual activity with any person who appeals to us.

The meal, with its elaborate culinary preparations and social conventions is a far cry from wolfing down foods. There is actually a more elaborate cultural transformation of our relationship to food than there is to sex. This results, in part, from the fact that we are much more inclined to eat than to have sex in public.

These are the sorts of profound observations that form the building blocks of ever-shifting public-health policies delivered (at jaw-dropping cost) to (mostly indifferent) consumers.

"Anthropology teaches us there is nothing ordinary about the ordinary, that is, if by ordinary, we mean 'usual' or 'normal,'" says anthropologist Judith Friedlander, "still, every culture believes their way of doing things is normal." The study of anthropology may help us understand why otherwise rational people opt to pig out on various weird dietary aberrations, when they could just as easily choose to eat a "normal," "usual" diet.

It is vitally important to increase our understanding of why people eat what they eat, within the limitations of their own geography, history, religious beliefs, and economic conditions. When experts study the amalgamation of old and new facts their knowledge serves as a guide to formulating public policy, which, among other things, tries to ensure that when food relief is sent to those in need, we offer food that is both acceptable and palatable to the recipients. At the other end of the spectrum, a respect for exactly what it is their guests like to eat helps chefs decide what to put on the menu.

For More Information

CASC, http://www.sciencesite.com/casc

Access the American Anthropological Association Web page at http://www.aaanet.org and go to the careers section. There you will find information about becoming an anthropologist. They also publish a directory of anthropology departments, which you may be able to find, or order, from your school library. You can check the local natural history museum to see if there are people you can talk to—or, if you live in a big enough city, look for your state archeologist. But the best way to track down a good program is to talk to people—they're your best resource, overall.

Recommended Books

Camporesi, Piero. *The Magic Harvest, Food, Folklore and Society*. Polity Press, 1980.

Farb, Peter, and George Armelagos. *Consuming Passions: The Anthropology of Eating*. New York: Pocket Books, 1983.

Harris, Marvin. *The Sacred Cow and the Abominable Pig*. New York: Simon and Schuster, 1985.

Sokolov, Raymond. *Why We Eat What We Eat*. New York: Simon and Schuster, 1991.

Visser, Margaret. *Much Depends on Dinner*. Collier Books, 1986.

Wood, Roy C. *The Sociology of the Meal: Food and Social Theory*. Edinburgh: Edinburgh University Press, 1995.

• RECIPE FOR SUCCESS •

FOOD ANTHROPOLOGIST

by Sydney Mintz,
professor emeritus of anthropology at Johns Hopkins University

I NEVER INTENDED to study food. I specialized in the social history of the Caribbean islands. Because my dad was a cook, I thought of food simply as part of my identity. I began to write about food by writing a book about sugar, which I'd studied in the Caribbean. When it was well received, I began to feel blessed by that discovery. *Sweetness and Power*, the book about sugar, came just twenty-five years after *Worker in the Cane*, the life history of a Puerto Rican cane cutter, and another book about sugar. But I believe that they are really one book, imbedded in each other—rather like combining a telescope and a microscope, I would say.

When you look at a particular country, whether it is France or Uganda, you see distinctive patterns for eating, and you can use those patterns as a way of grasping how that society is divided up. Every society divides children from adults and feeds them differently. Hence food is an instrument of social distinction, and a tool for understanding as much.

Things that we learn when we are young persist in our memories and we may hold them with affection. The foods of our childhood are associated with those who cared for us. Such memories are burned into the practices of daily life. What is more, one society may judge another society's behavior, including its foods and ways of eating, as quite irrational. Such judgments are usually reciprocated! Societies with what we consider all sorts of irrational beliefs may think the same of us, yet function quite well.

GARBAGE ANTHROPOLOGIST

WILLIAM RATHJE IS professor of anthropology at the University of Arizona, where a study called the Garbage Project has existed for many years. Says Rathje, "The food that we throw away can be very revealing." Among the study's findings:

- Halloween garbage contains candy wrappers but no candy, while Valentine's Day garbage contains both wrappers and candy. "On Halloween what's important is the candy; on Valentine's Day what's important is the gesture," says Rathje. (One could also conjecture that children do not throw away candy, but some adults do.)
- The more repetitious a family's diet is, the less food they throw away. (They keep buying the same limited number of foods and eating them without wasting any surplus.)
- Paradoxically, more food that is considered in short supply is discarded than foods considered abundant. This is because consumers tend to overbuy the "scarcer" foods, which then go bad before they are eaten.
- Buying processed foods such as individual frozen pot pies does not mean that other foods won't be thrown out. Single-portion dinners are eaten in preference to fresh food that requires work to prepare. More fresh food is thrown out—eventually.

Alan Shawn Feinstein, director of the World Hunger Program at Brown University, noted in *The Hunger Report* that only 60 percent of all the world's harvested crops are actually eaten by human beings, and 25 to 30 percent of the remainder is wasted in various ways. "Simply improving storage and distribution systems would automatically result in a great deal more food becoming available for everyone," he writes.

There are plenty of jobs for specialists in many different disciplines to enter this field of endeavor. As Wendell Berry, author of *The Unsettling of America*, said, "The enormous productivity of industrial agriculture cannot be denied, but neither can its enormous ecological, economic, and human costs."

Recommended Books

Rathje, William, and Cullen Murphy. Rubbish! *The Archaeology of Garbage: What Our Garbage Tells Us About Ourselves*. New York: Harper Collins, 1992.

Royte, Elizabeth. *Garbage Land: On the Secret Trail of Trash*. New York: Little, Brown, 2005.

▶ Folklorist

In his obituary in the *New York Times*, it was noted: "The late Alan Dundes was a renowned folklorist who, rigorously, engagingly and often provocatively, explored a vast spectrum of human customs and beliefs.

"He is widely credited with helping to shape modern folklore scholarship. As a popular and award-winning University of California, Berkeley, professor of anthropology and folklore, he earned an international reputation for his Freudian deconstruction of everything from fairy tales to football to the Book of Genesis."

Said Dundes, "As a psychoanalytic folklorist, my professional goals are to make sense of nonsense, find a rationale for the irrational, and seek to make the unconscious conscious."

Professor Dundes and his devoted students believe folklore to be a serious subject that deals with the essence of life. In recognition of his work, he was the first in his area of study to be elected to the American Academy of Arts and Sciences. His *Study of Folklore* was designed to fill a void of textbooks about folklore and has gone through twenty-six printings. Another of his many books is *Never Try to Teach a Pig to Sing*, in which he and coauthor Carl Pagter analyzed modern folklore. Many ethnic stereotypes judge whole civilizations or parts of civilizations by what they eat or refuse to eat, he found. He observed: "Cultures are defined by their food customs."

Under his guidance, the anthropology department at University of California, Berkeley, established a master's degree program in folklore that houses an archive of more than five hundred thousand items. Students study the allure of violent sports, holiday traditions, why the Jews were expelled from Spain in 1492, and even the mystique of the vampire. Garlic has many venerable roots in social history and pop culture, too. This is a curious custom of opposing science by citing mythology.

ʃOHN T. EDGE, SOUTHERN HISTORIAN

by Anne E. McBride

EDGE SAYS HE is a foodways generalist. His background and approach is hybridized—folklore meets interdisciplinary academia. He uses food as a filter for studying his primary field of interest: the American South.

Through the work of the Southern Foodways Alliance, an institute of the Center for the Study of Southern Culture at the University of Mississippi—and through his own writing—Edge strives to tell the story of unknown cooks of the American South and writes about people through the prism of food. He says this interdisciplinary field is a burgeoning one.

At the University of Mississippi, he learned to take academic research with a firm sociological and historical backbone and present it to a lay audience. "The research you do shouldn't remain in a filing cabinet, squirreled away for posterity so that only five people in fifty years will chance to read it," he says. "The challenge, of course, is to find the right market for your research and writing. In graduate school, I learned to think about my native region in a critical fashion. That experience gave me the perspective I needed, the perch from which I could write."

To compile ideas—notions that might become projects—Edge uses a number of online research resources including the Southern Folklorist listserv, the Association for the Study of Food and Society listserv, the Southern Foodways Alliance blog, and Lexis-Nexus. He attends many conferences, including, for example, the Southern Historical Association Conference and the American Studies Association Conference. He reads a lot, including *Food History News*, *Gastronomica*, *Gourmet*, *Saveur*, and *Simple Cooking*. "I'm also a gatherer," he says. "I have bulging files of newspaper clippings. I have stacks of menus and ephemera. And I'm always writing in a notebook, fiercely, jotting down ideas, tangents, observations."

Recommended Books

Edge, John T. *Fried Chicken*. New York: G. P. Putnam and Sons, 2004.

Apple Pie. New York: G. P. Putnam and Sons, 2004.

1

science and technology

THE UNLIMITED POSSIBILITIES for employment in the field of food science loom large once you accept the premise that growing, preparing, and cooking food is a marriage of science and art. Whether you're more interested in the medicinal value of herbs or are fascinated by the idea that flavors can be developed in a chemistry lab, science and technology offer numerous ways to turn your appreciation of food into a profession. For example, automation is a major component of the food business. Sensors use refracted light to test the sweetness of preserves. Machines measure ingredients with uncompromising accuracy and mix, stir, and knead a dough or batter to achieve the correct texture every time. Radio waves detect the crispness of cookies before they burn. Machines weave breakfast cereals from oats, wheat, corn, and rice, or engineer blends of multigrains, and extrude them in a triumph of physics and technology married to food chemistry. Food technologists and engineers have their fingers in many pies.

Science reaches even more extensively into the world of food, too. As nations address issues of world hunger, there is an ever-increasing need to grow more efficiently, to plant seeds in inhospitable land, and invent new methods of irrigation.

Health issues connected to food also will require trained scientists as the twenty-first century progresses. Childhood obesity in the

U.S. alone is a major challenge to the medical community and will not be conquered without the help of scientific research. Other important topics include: how to minimize the use of additives, hormones, and the extensive use of antibiotics in intensive farms; how to provide diets beneficial to cancer patients, diabetics, and others with specific food intolerances; how to deliver medications through food; and how to treat allergies. The possibilities are limitless for food professionals with an interest in scientific research.

▶ Obesity Researcher

Is body weight inherited, or is obesity more of an inadvertent, almost unconscious response in a society where food is cheap, abundant, and tempting? An extra hundred calories a day will pile on ten pounds in a year, public health messages often say. In five years that is fifty pounds.

Richard Webb, director of the New York Obesity Research Center Weight Loss Program, writes, "No one disputes that genetics plays a role in obesity, but the worldwide rise that has occurred over the past 50 years isn't due just to genes. Genes haven't changed in the past 50 years; the environment has. There are food and labor saving devices everywhere. The good news is that there are people who lose weight and keep it off. The mean weight loss among more than 5,000 men and women in the national Weight Control Registry is 60 pounds, and the group has maintained that loss for roughly five years. They work hard at it, and no one claims it's easy, but they do it."

Weight-loss clinics offer food professionals the opportunity to guide clients into more healthy eating patterns by conducting counseling and cooking classes.

MINDLESS EATING

On the jacket of his fascinating book, *Mindless Eating*, Brian Wansink, PhD, is identified as the John S. Dyson professor of marketing and nutritional science at Cornell University, where he serves as director of the Cornell Food and Brand Lab. He says, "I have designed and conducted over 250 studies, written over 100 academic articles, and made over 200 research presentations to governments and governors, to top universities and companies, to culinary institutes and research institutes, and I have presented my research results on every continent but Antarctica."

But what exactly does he do? He describes the work of his lab as follows:

> Using precise methods of weighing foods eaten or discarded, psychologists test the accuracy of food claims and consumers' perceptions. So despite our demonizing fast food restaurants (and all other food processors), they don't care a jot whether you eat their stuff—only that you buy it. If starting tomorrow at noon, we all went to Taco Bell and Burger King and ordered only salads, their menus would change faster.
>
> It takes 3,500 extra calories to equal one pound weight gain. It doesn't matter if we eat these extra 3,500 calories in one week or gradually over the entire year. They'll add up to one pound. This is the danger of creeping calories. Just 10 extra calories a day—one stick of Double mint gum or three small Jelly Belly jelly beans—will make you a pound more portly one year from today. Only three Jelly Bellys a day! Drinking one can of Coca-Cola, (130 calories) each day would amount to 101,470 calories—29 pounds—over a two-year period. Fortunately, the same thing happens in the opposite direction.

Mindless Eating is filled with fascinating fallibilities that affect our eating decisions even when we think *we* would never fall for foolish tricks that lead us to gain weight by eating mindlessly.

If you are interested in becoming a researcher, check out employment opportunities at the Consumer Behavior program at Stanford University, the Tuck School of Business at Dartmouth College, the University of Illinois Hospitality Management Program, the Penn State Department of Nutritional Science, University of Maryland College of Behavioral and Social Sciences, eLab at Vanderbilt University, and the U.S. Army Natick Labs. And look up consumer-behavior research programs on the Internet.

PRODUCT DEVELOPMENT
By Erica Murphy, culinary student

Does the idea of having thirty-eight different types of grape flavor available in a powder or liquid form excite you? Are you comfortable with meticulous measuring and recording? Is the cutting edge where you want to be? If so, product development could be the career for you. I learned a lot when I spent my cooking school externship working in the product development department of M&M Mars.

Product development within the corporate food industry is becoming popular for trained cooks with a background or an interest in food science. Sometimes referred to as research chefs, product developers also understand and apply methods of food preservation, mass production, and the technical terms used by scientists and business people. The term *culinologist* is being used to describe this new field and several universities, including the University of Nebraska, are granting degrees for research chefs.

The primary skills necessary for product development include the ability to think creatively and solve problems. If you are innovative as well as patient, a decent mathematician, a meticulous record keeper, scientifically oriented, enthusiastic, a persuasive communicator, and a trend watcher, you may have found your niche. Possible jobs include working in test kitchens for chain restaurants, grocery store chains, magazines, or food manufacturers. Researchers toil in every segment of the food-processing industry, including snack foods, candy, baked goods, drink manufacturers, frozen/prepared foods, and coffee.

Product developers have degrees in food science or another science-based field. For the culinary side, it is best to have a degree from an accredited culinary program either in culinary arts or baking and pastry arts. An undergraduate degree combined with a culinary degree will open many doors. Most importantly, you must have a firm grasp of cooking techniques, ingredient performance, and have a consumer-oriented mind.

To get started in product development, it is a good idea to do an internship with a food company or try for an entry-level job. Typical entry-level positions include food technicians, food researchers, and developers. You might want to consider starting your career with a flavor company or a small ingredient company or supplier that supports the major food corporations. This way, you can gain experience and exposure in the field with a company that will back you when you move to a larger corporation.

Companies that are known for hiring research chefs include Starbucks, Subway, and Panera restaurants. The work appeals to chefs who have an analytical mind and a nose for sniffing out food trends. It is an advantage to have both business and technical knowledge.

The Research Chefs Association was founded in 1995, and it currently has twenty-one hundred members, including forty-five certified research chefs and 170 student members. It has become an important source for the food industry, and its members include chefs and food scientists working in nearly every field, from restaurants to manufacturing and academia.

For More Information

Books

Brown, Alton. *I'm Just Here for the Food*. Stewart, Tabori and Chang, 2002.

Corriher, Shirley O. *Cookwise: The Hows and Whys of Successful Cooking*. New York: William Morrow, 1997.

McGee, Harold. *On Food and Cooking: The Science and Lore of the Kitchen*. New York: Scribner, 2004.

Wolke, Robert L. *What Einstein Told His Cook*. New York: Norton, 2005

Web Sites

American Institute of Baking, http://www.aibonline.org

American Dietetic Association, http://www.eatright.org/Public/

Food and Nutrition Information Center, http://www.nal.usda.gov/fnic

Research and product-development opportunities can be viewed at http://foodscience.co

National Center for Food Safety and Technology http://www.iit.edu/~ncfs

US Food and Drug Administration Center for Food Safety and Applied Nutrition http://vm.cfsan.fda.gov/list.html

Professional Organizations

Institute of Food Technologists, http://www.ift.org
Research Chefs Association, http://www.culinology.com

UNIVERSITIES WITH FOOD-BASED CURRICULUMS

Food Science

University of Georgia, Athens, Georgia
Rutgers, New Jersey
Purdue, Indiana

University of Florida, Gainesville, Florida
University of California, Davis, California
Kansas State University, Manhattan, Kansas
Oregon State University, Corvallis, Oregon

Product Development
Pennsylvania State University, State College, Pennsylvania
University of Nebraska, Lincoln, Nebraska
University of Cincinnati, Cincinnati, Ohio
Clemson University, South Carolina

SCHOOLS TO CONSIDER FOR CULINOLOGISTS

Culinary Institute of America (CIA).
Research Chefs of America (RCA) specialists teamed with
top-notch CIA chef instructors to offer students five-day
courses. Courses are offered at both CIA campuses in
Hyde Park, New York, and Greystone, California.

KENDALL COLLEGE.

The Culinary Arts Seminar for Food Technologists at Kendall
College is designed for food scientists and those involved in food-
related research and development. This intensive course helps
students gain an understanding and working knowledge of the
basics of the culinary arts in order to expand upon an R & D
(research and development) or food-science background. Classes are
taught by American Culinary Federation–certified chef instructors
in conjunction with a chef who specializes in the field of food-
related research and development. All classes consist of both lecture and practicum.

JOHNSON AND WALES PROVIDENCE CAMPUS.

The RCA, in collaboration with the College of Culinary Arts
at Johnson and Wales University, Providence campus in Rhode
Island, provides food technologists with the fundamentals of culinary arts. RCA specialists teamed with JWU chefs in order to conduct a three-day hands-on training program on the utilization of
commercial cooking equipment as well as proper food handling
and preparation techniques.

▶ Flavor Maker

As the demand for reduced-calorie and special-diet foods and beverages surges ever onward, large companies that concentrate on creating flavors are expanding their operations. Adding tastes that are lost when foods are processed to reduce their fat content is just a small part of the flavor makers' capabilities. All foods that are to be frozen must be given heightened flavor, because freezing mutes their tastes.

Flavor makers create roasted, baked, and fried flavors for hundreds of uses ranging from barbecue flavor for potato chips to deep, dark woodland flavor for "wild" mushrooms. Research chefs create "authentic" tastes for everything from ice cream to apple pie and iced tea. In fact, if a packaged food has a distinctive taste, the chances are good that it has received its flavor not from a farmer in a bib overall, but from a white-coated scientist in the laboratory. The interesting thing is that, given a choice, we often prefer what we have come to accept as the "real" taste of artificial or synthetic flavors to the *real* thing. (Ask many people to choose between homemade mayonnaise or vegetable juice and they will be very likely to reach for the Hellmann's or V-8.)

An expert tells us, "Flavors are extremely complicated things. A flavorist may sit down with, say, mango flavor and notice sweetness, a tang, tartness, a whole range of things. Then he'll go to a shelf and say, 'Well, citric acid has one of these flavor components, another type of acid has another component,' and on and on. After a long time and dozens of ingredients, he'll assemble the entire mango. It's quite remarkable when it all comes together into a complete flavor."

International Flavors and Fragrances (IFF) is the world's leader in creating and producing the intense tastes found in many of the new clear beverages and other products we eat and drink. Think of onion, sour cream, vinegar, and literally dozens of other savory flavors that increase the impact of many snack foods. Think of chicken, shrimp, beef, pepperoni, mushroom, scallion, garlic, sesame, and other flavors that make snacks taste good and IFF's got it.

Food scientists create an intricate amalgam of flavors and fragrances for literally thousands of foods. Each element is included for a reason. This is a formula for artificial strawberry flavor:

"As long as consumers demand convenience and processed foods, additives will be a part of those foods."

—**RITA STOREY**, RD, ConAgra
Foodservice Companies

■

Amyl acetate, amyl butyrate, amyl valerate, anethool, anisyl formate, benzyl acetate, benzyl isobutyrate, benzyl acid, butyric acid, cinnamyl isobutyrate, cinnamyl valerate, cognac essential oil, diacetyl, dipropyl ketone, ethyl butyrate, ethyl cinnamate, ethyl heptanoate, ethyl heptylate, ethyl lactate, ethyl methylphenylglycidate, ethyl nitrate, ethyl propionate, ethyl valerate, heliotropin, hydroxyphrenyl-2-butanone (10 percent solution in alcohol), alpha-ionone, isobutyl anthranilate, isobutyl butyrate, lemon essential oil, maltol, 4-methylacetophenone, methyl anthranilate, methyl benzoate, methyl cinnamate, methyl heptine carbonate, methyl naphthyl ketone, methyl salicylate, mint essential oil, neroli essential oil, nerolin, neryl isobutyrate, orris butter, phenethyl alcohol, rose, rum ether, -gamma undecalactone, vanillin, and solvent.

• MATTERS OF FACT •

𝒮URIMI IS MADE from the minced, rinsed, mild-white "meat" of Alaskan pollock. The rinsing process dissolves water-soluble elements, leaving behind a residue of tightly bonded proteins with such extraordinary "gel strength" that it can be molded into any shape and colored to approximate the appearance of crabmeat.

Some time ago, the story goes, when surimi was brand new on the market, a salesman left samples of it with a retail buyer whose staff members offered some to a seagull that regularly perched outside the office window. The seagull wouldn't touch the stuff. Subsequent offerings got the same turn down.

Finally, the salesman came by again with samples of a new and improved version. "If our resident expert likes it, I'll take some," the buyer told him. The office window was opened, the surimi treat was presented, the seagull gobbled it up and looked around for more—and the buyer gave the astonished salesman his first-ever order for surimi.

RARE JOBS
FOOD TASTERS

VINEGAR TASTER. Heinz employs a vinegar taster to examine the company's vinegars for clarity, color, and aroma. The taster dips a sugar cube into each sample and sucks up the vinegar. To keep his taste buds up to snuff, he nibbles unsalted crackers and drinks plain water between sips. Faced with Heinz's new super vinegar, 50 percent stronger than any of its predecessors, the resident taster turned up his toes and declared himself to be in heaven.

OLIVE OIL TASTER. Melissa Swanson, a freelance food-and-wine writer based in Oakland, California, tells us:

> For the past two years, I've served as a taster for the California Olive Oil Council's taste panel. We are a group of people with sensitive palates trained to detect defects in olive oil. The panel functions as part of the process a California producer might want to pursue in order to put an extra-virgin label on his or her oil. For an oil to be considered extra virgin, it must have certain fatty acid and peroxide levels, but it also must be deemed by our panel to be defect-free. Twice a month, we taste and smell between eight and fifteen oils.
>
> Our panel is the only one of its kind in North America. Because it is still a relatively small industry in the United States, the olive oil business is virtually unregulated here. In Europe, however, the International Olive Oil Council regulates oil from Europe and awards seals, just as we do. As tasters, we are selected and trained by the IOOC's standards.

ICE CREAM TASTER. Every morning a taster must confront sixty containers of Edy's ice cream and taste every flavor at the beginning, middle, and end of its run. The taster tastes vanillas first, then chocolate chip cookie dough, mocha almond fudge, and mint chocolate chip. John Harrison, taster extraordinaire, has his taste buds insured for $1 million.

CHEWING GUM CHEWER. Cadbury employs a professional chewer to report on the taste of its gum. It is not known if this is a full-time position nor whether it is required for the chewing to take place on the premises only.

TEA TASTER. Tasters sip two hundred to three hundred cups of tea a day for the Lipton Tea Company. A skilled sipper can determine the country

"At the turn of the last century, government, science, industry and technology changed not only what we ate but also how we thought about it. Food was reduced to those physical properties that could be analyzed and synthesized chemically."

—**BETTY FUSSELL**, food writer

■

a tea comes from, the specific plantation on which the tea was grown, and even the hillside from which the leaves were harvested. Experts create the consistent blend that issues forth from Lipton in 40 million tea bags daily.

According to the Tea Man's Tea Talk (http://teatalk.com), "a tea taster evolves after years and years of very specialized training, which comes toward the close of a career of even more specialized experience within the tea industry. He or she has elevated tea evaluation to more than a science and raised it to an art. The tea taster has honed all five senses to the point where they act in unison, simultaneously, as one sense organ whose sole purpose is to make an evaluation, a judgment, on one specific tea at a time (though hundreds of teas may be cupped or tasted during a single day). A taster uses the senses of smell, sight, touch, taste and hearing to form subjective and objective decisions about tea." No sugar, thank you.

COFFEE TASTER. Every couple of years, the New York Board of Trade conducts a two- to three-hour examination in its search for new professional coffee tasters. Writing for *Fast Company* magazine, Nick Reding reports, "Since taking his first job 30 years ago in Toronto with General Foods, the founder and sole employee of L. E. Faubert and Co. has become not only a coffee broker and a private taster, but also a NYBOT-certified 'cupper,' or grader. His ability to occupy all three roles puts him at the choke point of the entire $19 billion industry, a slim bridge between the hundreds of importers, exporters, manufacturers, growers, and shippers, and the tens of millions of U.S. coffee drinkers."

• MATTERS OF FACT •

- In 1995 we still had an official federal tea taster with an official tea-tasting room in Brooklyn, New York. Between salary and operating expenses, the federal government was still spending $120,000 a year to taste tea. Despite the valiant efforts of the federal tea taster in rejecting 1 percent of all tea tasted in 1995, the Clinton Administration ousted the position in 1996 as part of its reinventing-government plans.
- In his fascinating and highly recommended book, *A History of the World in 6 Glasses*, Tom Standage tells us, "The idea that coffee is the antidote to alcohol was put forth in 1671. In fact the opposite is true. It may make the inebriated person 'feel' more alert—but it actually reduces the rate at which alcohol is cleared from the bloodstream."
- Jesse Sartain, a professional chef, food and beverage taster, and marketing

executive, has tasted more than 150,000 products since 1985 when he founded the American Tasting Institute.

- The olfactory system is in the part of the brain that is the center for memory and emotion (hence the resonance between Marcel Proust and his madeleines).
- The human nose is a powerful possession. It detects an odor measuring one billionth of an ounce as it floats in the air.
- Our taste buds can detect sweetness in 1 part in 200. We can detect saltiness in 1 part in 400. Sourness is perceived in 1 part in 130,000. Bitterness can be tasted in 1 part in 200,000. An odor can be detected by the taste buds even when diluted to 1 part in a trillion. This is a protective mechanism. More poisonous foods are bitter than sweet.
- When an infant refuses to taste even a teeny tiny little bit "for Mommy," it is because the child has smelled the food and is repelled by it. It is not even remotely necessary or advisable therefore to proceed to tasting it.

For More Information

To apply for work as a professional taster, contact www.stayfreemagazine.org/archives/23/ flavor-chemists.html

If you've got a taste for the sweet and the salty, then International Flavors and Fragrances is your kind of company. http://www.iff.com

The Monell Center is a nonprofit independent scientific institute dedicated to interdisciplinary basic research on the senses of taste, smell, and chemosensory irritation. http://www.monell.org

▶ DIETITIAN

By Joyce Marcley Vergili, MS, RD, CDN, CDE, PhD

Do you like to work with people one-on-one? Do you prefer doing cooking demonstrations for an audience? Does developing a menu for a patient newly diagnosed with diabetes sound appealing to you, or would you prefer to help an athlete find the eating plan that will maximize his performance? Do you like flexible schedules, or are you more comfortable with the structure of a nine-to-five job? Do you enjoy being an integral part of a health-care team, or would you rather be a one-man show? As a registered dietitian (RD), the choice is yours.

QUALIFICATIONS

Registered Dietitians are food and nutrition professionals who have earned a minimum of a bachelor's degree in a food- or nutrition-related field from an accredited college or university, completed nine hundred hours of American Dietetics Association (ADA)–supervised practical experience, and passed the Commission on Dietetics Registration's (CDR) written exam. While earning a master's or doctoral degree is not required, over 50 percent of ADA members have degrees beyond a bachelor's.

In order to maintain their credentials, RDs must earn seventy-five hours of continuing professional education every five years. Those who have graduated with a bachelor's degree, but have not completed the ADA practice experience and/or passed the exam, often refer to themselves as graduate dietitians, nutritionists, or registration eligible. Only 10 percent of graduates opt against becoming registered, however, as many employers will not hire a dietitian, and many insurance companies will not reimburse the dietitian for his services, unless he is registered.

In addition to becoming registered, a dietitian may also become certified or licensed through his state's education department. The requirements for licensure or certification vary from state to state but are similar, if not identical, to the requirements for becoming an RD. In many states, obtaining this credential is optional. However, without it, the dietitian may not use the term licensed dietitian (LD) or certified dietitian (CD). The dietitian may refer to himself only as a dietitian, nutritionist, or RD, as appropriate. If you find this confusing, you are not alone! The ADA is working toward streamlining the credentialing process, including the standardization of the initials.

Some RDs hold additional certifications in specialized areas of practice, such as hospitality education and diabetes education. While these certifications are recognized within the profession, they are not required.

Those interested in attending a four-year college to earn a degree in food, nutrition, or dietetics have many options. Some students first earn an associate degree in dietetics technology, food science, or a similar field, land a job with a firm that offers tuition reimbursement, and then finish the four-year degree with the financial help of the employer. More colleges and universities are offering bachelor's degrees, either entirely or partially, as online or distance-learning programs. Students can concentrate on any number of areas, including food science, public health, research, clinical nutrition, journalism, global food systems, education, or food service.

WHAT IS A DIETICIAN?

One of my favorite definitions of a dietitian is, this: a person who translates the science of nutrition into food on the plate. Therefore, an important area of competency is meal planning and food preparation. When a client comes to an RD for medical nutrition therapy, the first utterances the RD will hear are:

- "What can I eat?"
- "Can you give me some recipes?"
- "Will it taste good?"

Because fewer people cook meals from scratch than ever before, the RD's ability to educate clients on basic cooking skills is becoming increasingly important. Many people do not possess even such elementary food knowledge as the difference between parsley and basil. RDs cannot, therefore, off-handedly advise a client to "use herbs and spices instead of salt." The demand to learn food preparation skills is so great that some dietitians make a career of teaching both clients and fellow dietitians how to cook. They can be found on the faculty of culinary schools, as culinary nutritionists in private practice, coordinating international culinary adventures, writing and editing cookbooks, and even on their own television cooking shows. (Visit the Food and Culinary Professionals Web site at http://www.foodculinaryprofs.org.)

The second core of educational requirements includes the sciences—biology, chemistry, biochemistry, and microbiology. Many nutrition majors find these courses rather challenging, if not overwhelming. Some will even forgo majoring in nutrition to avoid the imagined horrors of chem lab. Don't let such fears keep you from reaching your goal. In most cases you only have to get a C in these tough courses!

The last area of competency is the psychosocial sciences. When advising people to change their eating habits, RDs are advising changes of an extremely intimate nature. RDs must, therefore, be sensitive to personal food preferences and the culture through which a person views his world. Counseling a forty-five-year old overweight female who has just been diagnosed with high blood pressure to lose weight is likely to be ineffective if she believes that being "a little plump" is pleasing to her husband. Encouraging her to eat more vegetables and spend more time working in the garden may be a better approach.

"People who have little or no knowledge of nutrition will, within a given meal, seek a healthy variety. Animals, children, everyone, seem to have this instinct."

—**BARBARA ROLLS**, PhD, author, with Robert A. Barnett, of *Volumetrics: A Systematic Lifetime Approach to Eating*

"I'm wary of health faddists. When they're done talking, you can't eat *anything*. We need a nutritionist who loves good food."

—**JULIA CHILD**

NETWORKING

Networking on the local and national levels, exploring different roles (such as by shadowing other RDs), lifelong learning, self-confidence, and viewing the world as your oyster are the keys to success. One of my most fulfilling accomplishments, the opening of a Diabetes Center, began when I called the local hospital's CEO to suggest that the hospital should open a diabetes center. He not only whole-heartedly agreed, he hired me to do it! Although I had never before written a business plan or pitched a proposal to a finance committee, I was confident that I could do it. The education and experience required to become an RD laid the solid foundation upon which these new skills could be, and were, honed. Challenging? To say the least. Worth it? Absolutely!

WHERE THE JOBS ARE

RDs are found in a variety of jobs, with their scopes of practice continuously expanding. To get a sense of the many directions an RD's career can take, log on to the ADA Web site, http://www.eatright.org. There you will find twenty-eight specialty groups, known as Dietetic Practice Groups (DPGs), to which dietitians may belong to help them advance in, or even decide upon, their area(s) of expertise. Examples of DPGs include:

- Food and Culinary Professionals—for members who promote food education and culinary skills to enhance the health of the public.
- Dietitians in Business and Communications—for professionals employed by, seeking employment in, or self-employed in the profit-making organizations of the food and nutrition industry.
- Nutrition Entrepreneurs—for consultants in the business of developing and delivering nutrition-related services and/or products. Membership ranges from veteran business owners to members establishing new practices.
- Diabetes Care and Education—for members involved in patient education, professional education, and research for the management of diabetes mellitus.
- Dietetics in Developmental and Psychiatric Disorders—for nutrition professionals whose work

involves clients with physical and mental disabilities, substance abuse problems, and eating disorders.

■ Hunger and Environmental Nutrition—for members who promote optimal nutrition and well-being for all people, now and in the future, acknowledging the interdependence of food security, health, agriculture, and the environment.

■ Nutrition in Complementary Care—for dietetics professionals interested in the study of alternative and complementary therapies.

■ Sports, Cardiovascular and Wellness Nutritionists— for nutrition professionals with expertise and skills in promoting the role of nutrition in physical performance, cardiovascular health, wellness, and disordered eating.

■ Vegetarian Nutrition—for nutrition professionals in community, clinical, education, or food-service settings who wish to learn about plant-based diets and provide support to individuals following a vegetarian lifestyle.

■ The Weight Management Group—founded to support the highest level of professional practice in the prevention and treatment of overweight and obesity throughout the life cycle.

• MATTERS OF FACT •

● The ADA's Web site provides links to facilitate exploration of how to become an RD, including information on the over two hundred colleges that offer ADA-approved programs, as well as statistics regarding job outlook and salary expectations.

● According to the ADA's 2002 Dietetics Compensation and Benefits Survey, half of all RDs in the U.S. who have been working in the field for four years or less earn between thirty-three and forty-two thousand dollars per year. As with any profession, salaries and fees vary by region of the country, employment settings, scope of responsibility, and supply of RDs. Salaries increase with years of experience and many RDs, particularly those in management, business, and consulting earn incomes above fifty thousand.

● The U.S. Bureau of Labor Statistics reports that employment of dietitians is expected to grow about as fast as the average for all occupations as a result of increased emphasis on disease prevention, an aging population, and public interest in nutrition. Employment in hospitals is expected to show little change because of anticipated slow growth and reduced patients' lengths of hospital stay. Faster growth, however, is anticipated in nursing homes, residential care facilities, and physician clinics.

Competitive Enterprise Institute, http://www.org

The International Food Information Council's (IFIC) mission is to communicate science-based information of food safety and nutrition to health and nutrition professionals, educators, journalists, government officials, and others providing information to consumers. Its newsletter, Food Insight, reports current topics. http://www.ific.org and http://ific/healthy.org also http://ificinfo.health.org

Nutrition News Focus, run by David Klurfeld, editor in chief of the *Journal of the American College of Nutrition*, offers daily analysis of nutritional research and dietary claims. http://www.nutritionnewsfocus.com

Writing about Health Risks: Challenges and Strategies, by Michael Kamrin, PhD, and Marilynn Larkin, MA, American Council on Science and Health, is an excellent guide to the evaluation of scientific studies of all types. Free download:
http://www.acsh.org/publications/reports/factsfears.html

Internet Sources for Sound Nutrition and Health Information

The American Dietetic Association, http://www.eatright.org

Government Healthfinder, http://www.healthfinder.gov

Johns Hopkins Health Information,
http://www.intelhealth.com/IH/inhhtIH

Mayo Health Oasis (of the Mayo Clinic),
http://www.mayohealth.org

Medline http://www.nlm.nih.gov/datbbases/freemedl.html

National Institutes of Health, http://www.nih.gov

Tufts University Nutrition Navigator,
http://navigator.tufts.edu

The U.S. Food and Drug Administration,
http://vm.cfsan.fda.gov

World Health Organization, http://www.fao.org

- Former Surgeon General C. Everett Koop claims 75 percent of deaths in the United States are related to diet.
- In 2006, 177,000 people had gastric stapling surgery. It costs between fifteen thousand and twenty thousand dollars.
- According to Packaged Facts, the market for gluten-free products was valued at $210 million in 2001. In 2006, the sales escalated to an astonishing new high of $696.4 million and are anticipated to reach $1.7 billion in 2010.
- Hardee's Monster Thickburger is a 1,420-calorie burger consisting of two beef patties, three slices of cheese, and four strips of bacon on a bun smeared with both butter and mayonnaise. Would you like fries with that?
- A fast-food chain advertises its high-calorie food for "people on the go." It doesn't specify where they might be going.
- There are 25 million overweight people in America. Many will have shorter life expectancies than their parents.
- It costs $14 billion a year to treat overweight children.

▶ Seed Scientist

Scientists have high regard for ancient seeds, although they always seem to want to tinker with them. There was a lot of excitement recently when it was discovered that, under ideal conditions, seeds could remain viable for four hundred years. Israeli scientists have succeeded in germinating a date seed nearly two thousand years old, and one startling experiment reported that some barley seeds had sprouted after being dormant for thirty-three thousand years. This Lazarus-like discovery has greatly spurred international cooperation into efforts to preserve as many heirloom specimens as possible.

Collecting the seeds of the past is not just a hobby for dedicated gardeners who relish the vibrant tastes to be obtained from hardy nonhybrid varieties that are fertilized the old-fashioned way, by breeze or bees. In the past three years, sixteen hundred varieties of open-pollinated seeds have been saved from extinction and replanted to expand the inventories of small companies such as Native Seeds/SEARCH in Tucson, Arizona. The Seed Savers Exchange, headquartered in Decorah, Iowa, has eight thousand members involved in rescuing endangered vegetable and fruit varieties, including traditional Native American crops, as well as Mennonite and Amish vegetables. Each season, the seed savers select seeds from the hardiest, tastiest varieties to replant, and then deliberately let them go to seed so that they can extract the best ones to send back to the exchange.

If you are interested in becoming a seed scientist, you may want to consider enrolling in a school of agriculture. Your culinary knowledge combined with information about seeds will open a gate to future employment in both the food industry and hunger-relief agencies. Chefs are increasingly enthusiastic about putting heirloom varieties of vegetables and fruits on their menus, so you could consider planting a garden for restaurateurs and other connoisseurs.

Recommended Book

Katz, Solomon H., and William Woys Weaver, eds. *Encyclopedia of Food and Culture*. New York: Scribner, 2003.

8

farming

N THE NEXT three generations, world agriculture will be called on to produce as much food as has been grown in the entire twelve-thousand-year history of agriculture. The lessons learned during the past fifty years, underscored by public pressure, can help farmers preserve the integrity of the ecological system on which they depend, while simultaneously developing economies of scale essential for an abundant food supply. To do so, farmers must graft new technology onto their own understanding of seed selection, plant preservation, and nutrient recycling.

Farmers form the largest group of environmental decision makers in the world, and they need to make the right decisions on our behalf. Otherwise, says biologist Edward O. Wilson, "our descendants are going to be mightily peeved to learn that they're going to have to wait 10 million years—or five times the length of the entire history of the human species since its evolutionary origin—to see biodiversity recover from what we've done in less than one hundred years."

Our agricultural expertise has increased so dramatically that today's farmers are among the most sophisticated and highly educated of any segment of society.

Few among us realize just how technologically advanced the modern U.S. farming operations are and how far ahead we are of other countries in our ability to produce colossal quantities of food. The farmer's mission, not surprisingly, is to increase production while reducing costs.

When technology entered beef production, it increased the efficiency and reduced the cost of meat (and poultry) for the consumer. Today's ranchers can analyze their herds from conception to carcass. Monitors detect white-blood-cell counts that indicate the onset of infection. Ear tags maintain records of immunizations and drug dosages. Heat sensors detect when a heifer is ready to reproduce. Computerized scales and electronic eyes record steers' weights and heights. Digitized ultrasonic images reveal the distribution of the marbling of the meat on the live animal. Computer chips record how often and how much feed is consumed and adjust each animal's diet accordingly. The high-tech approach and scope of farming in the twenty-first century may spell trouble for the family farmer, but there are still many opportunities to work the land. The modern-day farmer needs to be creative, innovative, and, as farmers have always been, industrious.

Both down on the farm and in distant laboratories, there are farm-related jobs for scientists, engineers, economists, and, of course, lobbyists, politicians—and chefs.

FOR MORE INFORMATION

In 1891, Cornell University in Ithaca, New York, became the first agricultural college to offer a formal course in poultry husbandry. Its Institute for Biotechnology and Life Science Technologies is among the top schools in the U.S. It is also the home of the prestigious School of Hotel Administration. Some graduate students of the nations' leading culinary schools who are seeking senior positions in the hospitality industry attend the university.

Undergraduates learn about sustainable agriculture and organic farming at the Student Experimental Farm Children's Garden at University of California, Davis. This is also home to the department of viticulture and enology for those who long to grow grapes, manage vineyards, or make their own wine. Land grant universities throughout the country offer undergraduate and post-graduate degrees in every branch of agriculture, and all can be accessed on the Internet to obtain more information.

A listing of agricultural colleges can be found at http://www.oneglobe.com/agriculture/agcolleg.html#usacol.

Advocates of so-called smart plants agree with former president Jimmy Carter's assertion that "responsible biotechnology is not the enemy; starvation is." Julia Child once said that "genetic modification of food is one of the greatest discoveries of the last century. If biotechnology can give us a better tomato, I'm for it."

"Those who are blindly in favor of it speak of genetic engineering as if it were agriculture's salvation. Those who are opposed believe it will undermine organic farming. It will do neither. Like any other technology, it will be useful for solving some problems and not others," says biochemist Michael A. Lawton. He continues:

If we are to address the needs of the growing population on a decreasing area of arable land, while attempting to maintain pristine ecosystems (such as forests and swamp lands) from encroaching agriculture, then we will need to use all the tools that we can lay our hands on. Biotechnology is just one item in the agronomic tool kit that we will need if we are to address problems of production and sustainability in agriculture.

To solve these problems, biotechnology will need to be positioned alongside conventional breeding programs, integrated pest management programs, practices aimed at reducing soil erosion and (believe it or not) biotechnology will need to be deployed *alongside* organic farming, with which it is compatible (scientifically, if not politically).

Martina McGloughlin promotes and coordinates an unusually rich variety of biotechnology-related activities in research, graduate education, and community outreach and is adept at demystifying the growing role and impact of biotechnology in society. (She holds three master's degrees: molecular genetics, biotechnology, and business and serves as director of the biotechnology and life sciences informatics programs at the University of California, Davis.)

She simply states, "What has made us humans unique in the animal kingdom is the ability to manipulate our world. The many and varied tools of biotechnology hold great promise for increasing the efficiency and sustainability of productive agriculture, and assuring the abundance, variety, quality, and safety of food. For most crops, the seed is the delivery system through which advances

"Agriculture cannot be an industrial process any more than music can be. It must be understood differently from stamping this metal into that shape. The major workers—the soil microorganisms, the fungi, the mineral particles, the sun, the air, and the water—are all part of a system, and it is not just the employment of any one of them but the coordination of the whole which achieves success."

—**ELIOT COLEMAN**, environmental writer

"We must plant the sea and herd its animals using the sea as farmers instead of hunters. That is what civilization is all about— farming replacing hunting."

—**JACQUES YVES COUSTEAU**

• MATTERS OF FACT •

● Every week, 330 farmers leave their land. As a result, there are now nearly 5 million fewer farms in the U.S. than there were in the 1930s. Of the two million remaining farms, only 565,000 are family operations. Paradoxically, farmers' markets are flourishing.

● Food in the U.S. typically travels between fifteen hundred and twenty-five hundred miles from field to fork. A lettuce with relatively little nutrient value and high water content that is grown in the Salinas Valley is shipped more than thirty-one hundred miles to the East Coast. The lettuce requires thirty-six times as much fossil fuel energy in transportation energy as it provides in caloric food energy when it is eaten.

in plant genetics and biotechnology are transferred into agricultural production. Genetically modified seeds can better protect crops against diseases, pests, and weeds, and can generate improved or novel products."

Food professionals who hold informed views on many issues relating to food production can find work as advocates who write and speak to audiences made up of consumers, chefs, and government and industry groups.

FOR MORE INFORMATION

There are literally hundreds of advocacy organizations. Among the most prominent is the Center for Science in the Public Interest (CSPI), a nonprofit education organization. It has been a strong advocate for nutrition and health, food safety, alcohol policy, and sound science since it was founded in 1971. Its award-winning newsletter, *Nutrition Action Healthletter*, claims nine hundred thousand subscribers in the United States and Canada and is the largest-circulation health newsletter in North America. http://www.cspinet.org

If you are considering seeking work with an advocacy group, check first with the U.S. Department of Labor Bureau of Labor Statistics Career Guide to Industries, found at http://www.bls.gov. Search the Career Guide section to find answers to frequently asked questions. When checking this site you will be led to advocacy, grant-making, and civic organizations. The following list will provide answers to many frequently asked questions.

■ Nature of the industry
■ Working conditions
■ Employment
■ Occupations in the industry
■ Outlook
■ Earnings
■ Sources of additional information

FOR MORE INFORMATION

http://www.producecareers.com is a food job recruitment site.

ORGANIC AND SUSTAINABLE AGRICULTURE FARMING

Sustainable agriculture is to farming what recycling is to manufacturing. Everyone is for it, as long as it is convenient and doesn't cost anything—or not too much. But when the National Academy of Sciences took a hard look at our current ways of farming, they discovered that "it is the policies passed into law by politicians, not the activities of farmers, which are getting in the way of developing sound biological systems that feed the earth instead of starving it."

Organic farmers produce high-quality, pesticide-free vegetables and fruits. They raise poultry and livestock without using hormones or antibiotics and feed them grain that is grown organically. This is what many people say they want, yet, according the U.S. Department of Agriculture, organic farming currently accounts for less than a tenth of 1 percent of food produced in the United States, where it has its strongest foothold. But our attitudes are changing. The good news is that more people are agreeing with the principles of sustainable agriculture.

Sustainable agriculture and organic farming are not synonymous, although they frequently go hand in hand. Sustainable agriculture is a style of farming that protects the land and natural resources and very often means a reduction—or elimination—of pesticides. Crops are rotated so they do not deplete the soil, and planned companion-planting controls pests. In short, this is old-fashioned farming that relies on up-to-the-minute knowledge.

Just as health foods became mainstream, so support for restructuring our entire food system is gathering steam. As the demand grows for organically grown, sustainably produced crops and humanely raised animals, so do the numbers of farmers and retailers who are eager to supply them to the buyers.

In the final reckoning, every crop in every part of the world is dependent on the same four elements—clement weather, a reliable supply of clean water, healthy soil, and the ability to control pests. Well, make that five elements: the skill of the farmer counts for a lot, too. Finally, it must make economic sense, or there is no use discussing any kind of agriculture at all. So, actually, there are six elements—good stewardship must also take responsibility for the farm workers and their living conditions. Sustainable agriculture is an integrated regenerative system that can feed all the

"I think there is a gathering sense that organic and local are not the same. Buying national organic products does very little for the local economy. Local food chains are very, very important. Organic has important values having to do with pesticides and how land is treated, but now that it is industrialized, buying organic doesn't necessarily support living in a place that still has farmers consuming less energy. Moving organic food across the country uses just as much energy as conventional. I think this is becoming more important."

—**MICHAEL POLLAN**, the author of *The Omnivore's Dilemma*

people at a cost that does not put the land or the laborers in servitude to the landlord.

Chefs are turning to small organic and sustainable farms that are now producing everything from goats and rabbits to ducks and free-range chickens, grass-fed veal, and lovingly nurtured Kobe beef, as well as fruits vegetables, specialty mushrooms, pear and apple ciders, olive oils, farmhouse cheeses, and literally dozens of uncommon foods that are native to other lands but which, one hopes, do not prove destructive when introduced to an unfamiliar ecosystem.

NICHE FARMING

Niche farmers have many interests. They might raise vegetables, fruits, or flowers. They make cheese—goat, sheep, or cow—honey, and preserves. They might raise a specialty breed of cattle such as Miniature Herefords, Dexter, or Ayrshire; sheep such as Cotswold, Lincoln, and Leicester Longwool; or hogs such as Tamworth or Red Wattle. Some are raising free-range or pasture-raised chickens, turkeys, pheasant, or quail to meet the growing demand for this kind of poultry. The attraction of niche farming is that it often does not require a lot of land and the work can be sandwiched between earning a living in the commercial sector.

The opportunity to sell locally has kept some area ranchers from going out of business. Doc and Connie Hatfield, who founded the Country Natural Beef cooperative in Oregon in 1986, say the co-op now has seventy ranchers, who raise beef on a vegetarian diet free of hormones, antibiotics, and genetically modified feed. "Nineteen years ago we were going broke," Hatfield says. "Now we are paying income taxes."

Hatfield was just as pleased about an unexpected byproduct of selling locally: the bond forged between rural and urban residents. "Most of the ranchers are rural, religious, conservative Republicans," he says. "And most of the customers are urban, secular, liberal Democrats. When it comes to healthy land, healthy food, healthy people, and healthy diets, those tags mean nothing. Urbanites are just as concerned about open spaces and healthy rural communities as the people who live there. When ranchers get to the city, they realize rural areas don't have a corner on values. I think that's what we are most excited about."

The nature of farming is changing for the better in many places, and new opportunities for food professionals are appearing in the most unlikely places. For example, some farmers are offering prepared meats and poultry for purchase on the Internet. Food professionals develop accompanying recipes and cooking directions, maintain the Web sites, and promote the farms. This area provides a rich harvest for many food professionals.

FOR MORE INFORMATION

Many farm internships are available and awarded after an applicant completes a trial work period on a farm. Educational and training opportunities in sustainable agriculture can be accessed at:

Alternative Farming Systems Information Center (AFSIC), http://www.nal.usda.gov/afsic/AFSIC_pubs/edtr.htm. This directory includes contact information for farm-related multinational exchange programs as well as U.S. and non-U.S. agencies, institutions, and organizations that offer agriculture-related internships and training. For more information contact AFSIC staff by email at afsic@nal.usda.gov

• MATTERS OF FACT •

- The latest buzzword in farming is shifting from *organic* to *home grown*, as big businesses co-opt and loosen the standards of the organic legislation.

- Consumers are concerned about having no hormones, no pesticides, and no antibiotics in their food so it comes as something of a surprise to realize we have become remarkably casual about the use of the word *fresh*. When a basket of twenty fresh foods from a major "natural" food market was recently examined, the "fresh" items included apples from the United States; pears from Argentina; chicken from Thailand; fish from the Indian Ocean; lettuce, broccoli and strawberries from Spain; baby carrots and garden peas from South Africa; sugar-snap peas from Guatemala; asparagus from Peru; and grapes from Chile. In all, the basket contents had racked up 100,943 miles during their considerable travel time. If you define fresh as being recently harvested or slaughtered, it's a stretch to call this food fresh.

- According to the Community Food Security Coalition in Venice, California, over the past few years, more than two hundred schools have signed up with farm-to-college programs, which match up local farmers with area universities, The University of Montana in Missoula, for example, allocates about $425,000 to buy local meat, dairy and wheat products. This amounts to about 17 percent of the school's overall food budget.

"People have come from many countries to farm in America. Agriculture in California is only 100 years old. If there is any tradition in California, it is a tradition of innovative change. Our agriculture is founded on change; it grew and prospered on change. What worked for a parent will not work for his child. In the last century, change in American agriculture was like a revolution, toppling old structures with new technologies, creating new products, new markets and new farms."

—**DAVID MAS MASUMOTO**,
author of *Epitaph for a Peach*

■

ℂITRON FARMERS

 "SHOULD IT BE esrog, etrog or ethrog?" Shirley Kirkpatrick asked herself while making point-of-sale posters for two Bay Area markets. She says the fact that she even knew there was a spelling nuance is only part of the amazing journey she's traveled to become one of the first United States producers of kosher citron fruit, cherished by the Jewish community for Succos (or Sukkot or Succoth, depending on your Jewish heritage). Imagine the chutzpa. A Protestant family in remote California aligning with an Orthodox Jew in Brooklyn to grow a fruit most Americans know nothing about.

Entry into this unusual farming niche began in the fall of 1980 when John Kirkpatrick answered a chance phone call. A working farmer, he also was then associated with an agricultural consulting firm. On the line was a young man looking for someone to grow esrog citrons for him to sell. (The Kirkpatricks later learned he was only eighteen and had randomly selected their number from the Yellow Pages.)

The esrogim had always been imported, but the young New York entrepreneur wanted to establish a domestic supply. Since the Kirkpatricks already grew lemons, tangelos, oranges, and avocados, they agreed to accept the seeds for the esrog, along with branches of palm, willow, and myrtle, also required by Jews to fulfill the Biblical commandment for Succos, the Festival of Booths, or the Festival of the Tabernacle, again depending on your heritage.

The citron for the holiday must be perfect and only about one in twenty fruit makes the grade. According to Judaic laws, the tree must be grown from seeds under rabbinical supervision. Because they're on their own roots, they do not respond like other commercially grown grafted citrus, which proved to be a major source of frustration for the farmers. Finally, in 1994, Ysroel's brother-in-law Yaakov joined the struggling enterprise. He engaged an esrog grower in Israel to serve in an advisory capacity. Yankel came to the California grove and passed on the farmer's traditional methods, handed down through the centuries.

Finally, the fruit was a hit, remembers Shirley Kirkpatrick. It commanded good prices and gained a following. Even in California the story began to spread, and the family agreed to be interviewed by a

West Coast writer from the *Wall Street Journal* who wanted to explore this unique Judeo-Christian relationship. The resulting front-page article, accompanied by the journal's trademark dotty graphics, provided their fifteen minutes of fame.

Other interviews followed. Because of the extremely high standards, only a small part of the crop meets the requirements for holiday use. The Kirkpatricks agreed it was "too nice to waste," and so they searched for secondary markets. Today, some is bought by green grocers, restaurants, and preserve makers (it's great in marmalade), but the bulk of it goes to a distiller who infuses the citron essence into vodka. The citron is a wonderfully fragrant fruit; the family is still exploring its use in perfumes, essential oils, teas, and cleaning products.

What does the future hold? The Kirkpatrick's son joined the business and is planning for sales to an expanded market. Many Reformed and Conservative Jews and Messianic Christians are on the path of rediscovering their religious heritage. They're learning about and celebrating Succos. Which leads to their latest citron fantasy: providing kosher accommodations for farm-stay visits for those who want to see how and where their fruit is grown.

• MATTERS OF FACT •

- The Organic Trade Association is the leading business association representing the organic industry in the United States, Canada, and Mexico. Its more than fifteen hundred members include growers, processors, shippers, retailers, certification organizations, and others involved in the business of producing and selling certified organic products.

- A growing number of organic farms offer bed and breakfasts to guests. At the Apple Farm in Philo, California, weekend visitors attend cooking classes and pick their own apples, pears, and tomatoes. Other farms offer mushroom gathering in addition to the traditional pumpkin and strawberry picking farms.

"The best fertilizer is the footprint of the farmer."

—ANONYMOUS

"The earth does not belong to man; man belongs to the earth. This we know. Whatever befalls the earth befalls the sons of the earth. Man did not weave the Web of life; he is merely a strand in it. Whatever he does to the Web, he does to himself."

—CHIEF SEATTLE, nineteenth-century Native American

FRIEDA'S

by Karen Caplan.

MY MOM KIND of fell into the produce industry. Shortly after I was born, she found a job with flexible hours (important for a new mom) in the wholesale produce market. It turned out, she was a natural and was the only woman working in sales. One thing led to another, and by 1962, and the birth of her second daughter, she launched Frieda's, her own wholesale produce company. I fell in love with the produce business as I grew up. Our company's niche was "the unusual." Specialty, gourmet, and ethnic produce is our thing. My mother imported the first kiwifruit to America and is credited with launching the worldwide industry—and she actually named the fruit! (It was formerly called the Chinese gooseberry and in some parts of the world still is.)

I am now company CEO and president and am not as involved in the day-to-day as before. I spend most of my time on strategic issues and establishing and building relationships with our suppliers worldwide—we actually don't grow anything, but work with those who do. I do a lot of public speaking, promoting not only our company, but also the importance of specialty and ethnic produce in the retail and food-service business. As a woman-owned business, we are still in the minority. Many large clients are looking to expand their supplier base to include more minorities and women, so I am frequently called upon to speak about this.

I am often asked about the importance of a college education. For me, my college education was critical and I learned important skills and disciplines. I had a real advantage in college because I had worked for so many summers in my mom's business that I was able to apply real-life knowledge to the book learning.

I recommend a course of study that includes both some aspect of agriculture and business or psychology. (Psychology comes in handy when you're dealing with customers and suppliers.) As far as on-the-job training, my mother wisely insisted I learn every job in the company and I started at the bottom.

One of my secrets is that I am a lifelong learner. I made sure, especially early in my career, to attend as many workshops and developmental seminars as I could. I read a lot of books on business, trends, marketing, and management. Finally, I am passionate about food! I love to cook. I love to experiment. And I love to talk! That means my best performance is when I am either selling our products or doing cooking shows or radio or television interviews.

The books that hold the most interest for the cookbook writer and the scholar are the well researched, painstakingly executed ones that represent real contributions to our knowledge of food and cooking. Two titles that belong in every home and institutional library are Elizabeth Schneider's *Uncommon Fruits and Vegetables* and *Vegetables from Amaranth to Zucchini: The Essential Reference*. The latter book is a guide to more than 350 vegetables, both exotic and familiar. Each encyclopedic entry includes a full-color identification photo, common and botanical names, and an engaging vegetable biography that distills the knowledge of hundreds of authorities in dozens of fields.

THE RODALE INSTITUTE

The Rodale Institute believes that many of the problems that threaten humankind's very survival—famine, soil erosion, pollution of soil and water, loss of biodiversity, and rural poverty—have their roots in our misuse of land, energy, and technology. And the time remaining for effective corrective action is shrinking rapidly. The institute focuses on making connections between ideas such as regenerative agriculture and public health. Its purpose is to combine the latest scientific advances with traditional wisdom in order to create food and agricultural systems that are productive both in the short and long term, while enhancing the environment and our own health. The late J. I. Rodale himself predicted that farmers would someday be seen as health practitioners, and as partners with other professionals in the maintenance of good health. To find out about job opportunities at Rodale, go to http://www.rodale.com.

FARMERS' MARKETS

During Roman times it was considered the height of luxury to eat foods out of season. Now it is the reverse. Americans are, today, preponderantly an urban people. American children seldom if ever see a newborn lamb or watch the hatching of a baby chick. There is a fee to be paid to see live animals—in the zoo. Perhaps this is why there is something in our genes that sparks our ongoing love affair with farmers' markets. We flock there to gaze at and

"I like to be around on Wednesdays because that's the day the vegetables come in from the Chinos family down in Rancho Santa Fe. The Chino family has the most beautiful farm in the world. There are just rows and rows of every sort of vegetable. You never know exactly what the Chinos are going to send so opening the boxes is like opening a big surprise treasure chest. Sometimes there are striped tomatoes or yellow ones with orange veins or little tiny mini-red tomatoes that are littler than peas. Sometimes there are all these different peppers that are every color of the rainbow. Sometimes there are even brown ones. In the summer there's big and little corn and all different color basils or beets or whatever else the Chinos have been growing."

—**ALICE WATERS**

to buy fresh-picked fruits and vegetables, and to talk to the farmers. Anyone associated with farmers' markets will be very busy. Whether you rent space, organize the market, or promote it, you will be rewarded with a challenge and the chance to meet and work with like-minded people.

Twenty-four thousand visitors flock to farmers' markets every year, and every year the numbers increase. As was true on market days of old, farmers bring their produce and other items to a central location where they congregate and meet with the public. This may be a parking lot, town square, or a roadside open space.

A few farmers still set up stands on their farms and, once their presence is known, attract loyal customers. To maintain solvency, many small farmers have built mazes into cornfields. (One clever captioner named the adventure "hey daze.") A few have installed petting zoos for the children. Farmers encourage guests to learn how to milk a cow, collect the eggs, pick the apples and pumpkins, and learn how to bake a pie or make ice cream and farmers' cheese. Word of mouth is a big part of their success. And for a few lucky farmers, chefs are opening restaurants on their land. They harvest happiness.

HYDROPONIC FARMING

Growing plants in water is described in ancient Egyptian writings. Aztecs cultivated floating gardens in Mexico, as did the Chinese, who hundreds of years ago perfected new methods for growing plants without soil and using nutrients dissolved in water. Modern hydroponic farming began in the 1930s as an outgrowth of the techniques used by plant nutrition specialists. The field is expanding relatively quickly. The United States and Canada each have between fifteen hundred and two thousand acres of hydroponic greenhouse vegetable production. This is small in comparison with the Netherlands, where there are more than twenty-five thousand acres in greenhouse cultivation. North America may come to rely on this style of farming even more in coming years. It's a style of farming that does not require open fields and yet under controlled conditions in greenhouses, crop yields are impressive.

Hydroponic farmers raise plants without soil. The crops are raised without pesticides in greenhouses in which the light, air, water, plant nutrients, and spacing between plants are carefully monitored to achieve optimal growth in the least amount of time and at the lowest cost. The work requires the skills of a scientist and the devotion of a mother, but there is a viable commercial market in this watery way of farming. The seeds are nursed from germination through maturity in an inert growing medium, usually gravel, through which water containing a balanced mix of nutrients is pumped. As the plants grow, they travel in cradle-troughs along a moving conveyor belt. The cradles expand, allowing them more breathing room as they need it.

It is not economical to raise potatoes or root vegetables in such an environment because they take up too much room; however, a dozen heads of lettuce can grow in a space where only three would thrive in an open field. But the real jackpot is the tomato. Farmers can expect to gather slightly more than a pound of tomatoes in a week from a single plant. And discerning customers are willing to pay a premium for a pesticide-free, red-ripe, juicy tomato.

▶ Cowboy

The beef-eating cowboy is one of America's most enduring myths. His was a life of freedom and adventure spent among craggy peaks, green valleys, galloping horses, and grazing cattle. When he came to town, his days were filled with reckless drinking, scarlet (but big-hearted) women, and hand-to-hand combat on dusty, unpaved streets at high noon. Despite the liberties he took with the law, he usually emerged unscathed—in the movies, anyway.

• MATTER OF FACT •

- When the *Wall Street Journal* rated the best and worst jobs, cowboy was listed as the second-to-worst.
- Career prospects for cowboys are not terrific. At best you can hope to earn about twelve thousand dollars a year, you have to sleep on the ground, and "you get bit a lot by a lot of wild critters."

For More Information

If you are looking for work as a cowboy check out-
http://www.razorcreek.com/BulletinBoard_toc.htm

King Ranch in Texas covers almost thirteen hundred square miles. It is larger than the entire state of Rhode Island. It was founded in 1853 and still employs a few meat-eating cowboys. http://www.king-ranch.com/index_ie.htm

RARE JOBS
WILD-GAME FARMING

MIKE HUGHES OF the Broken Arrow Ranch in Ingram, Texas, is making serious efforts to harvest antelope humanely without having to trap them. The ranch supplies restaurants with free-range venison, antelope, axis deer, fallow deer, sika deer, and wild boar. *Wild* is the word used in the industry, but that's a bit of a false moniker. It is illegal to sell real wild birds or game, but the term is rather more romantic than *farmed*, which connotes big business. Hughes points out that his deer roam over thousands of acres and fit the definition of farmed only because the land is *his* land.

MacFarland Pheasants Inc. ships thousands of cultivated, nicely dressed pheasants to restaurants and caterers every month during the game season, which lasts from the early autumn through the holidays. The pheasant joins gaggles of geese, quail, duck, turkey, venison, elk, rabbit, bison, and other exotic "wild" things that appear on menus with increasing frequency. (Licensed recreational hunters are permitted to share their bounty with friends, but they are not allowed to sell it on the commercial market.)

> "Bees are the glue that holds modern agriculture together. If all the bees disappeared, man could live for only four years."
>
> —ALBERT EINSTEIN

■

RARE JOB
$\mathcal{B}$EEKEEPING AND HONEY MAKING

WHILE BEEKEEPING IS a difficult job with little financial reward, the connection it allows with nature makes it worth it for its practitioners. It's a surprisingly popular hobby, although many hobbyists also make a small income, too. Most beekeepers, as exemplified by David Graves of Berkshire Berries in Massachusetts, stay in the game because they feel that beekeeping perpetuates the presence of bees, which are essential to agriculture because the bees pollinate crops.

▶ **Mushroom Growing**

If you enjoy cultivating the unusual, specialty (or "wild") mushrooms offer many possibilities. The term *specialty* refers to any mushroom except the white button mushroom commonly found in supermarkets. Specialty mushrooms include shiitake, oyster, enoki, wine cap, maitake, and pompom, among many others. Small-scale cultivation of specialty mushrooms could be a profitable addition to your farming enterprise.

For More Information
For a more detailed discussion on growing many mushroom species outdoors, check out *Mushrooms in the Garden*, by Hellmut Steineck (Mad River Press).

For details on both outdoor and indoor cultivation: *The Mushroom Cultivator—A Practical Guide to Growing Mushrooms at Home* by Paul Stamets and J. S. Chilton (Agarikon Press).

For more details on more species: *Growing Gourmet and Medicinal Mushrooms* by Paul Stamets (Ten Speed Press).

For a comprehensive mushroom guide with over one thousand color photographs: *Mushrooms of North America* by Roger Phillips (Little, Brown).

For a monthly update on prices, marketing information, and production techniques: The Mushroom Growers' Newsletter, P. O. Box 5065, Klamath Falls, OR 97601, published monthly, eight to ten pages, $24 annually.

► Fish Farming

Fish farming is one the world's fastest-growing businesses. Annual global sales are already approaching the $45 billion mark, an astonishing sum in view of the rapid decline in stocks of wild fish. Salmon is now farmed in nearly every country with a cold deep-water coastline. Already more than half of the salmon eaten in the United States comes from fish farms.

A well-managed farm is a place where the advantages of aquaculture are most clearly seen. Experts decide when the fish have reached the desirable size and weight. At that moment, thousands of identical fish are channeled into a filleting factory where they are cleaned and sent off on their way to market. The fish farmers can go home for lunch and never need invest in sou' westers or even own a pair of waterproof boots. And the sparkling fresh fish is delivered clean and safe to eat on a predictable schedule and at a predictable weight and price. In contrast, commercial deep-water fishing is the most dangerous trade in the world. More men die at sea than in coal mines.

The rapid growth in fish farming was made possible with the development of super-technology—growth lights, nutritional food pellets, vaccines to protect the fish against bacteria and viruses, and underwater video monitors to watch over them. Like farm animals, "factory" fish depend on the farmer to ensure that they don't become sick, overcrowded, or hungry. Robots feed the

"Fishing has evolved into an art as well as a science."

—**IZAAK WALTON**,

author of *The Complete Angler* (1653)

• **MATTERS OF FACT** •

● In 1873 Alexandre Dumas calculated that if nothing prevented the
hatching of every egg from every
cod for three years, they would fill
the sea so we could walk dry-shod
on the backs of cod. Now cod is
endangered.

● Populations of groupers and snap-
pers have declined 80 percent;
blue fin tuna are down 90 percent
since the mid-1970s. Swordfish are
now endangered; they were once
fifteen feet long and long weighed
one thousand pounds, but now
are caught at only fifty pounds.

● When the National Marine Fish-
eries studied 153 species, they discovered more than 50 percent are
overfished.

fish on a strict time schedule with precisely measured quantities of formula. Special mechanized equipment creates movement of the water in the pens so the salmon develop firmer flesh by swimming against man-made waves.

Think of aquaculture as the aquatic counterpart of agriculture. We evolved from hunters to farmers, and just as we decided to cultivate food rather than venturing out to capture savage animals, a parallel can be drawn between those who farm fish rather than braving stormy seas in search of wild ones. An added bonus of fish farming is that each species is raised separately without needlessly catching and destroying other unwanted species.

Further, farmed fish tend to be higher in fat than their free-swimming brethren. They are not as reliable a source for the valuable-for-your-health omega-3 essential fatty acids, either. Because of their diet, many farmed fish are not considered nearly as beneficial as fish caught in the wild. Fish farming is not yet a panacea that solves our problem of over-fishing, but it is a growing and useful segment of agriculture, or more correctly, aquaculture. It's the wave of the future and when responsibly operated, lets the natural life of the oceans regenerate. Surely, there are great food job opportunities here.

GETTING STARTED

Entry-level positions on fish farms involve assisting with the growing and cultivation of fish and the maintenance of fish farm premises and equipment. Fish farmhands may be employed in either finfish or shellfish farming. They usually work outside, either on or in the water, or at shore-based facilities located in sheltered waters. Most fish farmhands are expected to work long hours, particularly in the summer months. Some employers also require a diving qualification and/or a license to operate a barge. This means that to work on a fish farm, employees must enjoy being outdoors and have a reasonable level of physical fitness. It is not necessary to be able to swim.

9

cooking schools and culinary education

DO YOU NEED professional training to find a food job? The maddening answer is yes—and no. Julia Child attended Le Cordon Bleu School in Paris, but she didn't need a journalism degree to write several best-selling books, nor did she attend drama school before setting her foot on the path to becoming a television culinary icon and a national folk hero. Her background as a file clerk and her passion for precision proved to be excellent training for her later-in-life insistence on accurate recipes and detailed instruction. Neither James Beard not Jacques Pépin went to cooking school. They learned their craft on the job, as have many food celebrities. Many successful stars of the culinary world arrived on the scene having started their professional life in an entirely different field.

There is no degree program currently available anywhere to qualify as a restaurant critic or a freelance food writer, though training at a professional cooking school or having a journalism degree or BA in liberal arts is undeniably helpful. It is useful, too, to have some business knowledge before setting out as an entrepreneur.

This means that the short answer is yes, it is wise to obtain formal qualifications for certain positions, but it is also important to gain experience on the job and to keep learning. To stay a heartbeat ahead of the competition means following food trends and keeping up with what is happening in all sectors of the food universe. And bear in mind that, in the end, it will be your charming personality that lands you the job.

As I mentioned in the Introduction, ask someone at the reference desk of your local public library for the *Occupational Outlook Handbook*. It lists all kinds of information you would need to know (including the salary) of just about any occupation you can think of. http://www.bls.gov/oco

WHO GOES TO COOKING SCHOOL?

Students from all over the world attend American cooking schools. They arrive from Thailand, Vietnam, Korea, China, Japan, Singapore, India, Mexico, Peru, Brazil, Israel, Canada, Belgium, England, and many other countries. Even the sons and daughters of illustrious French, Michelin-starred chefs attend U.S. and Canadian cooking schools.

Dorlene Kaplan, editor of ShawGuides' *Guide to Cooking Schools* says, "Over the past decade and particularly since 2001, enrollment at schools with professional culinary programs has jumped anywhere from 20 percent to 100 percent." And Meredith Moore, a culinary school spokeswoman, says, "Applicants are entering professional cooking schools with high SAT scores and impressive records of extracurricular activities that could easily earn them admission to top colleges."

Gone are the days when fourteen-year-old boys sweated through apprenticeships in cramped kitchens ruled by menacing ogres before beginning their painstakingly slow ascent up the ladder to the fish station. Nonetheless, students who have completed courses at culinary schools and gone on to successful careers tell new cooking school graduates to be realistic. Restaurant work is back-breaking. It requires considerable physical effort and emotional stamina. It's stressful. The hours are long—and few restaurants close on holidays and weekends.

Many students are admitted to professional cooking school straight from high school and are armed with little more than a diploma and a willingness to learn, though some professional cooking schools may require at least a year of experience, preferably working in a restaurant kitchen.

As many as one-third of the culinary-student community are career changers in their mid- to late-thirties and older. They come from all walks of life and include former airline pilots, lawyers, advertisers, engineers, scientists, nurses, and entertainers. They previously worked in offices, schools, hospitals, and even in prisons. Some have served in the military and civil service. Many have already worked in restaurants and decided the in-depth education from a cooking school will advance their career options. What they all share is a passion for food, though not necessarily for cooking.

> "The school of hard knocks teaches you a lot, but college teaches more, like managing, ordering, and sanitation. I've hired many people with formal training."
>
> —**DREW NIEPORENT**, chef and restaurateur

• MATTERS OF FACT •

- Professional cooking schools are among the fastest-growing educational sectors in America.

- There are close to seventy-five thousand students attending 274 or 475 schools, depending on who is counting. (Some institutes offer a limited curriculum and may not be fully accredited professional schools.)

- One of the most popular resources is *The Guide to Cooking Schools*, compiled by ShawGuides (http://cookingcareer.shawguides.com). It lists 881 culinary programs worldwide. Of those, 358 are geared toward professional training. The courses are listed with such detailed information as the type of instruction, faculty credentials, tuition costs, student profiles, and status of accreditation. ShawGuides also offers a free job-matching site: http://www.chefjobs.com.

- Another excellent resource is *Becoming a Chef*, Andrew Dornenburg and Karen Page. John Wiley & Sons, 1995. This book lists cooking schools, apprenticeship programs, food-related organizations, recommended reading and guidance for chefs who are planning to open a restaurant. There are also interviews with chefs who give readers personal advice.

- The American Culinary Federation Educational Institute has a three-year apprenticeship program in which students can learn on the job while still earning an income. The designation of certified cook is received when an apprentice successfully completes the program.

- The Institute of Culinary Education offers 760 cooking courses for both professionals and food enthusiasts at its campus in New York City. http://www.iceculinary.com

- Of course, a good number of the students who take courses at large and small cooking schools are not in degree programs. Teaching these eager hobbyists appeals to many trained cooks.

- Most school career offices report that more than 90 percent of graduates secure a full-time position after being offered an average of three jobs. The job-placement record for all cooking school graduates has become an important part of their programs.

CHOOSING A COOKING SCHOOL

Which cooking school you apply to is a personal choice largely determined by the goals of each student. High-profile schools offer more in terms of visits and cooking demonstrations by superstar chefs, but smaller schools may provide more nurturing environments and are less of a financial burden. School location, course schedules, and class size are also very real considerations for many would-be culinary students. Unlike traditional colleges, culinary schools attract students of all ages. Some have special needs that are not always anticipated by other institutions of higher education.

Many professional schools have three divisions: culinary skills; baking and pastry, and hospitality management. Students at some, though not all schools, are able to combine programs. A degree program can extend for anywhere from six to thirty-eight months, with tuition costs varying from ten thousand to more than seventy thousand dollars. Financial aid is readily available.

The schools with large endowments often have a more highly qualified and experienced faculty, better-equipped kitchens, a more extensive library, and even sports facilities. These schools may offer student housing. They attract students from around the world and tend to have higher tuition fees than smaller nonresidential schools. There are many factors to consider before enrolling, and prospective students are urged to take their time before making a decision about what is best for them.

An Associate of Occupational Studies (AOS) degree from a top-tier school is believed to carry more weight when seeking employment, but this is not necessarily so. Great students with a good attitude are offered terrific jobs, no matter which school they attend.

You may prefer to enroll in a small school where there is a strong focus on the individual and a small class size. In the culinary program at Paul Smith's College in Lake Placid, New York, for example, there is a fourteen-to-one student-to-faculty ratio and teachers, mentors, and advisors are always on hand. The college has a magnificent library, and its lakeside campus nestled in the magnificent Adirondack Mountains is an excellent destination for winter and summer sports enthusiasts.

Community colleges in every part of the country offer degree programs in culinary arts. In addition to more affordable tuition, they allow students to live at home—another cost-saving consideration.

As you will see from the following writings, professional culinary schools vary considerably. This is just a small sampling among many widely different opportunities for study.

A STUDENT DESCRIBES BOSTON UNIVERSITY'S CULINARY ARTS CERTIFICATE AND MASTER OF LIBERAL ARTS PROGRAMS

By Shaun Chavis

I had planned to attend another culinary school when I learned about Boston University's culinary arts certificate and master of liberal arts in gastronomy programs. For my goals, BU offers the perfect combination of culinary instruction and the academic food studies.

BU's Culinary Arts program is great for a career changer like me. It's a short sixteen-week course. From day one, you're in the kitchen learning knife skills. The five primary instructors all have distinguished careers in the business. They teach you classic principles, along with the techniques and skills it takes to make it in a professional kitchen. The program exposes you to a wide variety of international cuisines and various aspects of the industry. For example, we toured a vineyard and a meat-processing company.

The rest of the course is what makes Boston University's program unique: the instructors are working chefs who spend a day or two teaching you their specialties. My instructors included Jody Adams, Jacques Pépin, Michael Leviton, Ana Sortun, and Helen Chen. (Can you imagine an experience like Chef Pépin standing next to you, coaching you through making omelets?)

It's a great placement program: not only are you learning, the chefs get to know you and see how you work. Because of this relationship, I got a job in the business before I graduated. Every class is limited to twelve students, so you're not lost in the crowd, and you can get your instructor's assistance and feedback when you need it.

BU's culinary arts program is also a better bargain: the school I had previously considered cost nearly three times as much for six months of instruction, the main difference being a six-week internship. (With a built-in placement program, why pay to work?) BU's program includes evening seminars in subjects like wine, cheese, and food writing, and you can also study these subjects further through additional certificate programs.

Many people don't know that Julia Child started this program. She held graduation meals at her home. It was her dream for students to learn the foundations of French cooking and also be able to study food academically.

Because of Ms. Child, Boston University offers the only master's degree in gastronomy in the U.S. The culinary arts certificate and MLA gastronomy programs are offered separately; you don't have to do them both, but it was the ability to do both that sold me. Food impacts our economy, health, politics, and culture. I am studying food history, food anthropology, and foodways in various cultures. Classmates and professors are both supportive and ambitious. Because this is a liberal arts degree, I can take courses offered in other BU departments that relate to my career goals.

I believe the study of food is picking up momentum as an academic field among American colleges and universities. With its two programs, Boston University is on the cutting edge.

CALIFORNIA CULINARY ACADEMY, SAN FRANCISCO, CALIFORNIA

California Culinary Academy (CCA) literature tells us this school can help you gain the skills you'll need for a successful career in the culinary and hospitality industry. Founded in 1977 as one of the West's first culinary training institutions, the CCA is dedicated to providing the highest standard of education to all students in preparation for careers in the culinary and hospitality industries.

California Culinary Academy is located in one of the greatest culinary and hospitality capitals of the world—San Francisco. The city boasts one of the largest concentrations of hotels and restaurants in the country, providing a great "living classroom" and a large pool of resources when handpicking instructors. You'll also have the unique opportunity to work with these local establishments during your externship.

A STUDENT FROM THE CULINARY INSTITUTE OF AMERICA (CIA) RESPONDS TO FREQUENTLY ASKED QUESTIONS

By Lynne Jewell, bachelor's degree student

Q: What does the Culinary Institute of America offer to a student that makes it unique?

LYNNE JEWELL: At the CIA, we are proud of our programs that give prospective students the opportunity to experience what our college has to offer. You can attend a class for the day. You are given a chef jacket and have a hands-on experience by helping out in the kitchen. We also have a career discovery program that provides high school students the chance to spend a week with other students who are interested in attending the CIA. During this time, you will team-build, spend time with students from the college, and you can attend classes.

Q: What if I can't afford to spend a week at the school? How else can I find out about what the college has to offer?

LJ: If you can't make it to one of our programs, don't worry; the CIA has an open house several times a year. You can talk to admissions representatives, hear students talk about their experiences at the school, take a tour of the campus, and fill out an application to receive information in the mail. If you can't get to New York, visit our Web site at http://www.ciachef.edu and check out what we have to offer. No access to a computer? Call us at 1-800-CULINARY, and talk to one of our student telecounselors.

Q: Do I have to have experience in a restaurant before applying to the CIA?

LJ: No, it is not necessary to have experience while going through the application process; however, it is highly recommended that you have some experience in the field before making up your mind to attend the CIA.

Q: What degrees does the CIA offer?

LJ: The Culinary Institute of America offers four degree programs:

- Associate degree in culinary arts
- Associate degree in baking and pastry arts
- Bachelor's degree in culinary arts management
- Bachelor's degree in baking and pastry arts management

Q: How long will it take to earn an associate degree and a bachelor's degree?

LJ: An associate degree will take twenty-one months and a bachelor's degree will take thirty-eight months. Eighty-six percent of full-time students receive aid. The average amount per student is eighty-five hundred dollars. An accelerated fifteen-week course is also offered.

The Culinary Institute of America includes two unique features during the associate program and bachelor's degree programs. While studying in the associate program, you will look for job placement at an establishment of your choice, in what we call an externship. You will spend eighteen weeks working alongside culinary professionals, while increasing your skills in the kitchen or bakeshop.

In the bachelor's degree program, you will take a six-week tour of California where you visit organic farms, artisan bread and cheese makers, coffee roasters, candy factories, and some of the best-known wineries in the world. Culinary study is also available in Italy and Spain and other countries are being added to the curriculum. These experiences are among the reasons so many students attend our college, but for me they are only the tip of the iceberg!

Q: How will I find a job for an externship position, as well as a job when I graduate?

LJ: During your course of study at the CIA, you will meet with our career counselors in order to create or modify your cover letters and professional résumé. You will also get advice about finding a place to work. After graduating, you will have as much access to the school's career services as you want. We offer an online job search engine that enables graduates to contact prospective employers directly. Over three hundred employers attend frequent career fairs and recruit students on campus.

Q: What is the student body like?

LJ: Our student body consists of men and women from all over the world. Our college hosts students from all fifty states, and many other countries. Some have years of experience working in a restaurant, some come directly from high school, and others are career changers. It is one of the most diverse environments you can imagine.

Q: Can I double major in culinary arts and baking and pastry arts?

LJ: We do not offer a double major program at our Hyde Park, New York, campus, but our culinary students are able to receive a certificate in baking and pastry arts by attending the thirty-week certificate program at our Greystone campus in the Napa Valley, California.

Q: What does the CIA offer in terms of extracurricular activities?

LJ: Our college has several student clubs; we have a gourmet society, Bacchus society, beer and ale club, Eta Sigma Delta Honors Society, paintball team, basketball, swimming, and many other clubs. We have a fabulous pool where you can do laps while keeping an eye on the majestic Hudson River. We also have tennis courts, squash courts, and a fully equipped gym in our recreational center. We are a train journey or bus ride from New York City, Boston, and Montreal, so students can go skiing and also experience the culinary and cultural opportunities from these great cities.

Many of the best known and most successful chefs, entrepreneurs, and hospitality executives received their training at the CIA.

THE INTERNATIONAL CULINARY CENTER, HOME TO THE FRENCH CULINARY INSTITUTE AND THE ITALIAN CULINARY ACADEMY

In 1984, Dorothy Hamilton founded the legendary French Culinary Institute with a single goal: to create a world-class culinary school that blended classic French techniques with American inventiveness in an exciting, fast-paced curriculum. Over the years, Ms. Hamilton built on that goal, and in 2006, she opened the doors to the world-class International Culinary Center, which serves not only as the home to The FCI and its new sister school, The Italian Culinary Academy, but as a culinary arts center where aspiring chefs, sommeliers, restaurateurs, bakery owners, caterers and food writers can be inspired by and learn from the best.

Today, the schools' roster of deans, instructors, and graduates is incomparable. Our world-class faculty includes master chefs Alain Sailhac, Jacques Pépin, André Soltner, Jacques Torres, and Cesare Casella; award-winning food writer Alan Richman; acclaimed culinary technology experts Harold McGee and Dave Arnold; and noted wine, beer, and spirits expert Marnie Old. Star alumni including Bobby Flay, Dan Barber, and David Chang stop by regularly to give insightful and entertaining lectures. Right here, right now, the next generation of culinary leaders are honing their craft and shaping their dreams. Chefs and pastry chefs. Bread bakers and sommeliers. Restaurant/bakery owners and managers, food stylists, and food writers. They're all launching bright careers with the unmatched training, experience, and career connections of The International Culinary Center.

Using a rigorous, hands-on curriculum called *Total Immersion*^{TM}, instructors of our career programs propel students into the workplace after just six intense months of classes; nine if training is completed at night. All of our porgrams, including our extensive catalog of short courses, are fast and in-depth:

- In The French Culinary Institute's culinary career courses, students learn not just French cooking, but instead, the building blocks of all modern Western cooking, including the skills needed to keep them on the cutting-edge. And, they'll sharpen their skills with real time, hands-on cooking in the middle of the action at L'Ecole, our critically-acclaimed restaurant in the heart of New York's restaurant scene.

- In The Italian Culinary Academy's comprehensive "Italian Culinary Experience" program, students jet to Italy to live, work and absorb the culture and language as a component of their culinary learning at The ICA, sister school to The French Culinary Institute.

- Our Pastry Arts curriculum is the only one in the world created by the renowned Jacques Torres. Students master the full repertoire from breakfast pastries to desserts, and graduate ready to step into today's highest-end kitchens and bakeries—or to open their own. Our Art of International Bread Baking course is one of the world's most highly sought career programs of its kind.

- Our challenging Advanced Studies courses helps students gain the skills necessary to enter the competitive fields of food writing, restaurant management and wine/beverage management.

Upon graduation, our students are scooped up by top-rated employers. Companies who want the best know they'll find it here. Our world wide network of more than 6,000 industry professionals represents the world's top restaurants and food-related businesses—and when they're out to hire fresh talent for internships or full-time positions, they often call us first. Graduates of our career programs can count on ongoing job placement assistance and support.

And best of all, students learn at the center of today's culinary scene. Aside from the culture, education, and entertainment that make New York City unique, we're also home to top international chefs, food experts, and many of the world's most famous restaurants. The International Culinary Center is situated in the heart of SoHo, an enclave of art, fashion, and culture that's at the pulse of the city's freshest restaurant scene. Our industry is evolving here as we speak, and our students are at the edge of this dynamic evolution.

I invite you to meet our faculty, tour our facilities, and delve into our programs. And if you have any questions, please visit www.internationalculinarycenter.com, or call us at 1-888-324-CHEF. For more insight into food-related careers, we recommend you read *Chef's Story: 27 Chefs Talk About What Got Them Into The Kitchen,* the companion book the Public Television Series, Edited by Dorothy Hamilton (Founder and CEO of The French Culinary Institute) and Patrick Kuh. Ecco. 2007.

A STUDENT AT THE INSTITUTE OF CULINARY EDUCATION IN MANHATTAN RESPONDS TO FREQUENTLY ASKED QUESTIONS

By Anne McBride

Q: Why go to culinary school? What can I expect to learn?

A: Sometimes prospective students ask us why they should enroll in culinary school. Why not simply find a good restaurant and learn on the job? While working in a restaurant helps you decide whether the field is indeed for you, a drawback to on-the-job training is that your culinary education is limited to the repertoire of a single employer. You may learn the *hows* of cooking by working in a restaurant, but your employer probably wouldn't have time to teach you the *whys* of cooking. That's where culinary school comes in. We consider questions such as: Why does a sauce break? Why does a cake fall? What makes a stock cloudy?

Q: What can I do with a culinary diploma?

A: The food-service field is one of the fastest growing job sectors in the United States today, and employers increasingly see a culinary school diploma as an essential credential for a job in their kitchens. But working as a food professional can mean more than just working in a restaurant.

Q: How long will it take me to earn a diploma?

A: The culinary arts and pastry and baking arts programs run 610 hours—400 hours in class and 210 hours on externship. The culinary management diploma program runs 316 classroom hours. In all cases, a single class lasts four hours. Schedules are varied, allowing you to take classes two, three, four, or five times a week. Because of these schedule options, the total program length ranges from twenty-eight to forty-three weeks.

Q: Can you describe the students?

A: We see a broad range, from nineteen-year-olds just out of high school to career changers with many years of experience in fields from medicine to music, and computers to construction. They come from all over the United States and the world, including countries such as Brazil, the Philippines, Israel, England, and Korea, and from all walks of life. Our student population is approximately 50 percent men and 50 percent women.

Q: Do I have to have culinary experience before I enroll?

A: No, it is not necessary. Some of our students are at the start of their working lives, dreaming of becoming executive chefs in the nation's top restaurants. Others have already worked in professional kitchens and are seeking a way to deepen their knowledge and advance their careers. Career changers, too, have long made up an important part of our student body. Among our graduates are former lawyers, medical technicians, bankers, computer programmers, truck drivers, carpenters, journalists, and actors.

Q: What is the tuition cost? Is financial aid available?

A: Currently, culinary arts tuition is $24,067, pastry and baking arts tuition is $23,584, and the culinary management diploma program is $12,900. We have a variety of financial aid options, including those offered by Sallie Mae (SLM Financial Corporation). The loan period is from one to ten years and can include up to 100 percent of the student's tuition (subject to credit approval). Information and applications can be obtained from the admissions department.

Q: Can students take two programs at the same time, and is there a discount for doing so?

A: Yes, our schedules are arranged so that students can get a combined diploma in culinary arts or pastry and baking arts and culinary management by attending ICE mornings and afternoons or afternoons and evenings. Twenty percent tuition discount is offered on the CMD program if enrollment is concurrent with a culinary arts or pastry and baking arts program.

Q: How will I find a job when I've finished?

A: Our department of career services makes job placement available to all graduates and alumni. While in the program, you will benefit from job fairs, résumé workshops, interviewing seminars, counseling sessions, and volunteer opportunities. We maintain extensive job listings, from entry-level to advanced positions, through our established network of graduates, chefs, and other culinary contacts in New York City and elsewhere. Alumni have access to a weekly e-mail that lists a wide range of job opportunities at all levels.

Q: Why go the Institute of Culinary Education?

A: The institute received accreditation from the Accrediting Commission of Career Schools and Colleges of Technology (ACCSCT) in 1999. Prior to that, an ACCSCT team made up of industry experts and educational experts visited the institute for a two-day inspection. In their report, the accrediting team cited ICE for four separate "items of excellence":

1. One hundred percent student satisfaction: all students surveyed would "recommend the school to a friend."
2. Outstanding faculty and faculty commitment to students.
3. The school's facilities and equipment.
4. The school's involvement in community service.

The Institute of Culinary Education was the 2003 winner of the International Association of Culinary Professionals Cooking School of the Year Award. For more information and to see the extensive offerings of classes for recreational students log onto http://www.iceculinary.com.

JOHNSON AND WALES

The Johnson and Wales culinary school in Providence, Rhode Island, has several satellite campuses in other cities. Karl J. Guggenmos, MBA, AAC, the university's dean of culinary education and German certified master chef, has a message to students considering enrolling in the Johnson and Wales culinary program:

> The associate degree program provides students with practical education in baking and pastry production, while developing professionalism and excellence in academic achievement. An associate's degree in science and bachelor's of arts degree in culinary arts are offered. A bachelor's of science degree is also available in culinary nutrition. It combines practical education in culinary nutrition with rigorous academic and professional studies to prepare students as chefs possessing strong skills in nutrition management.
>
> Our educational programs were founded in 1974 and, from their humble beginnings, are considered leading programs in our industry. Currently, we have over fifty-six hundred students enrolled in our various culinary programs delivered on four world-class campuses. We offer associate degree programs in culinary arts and baking and pastry arts at all our campuses. Bachelor's degree programs in culinary arts, baking and pastry arts, and culinary nutrition are offered at our Providence campus. The bachelor's degree program in culinary arts is also offered at our Florida campus. The New England Association of Schools and Colleges (NEASC) accredits all of our culinary programs.
>
> Together, our faculty combines over eighteen hundred years of industry experience and has advanced educational degrees and certifications. Above all, they are passionate about their profession, dedicated to education, and driven by commitment to quality. They take a sincere and personal interest in the success and well-being of every student.
>
> Our students are educated in state-of-the-art facilities. They receive career guidance and direction in making "best fit" career choices. Students are given opportunities to gain both national and international industry experiences through our co-operative education programs, and internship programs. They are also exposed to the industry on a regular basis.

As the University Dean, I lead the culinary activities on all of our campuses and it would be my pleasure to welcome you to this dynamic group.

The Johnson and Wales University Web site is http://www.jwu.edu.

CULINARY STUDENT PATRICK WILLIAMS DESCRIBES CHICAGO'S KENDALL COLLEGE

There are two people who have had a great influence on my decision to attend culinary school. They are my grandmother and grandfather. Even though they passed away several years ago, they have always been more than just grandparents to me; they have been teachers, friends, and mentors. I have learned from them the importance of being a patient, caring, and understanding person in all aspects of life. My grandparents showed this in many ways, but I think the most memorable is how they shared their love of cooking food and entertaining with family and friends.

My grandmother spent hours cooking from scratch, making a spread big enough for fifteen to twenty people for our family and anyone who happened to stop by (and it seemed as if a lot of people did "just happen to stop by"). If there wasn't enough (but it seemed as if there always was), my grandparents would say, "We'll just make some more."

I remember watching how happy and content everyone seemed sharing the great food my grandparents prepared: the homemade sweet potato pies, the fried catfish, the fresh buttermilk biscuits, and barbecue with my grandfather's secret sauce. Seeing this scene year after year taught me that if a person is genuine, and shares a passion with those around them, the outcome would most likely be positive. So it was only natural for me to pursue my dream of attending culinary school and becoming a chef.

Kendall College was the perfect place to make my dream a reality. The admissions staff was more than helpful to me and made the application process simple. They were able to fully answer all my questions about the facilities and the curriculum.

What impressed me most about Kendall is their network of alumni and the success they all share in the food-service industry. Many of them work for some of Chicago's (and even the world's) top restaurants, including Ambria, Charlie Trotters, Roy's, Green Zebra, and the Big Bowl, just to name a few. To see these Kendall graduates as highly respected chefs and restaurant owners is not only impressive, but also encouraging to anyone who strives to do the same. The connections Kendall has with the food-service and hospitality industries allow students to find great internships at many of the leading businesses, restaurants, and hotels in the world.

The state-of-the-art kitchens and technology that we work with each day give us the experience we need to become leaders in this industry. I know that Kendall will provide me with the knowledge and skills necessary to accomplish my dream of becoming a great chef.

L'ACADEMIE DE CUISINE

Since 1976 L'Academie de Cuisine has been the premier source of cooking talent for fine dining establishments in the Washington area. Professional career training programs are offered both in the culinary and pastry arts that provide students with a comprehensive understanding and thorough training in classical French techniques. L'Academie de Cuisine's mission is to provide students with the skills needed to join the ranks of great chefs everywhere. The school has small class size so students receive personal attention and expert instruction under the direction of European and American trained chefs.

L'Academie's curriculum stresses the importance of the "Four P's": the best and freshest ingredients (purchasing), organization of the kitchen (preparation), the artistry of (presentation), and the development of taste (palate). Together, these four P's provide the foundation for creating the complete chef and pastry chef.

In 2005, L'Academie de Cuisine was recognized as one of the top ten culinary schools in the United States and Canada by CookingSchoolsCompared.com. It has distinguished itself among the best schools in the country through its focus on the techniques and the philosophy needed to become a great cook and ultimately a fine chef.

We differ from most culinary schools in two main areas: our teaching methods and our cooking philosophy. L'Academie's emphasis on daily meal preparation and cooking is unique among culinary schools. In the twelve-month culinary arts program, students cook full menus every day, focusing not just on one ingredient, but the entire composition of the meal, and the numerous techniques involved in preparing it. Using this integrated menu format, students receive a comprehensive understanding of the many elements, both techniques and ingredients, of meal preparation.

The eight-month pastry arts program begins with the fundamentals such as basic doughs, cakes, fillings, and décor, and culminates with a buffet of fine French pastries showcasing all the classical techniques that are learned during the program.

Second, our philosophy toward cooking encompasses basic hard work and a deep respect for the profession. We believe that cooking is a team effort, choosing the right ingredients is the first step to becoming a good cook, techniques are more important than recipes, creativity can come only after you have mastered the fundamentals, and there is never an end to learning from those around you.

Students at L'Academie are highly sought after for positions in fine dining kitchens throughout the United States and have the opportunity to work with some of the best chefs in the business. Many of L'Academie de Cuisine's externship sites consider our students future staff members and are always willing to serve as mentors to students as they move ahead in their culinary and pastry careers.

L'Academie de Cuisine is located about fifteen miles from downtown Washington, D.C., in Gaithersburg, one of the best communities in the United States to live according to *Money* magazine. More than just monuments, embassies, and museums, Washington has many lively historic neighborhoods and a vibrant music and arts scene. Our nation's capital is rich in culture and tradition, and you can experience a wide array of international cuisines with some truly great chefs in our world-class restaurants and hotels.

Culinary and pastry arts programs begin each January, April, July, and October. Visit us at http://www.lacademie.com or call 301-670-8670 or toll free: 800-664-2433.

In addition to traditional restaurant roles, graduates from L'Academie de Cuisine include:

Kris Larsen, partner at Fresh TV, LLC, an independent Producer for the Food Network

Pablo Solanet, owner and cheese maker for Firefly Farms that produces artisanal cheese in Allegheny County, Maryland

Beryl Shehan, owner of Beryl's International Decorating and Pastry Supplies Company

Virginia Willis, principal of Virginia Willis Culinary Productions, TV producer at *Martha Stewart Living*, *The Main Ingredient with Bobby Flay*, Epicurious, and TurnerSouth's series *Home Plate*

John Kessler, food critic for the *Atlanta Constitution*

Jennifer Cohen Siegel, culinary specialist at Hisaoka Public Relations

Thy Tran Parra, director of social catering at the Mandarin Oriental Hotel

Cheryl Haser, online producer at *Washingtonian* magazine

Rachel Hayden, marketing manager at the Inn at Little Washington

LE CORDON BLEU COLLEGE OF CULINARY ARTS

Few institutions of any kind possess the prestigious reputation of Le Cordon Bleu. The expression *cordon bleu* originates from the blue ribbon from which was suspended the cross of the knights from the Order of the Holy Spirit, established in 1578 by King Henri III of France. In 1895, journalist Marthe Distel introduced the weekly magazine, *La Cuisinière Cordon Bleu*, and the school was opened shortly thereafter.

This internationally renowned school for the culinary arts has become synonymous with expertise, innovation, tradition, and refinement—qualities that are painstakingly nurtured by the school. There are thirteen locations to choose from in the United States: Atlanta, Georgia, Austin, Texas, Chicago, Illinois, Dover, New Hampshire, Las Vegas, Nevada, Miami, Florida, Minneapolis, Minnesota, Orlando, Florida, Pasadena, California, Pittsburgh, Pennsylvania, Portland, Oregon, San Francisco, California, and Scottsdale, Arizona. In addition, there are schools in Paris; London; Ottawa; Tokyo; Sydney and Adelaide, Australia; Peru; Seoul, Korea; and Mexico City.

Le Cordon Bleu Colleges of Culinary Arts in association with Le Cordon Bleu parent company represents a union of European and North American culinary arts training programs. It prepares students for professional opportunities and career success by providing a personalized, hands-on education in the classic and modern culinary arts. Students are exposed to international culinary techniques that focus on demonstrations followed by practical application. Upon completion, students graduate with an associate of occupational science degree in culinary arts.

Le Cordon Bleu College of Culinary Arts offers a fifteen-month course leading to an associate of science degree in culinary arts. The school provides the training and expertise you need to become a professional chef. You'll spend twelve months on campus and three months in an externship that will expose you to a real-world culinary environment. You will also accomplish the following:

- Train in classical cooking methods
- Become proficient in standard techniques
- Study nutrition as it relates to food preparation
- Learn front and back-of-the-house operations
- Become skilled in proper procedures

The Le Cordon Bleu master of business administration in international and hotel and restaurant is different from other MBAs in that every aspect of the program is created around the hospitality industry. This means a program specifically designed to prepare graduates to be future managers and leaders of international hotels and resorts, hospitality and restaurant businesses.

The master of arts in gastronomy program has been developed for food professionals seeking related careers in hospitality, media, or tourism. Topics range across culinary history; food and its symbolism; twentieth-century restaurants and menus; and food in art, literature, and film.

Combining coursework and research, the program is designed to provide a general appreciation of the history and culture of food and drink, with a strong focus on contemporary issues. Classes are enriched through the contributions of students from many countries with a diversity of backgrounds, all sharing a common interest. It is one of the few programs leading to an advanced degree in gastronomic studies, and the only one available for online study. The normal minimum entry requirement for the program is a bachelor's degree plus English-language proficiency.

Graduates from the program have careers in teaching, research, and tourism, with some students continuing study toward a PhD. Find out more at http://www.LeCordonBleuSchoolsUSA.com.

NEW ENGLAND CULINARY INSTITUTE

A culinary education is a fine art—and few culinary schools practice the art as well as New England Culinary Institute. Although we began twenty-five years ago as a small cooking school offering a professional degree in the culinary arts, today a New England Culinary Institute education can transform your passion for food into a twenty-first-century career in the fast-growing world of food service and hospitality

The award for outstanding vocational cooking school is given to an International Association of Culinary Professionals (IACP) -member cooking school that provides a superior educational experience for students pursuing a career in the culinary industry. The recipient of this award in 2005 was New England Culinary Institute, in Montpelier, Vermont.

Whether you envision a job as a chef, food and beverage manager, pastry chef, food writer, or fulfilling any other food-oriented positions, New England Culinary Institute can give you the hands-on cooking experience and education you need and a professional degree that can help open doors. Degrees in culinary arts, baking and pastry arts, and food and beverage management are available.

Our location in the heart of Vermont's Green Mountains provides plenty of opportunity for outdoor recreation in an area of great natural beauty. Our goal is to train you to have the hands of an artisan, the eyes of an artist, the mind of an entrepreneur, and the knowledge, skills, and real-world experience to be successful.

The New England Culinary Institute (NECI) provides one of the most intense educational experiences of any cooking school in the world. Unlike others, NECI uses a standards-based approach. Students are not graded on their culinary skills or knowledge; rather, they have to meet or exceed a high standard of competence in each and every skill.

NECI's small class size, averaging seven students to one instructor, provides an exceptionally rare opportunity for personalized instruction, three-quarters of which is spent on the line in eleven real restaurants and food-service operations in Vermont. Programs include an AOS in culinary arts, an AOS in food and beverage management, a BA in food and beverage management, and a certificate in culinary arts. The AOS in culinary arts requires a two-year commitment and 113 credit hours, as compared with other programs that require just seventy to eighty credit hours. The demands are high at NECI, but graduates are prepared to be leaders in their chosen fields

Our cooking classes are small and intense, and our unusual student-to-teacher ratio (an average seven-to-one student/teacher ratio in production classes with a maximum of ten) means your instructors can give you personal attention. The unique hands-on learning experience in our celebrated restaurants and on paid, professional internships equips you with all the skills you need to make your passion your profession.

Alton Brown, host of the Food Network's *Good Eats* program and 1997 NECI graduate says, "Food connects to everything in our lives. If you have a good culinary background, you will have tremendous opportunity in the food industry. I chose NECI because of the intense education that I knew would prepare me for any path I chose." For more information, log onto http://www.neci.edu.

RUTGERS, THE STATE UNIVERSITY OF NEW JERSEY CONTINUING PROFESSIONAL EDUCATION, COOK COLLEGE

The Cook College Office of Continuing Professional Education provides quality outreach and public service programs. Cook College offers courses in agricultural production and competitiveness; food science and engineering; nutrition, health and safety; marine and coastal resources; natural resources and the environment; human and community resource development. Course topics include better process control, food safety, microbiology, culinology, the art and science of new food development, food protection, sensory evaluation, real-world techniques and applications, food service and safety, and HACCP verification and validation. Their Web site is http//aesop.rutgers/edu.

THE WASHBURNE TRADE SCHOOL
by Bill Reynolds

With the abundance of high-quality culinary schools in the United States today, it is difficult to image a time without them. The effort to develop formalized culinary education didn't take shape, however, until the first part of the twentieth century. The motivation, in part, was the need to train cooks for the army during World War I. Public funding for chef training programs through the Smith-Hughes Act of 1917 fueled further development, as did vital support from the hospitality industry and chef's associations.

Chefs at that time, who were mostly trained in Europe, were anxious to improve the low prestige of their profession in the United States. Developing a system for culinary training was the chosen way to improve their status. Schools began to develop around the country especially in California, Washington, New York, Connecticut, and Illinois. Chicago's Washburne Trade School Chef Training Program, founded by Swiss chef August

Forster in 1937, was the most successful of these early forerunners.

Keith H. Mandabach, author of *Professional American Culinary Arts Schools 1927-1940*, writes, "The Washburne program successfully negotiated the political winds of the public school system in Chicago to become the most successful and prolific program outside of the Culinary Institute of America, (founded in 1946). Washburne was founded on European principles, espoused professionalism and believed in an analytical approach to teaching cooking. Industry leaders from all the associations supported the program. During the war the program trained cooks for the Navy. The high standards of the program were maintained, and after the war many GI's returned wanting a higher level of culinary education. August Forster successfully reinvented the program as a technical school."

Culinary training was one of sixteen programs taught at Washburne's mammoth building at Thirty-first and Kedsie, where it continued until July 2000. The culinary program remained strong throughout the years despite cuts in funding, a dilapidated building, and worn-out equipment. The faculty, mostly made up of Washburne alums, was able to create an environment where students felt that these hardships actually made them better chefs. Their philosophy was that anyone could cook with flat-bottomed pans and a stove that has all burners working. Washburne students believed they could cook under any conditions and were all the stronger for it.

In 1993 the Chicago Board of Education, which had operated the Washburne Trade School since 1919, closed the tuition-free school for financial reasons. The City Colleges of Chicago picked up many of the existing programs, including the culinary program. Wayne Watson, chancellor for the City Colleges, brought me in as a twenty-five-year veteran of the Culinary Institute of America, to update the program. At that point the name was changed to the Washburne Culinary Institute.

Changing the trade-school curriculum to accommodate an associate's degree and building a new world-class facility housed in Chicago's historic South Shore Cultural Center overlooking Lake Michigan has helped bring this pioneer school into the twenty-first century. Although the program is no longer tuition-free, Washburne offers a competitive training program at one-third the cost of private culinary arts colleges. The affordability allows for a diversity of students, from single parents to older adults seeking a career change. Graduates continue to find excellent career opportunities because of the school's national

Words of Caution from a Culinary Student

by Drew Mullins

 I STARTED MY career at a local junior college in Dallas, Texas, that offered a degree in the culinary arts. After a year, I left the school to work as an apprentice under a well-known chef. And then, with industry experience and a small amount of formal education, I decided to follow my lifelong dream of earning a degree from one of the top professional cooking schools. Seventy-six thousand dollars and three and a half years later, I received a bachelor's degree in hospitality management.

Attaining a great job is easier with my degree, but repaying the student loans at a 10 percent variable interest rate is financially discomforting. Thirty thousand dollars of the total debt I accrued while financing my education can be consolidated at a fixed interest rate of 3.3 percent. The other forty-six thousand dollars will remain at a variable interest rate, which is raised quarterly and at the time of this writing is pegged at 10.75 percent. As is the case with a large portion of all educational loans, these are considered private loans and cannot be consolidated into lower-interest-rate loans. This means that these private loans have an interest rate 7.75 points higher than the national average for student loans. Over the course of my agreed loan term, which is twenty years, I will have paid $64,646.40 in interest just on the forty-six-thousand-dollar portion of my loan.

Unfortunately, the school's financial aid department didn't provide the guidance that I had anticipated in steering me to the most economical loan choices. I am not trying to discourage anyone from attending an institute of higher learning. I am trying to give a prospective student a piece of advice, just as my mentoring chefs have done for me. By doing a little more homework before borrowing money for college, I could have avoided many of the negative aspects of my personal loan agreement.

Fortunately the laws pertaining to student loans have come under government scrutiny and it is hoped, will become less burdensome in the future.

reputation. The Washburne name also has symbolized the struggle to open trade schools to students of all ethnic backgrounds, a legacy that continues today on Chicago's south side. The school has a long, rich tradition and is now well positioned to continue to make its mark on the culinary education scene.

THE CURRICULUM

It is important—indeed, essential—to study the curriculum carefully before making a commitment to attend a professional cooking school. Detailed information can be obtained by sending an inquiry letter to each school, and many schools post information online. Almost all cooking schools maintain a Web site. Identify all the schools that interest you using an online listing of professional schools and look into each one carefully.

All accredited schools require students to study fundamental cooking techniques and a variety of cuisines. Some institutes allow students to combine culinary programs with instruction in baking and pastry techniques, but others concentrate on only one branch of cooking in order to achieve the greatest possible breadth and depth of knowledge.

The top schools have mandatory classes in restaurant math, food purchasing, and budgeting and cost control. These are all important courses for anyone hoping to enter the field of hospitality management. There may also be compulsory classes in interpersonal communications, professional food writing, restaurant criticism, nutrition and food safety, product identification, and sanitation procedures. Students may also be required to study a second language such as Spanish, French, or Italian.

Included in the curriculum of some schools are training for front-of-the house management and waitstaff. Some may offer instruction in buffet catering, charcuterie and meat and fish fabrication, ice carving, menu and facilities design, and computer skills.

A few schools offer elective classes on subjects such as food photography and food styling. Some institutes offer extensive instruction in wines and spirits and beverage management. In addition to the scheduled classes, there are visits from celebrity guest chefs who give cooking demonstrations and provide students with the opportunity to observe and meet the leaders in the field. These are often memorable experiences.

When you decide on a school, plan to meet with the instructors early and, if necessary, often. They are there to help. Also, take as many electives as you can fit into your schedule. You never know when a class in food writing or food styling will come in useful, even if you never plan to leave the restaurant kitchen.

TUITION AND FEES

Make sure you know how much your education will cost beyond tuition fees. Don't forget the additional expenses of books, lab fees, and the cost of owning your own knives and other utensils. Check to see if the school fees include housing and one or two meals a day.

Ask if the school you are considering offers any financial incentives for you to enroll at a particular time of the year. In January,

A GOOD EXAMPLE of a student who has been helped by a C-CAP teacher and the program is Lasheeda Perry. Lasheeda had a difficult life growing up. She was one of eight children brought up by a single mother who was in and out of prison during Lasheeda's early years. During this time, she lived sith other family members, and foster families, never staying anywhere for very long. At the age of twelve Lasheeda, along with two of her siblings and her mother ended up in a homeless shelter.

Things didn't get better until she was in high school and discovered a C-CAP teacher by the name of Wilma Stephenson.

Lasheeda had the desire to attend college, but it was Mrs. Stephenson who made it happen.

Being a top winner in the C-CAP competition four years ago started a chain of events that have changed her life. Her first award was a full-tuition ($80,000) scholarship to Johnson & Wales University. Upon graduation from high school, she and two other girls were taken on an eight-day whirlwind trip to China with her Chef/mentor Joseph Poons.

While at Johnson & Wales Lasheeda won a 3-week trip to Australia, and did a three-month externship at a Relais & Chateau property in Ireland. In February, 2008 she graduated Summa Cum Laude with a BS in Pastry Arts and Food Service Management. Upon graduation Laaheeda was hired to start her full-time job as a pastry cook at the Four Seasons Hotel in Dallas, Texas.

Lasheeda is one of many underserved students whose career in the culinary world has been guided and helped by C-CAP.

"Pressure Cooker" a feature documentary, that follows Wilma Stephenson and her high school class as they prepare for the C-CAP competitions and awards, will be released in the fall of 2008. The film was produced and directed by Jennifer Grausman, and Participant Productions is the Executive Producer.

for example, there may be smaller class sizes and a fast-track application process because a number of the enrolled students may be off campus pursuing paid or unpaid internships—or, more accurately, "externships."

A few schools, including Culinary Institute of America and Johnson and Wales, offer accelerated Associate of Occupational

Studies (AOS) programs that omit the externship requirement. These programs appeal to those who already have industry experience.

APPLYING FOR A SCHOLARSHIP

A scholarship may be waiting for you right now, but unless you ask for it, you may never even know you could have benefited from it. Dan Traster, academic director of culinary arts at the Art Institute of Washington in Arlington, Virginia, urges would-be students to search diligently for financial assistance.

"Concentrate on researching the organization that offers or administers the kind of scholarship you want. For instance, the National Restaurant Association promotes the entire restaurant industry, so it considers applicants who want to be managers, dieticians and marketers, as well as cooks and pastry chefs," he says.

Read the fine print when you apply for scholarships. For instance, some are available only to high-school students, while others let you apply after you are in college. Some require a certain grade-point average; others give more weight to culinary skills or experience. Many scholarships are given only after completing a certain amount of time working in the industry. It is important to show you are really serious about continuing to stay in the field and won't change your mind and drop out if you find the work too hard or if it fails to live up to your expectations. You may need to provide proof of your experience, such as a copy of a paycheck stub.

Check the deadlines for applications and allow plenty of time to meet them. While you are looking for scholarships, think about where you want to study. Look at more than one school and study their programs carefully. Ask what kinds of scholarships they offer, how many are available, and what you have to do to get one.

To receive a scholarship from an organization such as the American Culinary Federation or the American Dietetic Association, you will get special attention if you send one or more references from a member of the organization to which you are applying, advises Traster. Be sure that person knows your work, or the recommendation will not carry enough weight.

It may seem obvious, but it's extremely important to follow the instructions on the application form carefully and answer every question. Judges say many applicants are dropped simply because some questions are left blank.

Be realistic. If you are asked to write an essay describing your goals, it is best to say you hope to find a job as a line cook in a restaurant rather than suggesting you want to start your career as a consultant to Emeril Lagasse or Thomas Keller. In other words, says Traster, "focus on an achievable goal and explain how the scholarship will help you to meet that goal. For instance, you may want to go to Italy to study the food of a specific region. That is a reasonable and understandable purpose and there are organizations that offer scholarships for just such a purpose. You may receive a grant that will give you enough funds to stay alive while working as an unpaid intern in a television studio. If you want to apply for an unpaid internship in a photography studio, enclose samples of your own picture taking to convince the awards committee of your talent. If you yearn to work as an intern at a magazine send along samples of your writings that have been published in the school newspaper or other publication."

Plenty of scholarships are available, but you have to work hard to get your hands on the big prize money.

THE CAREERS THROUGH CULINARY ARTS PROGRAM

Careers through Culinary Arts Program (C-CAP) has grown dramatically since its inception in 1990. From a pilot program founded by Richard Grausman in 12 New York City public schools, C-CAP has developed into a national organization with seven locations reaching 10,000 young people in 200 schools a year.

SCHOLARSHIP

Through its Cooking Competitions for Scholarships program C-CAP has awarded $25 million in post-secondary school scholarships to 2,300 students. It also offers career and college guidance, job training and internships.

The "C-CAP Approved," certification program for entry-level skills leads students to jobs. All C-CAP services are free-of-charge to students. The program is funded by donations from individuals, foundations, corporations, public school systems and by culinary schools, product sponsors and the volunteer services of hundreds of chefs.

The program provides awards and scholarships ranging from $1,000 to full-tuition and helps students to make informed college and career choices. The C-CAP Cooking Competition for

Scholarships provides an opportunity for motivated young people who decide to pursue a career in a culinary or hospitality related field. The competition consists of two parts; the Preliminary Competition and the Final Competition.

WHO'S ELIGIBLE?

C-CAP is a school-to-career program that links public high schools to the foodservice industry. Its comprehensive approach prepares students for a successful education and career. Both juniors and seniors from any participating C-CAP high school who have completed at least one culinary, cooking, or home economics class are eligible to compete in the C-CAP Preliminary Competition. Only seniors who successfully pass the C-CAP Preliminary Competition are eligible to go on to the C-CAP Cooking Competition for Scholarships.

JOBS AND INTERSHIPS

C-CAP provides job readiness training, job shadowing and places students in jobs and interships with local restaurants, hotels and other foodservice establishments.

COLLEGE AND CAREER ADVISING

C-CAP offers long-term support to scholarship recipients through financial aid assistance, career building workshops, job referrals and placement.

AFTER-SCHOOL PROGRAM

A specially designed curriculum allows middle-school and high-school age students to participate in C-CAP after the school day.

COLLEGE AND CAREER ADVISING

C-CAP offers long-term support to scholarship recipients through financial aid assistance, career building workshops, job referrals, and placement.

FOR MORE INFORMATION

Scholarships have recently been offered by these organizations:

- The Culinary Institute of America (http://www.ciachef.edu) awards more than $1.1 million through 769 scholarships. Recipients of Cream of the Crop scholarships are selected based upon their leadership skills and academic record. Recipients earn five thousand dollars, renewable for each year of study at the CIA, provided they maintain at least a 3.2 grade point average.
- The National Restaurant Association Foundation (http://www.restaurant.org) awards scholarships totaling more than $5 million.
- The Culinary School of the Rockies Scholarship (http://www.culinaryschoolrockies) in Boulder, Colorado, awards one five thousand dollar tuition-credit scholarship to a pre-enrolled student or career professional toward the six-month diploma of culinary arts.
- The Institute of Culinary Education Scholarship, New York, New York, http://www.iceculinary.com.
- International Association of Culinary Professionals (IACP) awards twenty-one scholarships ranging from four thousand dollars in tuition credit to full tuition at culinary schools worldwide. The IACP culinary trust grant program also assists food writers who need help covering travel and research expenses. http://www.iacp.com
- Le Cordon Bleu (international locations), http://www.condonbleu.edu
- New England Culinary Institute Scholarship, Montpelier, Vermont, http://www.neci.edu
- The French Culinary Institute Scholarship, New York, New York, http://www.frenchculinary.com
- L'Academie de Cuisine Scholarship, Gaithersburg, Maryland, http://www.lacadamie.com
- Kendall College Scholarship, http://www.kendall.edu
- American Culinary Federation's American Academy of Chefs, http://www.acfchefs.org
- New England Culinary Institute Scholarship, http://www.neci.edu
- American Dietetic Association, http://www.eatright.org

- American Institute of Wine and Food, http://www.aiwf.org
- International Foodservice Editorial Council (IFEC) provides money to students interested in culinary marketing, public relations or food writing. http://www.ifec-is-us.com
- Sullivan University, Louisville, Kentucky, http://www.sullivan.edu
- International Food Service Executives Association, http://www.ifsea.com
- Susanna Foo Chinese Cuisine Scholarship, http://www.womenchefs
- Women Chefs & Restaurateurs, http://www.womenchefs.org
- Culinary Trusts's Julia Child Endowment Scholarship, http://www.theculinarytrust.org
- The eGullet Society for Culinary Arts and Letters scholarship, http://www.egullet.org
- Zwilling J. A. Henckels, Inc. Scholarship, http://www.jahenckels.com
- The Charlie Trotter Culinary Education Foundation awards scholarships to individuals seeking careers in the culinary arts who otherwise would not have the means to pursue their dreams. Through his foundation, Chef Trotter has taught students how to cook and how to reach their personal goals through post-secondary education. He has donated over thirty guest-chef-for-a-day certificates each month for the past ten years and awarded over $150,000 in scholarships. http://www.charlietrotters.com/about/foundation.asp

• RECIPES FOR SUCCESS •

AS A HIGH school senior, Alfred Stephens spent nights and weekends practicing his culinary skills to compete for a scholarship awarded by the New York–based Careers through Culinary Arts Program (C-Cap). His expertise with a French-style omelet with potato filling earned him a full scholarship to the French Culinary Institute.

Caterer and private chef Mary Ladd says volunteering helped her win five thousand dollars toward study at the California Culinary Academy in San Francisco through its foundation. She planned weekend field trips for students, wrote a food news column for the school newspaper, and helped bring guest chefs to the campus.

Former public relations executive David Lenweaver took a contrary approach in the Culinary Institute of America's All-American Apple Pie Recipe Contest. While others were using an almond flour crust or adding litchi nuts, Lenweaver stuck to homey ingredients for his apple pie and also concentrated on writing a clever essay. He won a scholarship worth twenty-five thousand dollars.

Jessica Bride, director of marketing from Smith and Wollensky Restaurant Group, headquartered in New York City, spent a lot of time on the Internet looking up culinary associations and associations for women. She applied for and received a five-thousand-dollar scholarship from Women Chefs and Restaurateurs.

TEACHING THE CULINARY ARTS

It's one thing to attend a culinary school and go on to work in a restaurant, for a caterer, or a food company. It's another to teach.

Most chef/instructors draw on their own experiences and the love of teaching. Some who teach academic subjects have a degree in general education, which is useful. They may have taught other subjects before switching to or adding the specialty of culinary teacher. Many start by teaching avocational classes, catch the bug (most good teachers simply love to teach), and go on to teach at higher levels. There are no formal teachers' colleges for cooking instructors, though increasingly the outside-the-kitchen faculty of the top schools have earned not only undergraduate college degrees, but PhDs too.

▶ The Job of Chef Instructor

Chef instructors at cooking schools are responsible for training students and providing continuing education for experienced working chefs. Teachers provide practical, hands-on instruction in cooking and also in purchasing, cost control, and budgeting, menu development, product utilization, time management, ethics, and professionalism. The job entails developing curriculum, writing lesson plans, grading homework and class assignments, administrating tests and examinations, and evaluating students' performance.

Classically trained chef instructors draw from their hard-earned experience to teach others. A minimum of five years' experience working as an executive chef in a restaurant kitchen, bakery, catering company, or other branch of the hospitality industry is usually mandatory, and as part of the interview process, prospective instructors may be asked to prepare several dishes and demonstrate their ability to convey knowledge to students. They may have no formal academic qualifications, although people entering the field now generally do.

A successful chef instructor must be able to solve problems and maintain discipline in the classroom. As with all teachers, chef instructors acknowledge that classes vary from one another. A significant indication of their competency lies in their ability to transform the bad or bruised apples into polished chefs, not just make the already shiny ones shinier. In other words, a teacher combines the attributes of sainthood with the benign affection of motherhood.

▶ Cooking School Director

Cooking schools run the gamut from large institutions such as Johnson and Wales and the Culinary Institute of America to small schools and programs administered by community colleges. Directing a school demands keeping your eye on the prize, which is to produce well-trained graduates who go out in the world and make the school proud. This means understanding the need to teach basic techniques to give students a strong foundation in the culinary arts but also to offer classes that appeal to their desire to soar. A good director keeps abreast of trends and shifts in the marketplace, and a great director knows how to hire the right teachers who have the needed flexibility and knowledge to inspire the students.

$\mathcal{A}$NNE WILLAN

I FOUNDED ECOLE de Cuisine La Varenne in Paris in 1975. With the encouragement and expert advice of three food authorities, Julia Child, Simone Beck, and James Beard, we opened our doors in an old building with five students and one teaching chef. I was terrified. I discovered it is a quantum leap from cooking professionally and writing about food, as I had been doing, to planning and running a school.

Choosing the name was the least of it and even that took several months. François Pierre de la Varenne was the first cookbook writer to define classical French cooking, and I had been trained in that discipline. I started at the London Cordon Bleu under Rosemary Hume where the style was robustly domestic, with an overlay of French technique. The Paris Cordon Bleu, where I went next, transcended time. The syllabus covered exclusively the grand classics, the blanquettes and braises, the sauces and soufflés of Escoffier. We cooked in a basement with a single oven without a thermostat, which heated top, bottom, or both together, take your choice. On a good day, the cantankerous old chef would pinch my knee, on a bad day he simply yelled. It was excellent experience as a soufflé that rose there would rise anywhere. My mother, arbiter of progress, remarked how much my cooking had improved.

I was raised during World War II in the depths of north Yorkshire, half a mile from the nearest farmhouse, a happy, solitary childhood full of books and folklore. Even then I was excited by food; for me baking day was the big event of the week when our old cook fired up the range and baked pastry and cakes for the seven days to come. Boarding school led to the intoxication of Cambridge University, where I was one of two women studying economics. I was quite unsuited to academic life, but loved it all the same. Looking back, it was when I moved to France that I grew up, escaping from a cozy, predictable world as the much-loved only child of well-to-do parents.

Fifteen years after that first immersion into French food, I moved back to Paris from the United States, now an American citizen with a husband and two little children. The 1970s were revolutionary times in the cooking world: nouvelle cuisine was just beginning to oust the stately Escoffier classics that had reigned since the start of the century. When we opened La Varenne, I was determined to teach the full French range—the classics, the regional dishes, a little bit of history, and also those novelties such as fish pot-au-feu or warm salad of foie gras with raspberry vinegar that were taking Paris by storm. I knew what it was like to be a stranger in France, and La Varenne, we knew, would draw on foreign students. We needed to allow for national tastes, not to mention foodstuffs back home. There would be strong insistence on practical training, on putting *la main à la pâte* (hand to dough). We would provide *stagiaires* (bilingual teaching assistants) to give instant meaning to the chef's words.

Ten years later, the scene had changed again. American students no longer needed to come to France to learn basic knife skills and how to make stock. Sound basic training was available back home. The graduate experience was what was needed, an immersion in the cultural aspects of food in France as well as advanced practical expertise in the kitchen. I would like to think that I had already sensed the return to tradition that became so characteristic of the 1990s, with its bistros and emphasis on *cuisine de grand'mère*. We made courses shorter, more diverse, more demanding. A new breed of student also appeared: the culinary tourist who comes

continued

continued from page 299

for a week or two to learn a few amusing dishes, to hobnob with the pros, and enjoy some memorable meals. Many are serious cooks, technically adept in the kitchen, and a few have gone on to turn professional, the classic career changer. It was to this group that we appealed more and more.

Here's where Château du Feÿ comes in. It is the idyllic seventeenth-century property in northern Burgundy where our family has been based for the last twenty-five years. We are surrounded by fine restaurants and top chefs, the region is a source of outstanding ingredients, and we are within a short distance of Chablis, the Côte d'Or, Champagne, and the Loire, with their world-class wines. It is above all the people—not only the chefs, but the vintners, the growers, the truffle producers (yes there are truffles here in Burgundy), the cheese *affineur*, and the local artisan community generally who add the insiders' view to our current culinary programs.

We used to wonder what careers our students would choose, and we soon found out. Only a few have followed the traditional restaurant route of sous chef followed by chef and, finally perhaps, restaurant owner. Many, like me, have combined their cooking experience with writing, so that there is now scarcely a food magazine in the U.S. that does not have a La Varenne graduate on the masthead. I like to think they pursue my insistence on accuracy with a leavening of lighter comment.

Cooking careers have blossomed in the past two decades, particularly for women, with openings in food styling, recipe development, catering, culinary newsletters, marketing, and most recently, on the Internet, to name a few. The La Varenne culinary training, with its emphasis on history, cultural background, and the importance of writing skills, helps students to escape from the heat of the kitchen to the wider world of the food and wine arts.

For information about ongoing three- and five-day classes at La Varenne in Burgundy, please visit http://www.chateaudufey.com and http://www.lavarenne.com.

CULINARY TRAVEL AND LEARNING

As the world shrinks, the interest in different cuisines expands. We travel more easily than ever before, and while all this movement has meant cross-pollination of food cultures, it also has spurred interest in learning about "authentic" cooking customs. Destination cooking schools and culinary tours, directed at cooking hobbyists, are a growing business.

COOKING SCHOOLS ABROAD

The following cooking schools are a tiny sample among many that are primarily designed for people who cook as a hobby, though professionals are always welcomed. More information can be found about them on the Internet. Learning about these schools could spur you on to create a similar school in your corner of the world.

BALLYMALOE COOKERY SCHOOL

Cookbook author Darina Allen offers wonderfully inspiring and practical kitchen instruction from a converted eighteenth-century farm building in Shanagarry, County Cork, Ireland. Classes (ranging from a half day to five days) are mostly hands-on, and vary from basics like bread baking and seafood cookery to cuisines of other countries. Allen CCP (Certified Culinary Professional) was the recipient of the International Association of Cooking Professionals Cooking Teacher of the Year award in 2005. http://www. cookingisfun.ie

GEORGEANNE BRENNAN'S HAUTE PROVENCE

Cookbook author Georgeanne Brennan offers week-long, hand-on cooking vacation classes in a beautifully restored convent in the Provencal village of Aups. The week includes daily market shopping, visits to artisinal honey and cheese producers, and more. Because the week is limited to only seven people, instruction is highly individualized. Georgeanne is the recipient of both a James Beard Award and an IACP Julia Child award. Her brilliant book, *A Pig in Provence*, was published by Harcourt in 2008.

THE FRENCH KITCHEN IN GASCONY

Students of gastronomy can study year-round in southwestern France with writer/cook Kate Hill at her enchanting canal-side *auberge* and gardens in Camont, France. Hill offers a celebration of authentic and simple French recipes to welcome each season. Her classes feature techniques used in every French home kitchen: making easy pastries, sautéing, braising, and cooking with fresh herbs. She is the captain of the eighty-five-foot barge, *Julia Hoyt*, and owner-director of the French Kitchen Cooking School in Camont. She is also author of *A Culinary Journey in Gascony: Recipes and Stories from My French Canal Boat*. http://www.thefrenchkitchen.com

TASTE OF CULTURE

Japanese-food specialist and *Gourmet* magazine contributor Elizabeth Andoh has a Tokyo-based program that includes customized programs of intensive study during six- to ten-day demonstration classes that concentrate on a wide range of cooking techniques, with tasting programs and excursions into neighborhood food shops. http://www.tasteofculture.com

UNLIMITED CUISINE COMPANY

Some of the best Chinese cooking classes are based out of Australia, and Malaysian-born chef Tony Tan's is among them. He has day and evening sessions at his school in Melbourne and conducts an eleven-day excursion to China and Macau with an intensive schedule of cooking demonstrations, tea tastings, and market tours. http://www.tonytan.com.au

THE WORLD OF REGALEALI

The school provides an introduction to Sicilian cuisine. It is located on the lush Regaleali-Tasca d'Almerita wine estate, about an hour and a half journey from Palermo, Italy, and offers one-, three-, and five-day programs. Cookbook author Countess Anna Tasca Lanza expertly guides students through the preparation of the day's meals. Some of the ingredients come directly from the property's farm. There are wine tastings and visits to local markets and trattorias. http://www.cuisineinternatioanl.com/italy/regaleali.

For More Information

Andrews, Colman. *Catalan Cuisine: Vivid Flavors from Spain's Mediterranean Coast*. Paperback edition. Cambridge, MA: Harvard Common Press, 2006.

Barranechea, Teresa, with Mary Goodbody. *The Basque Table*. Paperback edition. Cambridge, MA: Harvard Common Press, 2006.

The ShawGuides. The ShawGuides are the definitive source for information on recreational cooking schools. The 358-page 2005 (seventeenth annual) edition contains detailed descriptions of 509 career and 708 recreational programs worldwide. It's the largest edition to date, with 1,217 listings. It is "the Bible" according to the *New York Times. The Wall Street Journal, Forbes, BusinessWeek, Fortune,* and every leading food and wine publication recommends the guide. http://www.shawguides.com.

To locate American Culinary Federation–accredited culinary programs, check http://www.acfchefs.org/drctaccr.html.

Also access http://www.cookingschools.com listings of fourteen hundred professional and recreational cooking schools organized by state locations.

Chef2chef.net is a resource for chefs to find employment and also offers other useful information as well as an online index of culinary schools.

CULINARY TOURS

Faith Heller Willinger works with food professionals and intrepid eaters interested in learning about Italian food and wine by arranging itineraries, which include cooking lessons, winery visits, and artisanal food tastings as well as lodging and meals in Italy. Willinger is not alone. This is an expanding field and is even catching on domestically. Becoming a culinary tour leader or facilitator takes careful planning, thorough knowledge of your region, and an outgoing personality.

Willinger is the director of Canonica Cucina at Castiglione del Bosco, a private membership club in Montalcino. She used to direct the culinary programs at the Hotel Cipriani in Venice, Hotel Posta Vecchia in Ladispoli outside Rome, and was codirector of the Capezzana Wine and Culinary Center near Florence.

"I visited Italy in the early 1970s, armed with an American's knowledge of Italian cooking," she recalls. "I was familiar with supermarket Italian foods—parmesan in a green shaker, rubbery mozzarella, olive oil (forget about extra-virgin) in a tin. All this didn't prepare me for the wonders of Italian regional cooking and foods. I discovered risotto, polenta, tortellini, radicchio, peppers that weren't green, artichokes to eat raw, just-pressed extra-virgin olive oil and much, much more, and I was hooked. Italy became my obsession and I wanted to learn everything I could."

She moved to Rome, wrote to Julia Child for advice, telling her she wanted to learn about Italian food as Child had learned about French. Child suggested Willinger study with a professional chef and join the International Association of Culinary Professionals. Willinger took her advice. She worked in a restaurant in Rome, took notes, traveled, experimented at home, moved to Florence, learned about Tuscan food, and got turned on to wine. She studied with a master chef, Andrea Hellrigl, in the village of Merano, in Alto-Adige, and started tours of the Tuscan countryside, combining art, food, and wine. Today she says, "I have the best job in the world."

"No matter where you live, you can establish yourself in the community by giving tours of local markets, restaurants, cooking schools, cookware stores, food processing plants, farms, and farmers' markets," says tour guide Lisa Förare Winbladh. "Almost

● The New School Culinary Arts Program in New York City conducts culinary walking tours. Each program is limited to twenty people, and the fee that includes lunch is $65 per person. Call (212) 255-4141 NSCulArts@aol.com.

● The International Association of Culinary Professionals has a culinary tour special interest committee. Contact IACP.com.

everyone will welcome the publicity and you may also land a regular spot on radio or television and perhaps even decide to write a food column about the food entrepreneurs and unique services in your part of the country."

Winbladh says that when she moved to the south of Sweden, she decided to establish herself as a local food personality. She set up a two-hour guided walking tour of four to six specialty food shops. Establishing good relationships with the shopkeepers was the scariest part of this venture, she says. Cultural differences are a very real obstacle to communication and cooperation.

She offers this advice to anyone interested in becoming a culinary tour guide:

- Get a good name. I picked Food-Karavan because it conveys an exotic aroma of spices.
- Decide who you are. I present myself as the food nerd, a slightly obsessed person in eternal pursuit of culinary bungee jumps.
- Be consistent. Keep all your presentation materials and your Web site and your printed material in line with your image. A good design is essential to your business. It gives credibility and adds value.
- Be patient. Start with small groups so the shopkeepers and other businesses become comfortable with the idea. Always keep a few alternative shops in mind just in case a problem develops.
- Be humble. I always keep in mind that the shopkeepers got on fine before I started Food-Karavan. I need them more than they need me. Also, show gratitude and never expect to receive it. Pay (or offer to pay) for everything you sample in the shops.

TEACHING COOKING TO CHILDREN

The children's culinary industry is bubbling over with opportunity. Cooking classes for children have increased by more than 50 percent in the last three years, while 85 percent of children aged five to twelve are involved in an average of three after-school activities a year, and cooking classes are among these activities. Teachers who work with kids say that children and adolescents who learn to cook become educated on the nutritional value of foods and therefore are able to make more healthful food choices all their lives.

Barbara Beary, who teaches kids, says that the teacher and the kids together will master math, science, and reading. Learning to cook helps kids in other pursuits, too, she believes. It builds prediction and outcome skills and develops reasoning ability. It allows and encourages children to think outside the box and embraces creativity to its fullest. Emotionally, it instills self-confidence fostered in a noncompetitive environment.

"Your career in the children's culinary education profession will provide you with the opportunity to be an integral component in changing the way we think about the foods we eat," Beary says. The requirements are simple: a love of children and a passion for cooking. A background in childhood development and education are critical prerequisites, while a teaching certificate or teaching degree is a distinct advantage. Basic training in the culinary arts is important, but not essential, she says.

NEW YORK UNIVERSITY'S MASTER'S PROGRAM IN FOOD STUDIES AND FOOD MANAGEMENT

by Anne E. McBride

SINCE 1997, THE department of nutrition, food studies, and public health at New York University has offered bachelor's and master's degrees in food studies and food management and a doctoral degree in food studies. At any given time, approximately one hundred students are enrolled in the master's program in food studies and food management. There are students who have just finished their undergraduate studies and career changers in their forties and fifties. Most students are in their thirties, and their career goals vary widely. Some want to open a restaurant or other food business, while others hope to work as a food writer or public relations specialist.

Typically, the program takes two years to complete, but some finish it in a year and a half, and others go near the maximum allowed, which is six years. The schedule that will best fit you depends on your other commitments. For the most part, those who complete the program on the fast track came to New York with the sole purpose of attending NYU and then return to their home state or country, while students attending part-time, often work or wish to complete personal projects, such as writing a book, as they progress with their degree.

continued

continued from page 299

A large number of the students are career changers who have always loved food but were only able to work in it alongside other work, perhaps by catering small parties from their home kitchens. They start the NYU program because it allows them to add academic knowledge to their love of food, and hopefully will enable them to transition to a food-related occupation.

These transitions often come with considerable sacrifice, such as accepting lower wages, but the disadvantages are far outweighed by the satisfaction of working in a field they enjoy.

I was fortunate to start the program while already working in the food industry as a cookbook editor. In addition to the skills I developed in a professional capacity, my studies have vastly broadened my perspective on food and have allowed me to publish and present papers at conferences. My education contributes to my work. I am currently a writer and editor for a culinary school. It has also been immensely satisfying to meet like-minded people for whom food is more than a thrice-daily necessity, and who are as interested in cooking it as in discussing its origins and future. I have been accepted into the doctoral program, and eventually hope to have a career in teaching.

GETTING STARTED

To enter the program, you need to submit an application to the Steinhardt School's admission department (http://www.nyu.edu/education), which includes writing an essay detailing your motivations and goals. Take the essay as something you produce not only for NYU, but also for yourself, as it will allow you to map out the path you want to take once you start the program.

Students need to complete forty credits to graduate, or thirty-four if they have a degree from a culinary school. Some of the classes in the program include food history, food writing, contemporary issues in food studies and food management, international cuisines, entrepreneurship, food and culture, recipe analysis and development, research methods, and research applications. Based on their interests, students can then take further specialization classes such as food and film, field trips, food photography, and classes in other NYU departments to complement their program. Students typically have taken classes at Stern Business School—particularly those with an interest in food marketing and management—in performance studies, or in history. Every June, students can go to Tuscany for three weeks to obtain six credits. They take classes locally, visit food producers, attend lectures by prominent locally-based historians and writers, and write research papers when they return.

As for career prospects, current graduates and students work in education, media, public relations, catering, sales, marketing, product development, research, and writing, for example. Very often, students find that the skills they acquired in previous careers can be tailored to positions in the food industry, so they use those credentials, along with their newly acquired knowledge and skills, to find a position that suits them.

Networking is an important element of the program, and students tend to be supportive of their peers as they pass along job openings and circulate résumés. It is also important to take advantage of student rates to join organizations like the Culinary Historians of New York, New York Women's Culinary Alliance, the American Institute of Wine and Food, and Women Chefs and Restaurateurs, among others.

The department does not offer career services per se, but lists jobs as it learns about them, and NYU has a career service department that students can use.

For More Information

NYU Department of Nutrition, Food Studies and Public Health, http://www.nyu.edu/education/foodstudies

The Association for the Study of Food and Society is the academic organization of food studies, and when you join its listserv (which you can access without paying membership fees for the organization), you will be able to participate in conversations with leading food scholars. Again, because the field is still new, people are extremely supportive of one another, and every question receives a response.

Professional Organizations

Association for the Study of Food and Society,
http://www.food-culture.org

Culinary Historians of New York,
http://www.culinaryhistoriansny.org

New York Women's Culinary Alliance,
http://www.nywca.org

Women Chefs and Restaurateurs,
http://www.womenchefs.org

American Institute of Wine and Food,
http://www.aiwf.org

International Association of Culinary Professionals,
http://www.iacp.com

CORNELL UNIVERSITY OF NEW YORK SCHOOL OF HOTEL ADMINISTRATION

Cornell University's School of Hotel Administration is a service-oriented management school offering undergraduate, masters and PhD degrees in executive education. Each year about 150 industry leaders visit Cornell to lecture and offer guidance while more than one hundred companies recruit Cornell students for full-time and summer employment. The Cornell Hotel School has the world's largest group of scholars focused on hospitality service-oriented management, and as such is a significant representation of hotel and hospitality schools in general.

The Hotel School offers undergraduate programs with focuses on management operations and food-and-beverage management, to name a few. A master's of management in hospitality (MMH) program is a two-year graduate degree program specifically designed to develop leaders in the hospitality industry; MS and PhD programs for students who plan to teach at the college level or conduct research in hospitality-related fields; and a Summer Honors Program for high school sophomores.

The Hotel School's Office of Executive Education offers three programs for hospitality managers, from trainee through senior executive.

The Advanced Management Program focuses on managing the future; Anheuser-Busch Professional Development Program offers fifty intensive one-week courses in eight fields of study: food, beverage, and restaurant management; general and strategic management; human resources management; managerial accounting and finance; marketing; operations management and information technology; property-asset management and real estate; and rooms management. The General Manager's Program tackles strategic property-level issues.

For More Information
Hotel School Books provide recent releases on topics including management contracts, table service and restaurant management.

http://www.hotelschool.cornell.edu

RECREATIONAL COOKING TEACHER

Avocational classes are the most popular cooking classes in the country. Not everyone interested in food has the time or inclination to go to a professional cooking school, and so the next best thing is to take a few classes. Some avocational schools teach a wide array of classes and attract the same students class after class, and a few offer professional-level classes as well. Their students may go on to work as caterers, cooks in gourmet stores, food writers, travel tour guides, food stylists, and personal chefs and private cooks. Others just go home and throw fabulous dinner parties.

People who teach cooking have a passion for it. They love the creativity, the give-and-take of the class, and the interest their students bring to every session. They get their ideas from any number of places and shape these into cohesive classes. Not everyone who teaches cooking is brilliant at it, but those who are usually cultivate a loyal following.

Cooking teachers must keep up with the times. Last year's pasta class will be this year's whole-grain class, while a course on roasting morphs into one on cooking lean cuts of meat. Because the public is fickle and tastes change, cooking teachers must constantly keep up with the times.

Richard Ruben, a cooking teacher in New York City, says he gets ideas for classes from articles in food magazines, newspapers and periodicals, from movies, television, and music. He suggests cooking teachers walk through their neighborhoods and take a critical look at what is going on in local markets and restaurants. He looks at the hot holiday destinations to get ideas, and takes note of the demographics that mainstream advertisers are targeting, such as "tweens" and dieters.

"Without passion, a great idea can fall short," says Ruben. "Teach every class like it's your first and give back stories to the recipes." Do your homework, he says, and urges cooking teachers to collect curious food facts, anthropological insights, and germane scientific concepts.

"Always empower the student with information, encouragement, and your love of the topic," Ruben advises.

"As a cooking school teacher, I experience first-hand how my students react to instruction, how they take in information, and how they approach tasks," says Vicki J. Caparulo, who teaches cooking in New Jersey. "When I instruct a student who can barely butter toast, I must be detailed and nurturing or get a reaction similar to that of a deer paralyzed by headlights. If the student is unable to learn, I am not succeeding as a teacher," she says.

When Caparulo develops recipes for a class of beginners, she makes sure the instructions are very specific. The students come to class to learn what to do, she says. "Therefore I will instruct that onions and garlic be peeled and trimmed, or describe a technique from start to finish rather than just call it by its culinary name," she explains.

GETTING STARTED

If you want to teach cooking to hobbyists and others who simply want to spend a few enjoyable hours learning some new skills, start small and stay local. There are opportunities at large, established schools, mainly in cities, where professional students also take classes, but most teachers work in smaller venues. Building credibility is a lengthy process, but worth its weight in gold. Find your niche, and base it on your strengths and expertise.

"I began teaching children's cooking classes many years ago, teaching only two classes a week that were based in my home," says children's cooking teacher Barbara Beary. Gradually, she added classes and cooking camps, and then began hosting cooking birthday parties. Her best and only advertising was "word of mouth."

As critical as it is to start small, you should think big. Design a Web site, write about cooking for newspapers and magazines, and try to get a spot on a local morning television show or a weekend radio program. With perseverance, your reputation will grow. For instance, Beary was asked to be a guest on the Food Network as a children's cooking expert. Today, she is franchising her business, opening a retail flagship store and children's culinary school, and publishing a children's cooking magazine. Barbara Beary can be found at http://www.batterupkids.com.

Sur La Table offers excellent and hugely popular cooking classes conducted by such renowned teachers as Hugh Carpenter, Rosemary Barron, Joyce Goldstein, and Kate Hill. For more information about its culinary programs, call 866-328-5412 or visit one of the 48 Sur La Table locations. http://www.surlatable.com/cooking/index.cfm

Williams Sonoma offers dozens of exciting demonstration cooking classes at its stores throughout the country. Check the schedule online at http://www.williams-sonoma.com. The company has a selected collection of instructional cookbooks from masters in their fields in addition to their own excellent publications.

TEACHING ABOUT FOOD TO NON-CULINARY STUDENTS

There are a growing number of students who may have little or no interest in learning how to cook but are nonetheless intrigued by food and its impact on our world. They may be interested in the sociological, historical, and anthropological significance of food, how it impacts the environment or farming and fishing practices, or how it figures in literature.

Increasingly, food and cooking are being taken seriously in academia, something that a generation ago was unthinkable, except to a few visionaries. This means even more opportunities for anyone interested in teaching.

THE JOB OF UNIVERSITY PROFESSOR

Darra Goldstein, Professor of Russian at Williams College was dissuaded from writing her thesis on a food subject because until a few years ago food was not considered to be a serious topic. Things have changed now. She says: "What is mainly happening is that graduate students are getting degrees in the traditional fields but writing their theses on topics having to do with various aspects of food. This makes sense if they want to go into academia, since there aren't really gastronomy programs to house academics . . . at least not yet. I think that will change, but slowly."

Professor Goldstein describes her work:

Ever since the collapse of the Soviet Union, Russian departments nationwide have been starved for students so I decided to offer a new course to pique student interest: "Topics in Russian Culture: Feasting and Fasting in Russian History," designed to teach Russian culture through the prism of food. In the 200-odd-year history of Williams College, this was a groundbreaking course, as the college had never before listed a regular class in food studies. I have to admit I was nervous. Some academics still regard culinary history with heavy skeptisicism, deeming it a not-quite-serious discipline. To ensure that the class would not be perceived as a "gut," I ended up preparing one of the most rigorous syllabi I've ever used, with an extensive schedule of readings, papers, and exams.

The course used the methodology of food history to explore the broader historical, economic, and artistic conditions that gave rise to Russian culture. We examined not only culinary practice but also the social context of cooking and eating in Russia. Essentially, the class presented Russian culture from a domestic point of view that of the wooden spoon rather the scepter. Discussions of such issues as the domestic roles of women and serfs, the etiquette of the table, the roles of drinking and temperance movements, and the importance of feasts and fasts in the Russian Orthodox Church provided insight into the important interplay between culture and cuisine. Memoirs, cookery books, and wonderful fiction by Chekhov, Gogol, Saltykov-Shchedrin and Babel helped to illuminate class and gender differences, cooking techniques and the particular tastes that characterize Russian cuisine.

We began the course with some theoretical reading on how to define a culinary culture, and then moved quickly into the specifics of Russian cuisine with accounts of 16th-century travelers to Ivan the Terrible's "rude and barbarous kingdom," where the inhabitants reeked of garlic and onions.

The students learned about the significance of fasting in Russian peasant culture, as well as the ethos among the well-to-do. The dichotomy between rich and poor, feast and famine, was never far from our minds, especially as we moved into the 20th century with accounts of the forced hunger of Collectivization and the Siege of Leningrad, when people scraped wallpaper paste off the walls and boiled old shoes in an attempt to survive.

Less distressing were our studies of the symbolism of the Russian stove and of food imagery in Russian art. We also considered the problem of vodka consumption, ending the course with a look at post-Soviet society and the recurrent debate over western influence.

Because I also wanted my students to experience food as pleasure, I supplemented the class meetings with extracurricular events. We celebrated the Russian pre-Lenten Butter Festival with an all-you-can-eat blini dinner and went on a mushroom hunt, for which the students prepared by reading Tolstoy's evocative passage on mushrooms from Anna Karenina. We were thrilled to find an abundant patch of morels!

The seminar concluded with a four-course Russian feast. Each student researched and prepared a traditional dish, and the results were impressive. In addition to the familiar borscht and pirozhki, we enjoyed a 19th-century cold beverage made from pounded pistachios, homemade kvass (an effervescent drink made from fermented black bread), eggplant caviar, a large pie with four different fillings straight out of Gogol's *Dead Souls,* and varenki, Ukrainian sour-cherry dumplings.

This course proved popular beyond expectation—I had to cap enrollments at 50 to make it manageable. Approaching culture or history through food is an excellent way to engage students with vastly different interests, and for me this was one of the most exciting aspects of the class.

Very few Russian majors took this course; the students came from a wide array of departments. Their individual interests enabled them to bring divergent perspectives to both class discussions and their term papers. Thus we considered elements of social history, economic history, political history, and the history of science, cultural history, and culinary history, all of which enriched the class.

As the French semiotician Roland Barthes has said, "an entire world is present in food." Not only did my students conclude the course with a good understanding of Russian passions and politics and the ways in which food has affected both, they also started thinking about larger issues of influence and trade that increasingly determine our world today.

Students can learn a great deal about the domestic and political lives of nations by studying their food, with which they feel viscerally connected as they begin to think about their own food traditions. But perhaps the most important lesson they learned is that food is never neutral, it is always culturally marked.

Darra Goldstein is Professor of Russian at Williams College and founding editor of *Gastronomica: The Journal of Food and Culture* (http://www.gastronomica.org). Since earning her PhD in Slavic languages and literatures from Stanford University, she has published numerous books and articles on Russian literature, culture, art, and cuisine, and has organized several exhibitions, including *Graphic Design in the Mechanical Age* and *Feeding Desire: Design and the Tools of the Table* for the Cooper-Hewitt, National Design Museum. She is also the author of three cookbooks, *A Taste of Russia* (nominated for a Tastemaker Award), *The Georgian Feast* (winner of the 1994 IACP Julia Child Award for Cookbook of the Year), and *The Winter Vegetarian*. Goldstein has consulted for the Russian Tea Room and Firebird restaurants in New York and is currently Food Editor of *Russian Life* magazine. She is also General Editor of *California Studies in Food and Culture.*

WHAT IS GASTRONOMY?

Jacques Pépin was just thirteen when he began his culinary apprenticeship. Surely, he couldn't have imagined he would achieve such fame for his work as a chef, television star, and writer. His acclaimed La Technique and La Methode, describe the principles of culinary technique and artistry and earned him a place in the James Beard Foundation's Cookbook Hall of Fame, an honor bestowed each year on an author whose contributions to food literature have had a substantial and enduring impact on the American kitchen. Jacques is not only a beloved teacher but also a dedicated student. He studied at Columbia University where, in 1972, he was awarded an MA degree in eighteenth-century French literature. His résumé lists his many accomplishments but perhaps his enduring legacy will be as a founder of Boston University's Master of Liberal Arts in Gastronomy.

But what is this thing called gastronomy? Clearly, the material for gastronomy classes varies widely (and wildly) and is subject to interpretation by each instructor: A writer from the *New York Times* reported on a food-and-cultures class that was delving into the importance of Friday night pizza parties for parent-child bonding and discussing, What is it about New York Jews and Chinese food? Why are Jewish immigrants from Eastern Europe drawn to Chinese restaurants for Sunday supper? Who knows?

For one instructor, gastronomy means an in-depth study of classic French culinary traditions: nouvelle cuisine, modern and postmodern Cuisine featuring recently and soon-to-be-deceased French trailblazing chefs. Another teacher peers into the ethics of food production, scrutinizes the protocols of fine dining and explores and speculates on the evolving role of the contemporary chef. Yet another lecturer ponders the traditions of the biggest blowout days of the food year: Thanksgiving Day dinner and Super Bowl Sunday.

A conference at the New School dissected the complex inter-relationships between people and their food: "What we eat and why we choose the foods that make up our daily diet; the cere-monies that surround food; how it underscores our sameness and differences; its mythic and symbolic importance; the joy of plenty; the fear of famine and deprivation—all are occasions for reflections on the human condition. Why do we tolerate the prevalence of widespread hunger in a world of abundance? What roles do cul-turally determined food preferences or the power of science, pol-itics, or global trade play in determining who will be well fed and who will starve?"

The education of the professional chef is no longer limited to chopping carrots, celery and onions. Within the boundary of a sin-gle lifetime, Jacques Pépin can trace his own experience from indentured servant to celebrity and from strict traditional cook-ing to what was formerly known as molecular gastronomy, and could now be named ARTISENSE—a breathtaking gastronomi-cal revolution in which food is transformed into ART and Ingre-dients are deconstructed and reconstructed to appeal to each of our SENSES: sight, smell and exquisite taste and presented to the guest in a wondrous interpretation of sculpture and architecture. This is gastronomy indeed.

Our evening meal offers a unique opportunity to learn about our past, present and future. Imagine a menu consisting of Malpeque Oysters Garnished with Sevruga Caviar followed by Roast Beef, or Chilean Sea Bass in a Ginger-Saffron Broth. The salad course is Locally Grown, Organic Mixed Greens followed by a Cheese Plat-ter and for dessert, Flourless Chocolate Cake.

The meal forms the framework for discussing: the history of oys-ters, trade issues involving the banning of imported caviar, the car-nivore and the vegetarian diet, the role of chefs in boycotting endangered fish, the discovery of fire and its role in the evolution of the human race. Then there are the politics of organic farming and agricultural and marine biotechnology to consider along with the ecclesiastic symbolism of olive oil, the history of the spice trade in general and salt and pepper in particular. Here too is an oppor-tunity to talk about the physiology of taste and the long-term effects of chronic hunger. We could dwell on the economics of obe-sity, the impending water crisis (bottled water is offered to a guest by the waitstaff), which leads to an investigation of tipping opportunities that accompany the service of artisanal cheese.

The chocolate cake is just an excuse to talk about food fads and trends—and there is still time to talk about fair trade issues as they relate to tea and coffee as well as the impact of stock market gyrations on reservations at uptown restaurants. That's just a few crumbs for starters. We haven't even approached the subject of fast food.

The universe of food continues to expand: the more stars there are in the galaxy, well, the more stars there will be in the galaxy.

Finding, or inventing, a food job that brings you satisfaction and happiness is a voyage of discovery that begins with a telescope through which to look at the entire food world and ends with a microscope as you narrow the field and take your own personal seat at the bountiful table.

———

"I have found that the men and women who got to the top were those who did the jobs they had in hand, with everything they had of energy and enthusiasm and hard work."

—*Harry Truman*

Index

French Kitchen in Gascony, The, 301
French Laundry, The, 14
Fresh TV, 283
Frieda's, 260
Frito-Lay, 206
Fussell, Betty, xvii, 151, 161–162, 241
Futurist, xiv, 219, 224–225

• G •

Garbage Anthropologist, xiv, 230
General Manager, xiii, 13, 18, 39, 40, 308
Generation Green, 159
Georgeanne Brennan's Haute Provence, 301
Gift Basket Maker, xiii, 119
Glaser, Milton, xvii, xix, 123
Glover, Cynthia, xvi, xvii, 149
Golden Door, 78
Goldstein, Darra, xvii, 124, 311, 313–314
Good Cook Book Club, 163
Google, 194
Gramercy Tavern, 47
Grand Union, 123
Graphic Designer, xiii, xix, 14, 122–123, 131
Grausman, Richard, 293
Green Zebra, 281
Greenbrier, 148
Grimes, William, 190

• H •

Haber, Barbara, xvii, 177–178
Hacker, Carol, 176
Hamersley's Bistro, Boston, 18
Hamersly, Gordon, 18
Hamilton, Dorothy, 275, 277
Hannington College of Design, 133
Harbor Court Hotel, The, 150
Hardee's, 249
Harvard, 85, 177–178, 226
Harvest Grille and Cider House, 81
Healthcare Foodservice Management, 90
Heinz, 241
Heiss, Bob, 115
Herb and Speciality Crop Farmer, xiv

Hisaoka Public Relations, 284
Historian, xiv, 108, 151, 161, 219–222, 224, 232, 307
Home Baking Association, 175
Honey Producer, xiv, 264
Hospital Chef, xiii, 79
Hospitality Guild Private Club Management, 72
Hot-Dog Vender, xiii, 62
Hotel Cipriani, Venice, 303
Hotel Posta Vecchia, 303
Howard, Jim, xvii, 93
Humanitarian, xiii, 55
Hunter Public Relations, 215
Hydroponic Farmer, xiv, 262

• I •

IACP, xvii, 148, 176, 212, 286, 295, 301, 304, 308, 314
Ice Cream Namer, xiii, 114
Ice Cream Taster, xiv, 241
Indexer, xiv, 166–167
Inn at Little Washington, 284
INNexperience Internship, The, 73
Institute of Culinary Education, xx, 33, 102, 104, 143, 163, 268, 277–279, 295
International Academy of Design and Technology, 133
International Association of Culinary Professionals, 91, 148–149, 154, 174–175, 286, 295, 303–304, 308
International Caterers Association, 89
International Congress and Convention Association, 92
International Culinary Center, The, 275, 277
International Flavors and Fragrances, 239
International Food Group, 64
International Food Service Executives Association, 296
International Food, Wine and Travel Writers Association, 148
International Foodservice Editorial Council, 296

Media Trainer, xiv, 2, 197–198
MediaMentor, 215
Memorial Sloan-Kettering Cancer Center, 80
Menu Designer, xiv, 131
Metropolitan Museum, NY, 60
Meyer, Danny, xvii, 43, 47, 59, 210
Military Chef, xiii, 82
Military Hospitality Alliance, 82
Mintz, Sydney, xvi, 229
Minuta, Dana, xviii, 73–74
Mississippi University for Women, 128
MIT, 85
Modern, The (Museum of Modern Art), 47
Monell Center, The, 8
Morrison, 80
Motorola, 58
Mullins, Drew, 289
Murphy, Erica, xvi, 235
Murray's Cheese, 107
Mushroom Grower, xiv, 140, 264–265

• N •

NASA, 8, 239
National Academy of Sciences, 255
National Association for the Specialty Food
    Trade (NASFT), 98, 100
National Association of Catering Executives,
    89, 91
National Association of College and Univer-
    sity Food Services, 90
National Cancer Institute, 206
National Confectioners Association, 35
National Dialogue on Entrepreneurship, 95
National Kitchen and Bath Association, 134
National Meat Association, 26
National Restaurant Association, 90, 292, 295
National Writers Union, 148
Nation's Restaurant News, 30
Nestle, Marion, 244
New England Culinary Institutes, 285–286, 295
New School Culinary Arts Program, 304, 315
New York Public Library, The, 180
New York University, 179, 305

New York Women's Culinary Alliance, 307
Newsletter Producer, xiv, 154
Nieporent, Drew, 269
Niman Ranch, 112
Nischan, Michel, xvii, 78–79, 158
Norman Rockwell Museum, 220
North American Meat Processors Association,
    26
Northeastern University, 85
Nugent, Mat, 22
Nutritionist, xiv, 113, 214, 244–245, 247

• O •

Obesity Researcher, xiv, 250
Olive Oil Factory of Watertown, 187
Olive Oil Taster, xiv, 241
Oliver, Sandra, 154, 219, 224
Olives, 13
Olson, Deborah, 117
Omelet Maker, xiii, 60
Online Writing Lab, Purdue University, 163
Oregon State University, 238
Organic Trade Association, 259
Oscar Mayer, 206

• P •

P.C. Richard and Son, 134
Panera Bread, 8, 112, 236
Paris Cordon Bleu, 299
Parseghian, Pam, xviii, 153
Participant Productions, 291
Pastry Chef, xiii, 7, 12, 31, 34–37, 111, 121,
    124, 209, 275, 282, 286, 292
Paul Smith's College, 270
Payard, Francois, 37
Payard's Patisserie Bistro, 37
Penn State University, 235, 238
Pepin, Jacques, xvii, 19, 152, 199, 202, 215,
    267, 271, 275, 314–315
Per Se, 14, 107
Perfect Gift, The, 119
Personal Chef, xiii, 2, 13, 59, 64–68, 209, 309
Picnique, 28

San Diego State University, 211

Sandwich-Shop Owner, xiii, 113

Sausage Maker, xiii, 27

Scherber, Amy, 109

Scherzi, James, xviii, 126

School of Hospitality Business (Michigan State University), 92

Second Harvest, 55

Seed Savers Exchange, The, 249

Seed Scientist, xiv, 249–250

Segan, Francine, xviii, 220

Service Corps of Retired Executives, The (SCORE), 96

Shakespeare and Company, 220

Share Our Strength, 55

ShawGuides, 14, 16, 35, 268–269, 302

ShawGuides, 268

Sheraton, Mimi, xvii, 188

Sherlock, Richard, xvii, 226–227

Shore, Bill, 55

Silver Diner, The, 48

Silver Palate, The, 105

Silver Seas, 76

Sixth Star, 76

Small Business Administration, 99

Smartworks, 149

Smith and Wollensky Restaurant Group, 43, 297

Smith College, 85

Smith, Andrew, xviii, 147, 221

Society for Foodservice Management, 90

Sodexo, see Sodhexo

Sodexho, 59, 80

Soil Association, The, 187

Sokolov, Raymond, 207, 229

Sommelier, vii, xiii, 13, 46, 130, 275

Sonneschmidt, Fritz, 17

Sous Chef, xiii, 12, 20–22, 25, 29, 58, 74, 77, 300

Southern Foodways Alliance, 232

Spa Chef, xiii, 77

St. Luke Episcopal Hospital, Houston, 80

Stanford University, 235

Starbucks, 8, 33, 95, 225

StarChefs, 17

Steingarten, Jeffrey, xvii, 138, 147, 190

Steinhardt School, 306

Stern Business School, 306

Stonewall Kitchen, 103

Stowe Resort and Spa, 78

Stroot, Michel, 78, 79

Styler, Chris, xx, 203

Subway Restaurant, 236

Sullivan University, 296

Super Suppers, 113

Sur La Table, 311

Swanson, Melissa, 241

Symposium for Professional Food Writers, The, 148

Systems and Services Company (SYSCO), 64

• T •

Tabla, 47

Taco Bell, 206

Taillevent, Paris, 46

Tanner, Ron, xvii

Taste of Culture, 301

Tavern on the Green, 15, 53

Tea Shop Owner, xiii

Tea Taster, xiv, 241–242

Theater for a New Audience, 220

Tisch School of Arts, NYU, 130

Tower Suite, 15

Trader Joe's, 111

• U •

U.S. Army, 235

U.S. Bureau of Labor Statistics, 3

UCLA, 211

Unilever, 187

Union Square Cafe, 47

United Fresh Fruit and Vegetable Association, 91

University of Arizona, 230

University of California at Berkeley, 231

University of California, Davis, 238, 252–253

University of Cincinnati, 238

University of Florida, 238

University of Georgia, 237

University of Illinois Hospitality Management Program, 235

University of Maryland, The, 185, 235

University of Michigan, 179

University of Mississippi, Center for the Study of Southern Culture, 232

University of Nebraska, 236, 238

University of Pennsylvania, 227

Unlimited Cuisine Company, 302

Utah State University, 226

• V •

Vanderbilt University, 235

Veranda Flowers, 116

Vergili, Joyce, 243

Vinegar Taster, xiv, 241–242

Virginia Willis Culinary Productions, 283

Vivaldo, Denise, xviii, 86, 89

Von Hengst, Ype, 48

Vongerichten, Cedric, 24

Vongerichten, Jean-Georges, 107

• W •

Waitstaff, xiii, xvii, 13, 20, 39–42, 46, 48–50, 52, 63, 71, 81, 122, 130, 187, 290, 315

Wall Unit, Huntsville, TX, 81

Wallace, Candy, xviii, 68

Wansink, Brian, 234

Washburne Culinary Institute, 287–288

Washburne Trade School, The, see Washburne Culinary Institute

Waters, Alice, xvii, 53, 83–85, 202, 261

Waxman, Nach, xviii, 168

WCCO AM/CBS Radio, 196

Wegmans, 110, 140

Weinstock, Sylvia, xviii, 31, 34–35

White, Jasper, 197

Whole Foods Market, 111

Wholesaler, xiii, 99, 105, 107

Wild Edibles, 107

Wild Game Farmer, xiv, 263

Willams College, 311–313

Willan, Anne, xvii, 299

Williams Sonoma, 311

Willinger, Faith, xviii, 303

Wilton Company, The, 33

Winbladh, Lisa, 303–304

Windows on the World, xxi, 1, 15

Wish, 210

Witchcraft, 17

Women Chefs and Restaurateurs, 91, 109, 296, 308

Wonton Food, 139

World Association of Cooks Societies, 36

• Y •

Yahoo!, 194

Yale University, 85

Yannuzzi, Elaine, ii, xvi, 105–106

Young's Bluecrest Seafood, Ltd., 187

Yum! Brands, 8

• Z •

Zabar's, 112

Zelickson, Sue, xviii, 196

Zingerman's, 112

Zum Zum, 15